THE ENCYCLOPEDIA OF

REPTILES

AMPHIBIANS & INVERTEBRATES

A Complete Visual Guide

THE ENCYCLOPEDIA OF

REPTILES

AMPHIBIANS & INVERTEBRATES

CHIEF CONSULTANTS

Dr Noel Tait

Consultant in Invertebrate Biology

Sydney, Australia

Dr Richard C. Vogt

Curator of Herpetology and Professor

National Institute for Amazon Research

Manaus, Amazonas, Brazil

CONSULTANTS

Dr Hugh Dingle

Professor Emeritus

University of California, Davis, USA

RED
LEMON
PRESS

A Complete Visual Guide

This edition published in 2015 by:
Red Lemon Press
(An imprint of Weldon Owen)
Deepedene Lodge,
Deepdene Avenue,
Dorking, Surrey
RH5 4AT

Conceived and produced by Weldon Owen Pty Ltd
59 Victoria Street, McMahons Point
Sydney NSW 2060, Australia
Copyright © 2006 Weldon Owen Inc.

Chief Executive Officer John Owen
President Terry Newell
Publisher Sheena Coupe
Creative Director Sue Burk
Vice President International Sales Stuart Laurence
Administrator International Sales Kristine Ravn

Project Editors Stephanie Goodwin, Angela Handley, Jennifer Losco
Designers Clare Forte, Heather Menzies, Jacqueline Richards,
Karen Robertson
Cover Design Heather Menzies, Juliana Titin
Picture Research Annette Crueger, Jennifer Losco, Heather Menzies
Text Jenni Bruce, Karen McGhee, Richard C. Vogt

Species Gallery Illustrations MagicGroup s.r.o. (Czech Republic) –
www.magicgroup.cz
Feature Illustrations Guy Troughton
Maps Andrew Davies Creative Communication, Map Illustrations
Information Graphics Andrew Davies Creative Communication
Index Sarah Plant/Puddingburn Publishing Services

Editorial Coordinators Helen Flint, Irene Mickaiel
Production Director Chris Hemesath
Production Coordinator Charles Mathews

ISBN: 978-1-78342-062-9

Printed in Latvia

CONTENTS

8 Foreword
10 How to use this book

12 REPTILES
14 Reptiles
16 Reptiles through the ages
17 Classification
18 Biology and behaviour
21 Habitats and adaptations
23 Reptiles in danger
24 Tortoises and turtles
33 Crocodilians
36 Tuatatra
36 Amphisbaenians
37 Lizards
60 Snakes

82 AMPHIBIANS
84 Amphibians
85 Amphibians through
   the ages
86 Classification
87 Biology and behaviour
89 Habitats and adaptations
91 Amphibians in danger
92 Salamanders and newts
99 Caecilians
100 Frogs and toads

120 INVERTEBRATES
122 Invertebrates
123 Invertebrates through the ages
124 Classification
126 Biology and behaviour
127 Habitats and adaptations
129 Invertebrates in danger
130 Invertebrate chordates
131 Sponges
132 Cnidarians
135 Flatworms
136 Roundworms
137 Molluscs
144 Segmented worms
146 Arthropods
148 Arachnids
156 Horseshoe crabs
156 Sea spiders
157 Myriapods
158 Crustaceans
164 Insects
166 Dragonflies and damselflies
167 Mantids
168 Cockroaches
169 Termites
170 Crickets and grasshoppers
171 Bugs
175 Beetles
179 Flies
182 Butterflies and moths
186 Bees, wasps, ants and sawflies
191 Other insects
194 Insect allies
195 Echinoderms
197 Other invertebrates

200 Glossary
202 Index
208 Acknowledgements

FOREWORD

This lavishly illustrated book is an introduction to the natural history of three groups of animals: reptiles, amphibians, and invertebrates. The diversity of living reptiles and amphibians is amazing – there are more than 8,000 species of reptiles and 5,400 species of amphibians. Despite the constraints of their limited body forms, they have a remarkable array of behavioural patterns and survival strategies. Frogs, for example, exploit two very different niches – as tadpoles they are herbivores, as adults they become predators. The 3,000 species of snakes range from tiny burrowing blind snakes to huge constrictors more than 10m (33 feet) long. Their habitats encompass the subterranean, the arboreal, and the aquatic. The ways in which reptiles and amphibians move and reproduce are equally varied – their courtship, parental care, territorial defence and migration can rival those of mammals and birds.

Invertebrates, with more than 1.3 million species, constitute over 95 per cent of all known animal species, and countless more are yet to be discovered. They are unified and distinguished by what they lack: they have no backbone, no bones and no cartilage. In form, they are as diverse as brightly coloured butterflies, venomous spiders, floating jellyfish, porous sponges and a multitude of bugs and beetles. They are at home in the air, on land and in the seas. They swim, burrow, creep, run and fly. Yet, despite their impressive numbers, the behaviour and ecology of most of these animals have never been studied. In this volume we provide an overview of representative species in each major group.

Habitat destruction, environmental degradation, pollution, illegal collecting and the introduction of alien species threaten the existence of many reptiles, amphibians and invertebrates. If we are to ensure the survival of these creatures, we must control the impact of our own species on the environments in which they live. At the present time 80 per cent of the turtles and 30 per cent of the known species of frogs and toads are listed in the IUCN Red List of Threatened Species. If nothing is done, their status will have to be revised, as they slip from rare and threatened to endangered or extinct in the ponds they once inhabited. Without international cooperation among governments and the public will to preserve creatures such as these, life on our planet will become less diverse. Bleak will be the spring when there are no frogs singing.

DR RICHARD C. VOGT

Curator of Herpetology and Professor,
National Institute for Amazon Research, Manaus, Amazonas, Brazil

HOW TO USE THIS BOOK

This book is divided into three taxonomic parts, namely Reptiles, Amphibians and Invertebrates. Each part begins with an overview of the characteristics of the group, its evolution, classification, biology, behaviour, habitats, adaptations and conservation status. Then follow the species sections, which are broken down into chapters devoted to particular subgroups. The structure of these sections reflects the taxonomy of each of the featured groups. The section on Invertebrates, for example, profiles a larger taxonomic group than Reptiles or Amphibians to ensure that the diversity of Invertebrates is adequately conveyed. The book concludes with a comprehensive glossary and index.

HABITAT ICONS

The 19 habitat icons below indicate at a glance the various habitats in which a species or group can be found. It should be noted that the icons are used in the same order throughout the book, rather than in their order of significance. More detailed profiles of these habitats can be found at the beginning of each taxonomic part.

- Tropical rain forest
- Tropical monsoon forest
- Temperate forest
- Coniferous forest
- Moorlands and heath
- Open habitat, including savanna, grassland, fields, pampas and steppes
- Desert and semidesert
- Mountains and highlands
- Tundra
- Polar regions
- Seas and oceans
- Coral reefs
- Mangrove swamps
- Coastal areas, including beaches, oceanic cliffs, sand dunes, intertidal rock pools and/or coastal waters (as applicable to group)
- Rivers and streams, including river and stream banks
- Wetlands, including swamps, marshes, fens, floodplains, deltas and bogs
- Lakes and ponds
- Urban areas
- Parasitic

Section and chapter
This indicates the group of animals under discussion.

Classification box
This shows the taxonomic groups to which the animals belong in the animal kingdom.

Lavish photographs
Taken by leading wildlife photographers, these portray the habits and habitats of different species.

Detailed diagram
Where appropriate, diagrams are included to illustrate points about anatomy or adaptation.

Group global distribution
A map shows the worldwide distribution of the group being profiled, followed by text that discusses the distribution of particular groups in more detail.

24　**REPTILES** TORTOISES AND TURTLES

TORTOISES AND TURTLES

CLASS	Reptilia
ORDER	Testudines
FAMILIES	14
GENERA	99
SPECIES	293

Turtles and tortoises are the only vertebrates that house the pelvic and pectoral girdles within a shell made of ribs fused with bone. The first fossils to show this trait appeared 220 million years ago in the Triassic period, when dinosaurs roamed the earth. The shell design has since undergone various modifications. The African pancake tortoise has a flexible flat shell allowing it to wedge into crevices; it then inflates, after which it is impossible to pull out. Softshell turtles lack a hard shell; instead, the bones are covered with a smooth leathery shell, giving them more speed. There is still controversy as to whether turtles are derived from a different lineage to other reptiles.

Distribution Turtles are found on all continents except Antarctica, and in all oceans: 241 species of turtles have adapted to freshwater rivers, lakes, and ponds; 45 tortoises are terrestrial; only seven species live in the oceans.

Baby leatherback Leatherback turtles lay up to six nests of up to 200 eggs a year for decades. This hatchling has passed the first hurdle: 2 months incubating in the sand with predators digging around it. It now has to face the many threats in the sea.

Saddleback giant The Galápagos tortoise (above) has a saddleback carapace. This condition is more often seen in adult male tortoises, due to enhanced mating success, from populations on the drier and more barren islands of the Galápagos.

Turtle skeleton A turtle's shell has an outer layer of epidermal scutes (usually 38 on the carapace and 16 on the plastron). Under these, a shell of fused ribs (the plastron) supports the body. The vertebrae are joined to the inside of the carapace.

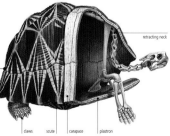

retracting neck

claws　scute　carapace　plastron

Swimming sea turtle The forelimbs of sea turtles have been modified into flipper-shaped paddles that move synchronously, resembling aquatic flying rather than swimming. Sea turtles are so adept in the water that they rarely leave it except to nest. Freshwater turtles swim using all four limbs in turn.

EVOLUTION SHELLED OUT
In addition to the shell, turtles and tortoises have evolved many unique features. Turtle muscles are able to withstand high levels of lactic acid, so they do not tire after swimming rapidly. They also fill their large urinary bladders with water for ballast to maintain buoyancy. Turtles and tortoises occupy niches as predators, grazers, croppers and scavengers. Some have gut flora to digest plant cells; others are seed dispersers. Wood turtles stomp on the ground with their front feet, then eat the earthworms that come out of the ground.

Some sea turtles and freshwater turtles nest within a few days in tremendous numbers on the same nesting beach. These mass nestings, known as arribadas, evolved to swamp local predators—it would be impossible for them to eat all of the eggs or kill all of the females. The success of these adaptations has helped turtles to survive over millions of years; now, as a result of human intervention, two-thirds of all turtle species are being carefully monitored by the IUCN.

CONSERVATION INFORMATION

Within the fact files, each profiled species is allocated a conservation status, using IUCN and other conservation categories, as follows:

† Indicates that a species is listed under the following categories:
Extinct (IUCN) It is beyond reasonable doubt that the last individual of a given species has died.
Extinct in the wild (IUCN) Only known to survive in captivity or as a naturalised population outside its former range.

✴ Indicates that a species is listed under the following categories:
Critically endangered (IUCN) Facing a very high and immediate risk of extinction in the wild.
Endangered (IUCN) Facing a very high risk of extinction in the wild in the near future.

The following categories are also used:
Vulnerable (IUCN) Facing a high risk of extinction in the wild in the foreseeable future.
Near threatened (IUCN) Likely to qualify for one of the above categories in the near future.
Conservation dependent (IUCN) Dependent upon species- or habitat-specific conservation programs to keep it out of one of the above threatened categories.

Data deficient (IUCN) Inadequate information available to make an assessment of its risk.
Not known Not evaluated or little studied.
Common Widespread and abundant.
Locally common Widespread and abundant within its range.
Uncommon Occurs widely in low numbers in preferred habitat(s).
Rare Occurs in only some of preferred habitat or in small restricted areas.

Snippets
These highlight distinguishing aspects or characteristics of the species, such as colour variations, behaviour, habitat, size and anatomical features.

Name labels
Labels provide the common and scientific names, as well as the species' family, order or class, where appropriate.

Conservation watch box
This provides information about the status of a particular species or group of animals. These boxes may also outline factors that threaten the animal's survival.

✴ **CONSERVATION WATCH**

Arachnid alert The conservation movement has paid little attention to arachnids. Only 18 species have been assessed by the IUCN, but all of these are on the Red List. Further research is needed, but arachnid diversity is no doubt threatened by habitat loss, pollution, pesticide use and invasive exotic species.

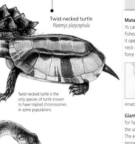

Matamata
Chelus fimbriatus

Matamata characterized by its long snorkel nose, which allows it to lie in shallow water and reach the surface to respire without frightening its prey

Common snake-necked turtle
Chelodina longicollis

Twist-necked turtle
Platemys platycephala

Twist-necked turtle is the only species of turtle known to have triploid chromosomes in some populations

Helmeted turtle
Pelomedusa subrufa

Giant Amazon river turtle
Podocnemis expansa

Chelidae Fitzroy turtle
Rheodytes leukops

Serrated turtle
Pelusios sinuatus

Hilaire's toadhead turtle
Phrynops hilarii

Victoria short-necked turtle
Emydura victoriae

FACT FILE

Matamata The matamata, relying on its camouflage, lies waiting for small fishes to pass. With lightning speed, it opens its mouth and thrusts out its neck simultaneously, creating a sucking force that pulls fishes into its mouth.

⬤ Up to 18 in (46 cm)
🌊 Aquatic
♀♂ Unknown
● 12–28
✴ Common

Amazonia (N. South America)

Giant Amazon river turtle Selection for fast incubation was influenced by the unpredictability of rising river levels. The eggs hatch in 45 days, and nest temperatures often reach 104°F (40°C), the highest known for any turtle.

⬤ Up to 42 in (107 cm)
🌊 Aquatic
♀♂ TSD
● 60–150
✴ Conserv. dependent

Amazon & Orinoco basins (N. South America)

BEGINNING OF LIFE

Sea turtles lay their eggs on the same beaches that their ancestors have used for millennia. Once the nest has been covered with sand, the eggs are left to chance to go undetected by predators. Hatchlings must race to the sea, running the risk of predation by hungry mammals and birds, to the dubious safety of waters filled with even more predators. Survival rates for some species may be as low as 1 in 50,000.

Hatchling flatback turtles
Hatchling turtles are on their own.
Their only chance of survival is to
scamper to the sea in a large group.

Fact file
This profiles several of the illustrated species or groups, with information about their characteristics and behaviour.

Distribution map
This shows the species' or group's range (and former range, where appropriate). A world or regional map is used according to distribution.

Habitat icons
The icons indicate the various habitats in which the profiled animal(s) can be found. A full list is on the opposite page.

Panel feature box
Illustrations and text provide information about an interesting aspect of a species or group of species.

FACT FILE STATISTICS
Important or interesting facts about a species or group use the following icons and information. All measurements are maximums.

Length
⬤ Reptiles: snakes and lizards: snout to vent; other reptiles: head and body including tail
⬤ Turtles: length of carapace
⬤ Amphibians: head and body, including tail

Weight/Mass
🔺 Body weight

Reproduction: Reptiles
● Number of eggs

Habit: Reptiles and Amphibians
◐ Terrestrial
◑ Aquatic
◐ Burrowing
⊕ Arboreal
◑ Varies between the above

Breeding season: Amphibians
⇉ When breeding occurs, e.g. spring

Breeding: Reptiles
⚲ Viviparous (producing live young)
○ Oviparous (producing eggs that develop outside the maternal body)
⊘ Ovoviviparous (producing eggs that develop within the maternal body)

Sex: Reptiles
♀♂ Indicates whether a species is temperature sex determined (TSD) or genetically sex determined (GSD)

Number of genera and species: Reptiles and Invertebrates
The number of genera and species in the relevant taxonomic group

REPTILES

REPTILES

PHYLUM	Chordata
CLASS	Reptilia
ORDERS	4
FAMILIES	60
GENERA	1,012
SPECIES	8,163

Modern reptiles are not simply relics from the age of the dinosaurs, now dwarfed in the shadow of their evolutionary heyday. Reptiles, like all other major animal groups, are continuously adapting to their environments. Today's species are the product of 300 million years of evolution that began with some of the earliest creatures to walk on land. They gave rise to two evolutionary lineages: one leading to mammals (Synapsida) and the other to birds and reptiles (Diapsida). Turtles were once thought to belong to the Anapsida, a sister group to the Diapsida. New biochemical studies suggest, however, that they are diapsids, and that the anapsids evolved later.

MODERN DIVERSITY

The diapsid reptiles diverged during the Triassic (248–206 million years ago) into two main groups: the Lepidosaura (scaly reptiles, such as lizards, snakes, amphisbaenians and tuataras); and the Archosauria (ruling reptiles, including crocodiles, pterosaurs, dinosaurs and ancestral birds). Turtles appear in the fossil record from 210 million years ago.

There were once as many as 16 major reptile orders; now there are just four. Squamata – the snakes, lizards and worm lizards – is by far the most diverse and widespread of the modern groups. It is also the group that displays the widest range of body size and form, from the largest lizard – Indonesia's Komodo dragon, up to 3m (10 feet) long, to tiny geckos no longer than 2.5cm (1 inch). Crocodilia includes the crocodiles, alligators and gharials, all of which have protective bony plates in their skin, short limbs, skulls with long snouts and long tails with deep sides adapted for swimming. Testudines contains the tortoises and turtles, most of which live in freshwater or terrestrial habitats. Seven species live in marine habitats and some tortoises exist in desert regions. Order Rhynchocephalia contains just two species of tuatara, both of which occur only on islands off New Zealand.

Reptiles, like amphibians and fishes, are ectothermic – they have a limited capability to generate their own body heat internally through metabolic activity. Instead, they are dependent on warmth from the external environment. Sea turtles, particularly the giant leatherback turtle that ventures into the Arctic Sea, can raise their body temperature above that of the water through their metabolic activity when swimming. Unlike mammals, reptiles are not able to control their internal temperature by sweating. To avoid excessive daytime heat, many desert species of snakes and lizards are nocturnal.

Lizard life Madagascar's panther chameleon relies on acute vision and lightning-sharp reflexes to capture prey – mostly insects, but also other reptiles and small birds. To heat their bodies, chameleons can darken their skin colour to better absorb and retain the Sun's warmth.

LAND INVADERS

Several key physiological developments freed reptiles from their aquatic beginnings. The evolution of the cleidoic – or waterproof – egg was pivotal, not only for reptiles but for vertebrates in general. A closed-system egg, in which water, nutrients and waste are stored until hatching, allowed reptiles to move away from water to reproduce. Still, the eggs of some modern species must be buried in a moist place to survive. Other species have developed thick shells to avoid dehydration. Although all turtles and crocodiles lay their eggs, some snakes and lizards retain theirs internally to give birth to live young. Other snakes and lizards are viviparous – they nurture their developing embryos through blood vessels connected to the mother.

Impermeable skin gave reptiles the chance to live permanently out of water without dehydrating. Salt glands on the side of the nose of some turtles, snakes and lizards also help to reduce water loss. These excrete unwanted salts to reduce the amount of water required in the urine. Snakes and lizards excrete urine as a near-solid waste, composed mainly of uric acid crystals. This is another key adaptation for water conservation. Internal fertilisation has also helped free reptiles from an aquatic life. Females have a combined urinogenital opening. In tuataras, males also have a similar vent that they bring up against that of the female to transfer sperm in a "cloacal kiss." Male crocodiles and turtles have a penis, while lizards and snakes have two functional hemipenes. This is somewhat like having two penises, although they use only one at a time. Reptiles such as snakes and lizards can remain bound together in copulation for hours. The intricate hemipenes are valuable identification structures in the taxonomy of snakes.

Devoted parent The mothers of many snake species stay with or near their eggs to deter predators. Most female pythons, including Australia's children's python, also coil their bodies around their brood, generating warmth by muscle twitching to hasten development of the embryos within the eggs. During the entire incubation time, which may take months, the female remains with her eggs and does not feed.

Misplaced survivor The Seychelles giant tortoise was believed extinct for at least 120 years until scientists rediscovered it in the late 1990s. Individuals from this species, including museum specimens and animals in zoos, were previously thought to have belonged to another giant tortoise species. Modern DNA analysis was needed to crack this case of mistaken identity.

Crocodile call Reptiles produce eggs within which the embryo develops and hatches (or is born, in the case of live-bearing species). A series of fluid-filled sacs cushion the developing embryo within a calcareous shell that is permeable to gases, such as oxygen and carbon dioxide, but which restricts water loss. While still in their eggs in an underground nest, Nile crocodiles call to their mothers when they are ready to hatch.

Skin replacement Most vertebrates lose skin cells continuously but snakes shed, or slough, their entire outer layer all at once at various times throughout the year. Snakes are particularly vulnerable to predators until their new skin layer, which is secreted beneath the old one, fully hardens. They will even shed their translucent eye caps. Timing is related to both internal and environmental cues.

REPTILES THROUGH THE AGES

The ancestral reptile group, the Captorhinomorpha, which gave rise to all reptiles, had probably appeared by about 315 million years ago. This group of rather small and agile lizard-like animals is known from fossils found in ancient tree stumps from the late Carboniferous, as well as in subsequent Permian sediments. These ancient predators did not have the powerful snapping bite of the early amphibians from which they probably arose. Instead, their crunching bite was better suited to deal with the chitinous armour of their insect prey. The Archosauromorpha – the ruling reptiles from which dinosaurs and crocodiles ultimately arose – was, and remains, the most diverse reptile group ever. Early representatives were the rhyncosaurs – herbivores which, along with synapsids (mammal-like reptiles), were the dominant land animals for about 60 million years until the rise of the dinosaurs. They did not take to the air until the late Permian, when *Coelurosauravus*, with a 30cm (12-inch) wingspan, took flight.

CONTINENTAL DRIFT

Extensive geological, palaeontological and biological evidence suggests ancient connections between continents and indicates that these land masses are still drifting inches apart annually. It is thought that about 300 million years ago, all today's continents were joined in one large supercontinent known as Pangea. This huge land mass began separating about 200 million years ago to create two great continents. Biological similarities between past species preserved in the fossil record and present species support evidence that Australia, India, Africa, South America and Antarctica were once part of a southern supercontinent known as Gondwana. Similarly, Asia, North America, and Europe were once joined in a northern land mass, known as Laurasia.

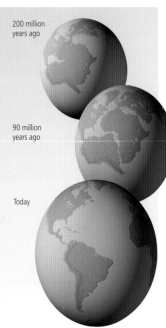

200 million years ago

90 million years ago

Today

Pteranodon, a pterosaur from the late Cretaceous, fed on fish like a pelican.

Coelurosauravus, from the Permian, could glide from tree to tree like a flying lizard today.

Pachyachis, from the Cretaceous, may be related to the ancestor of modern snakes.

Stegosaurus, from the Jurassic, was a dinosaur that ate plants.

Dimetrodon, from the Permian, was related to the ancestors of mammals.

Hylonomus, from the Carboniferous, is known only from fossils found trapped in fossilised tree trunks.

Proganochelys, from the Triassic, had much in common with living tortoises.

Planocephalosaurus

Deinosuchus, from the Cretaceous, could be the largest crocodile ever to have lived.

Archelon

Ichthyosaurus, from the Jurassic, was streamlined and ate fish like a modern dolphin.

Earliy reptiles, Reptiles were at their most diverse during the Cretaceous, 165–144 million years ago.

Elasmosaurus, from the Cretaceous, had the longest neck of any marine reptile.

DINOSAURS RULE

The earliest dinosaurs appeared around the same time as the lineage that led to modern reptiles. They were small, bipedal and carnivorous but the group diversified quickly. By the end of the Triassic, 206 million years ago, many herbivorous forms had appeared, including some that had begun approaching the massive sizes for which dinosaurs are renowned. The radiation of dinosaurs across Earth's terrestrial habitats coincided with the appearance and global spread of coniferous trees, the main source of food for the largest of these creatures.

Dinosaurs dominated the planet for 150 million years, reaching their peak diversity during the Jurassic. The last dinosaurs disappeared some 65 million years ago as part of the mass extinction at the end of the Cretaceous. Thought to have been caused by a catastrophic event, such as a meteor hitting Earth, this extinction also saw the demise of almost all other large reptiles. Two important exceptions were turtles and crocodiles. Lower temperatures may have exterminated the dinosaurs if they had temperature-controlled sex determination. Crocodiles and turtles may have survived as they produce females at both low and high temperatures, and males at medium temperatures.

CLASSIFICATION

As well as having discovered, described and given names to some 1.7 million modern species of animals, biologists include extinct species in their classification system. This is particularly significant for reptiles because current reptilian diversity is a mere shadow of what it has been during Earth's history. The classification process does two things: it provides a unique name for each animal, both extinct and living; and it sorts them into a hierarchy of increasingly inclusive groups, known as taxa, based on evolutionary relationships. In this way, all animals can be unequivocally recognised and associated with other species having a common ancestry. Much of the new taxonomy relies on biochemical studies of DNA to determine common ancestry and species divergence.

Naming rights Biologists use a system known as Linnaean classification to sort and organise living organisms. Its principal feature is that it assigns a unique two-part name to every organism, such as Crocodylus intermedius. The first part indicates the genus to which an organism belongs. The second part, combined with the first, is the species. Only one organism within any genus will ever be assigned this name.

Living fossils Two species of tuatara, Sphenodon punctatus and S. guntheri, are the only survivors of a large reptile group that was widespread more than 225 million years ago. Fossil evidence reveals the relict species, which are now confined to small islands off New Zealand, have changed little since their evolution. Tuataras were once threatened but now, through strict conservation measures, more than 60,000 thrive on 30 islands.

KINGDOM
Animalia
Orinoco crocodile, stick insect, sponge, sea urchins

PHYLUM
Chordata
Orinoco crocodile, fish, salamander, dinosaur, albatross, human

CLASS
Reptilia
Orinoco crocodile, turtles, lizards, snakes, tuatara, amphisbaenians

ORDER
Crocodilia
Orinoco crocodile, caimans, crocodiles, alligators, gharials

FAMILY
Crocodylidae
Orinoco crocodile, crocodiles, alligators, gharials

GENUS
Crocodylus
Orinoco crocodile, other crocodiles

SPECIES
Crocodylus intermedius
Orinoco crocodile

GROWING GROUP

So far, more than 8,000 reptile species have been described. Although some of the largest and most spectacular – such as the Komodo dragon, leatherback turtle and saltwater crocodile – are very distinctive, many closely related forms are characterised by only subtle differences. Sometimes, such intangible areas as vocalisations and behaviour can yield features of value in classifying reptiles. Internal attributes, including aspects of the skeleton and even tissues and organs, are also often used to differentiate between groups. Most often, though, attributes involving external appearance and structure are the keys to classifying reptiles. These include shape, size, body proportions and colouration. For example, differences in the number, shape, and structure of scales can be of great significance in snake and lizard identification and classification.

Because many modern reptiles are small and secretive, occur only across a localised range or inhabit unexplored regions, as many as 25 new species are still being discovered and described each year. Most of these new species are from the vast, uncharted regions of the Amazon rain forest.

REPTILES

Class Reptilia

Order Testudines
Tortoises and turtles

Order Crocodilia
Crocodilians

Order Rhyncocephalia
Tuatara

Order Squamata
Lizards and snakes

Suborder Amphisbaenia
Worm lizards

Order Testudines, page 24

BIOLOGY AND BEHAVIOUR

Because reptiles have internal fertilisation, species recognition is vital. In order to get together to mate, individuals need to be able to communicate clearly with others of their own kind. Some reptilian communication is visual, as occurs with displaying iguanid lizards. Most snakes employ a form of olfactory communication, which includes the use of chemical substances called pheromones. Crocodiles, alligators and some lizards use calls, grunts and other vocalisations to communicate with prospective mates. Signals provide information, not only for species identity, but also about the gender and reproductive fitness of individuals. The loudness and deepness of the crocodile's bellow is an indicator of its size and prowess.

TERRITORIALITY

Most male lizards both advertise and defend their territory with ritualised displays. Among the Iguanidae and Agamidae, this posturing emphasises body colouration and patterns. Displays can be reinforced by 'push-ups', head-bobbing or other movements. Territoriality is uncommon in snakes. However some, such as the vipers and pit vipers, have elaborate male combat rituals that may establish reproductive rights. Sparring male rattlesnakes, for example, raise their heads and bodies high, and twist against opponents, trying to topple them. Some male tortoises butt shells in strength tests to establish reproductive superiority. Larger aquatic turtles maintain their preferred basking positions on logs by aggressive behaviour.

COURTSHIP

In snake courtship, the male usually crawls repeatedly over the female to orient their heads in the same position, while also aligning his tail with hers. Some males hold females in place using a biting grip to the head or neck. Sometimes male lizards do the same, while bringing their tails into a mating position. Many turtles have well-defined rituals. Male false map turtles, for example, court females by vibrating the sides of their faces with long fingernails. A male identifies a female by head markings and then convinces her that he is the correct species by the speed of the vibrating and the number of vibrations per second. The gopher turtle circles his mate on land, sometimes butting her shell to induce passivity so he can mount her.

Colourful display Chameleons (below) are renowned for their ability to rapidly change their skin colour, a skill used more in communication than camouflage. Colour change can convey emotion and sexual status to prospective mates and is also used by males in defending territories. Sexual excitement can cause an explosion of colour.

Ready to mate New World anole lizards (above) are noted for displays of their colourful, sail-like dewlaps. Although both sexes have dewlaps, those of the males are usually bigger and more brightly coloured, and are used to advertise territory ownership. Mature males also use a back crest in breeding and territorial displays.

Mating ritual A male adder of the species Vipera berus will begin courting a receptive female with tongue flicks across her body. The pair's tails, and sometimes also their bodies, vibrate in unison. If another male approaches, the first will vigorously defend his mating rights. The two males will thrash about entwined in a dance-like duel.

MIGRATION

Reptiles are not normally noted for their migratory skills. Sea turtles are among the most spectacular exceptions, with all species swimming great distances between feeding grounds and nesting sites. Some populations of the green sea turtle migrate from the coast of Brazil to nesting beaches 5,000km (3,000 miles) away on Ascension Island in the mid Atlantic Ocean. Other, less spectacular, reptile migrators include prairie rattlesnakes, which can travel up to 15km (9 miles) from their hibernation den in the spring and return in the fall. Marine iguanas of the Galapagos Islands migrate hundreds of miles between lava reefs where they feed on algae, to nesting beaches where they lay their eggs.

Sophisticated travellers To reach their nesting beaches, sea turtles routinely migrate thousands of miles across open ocean. This involves sophisticated guidance mechanisms that are not yet fully understood by scientists. One popular theory suggests they may be able to detect and use Earth's geomagnetic fields, as some birds do. Celestial cues may also be important.

PARENTAL CARE

Female reptiles typically deposit eggs in nests dug in the sand or humus, or in burrows, leaving them to hatch unattended. Some female snakes and lizards retain embryos within the oviducts and bear live young. Parental care is rare, although there are some notable exceptions. Female North American skinks stay with their eggs, keeping them moist and protecting them from fungus and predators. When they hatch, the mother licks the young clean and they go on their way. Rattlesnakes stay with their newborn young for a week or more, and Indian cobras guard their nests from predators until the eggs hatch.

Precious mouthful Many species of crocodilians have extended parental care. As well as guarding their nests when the eggs hatch and their young start peeping, females open their nests and carry their young in their mouth to the water. Once in the water the group of hatchling crocs, called a pod, often stay with their mother for their first six weeks. This extended parental care helps crocodile populations rebound rapidly if hunting pressure is decreased.

Scare tactics The bearded dragons and frilled-neck lizards of Australia have elaborate throat fans, which they greatly enlarge when confronted by a potential threat. They can make themselves appear even more intimidating by opening their mouth and rising on their hind legs. If none of that works, they will flee at speed, running on their hind legs.

DEFENCE

Biting, the most common reptilian defence, is well developed in many snake families, especially the true vipers, pit vipers and elapids such as cobras and their relatives, all of which produce venom. The only venom-producing lizards are the bearded lizards of the Americas.

Body structure and habitat affect the way reptiles express aggression. Many lizards flatten the body while raising it high, making them seem larger to would-be predators. Snakes often inflate or enlarge their neck in a threatening manner, as most cobras do, while other snakes flash a bright colour on the underside of the tail to startle and confuse predators.

CATCHING FOOD

Most reptiles are predators. Smaller species tend to exploit insects and other invertebrates. Larger reptiles commonly feed on mammals, fishes and birds. The primary function of the venom of poisonous snakes is to immobilise prey so it can be consumed. Non-venomous snakes use other methods such as constriction with body coils, as boas and rat snakes do. Some reptiles actively hunt prey. Others adopt a sit-and-wait strategy, striking out only when a potential meal nears. Some even use lures to draw prey close. Australia's death adder, for example, has a modified scale at the end of its tail that it waves from side to side, simulating an insect.

Open threat Many snakes and lizards threaten potential predators by gaping their mouths widely. This display is intended to convey aggression but also makes snakes such as the parrot snake (below) appear larger.

Cryptic colouration Like many other reptiles, this short-horned lizard (below) avoids detection by being so well camouflaged it blends in with its rocky surrounds. Remaining still completes the deception.

Methodical predators The slow-moving gopher snake (bottom) hunts mainly by smell, flicking its forked tongue into rocky burrows and crevices in search of prey such as small rodents, lizards, birds and sometimes even other snakes.

HABITATS AND ADAPTATIONS

Being ectothermic makes reptiles largely intolerant of colder climates. As a result, species numbers in all groups decrease toward higher latitudes and elevations, until eventually they drop out altogether. Just one hardy snake and one lizard species occur above the Arctic Circle, in Scandinavia. On some mountains, lizards scurry around snow banks on their daily activities. Such examples, however, are unusual. There are two kinds of places where reptiles really excel. They are abundant in the tropics and they form a conspicuous part of the desert fauna. Turtles and crocodilians are mainly aquatic, whereas most lizards and snakes are terrestrial or arboreal. There are, as always, interesting exceptions: some tortoises not only live away from water but they do so in desert regions; and some sea snakes live a totally aquatic existence.

TERRESTRIAL REPTILES

The limbs of reptiles are highly adapted to the kind of environment in which they live. Fast-running terrestrial lizards usually have relatively long legs and well-developed toes and claws to help push against the ground. Some lizards with exceptionally long limbs increase their speed by rearing up and running on their hind legs. These lizards have extremely long tails that work as a counterbalance during bipedal running.

Being limbless, terrestrial snakes have a different suite of adaptations. They are able to move across the ground by bending the body and pushing backward against surface irregularities. The large transverse scales on the underside are firmly attached in front, but have a free edge behind where they overlap the following scale. These free edges catch against the ground to prevent the snake from slipping backward. In order to move over surfaces such as loose sand and soft mud, snakes adopt a method known as sidewinding. The snake uses a point of contact with the ground as purchase, then lifts its trunk clear of the ground to secure another point of contact. In sea snakes, which no longer need to grip on the ground, the belly scales are reduced and, in some cases, are no different in size and shape from the dorsal ones. Many terrestrial snakes are long and narrow with relatively long tails, attributes associated with rapid movement across the ground.

Cool pads Gecko feet are lined with millions of tiny hairs, called setae. Each seta ends in multiple branches and each branch ends in a flattened 'spatula'. When these are placed on a surface, intermolecular forces of attraction operate. These are weak in isolation but when multiplied by the billion contact points on a gecko's feet, they enable them to run across ceilings.

Running hot The collared lizards of North American deserts are among the world's fastest lizards. When threatened, they often rear back on their hind legs, the forward part of the body near vertical, and run. Using this bipedal gait, the lizards can reach a top speed of 26km per hour (16mph).

ARBOREAL REPTILES

Many tree-climbing lizards have sharp claws to grasp bark. Geckos grip, even on near-smooth surfaces, using expanded toe pads of ripple-like lamellae. Chameleons have opposable toes that can grasp twigs and a prehensile tail to curl, monkey-style, around branches.

Despite being limbless, many arboreal snakes are amazing climbers: some ascend vertical tree trunks without coiling, instead using crevices in tree bark for purchase. Other arboreal snakes are triangular shaped in cross-section. This provides greater strength and rigidity when the body is extended without support during climbing. Tree-dwelling requires the ability to judge distances. Most arboreal lizards and snakes have forward-directed eyes that can be focused in front to achieve stereovision.

Perhaps the most unusual adaptation of arboreal reptiles is the ability to glide. A genus of Asian lizards (*Draco*) has extended ribs which support the normally loose flank skin to form gliding 'wings'. If disturbed, these 'flying lizards' will escape out of their tree and glide long distances, either to the ground or to another tree trunk. At least one Asian 'flying' snake (*Chrysopelea*) leaps from trees and, by flattening its body, can glide and break its fall. No modern reptiles, however, match the soaring capabilities of the long-extinct pterodactyls.

AQUATIC REPTILES

Females of most aquatic reptile species must come to land to lay their eggs. Only some marine snakes give birth to live young in water and never emerge on land. All reptiles must rise to the surface to breathe periodically but some have evolved capabilities for prolonged diving. Nostril-closing valves, a tight-fitting mouth, and permeable skin that absorbs oxygen and releases bends-causing nitrogen bubbles, enable some sea snakes to remain submerged for up to two hours and dive to 100m (330 feet).

Aquatic reptiles with limbs have evolved webbed feet or, in the sea turtles, flippers. Sea snakes have a flattened, paddle-shaped tail, as do crocodilians and some semi-aquatic lizards. Reptilian kidneys cannot cope with high salinities, and life in the sea is possible for marine reptiles only by virtue of special salt-excreting glands. For example, sea turtles have a modified tear gland that excretes brine from the eye, and the saltwater crocodile has small salt glands scattered over the surface of its tongue.

Floating predator The nostrils and eyes of crocodilians and aquatic snakes are located high on the dorsal surface. This allows an animal to remain low in the water without obstructing either breathing or vision.

SUBTERRANEAN REPTILES

In a dark burrow where the head is in direct contact with the soil, eyes are of no use. Not surprisingly, some burrowing snakes and lizards have only rudimentary eyes. Most truly underground-dwelling reptiles have also lost their limbs. Although these can be useful for digging, they increase friction within a burrow and take up space. The skull bones of many burrowing lizards and snakes are fused into a solid compact structure to form a battering ram. Blindsnakes (family Typhlopidae) have a sharp point on the tail that provides an anchor as they push their smooth, highly polished body through the soil. Amphisbaenians have grooves around their bodies to provide traction so they can inch forward in their burrows.

The limblessness of snakes is probably explained by their ancestry. It is thought they arose from burrowing lizards with reduced limbs. Supposedly, they arose several times. That snakes did have legs at one time is attested for by the vestigial legs, or spurs, found in modern boas and pythons.

Tunnel life The worm lizards, or amphisbaenians, are among the very few completely subterranean and self-tunneling reptiles. None of the 150-plus species has hindlimbs and only a few have rudimentary forelimbs.

REPTILES ON ISLANDS

Many lizards live in and under driftwood that eventually washes out to sea and onto distant shores, carrying adults or eggs in crevices. Some geckos have salt-tolerant eggs that are sticky when laid but become firmly fixed to surfaces when dry. Dispersal by rafting is a relatively rare phenomenon, and a second member of the species may not arrive during the life-span of an individual reptile. Most arriving species would die out with the death of the colonising reptile unless both sexes were present.

Parthenogenesis, where females can lay eggs without insemination by a male, is one solution. Some gecko species characteristic of remote islands are parthenogenic and have few or no males. A colony could be established if just one individual or egg washed up on an island. A widely distributed Pacific blindsnake is also parthenogenic. Some of the parthenogenic whiptail lizards (*Cnemidophorus*) need courtship and pseudo-copulation from other females to stimulate the ovulation of their eggs.

Distant travellers The only relatives of the iguanas of Fiji and neighbouring Pacific islands are in South and Central America. Their ancestors rafted across the Pacific Ocean, and once isolated, evolved into the species of today.

REPTILES IN DANGER

Reptilian biodiversity, like that of most animal groups, is being eroded at an unprecedented rate. Many scientists believe reptile species are disappearing in higher numbers and more quickly than ever before. The last great reptile extinction occurred 65 million years ago, took the last of the dinosaurs, and was caused by a natural event. This time, blame is leveled at the human species and its rapid and massive population growth during recent centuries. Just over 60 per cent of all known reptile species are now included on the IUCN Red List of Threatened Species.

IMAGE PROBLEMS

The major causes of reptile decline are the same as for other animal groups: habitat clearing and fragmentation; poaching, hunting and overexploitation; and pollution. Reptiles, however, tend to suffer more indifference to their plight than groups with more 'cuddly' appeal. Giant pandas, Bengal tigers and humpback whales are all held up as flagship species to draw attention to the plight of disappearing mammals. Among reptiles there is no equivalent pin-up species embraced by the wider conservation movement. Reptiles often gain protection or attention as a by-product of attempts to save other species. Reptilian conservation is also hampered by the fear many people seem to have for these creatures. Only through grass roots educational programs will we appreciate the role of reptiles in the ecosystem.

Stop the traffic Trafficking in wild reptiles is a multimillion-dollar business. It feeds the demand for exotic creatures as pets, food and as material for decorative objects. Most die in transit. China has become the major importer of turtles, placing nearly all of the turtles in Southeast Asia on the IUCN Red List. Authorities intercepted the traffic of 1,500 live turtles (above) bound for China in 2002.

Snake losses Weak economies in several South American countries are contributing to anaconda declines. They are suffering habitat destruction to make way for unsustainable and badly planned forestry, agricultural and urban developments aimed at quick financial returns. Anacondas are also poached for their skins. Commercial farming could be a long-term solution.

TORTOISES AND TURTLES

CLASS	Reptilia
ORDER	Testudines
FAMILIES	14
GENERA	99
SPECIES	293

Turtles and tortoises are the only vertebrates that house the pelvic and pectoral girdles within a shell made of ribs fused with bone. The first fossils to show this trait appeared 220 million years ago in the Triassic period, when dinosaurs roamed the earth. The shell design has since undergone various modifications. The African pancake tortoise has a flexible flat shell allowing it to wedge into crevices; it then inflates, after which it is impossible to pull out. Softshell turtles lack a hard shell; instead, the bones are covered with a smooth leathery shell, giving them more speed. There is still controversy as to whether turtles are derived from a different lineage to other reptiles.

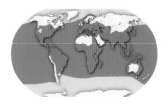

Distribution Turtles are found on all continents except Antarctica, and in all oceans: 241 species of turtles have adapted to freshwater rivers, lakes and ponds; 45 tortoises are terrestrial; only seven species live in the oceans.

Saddleback giant The Galápagos tortoise (above) has a saddleback carapace. This condition is more often seen in adult male tortoises, due to enhanced mating success, from populations on the drier and more barren islands of the Galápagos.

Turtle skeleton A turtle's shell has an outer layer of epidermal scutes (usually 38 on the carapace and 16 on the plastron). Under these, a shell of fused ribs (the plastron) supports the body. The vertebrae are joined to the inside of the carapace.

Baby leatherback Leatherback turtles lay up to six nests of up to 200 eggs a year for decades. This hatchling has passed the first hurdle: 2 months incubating in the sand with predators digging around it. It now has to face the many threats in the sea.

EVOLUTION SHELLED OUT

In addition to the shell, turtles and tortoises have evolved many unique features. Turtle muscles are able to withstand high levels of lactic acid, so they do not tire after swimming rapidly. They also fill their large urinary bladders with water for ballast to maintain buoyancy. Turtles and tortoises occupy niches as predators, grazers, croppers and scavengers. Some have gut flora to digest plant cells; others are seed dispersers. Wood turtles stomp on the ground with their front feet, then eat the earthworms that come out of the ground.

Some sea turtles and freshwater turtles nest within a few days in tremendous numbers on the same nesting beach. These mass nestings, known as arribadas, evolved to swamp local predators – it would be impossible for them to eat all of the eggs or kill all of the females. The success of these adaptations has helped turtles to survive over millions of years; now, as a result of human intervention, two-thirds of all turtle species are being carefully monitored by the IUCN.

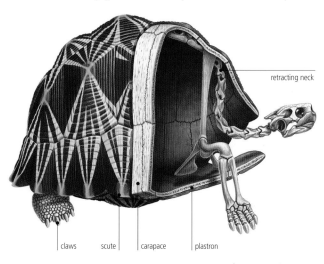

retracting neck

claws   scute   carapace   plastron

Swimming sea turtle The forelimbs of sea turtles have been modified into flipper-shaped paddles that move synchronously, resembling aquatic flying rather than swimming. Sea turtles are so adept in the water that they rarely leave it except to nest. Freshwater turtles swim using all four limbs in turn.

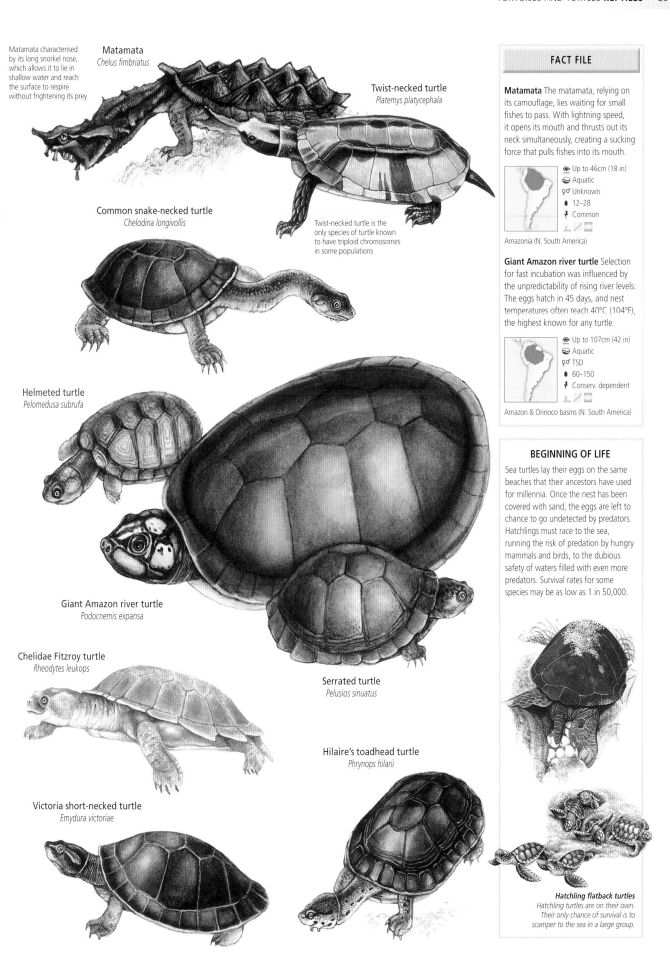

Matamata characterised by its long snorkel nose, which allows it to lie in shallow water and reach the surface to respire without frightening its prey

Matamata
Chelus fimbriatus

Twist-necked turtle
Platemys platycephala

Twist-necked turtle is the only species of turtle known to have triploid chromosomes in some populations

Common snake-necked turtle
Chelodina longivollis

Helmeted turtle
Pelomedusa subrufa

Giant Amazon river turtle
Podocnemis expansa

Chelidae Fitzroy turtle
Rheodytes leukops

Serrated turtle
Pelusios sinuatus

Hilaire's toadhead turtle
Phrynops hilarii

Victoria short-necked turtle
Emydura victoriae

FACT FILE

Matamata The matamata, relying on its camouflage, lies waiting for small fishes to pass. With lightning speed, it opens its mouth and thrusts out its neck simultaneously, creating a sucking force that pulls fishes into its mouth.

- Up to 46cm (18 in)
- Aquatic
- ♀♂ Unknown
- 12–28
- Common

Amazonia (N. South America)

Giant Amazon river turtle Selection for fast incubation was influenced by the unpredictability of rising river levels. The eggs hatch in 45 days, and nest temperatures often reach 40°C (104°F), the highest known for any turtle.

- Up to 107cm (42 in)
- Aquatic
- ♀♂ TSD
- 60–150
- Conserv. dependent

Amazon & Orinoco basins (N. South America)

BEGINNING OF LIFE

Sea turtles lay their eggs on the same beaches that their ancestors have used for millennia. Once the nest has been covered with sand, the eggs are left to chance to go undetected by predators. Hatchlings must race to the sea, running the risk of predation by hungry mammals and birds, to the dubious safety of waters filled with even more predators. Survival rates for some species may be as low as 1 in 50,000.

Hatchling flatback turtles
Hatchling turtles are on their own. Their only chance of survival is to scamper to the sea in a large group.

FACT FILE

Green turtle Green turtles migrate huge distances across the open seas between their feeding grounds and nesting beaches. They graze in shallow-waters on submerged vegetation. Adults are primarily herbivorous, while juveniles are more carnivorous.

- 🐢 Up to 1.5m (5 ft)
- 〰️ Aquatic
- ♀♂ TSD
- 🥚 50–240
- ⚡ Endangered

Tropical oceans worldwide & Mediterranean Sea

Olive Ridley turtle This species is characteristic of turtles that nest in arribadas. Most of the population comes to nest within a 2–3 day period on the same beach. Arribadas in Orissa, India, have numbered more than 100,000 turtles nesting each year.

- 🐢 Up to 79cm (31 in)
- 〰️ Aquatic
- ♀♂ TSD
- 🥚 30–168
- ⚡ Endangered

Primarily tropical regions of Pacific, Indian & Atlantic oceans

SHELL SHAPES

Tortoises are high-domed to protect them from predators and store water. Pond turtles are more streamlined so that they can swim with less resistance. Semi-terrestrial turtles have higher domes for predator protection. Sea turtles are designed for least resistance to glide through the water.

Land tortoise

Semi-terrestrial

Sea turtle

Pond turtle

Front feet modified as flippers; swim with a figure-eight stroke

Loggerhead
Caretta caretta

Green turtle
Chelonia mydas

Olive Ridley turtle
Lepidochelys olivacea

Kemp's Ridley turtle
Lepidochelys kempi

Leatherback turtle
Dermochelys coriacea

Carapace scutes used for making combs and hair ornaments

Flatback turtle
Natador depressus

Hawksbill turtle
Eretmochelys imbricata

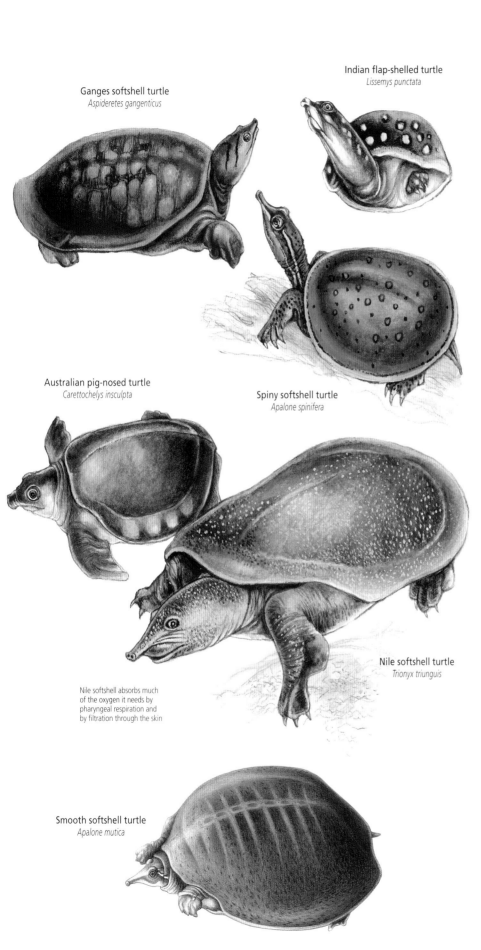

Ganges softshell turtle
Aspideretes gangenticus

Indian flap-shelled turtle
Lissemys punctata

Australian pig-nosed turtle
Carettochelys insculpta

Spiny softshell turtle
Apalone spinifera

Nile softshell turtle
Trionyx triunguis

Nile softshell absorbs much
of the oxygen it needs by
pharyngeal respiration and
by filtration through the skin

Smooth softshell turtle
Apalone mutica

FACT FILE

Ganges softshell turtle An important scavenger, this species helps to lower pollution levels in the Ganges River by consuming partially cremated human corpses that are thrown into the river in traditional funeral rites.

- Up to 71cm (28 in)
- Aquatic
- ♀♂ Unknown
- 25–35
- Vulnerable

N. India, N.W. Pakistan, Bangladesh & Nepal

HEAT AND SEX

Sex in some species of turtles, as in most vertebrates, is genetic (referred to as GSD, or genetic sex determination). In most turtles studied, some lizards, all crocodiles, and the tuatara, sex is controlled by the incubation temperature (referred to as TSD, or temperature sex determination). The temperature during the middle third of the incubation period determines what the sex of the hatchling turtle will be. Females are produced at extreme low and high temperatures and males at intermediate temperatures. Thus a female can control the sex of her offspring by where she lays her eggs: nests out in the full sunlight produce females, while nests in the shade produce males; the first nests in summer produce females, while the last nests in the fall produce males.

Wood turtle hatching
Wood turtles are one of the few North American turtles in the family Emydidae to have GSD; most others have TSD.

🏴 CONSERVATION WATCH

The 198 species of testudines on the IUCN Red List are categorised as follows:

7	Extinct
1	Extinct in the wild
25	Critically endangered
46	Endangered
57	Vulnerable
1	Conservation dependent
41	Near threatened
13	Data deficient
7	Least concern

FACT FILE

Diamond-back terrapin This is the only turtle to specialise in living in brackish water marshes. It was once driven to near extinction because of its popularity for the gourmet table.

- Up to 24cm (9½ in)
- Aquatic
- ♀♂ TSD
- 4–18
- Near threatened

E. seaboard & Gulf Coast (USA)

Ringed sawback This species thrives in fast-moving water, where it forages for aquatic insect larvae. It is endangered due to pollution of the Pearl River. The pet trade and target practice have also reduced its numbers.

- Up to 21cm (8½ in)
- Aquatic
- ♀♂ TSD
- 4–8
- Endangered

Pearl River, Mississippi (USA)

European pond turtle Only males hatch at incubation temperatures of 24–28°C (75–82°F), while at 30°C (86°F), 96 per cent of the hatchlings are females. At higher temperatures, only females are produced.

- Up to 20cm (8 in)
- Aquatic
- ♀♂ TSD
- 3–16
- Common

S. Europe & W. Asia

Painted turtle In spring, this cold adapted species can be seen swimming under the ice and mating in iceflows. Hatchlings overwinter in the nest, super-cooling yet not freezing at 4°C (20°F).

- Up to 25cm (10 in)
- Aquatic
- ♀♂ TSD
- 4–20
- Common

E. & C. USA

River cooter A complete herbivore, this species is often seen basking by the dozens on floating logs in order to raise its body temperature to speed digestion. Basking is also important for ridding the shell and limbs of fungal and algal colonies.

- Up to 43cm (17 in)
- Aquatic
- ♀♂ TSD
- 6–28
- Common

S.E. USA

Diamond-back terrapin
Malaclemys terrapin

Ringed sawback
Graptemys oculifera

Wood turtle
Clemmys insculpta

Eastern box turtle
Terrapene carolina

Cagle's map turtle
Graptemys caglei

Red-eared slider
Trachemys scripta

Red-bellied turtle
Pseudemys rubiventris

European pond turtle
Emys orbicularis

Scorpion mud turtle
Kinosternon scorpioides

Muhlenberg's turtle
Clemmys muhlenbergi

Painted turtle
Chrysemys picta

River cooter
Pseudemys concinna

Furrowed wood turtle
Rhinoclemmys areolata

Indian roofed turtle
Kachuga tecta

Caspian turtle
Mauremys caspica

Malayan box turtle
Cuora amboinensis

Malayan snail-eating turtle
Malayemys subtrijuga

Spotted pond turtle
Geoclemys hamiltoni

Black-breasted leaf turtle
Geoemyda spengleri

River terrapin
Batagur baska

One of the few freshwater
turtles to nest on ocean
beaches. The hatchlings
can live for at least
2 weeks in sea water

Painted terrapin
Callagur borneoensis

Feeds almost entirely
on terrestrial plants

FACT FILE

River terrapin During the breeding season, from September to November, the male's head colouration changes. The nostrils become blue, the iris white, the head deep black and the neck and front limbs deep red and black. Sand mining is destroying the preferred nesting beaches of this species.

⊕ Up to 60cm (24 in)
◒ Aquatic
♀♂ Unknown
● 12–34
⚡ Critically endangered

E. India & Bangladesh to Burma, Thailand, Cambodia & Indonesia

Painted terrapin Painted terrapins are exploited for their eggs, which fetch five times the price of chicken eggs. Habitat destruction is also exacerbating the decline of the species. Only one or two rivers harbor more than a hundred nesting females.

⊕ Up to 76cm (30 in)
◒ Aquatic
♀♂ Unknown
● 10–15
⚡ Critically endangered

S. Thailand, Malaysia, Sumatra & Borneo

LEG ADAPTATIONS

From the shape of the leg, foot and claws, it is possible to deduce what habitat the turtle was adapted for, but not necessarily where it is living today.

Sea turtle The forelimbs of sea turtles are aero-dynamically designed to fly through water. They are tapered from tip to base like the wings of an albatross. There is no webbing, as the toes are fused together within the flippers.

Land tortoise This animal is designed for walking with a load on land, not for swimming. The legs have armoured plates, the unwebbed toes are elephantine and the feet are flat to support the tortoise's weight on land.

Pond turtle The legs are only slightly paddle-shaped to navigate through aquatic vegetation and to walk on land. The toes are webbed, with long, claw-like toenails for traction when crawling up logs to bask.

FACT FILE

Leopard tortoise During courtship, the male trails the female, butting her into submission. After mounting, he extends his neck and releases a grunt-like bellow. Females lay 5–7 clutches of 5–30 eggs from May to October.

- 🐢 Up to 68cm (27 in)
- ◯ Terrestrial
- ♀♂ Unknown
- ● 5–30
- 🗲 Common

S. Sudan & Ethiopia to Natal & South Africa

African tent tortoise Nesting takes place from September to December, when up to three ellipsoidal eggs are laid in a single yearly clutch. The eggs hatch between April and May. The hatchlings are 2.5cm (1 inch) long.

- 🐢 Up to 16cm (5½ in)
- ◯ Terrestrial
- ♀♂ Unknown
- ● 1–3
- 🗲 Common

S.W. Africa to Cape (South Africa)

Texas tortoise This species feeds on the pads, flowers and fruit of cactus. In the Chihuahuan Desert, they are active early in the morning, and rest in the shade or in burrows during the heat of the day.

- 🐢 Up to 22cm (8½ in)
- ◯ Terrestrial
- ♀♂ TSD
- ● 1–4
- 🗲 Vulnerable

S. Texas (USA) to N. Mexico

COURTSHIP

Courtship occurs in turtles that have sympatric congeners to ensure intra-specific mating. Males come face to face with the female, and present head bobs or titillations with the foreclaws to the face of the female. The number of bobs or vibrations and the length of the bout are species-specific.

Titillating a female Red-eared slider males are smaller than females. A courting male vibrates his foreclaws against the sides of the female's head. If the number of beats per minute is correct, it identifies him as a suitable male to breed with.

Leopard tortoise
Geochelone pardalis

Dark blotches on carapace

Bell's hinge-back tortoise
Kinixis belliana

Marginated tortoise
Testudo marginata

Radiated tortoise
Geochelone radiata

Dark lines on carapace

Speckled cape tortoise
Homopus signatus

Elongated tortoise
Indotestudo elongata

Bright red scales on legs

South American red-footed tortoise
Geochelone carbonaria

African tent tortoise
Psammobates tentorius

African pancake tortoise
Malacochersus tornieri

Texas tortoise
Gopherus polyphemus

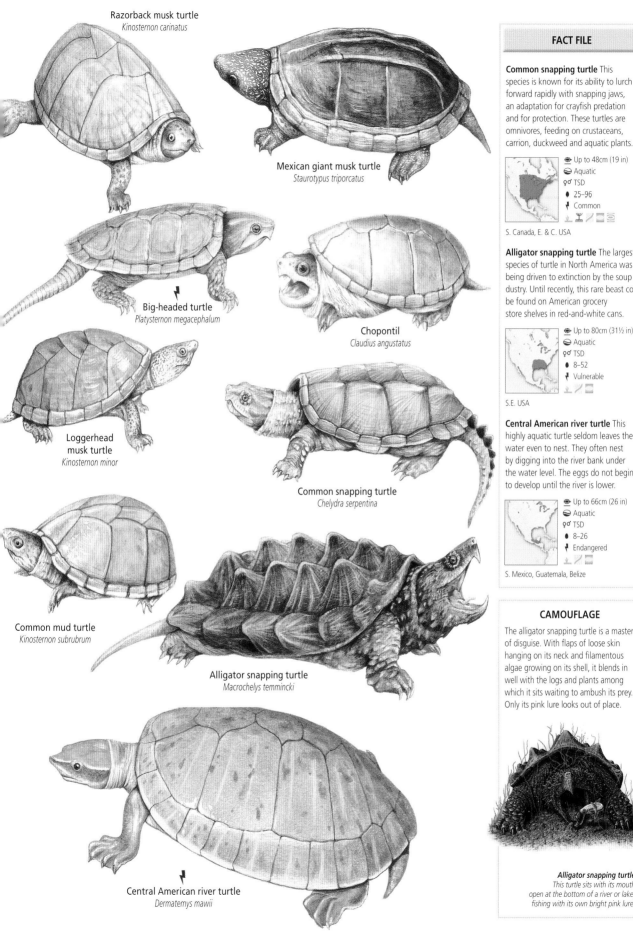

Razorback musk turtle
Kinosternon carinatus

Mexican giant musk turtle
Staurotypus triporcatus

Big-headed turtle
Platysternon megacephalum

Chopontil
Claudius angustatus

Loggerhead
musk turtle
Kinosternon minor

Common snapping turtle
Chelydra serpentina

Common mud turtle
Kinosternon subrubrum

Alligator snapping turtle
Macrochelys temmincki

Central American river turtle
Dermatemys mawii

FACT FILE

Common snapping turtle This species is known for its ability to lurch forward rapidly with snapping jaws, an adaptation for crayfish predation and for protection. These turtles are omnivores, feeding on crustaceans, carrion, duckweed and aquatic plants.

- Up to 48cm (19 in)
- Aquatic
- ♀♂ TSD
- 25–96
- Common

S. Canada, E. & C. USA

Alligator snapping turtle The largest species of turtle in North America was being driven to extinction by the soup industry. Until recently, this rare beast could be found on American grocery store shelves in red-and-white cans.

- Up to 80cm (31½ in)
- Aquatic
- ♀♂ TSD
- 8–52
- Vulnerable

S.E. USA

Central American river turtle This highly aquatic turtle seldom leaves the water even to nest. They often nest by digging into the river bank under the water level. The eggs do not begin to develop until the river is lower.

- Up to 66cm (26 in)
- Aquatic
- ♀♂ TSD
- 8–26
- Endangered

S. Mexico, Guatemala, Belize

CAMOUFLAGE

The alligator snapping turtle is a master of disguise. With flaps of loose skin hanging on its neck and filamentous algae growing on its shell, it blends in well with the logs and plants among which it sits waiting to ambush its prey. Only its pink lure looks out of place.

Alligator snapping turtle
This turtle sits with its mouth open at the bottom of a river or lake, fishing with its own bright pink lure.

DEATH ROW

During the last five years, the decimation of turtle populations has accelerated rapidly. The Turtle Survival Alliance (TSA) has been formed to monitor and attempt to reverse this trend. TSA shortlisted 25 of the most critically endangered species to raise awareness of the problem. Most of these species occur in hotspots for high biodiversity – areas that are important for the critical habitat of a number of other taxa as well. The turtles are in trouble because of over-exploitation for food or traditional remedies, the pet trade, restricted range and habitat degradation. Only five of these are suffering due to habitat degradation – 15 of the 25 are on the brink of extinction because of uncontrolled exploitation by humans.

Bogged down The bog turtle (*Clemmys muhlenbergii*) is endemic to acidic wetlands of the Piedmont and Appalachian mountains, USA. Habitat fragmentation and destruction; and the pet trade have decimated this species and others such as the yellow-blotched map turtle (*Graptemys flavimaculata*) from Pascagoula River, Mississipi, USA.

Reaping death There are now fewer than 400 ploughshare tortoises (below) in the wild; they are now restricted to the bamboo scrub near Baly Bay in northeastern Mada gascar. Local consumption, the pet trade and habitat degradation have led to their downfall. The tortoise's name comes from the long gular scute that extends under its head and is used in combat by the males.

Lonely giants Once there were 15 distinct island forms of Galápagos tortoises; some are extinct and now only one Abingdon Island tortoise (*Geochelone nigra*) remains. Human predation and feral mammals have had a devastating impact.

Rapid decline The painted terrapin (above) is extinct over much of Indochina due to harvesting of eggs and adults. A small population has been protected in Cambodia since 2001 and 30 hatchlings were released in 2002. However, the Mary River turtle (*Elusor macrurus*) of Australia, which was also on the verge of extinction, has been saved by conservation efforts.

THE WORLD'S MOST ENDANGERED TURTLES

1. MESOAMERICA HOTSPOT
Central American river turtle
Dermatemys mawii

2. CHOCÓ-DARIÉN–WESTERN ECUADOR HOTSPOT
Dahl's toad-headed tortoise
Batrachemys dahli

3. MEDITERRANEAN BASIN HOTSPOT
Egyptian tortoise
Testudo kleinmanni

4. MADAGASCAR AND INDIAN OCEAN ISLANDS HOTSPOT
Madagascar big-headed turtle
Erymnochelys madagascariensis

Ploughshare tortoise
Geochelone yniphora

Flat-tailed tortoise
Pyxis planicauda

5. SUCCULENT KAROO HOTSPOT
Southern speckled padloper tortoise
Homopus signatus cafer

6. CAPE FLORISTIC REGION HOTSPOT
Geometric tortoise
Psammobates geometricus

7. INDO-BURMA HOTSPOT
Striped narrow-headed softshell turtle
Chitra chitra

Chinese three-striped box turtle
Cuora trifasciata

Arakan forest turtle
Heosemys depressa

Burmese star tortoise
Geochelone platynota

Burmese roofed turtle
Kachuga trivittata

Leaf turtle
Mauremys annamensis

Yangtze giant softshell turtle
Rafetus swinhoei

8. SUNDALAND HOTSPOT
River terrapin
Batagur baska

Painted terrapin
Callagur borneoensis

9. PHILIPPINES HOTSPOT
Philippine forest turtle
Heosemys leytensis

10. WALLACEA HOTSPOT
Roti snake-necked turtle
Chelodina mccordi

Sulawesi forest turtle
Leucocephalon yuwonoi

11. SOUTHWESTERN AUSTRALIA HOTSPOT
Western swamp turtle
Pseudemydura umbrina

CROCODILIANS

ss Reptilia
DER Crocodilia
MILIES 3
JERA 8
CIES 23

Alligators, caimans, crocodiles and gharials are all crocodilians, belonging to the lineage of archosaurs, which includes the dinosaurs and birds. Crocodilians are much more closely related to birds than they are to other reptiles, and have existed for 220 million years, since the Triassic period. Part of their success is a result of being the top aquatic predator in their domain. As the body form of crocodilians has stayed the same, they are often called living fossils, but these beasts have been evolving for millions of years and are very different from their ancestors in the age of the dinosaurs. Unlike most reptiles, crocodilians are very vocal, especially during courtship.

Distribution Crocodilians are found in tropical, subtropical and temperate zones worldwide: Gavialidae in South Asia, and Alligatoridae in eastern North America, Central and South America, and eastern China. Crocodylidae inhabit estuaries and freshwater streams of Africa, India, Indonesia, Australia, northern South America, Central America and the West Indies.

Nile crocodile baby When about to hatch, the young call from the egg. Their mother responds by scraping away the material covering the eggs. When they hatch, she gently gulps them into a pouch that has developed in the floor of her mouth, then transports them to their wetland nursery.

Nile crocodile Despite their ferocious look, these animals feed primarily on fishes. Those over 1m (3 feet) mainly eat fishes that are predatory on human food fishes. Maintaining populations of this species in the wild may help the local fishing industry.

CANNIBALISM AND CARE

Crocodilians have an elongated, cylindrical body with short, muscular limbs and a laterally compressed tail. The massive skull is set on a short neck and features strongly toothed jaws. Crocodilians are aquatic, yet bask and nest on shorelines.

Crocodilians are oviparous, with internal fertilisation. Clutches usually contain 12–48 eggs; all species studied have temperature-controlled sex determination, in which females are produced at high and low incubation temperatures and males only at a narrow range of intermediate temperatures.

The eggs are laid in nests made of mounds of vegetation or in nests dug in the sand. Nest site selection can control the sex of the young. Both males and females of some species guard the nest. Females of some species are known to respond to the grunts of the nearly hatched embryos by opening the nests for them. The female will also carry the hatchlings in her mouth to the water, where she has bulldozed a nursery pond for them.

Females will protect their young for the first 2 months. However, males are also known to protect and maintain their territories and food supplies by killing and eating any young male crocodilian in their territory, so the female is often protecting her young from their own father. Female American alligators often stay with their young near the nesting site for 1–2 years.

⚡ CONSERVATION WATCH

The 14 species of crocodilians on the IUCN Red List are categorised as follows:

4	Critically endangered
3	Endangered
3	Vulnerable
2	Conservation dependent
1	Data deficient
1	Least concern

Walk
Crocodilians walking on land hold the limbs vertically beneath the body.

Crawl
Crocodiles crawl low to the ground when they are trying to conceal themselves from potential prey or predators.

Gallop
Australian freshwater crocodiles often gallop over rough terrain.

Crocodile gaits Although crocodiles are primarily aquatic, they use their legs for walking on land and the tail for swimming. On land, the use of ball-and-socket vertebrae allows crocodilians to have varied gaits.

FACT FILE

American alligator Populations of this species were low in the 1950s and protected as endangered in 1967. Populations rebounded in 20 years to over 800,000 animals. Hunting of some populations is now allowed, in order to control their numbers.

⟷ Up to 5.8m (19 ft)
◐ Aquatic
○ Oviparous
● 10–40
♛ Common

S.E. USA

Black caiman This species has recently been reclassified from endangered in Brazil. Conservation efforts over more than 10 years were highly successful, with populations recuperating rapidly. A program to sustainably harvest this species is being enacted.

⟷ Up to 6m (20 ft)
◐ Aquatic
○ Oviparous
● 35–50
♛ Conserv. dependent

Amazon Basin (N. South America)

Chinese alligator This species spends the majority of its life in a complex of underground burrows. The alligators build these systems with pools of water above and below ground as well as air holes for breathing.

⟷ Up to 2m (6½ ft)
◐ Aquatic
○ Oviparous
● 10–40
♛ Critically endangered

Yangtze Valley (China)

ALLIGATOR ACTIVITY

Alligators frequently forage for fishes beneath waterbird rookeries. On occasion, for a change in diet, they will launch themselves at birds as well, using just the propulsion of their tails. They can reach amazing speeds and heights, and it often appears as if they are walking on their tails.

American alligator
Alligator mississippiensis

Black caiman
Caiman niger

Cuvier's dwarf caiman
Paleosuchus palpebrosus

African dwarf crocodile
Osteolaemus tetraspis

Chinese alligator
Alligator sinensis

False gharial
Tomistoma schlegeli

Mugger
Crocodylus palustri

Saltwater crocodile
Crocodylus porosus

Orinoco crocodile
Crocodylus intermedius

Spectacled caiman
Caiman crocodilus

Black tail bands
are characteristic
of the caiman

Siamese crocodile
Crocodylus siamensis

American crocodile
Crocodylus acutus

Five clawed digits
are present on
the forelimb

Gharial
Gavialis gangeticuss

Only the male has
a distinct boss on
the tip of the snout

Nile crocodile
Crocodylus niloticus

FACT FILE

American crocodile This species was once abundant and widespread but was extirpated in many regions due to the skin trade and habitat destruction. Populations have not recuperated in many areas because of habitat loss and continued hunting.

- ↔ Up to 7m (23 ft)
- 🌊 Aquatic
- ○ Oviparous
- ● 30–40
- ⚊ Vulnerable

S. Florida (USA), Mexico to Colombia, Ecuador

Nile crocodile Maturity is reached in 12–15 years at 1.8–2.8m (6–9 feet). The female guards the nest, opens it at hatching and carries the hatchlings to the water. Both parents guard the young for up to 2 months.

- ↔ Up to 6m (19 ft)
- 🌊 Aquatic
- ○ Oviparous
- ● 16–80
- ⚊ Common

Sub-Saharan Africa

ANATOMY

Crocodilians have various adaptations to an aquatic life. The position of the eyes, ear openings and nostrils at the highest part of the body allows them to lie concealed just below the surface of the water when stalking prey. A secondary palate lets them breathe with the mouth closed. A flap of skin in the throat prevents water from entering the throat when the jaws are being opened to capture prey.

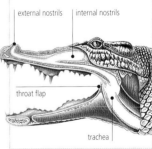

external nostrils | internal nostrils

throat flap

trachea

⚡ CONSERVATION WATCH

Fashion victims Skins from 15 species of crocodilians have been sold as luxury leather products. This has had a negative effect on wild populations of crocodilians. Crocodile farms, meanwhile, are vanishing due to high costs, lower demand and lower prices. Sustainable use of wild populations seems to be more feasible in the long term.

TUATARA

CLASS	Reptilia
ORDER	Rhynchocephalia
FAMILY	Sphenodontidae
GENUS	Sphenodon
SPECIES	2

The tuatara is often called a 'living fossil' and is now only to be found on the islands of New Zealand. It is the only survivor of a large group of reptiles that roamed with the dinosaurs over 225 million years ago, the rest of which became extinct 60 million years ago. Its tooth arrangement is unique: a single row in the lower jaw fits between two rows of teeth in the upper jaw. Lizards have visible ear openings but tuatara do not.

Distribution About 400 Sphenodon guntheri live on North Brother Island, New Zealand. More than 60,000 S. punctatus live on some 30 islands off the northeast coast of New Zealand's North Island.

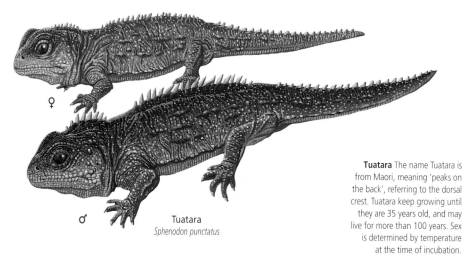

Tuatara The name Tuatara is from Maori, meaning 'peaks on the back', referring to the dorsal crest. Tuatara keep growing until they are 35 years old, and may live for more than 100 years. Sex is determined by temperature at the time of incubation.

♀

♂ **Tuatara**
Sphenodon punctatus

AMPHISBAENIANS

CLASS	Reptilia
ORDER	Squamata
SUBORDER	
Amphisbaenia	
FAMILIES	4
GENERA	21
SPECIES	140

These legless squamates have reduced pectoral and pelvic girdles. They have an annulated pattern of scutes, and short tails. Amphisbaenians are built for burrowing, with heavily ossified skulls. Their brain is surrounded by the frontal bones. The right lung of amphisbaenians is reduced in size, while in other limbless lizards and snakes the left lung is smaller. Three of the four families of worm lizards have no limbs whatsoever, while the remaining family has enlarged forelimbs, which help it with locomotion and digging.

Distribution Amphisbaenians are found in tropical and subtropical regions of southern North America, South America to Patagonia, West Indies, Africa, the Iberian Penisula, Arabia and western Asia.

Shovel-snouted worm lizard The illustration below shows how the worm lizard pushes its head against the ceiling of the tunnel to widen it. Worm lizards have large, interlocking upper and lower teeth, which allow them to grasp prey and drag it into their tunnel.

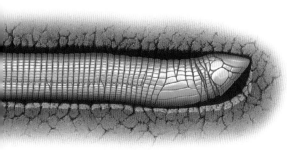

Two-headed legless lizard Amphisbaenians are often erroneously called two-headed snakes, as the tail is designed to mimic the head to confuse potential predators. A wound to the tail would be easier to survive than one to the head.

HOW THEY BURROW

The rings of scales behind the head are close together at the start of the stroke. During penetration the rings separate, pushing the head forward. To widen the tunnel, the head is lifted against the ceiling of the tunnel.

Round heads

Shovel heads

Keel heads

Chisel heads

LIZARDS

Today, lizards occupy almost all landmasses except for Antarctica and some Arctic regions. At the end of the Cretaceous period, some 65 million years ago, lizards survived when the dinosaurs and other large reptiles died out. With more than 4,000 species, they are the largest group of living reptiles. Although the largest lizard, the Komodo dragon, reaches an impressive length of 3m (10 feet), few lizards exceed 30cm (12 inches) and this is one reason for their continued success. Lizards tend to be restricted to specific habitat niches, as mountains and water are significant barriers to their movement.

ASS Reptilia
DER Squamata
BORDER Sauria
MILIES 27
NERA 442
ECIES 4,560

Distribution Lizards are found from New Zealand to Norway, and from southern Canada to Tierra del Fuego. They are also endemic to many islands in the world's oceans. The only continent they have not colonised is Antarctica.

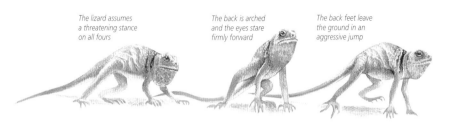

The lizard assumes a threatening stance on all fours

The back is arched and the eyes stare firmly forward

The back feet leave the ground in an aggressive jump

Territorial defence A defined territory provides an area in which an adult male lizard can hunt for food and find a female for mating. If a rival invades its territory, a collard lizard does a series of 'push-ups' to make itself look bigger and more threatening to the unwelcome interloper.

Lizard features *The cone-like spines on the crest of the forest dragon make it appear to be larger and more formidable than it actually is, and its multicoloured scales provide perfect camouflage in the mottled forest light.*

Prehensile-tailed skink The Solomon Island skink (*Corucia zebrata*) is arboreal and herbivorous. It uses its prehensile tail to hold onto branches as it feeds on fruits and leaves in the treetops.

DEFENCE AND ESCAPE

Lizards are preyed upon by spiders, scorpions, other lizards, snakes, birds, and mammals. The Gila monster and the Mexican beaded lizard are the only two venomous species, but even these will resort to scare tactics at the start of a confrontation. Many others have developed an impressive array of tactics to defend themselves or to escape an attacker.

Most lizards are extremely well camouflaged and may keep absolutely still until a predator passes by. Chameleons, in particular, are well known for their ability to change colour to blend in with their environment. Other lizards surprise or distract a predator to give themselves a chance to escape. The Australian frilled lizard, for example, opens its mouth, hisses loudly and flourishes its neck frill before scampering away.

Some species have sharp spines that can injure a predator's mouth, or slippery scales that make them hard to grip. The armadillo girdle-tailed lizard curls itself into a ball and protects itself with a prickly fence of spikes, while the basilisk escapes by skimming on water before diving in to safety.

Diurnal dragon *Boyd's forest dragon forages by day near streams or forest edges in tropical rain forests.*

Dragon lizard Boyd's forest dragon (*Hypsilurus boydii*), a chisel-tooth lizard from the rain forests of northeastern Australia, is one of the largest dragon lizards in the world. It can puff out its dewlap – a flap of skin on its throat – to communicate with other forest dragons.

tree-living chameleon

Lizard tails Some lizards have tails that mimic leaves; others mimic heads. Some are used to hold onto branches, and many are expendable. If a predator grabs a skink's tail, the tail stays in the predator's mouth and the lizard escapes.

skink

leaf-tailed gecko

Underwater grazers Marine iguanas on the Galápagos Islands are herbivores from the time they hatch. They dive into the ocean to forage on algae. Before and after diving, they bask to increase their body temperatures to help them more efficiently digest their food, and also to increase swimming stamina in the usually cold seas.

Lizards use their tails for defence. Monitors and iguanas beat their attackers with their tails. Skinks and other small lizards may give up a little piece of tail in return for their lives. These lizards often have brightly coloured tails that they will wave from side to side, inducing the predator to attack the tail and not the head. The tail continues to wriggle after the lizard has escaped. Shed tails grow back after time; the lizard loses some stored energy but remains alive to reproduce. In territorial bouts, some geckos attack and eat the tails of their opponents.

Horned lizards, when attacked by foxes and coyotes, will squirt a stream of bad-tasting blood out of their eyes to distract and discourage potential predators. Some lizards also attempt to scare off predators by sticking out their tongues. Australian skinks hiss and thrust their brightly coloured tongues out to startle predators. Even though the Gila monster is venomous and brightly coloured to warn predators of the risk of attacking, if molested it will display its bright purple tongue and hiss at its aggressor.

Rainforest ranch The common green iguana (above) is completely herbivorous after hatching. The low-cholesterol meat is eaten as a delicacy in Meso-America.

Predatory dragon The Indonesian Komodo dragon (left) tests the air for the scent of warm-blooded prey. These lizards grow to be more than 3m (10 feet) in total length and feed on large mammals such as deer, pigs, goats and even water buffalo.

Fiji banded iguana
Brachylophus fasciatus, family Iguanidae

West Indian iguana
Iguana delicatissima, family Iguanidae

Marine iguana
Amblyrhynchus cristatus,
family Iguanidae

Galápagos
land iguana
Conolophus subcristatus,
family Iguanidae

Rhinoceros iguana
Cyclura cornuta,
family Iguanidae

Black iguana
Ctenosaura similis,
family Iguanidae

The warmer male black
iguana (top) is lighter
in colour; the other male
is colder and darker

Green iguana
Iguana iguana, family Iguanidae

Family Iguanidae This family contains
terrestrial, rock-dwelling, marine and
arboreal species. They range from the
14cm (5½ inch) snout–vent length
Dipsosaurus to the more than 70cm
(27½ inch) Cyclura. Young iguanas
of some species eat insects, but later
become predominantly herbivorous,
feeding on leaves, fruit and even algae.
All species are oviparous.

Genera 8
Species 36

USA to Paraguay,
Galápagos Is., Fiji,
West Indies

Old salts
Marine iguanas spend
so much time at sea that
they have a special gland to
exude salt from their bodies.

Long time coming
The Fiji crested
iguana (Brachylophus
vitiensis) has a 30-week
incubation – three times
that of other iguanas.

LIZARD TONGUES

The long forked tongues of monitors
are used to capture scent information
from the air and to transfer it to the
Jacobson's organ for analysis. The
long, sticky tongues of chameleons
are used to capture prey, while the
blue-tongued skink (below) flashes
its tongue to deter attacking birds.

CONSERVATION WATCH

The 15 species of iguanas on
the IUCN Red List are categorised
as follows:

5 Critically endangered

2 Endangered

7 Vulnerable

1 Near threatened

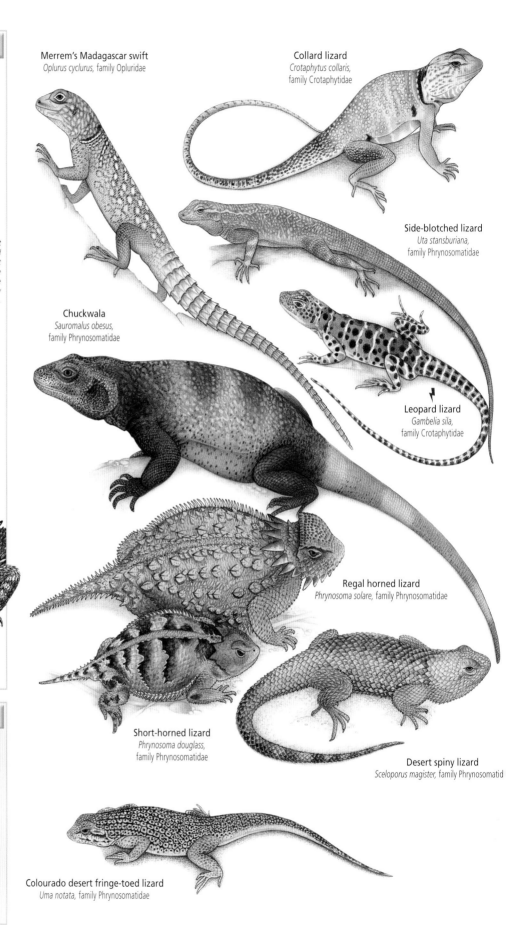

Merrem's Madagascar swift
Oplurus cyclurus, family Opluridae

Collard lizard
Crotaphytus collaris,
family Crotaphytidae

Side-blotched lizard
Uta stansburiana,
family Phrynosomatidae

Chuckwala
Sauromalus obesus,
family Phrynosomatidae

Leopard lizard
Gambelia sila,
family Crotaphytidae

Regal horned lizard
Phrynosoma solare, family Phrynosomatidae

Short-horned lizard
Phrynosoma douglass,
family Phrynosomatidae

Desert spiny lizard
Sceloporus magister, family Phrynosomatid

Colourado desert fringe-toed lizard
Uma notata, family Phrynosomatidae

Blue-throated anole
Norops nitens, family Polychrotidae

Male giving
compound
courtship display

Green basilisk lizard
Basiliscus plumifrons, family Corytophanidaee

Only males have
a head crest

Banded tree anole
Anolis transversalis,
family Polychrotidae

Knight anole
Anolis equestris,
family Polychrotidae

Vinales anole
Anolis vermiculatus,
family Polychrotidae

Bearded anole
Anolis barbatus,
family Polychrotidae

Green thornytail iguana
Uracentron azureum, family Tropiduridae

Common monkey lizard
Polychrus marmouratus, family Polychrotidae

FACT FILE

Family Corytophanidae All members
of this family are carnivorous. Crested
lizards are arboreal, living in rain forests
or tropical scrub forests. Up to 20cm
(8 inches) in snout–vent length, they
have a casque-shaped head, slender
body, long legs and long tails. Basilisk
lizards forage mainly on the ground,
returning to the trees for escape.

No problem Lamina along
the toes gives them more
surface area so that the
basilisk lizard can run
across the water surface.

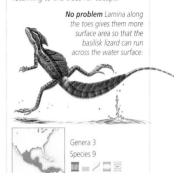

Genera 3
Species 9

Mexico to Colombia,
Venezuela

Family Polychrotidae All anoles
have subdigital lamellae for climbing
and a colourful dewlap for intraspecific
communication. Some species are
terrestrial, others are aquatic. Many are
arboreal. All will lose their tails if they
are grasped, and are oviparous, laying
one to two eggs per clutch. Most are
entirely carnivorous.

Territorial display
Male anoles have a gular fold,
or dewlap, that they inflate to
show their attraction to
females and to maintain
distance between males.

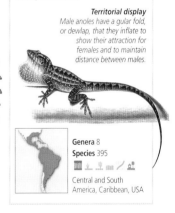

Genera 8
Species 395

Central and South
America, Caribbean, USA

⚡ CONSERVATION WATCH

In general, the diverse habitat
needs of basilisks and anoles ensure
abundant populations throughout
much of their ranges. However,
studies are lacking on many of the
species endemic to rain forests in
Mexico and Central America. As
these habitats dwindle, populations
may need protection. The four
species of Polychrotidae on the IUCN
Red List are categorised as follows:

1   Critically endangered
1   Vulnerable
2   Data deficient

FACT FILE

Family Agamidae Chisel-tooth lizards are from Africa, Asia and Australia. There are 52 genera, ranging from 5–35cm (2–14 inches) in length from snout to vent. Forest species are green; desert species are brown, grey or black. Sexual dimorphism in colouration is common; some can change colouration rapidly. The head is usually large, and distinct from the neck; the body form may be compressed, depressed or cylindrical. The thick tongue is notched.

Genera 50
Species 420

Australia, Indonesia, Asia, Africa

Frilled lizard This arboreal lizard is active diurnally in dry woodlands. When escaping, it runs bipedally. If threatened, it erects its huge frilled collar to appear much larger than it is.

✳ Up to 28cm (11¼ in)
➊ Arboreal
○ Oviparous
● 8–23
♦ Common

N. Australia & S. New Guinea

Carnivores
Frilled lizards feed on cicadas in the trees and will descend to the ground to feed on ants and crickets.

Thorny devil A hygroscopic system of grooves on this lizard's skin leads to the corners of its mouth, allowing it to drink the dew that falls on its back. It feeds only on ants, similar to the North American horned lizards.

✳ Up to 11cm (4½ in)
◐ Terrestrial
○ Oviparous
● 3–10
♦ Common

W. Australia

⚡ CONSERVATION WATCH

The five species of Agamidae on the 2003 IUCN Red List are categorised as follows:

2 Endangered
1 Vulnerable
2 Data deficient

1	Frilled lizard *Chlamydosaurus kingii*, family Agamidae	**5**	Ocellated mastigure *Uromastyx ocellata*, family Agamidae	**8**	Persian agama *Trapelus persicus*, family Agamidae
2	Banded agama *Laudakia stellio*, family Agamidae	**6**	Sinai agama *Pseudotrapelus sinaitus*, family Agamidae	**9**	Moroccan dabb lizard *Uromastyx acanthinura*, family Agamidae
3	Thorny devil *Moloch horridus*, family Agamidae	**7**	Iranian toad-headed agama *Phrynocephalus persicus*, family Agamidae	**10**	Common agama *Agama agama*, family Agamidae
4	Eastern bearded dragon *Pogona barbata*, family Agamidae				

FACT FILE

Sailfin lizard This semiaquatic lizard forages and basks along the edges of streams. When danger approaches, it runs bipedally across the surface of the water with the aid of a fringe on the toes of its hindlimbs. Populations are declining due to over-collection for the pet trade and its popularity as food.

- ✳ Up to 100cm (40 in)
- ⊛ Variable
- ○ Oviparous
- ● 6–12
- ⚑ Common

S.E. Asia, New Guinea

Chinese water dragon These lizards are semiaquatic, living along the shores of rivers, climbing into the lower branches of trees and sharing burrows in colonies of one dominant male and several females. Males have larger crests than females. Incubation time for water dragon eggs is 60 days.

- ✳ Up to 30cm (12 in)
- ⊛ Variable
- ○ Oviparous
- ● 7–12
- ⚑ Common

Thailand, E. Indochina, Vietnam, S. China

Common green forest lizard This arboreal lizard inhabits most forest areas to an altitude of 1,500m (4,900 feet), beyond which they are replaced by other species. Males, the largest lizards in Sri Lanka, have very vivid colouration.

- ✳ Up to 30cm (12 in)
- ⊕ Arboreal
- ○ Oviparous
- ● 10–20
- ⚑ Common

India & Sri Lanka

TREE DRAGON

The semiarboreal tree dragon (*Diporiphora superba*) is one of the most slender agamids. It measures 8cm (3 inches) in snout–vent length and its tail is up to four times its body length.

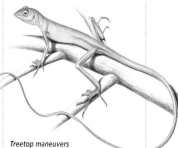

Treetop maneuvers
*The tree dragon uses its long
tail for balance while climbing
and scampering through the branches.*

1	Armoured pricklenape *Acanthosaura armata*, family Agamidae	**4**	Giant forest dragon *Gonocephalus grandis*, family Agamidae
2	Five-lined flying dragon *Draco quinquefasciatus*, family Agamidae	**5**	Chinese water dragon *Physignathus cocincinus*, family Agamidae
3	Sailfin lizard *Hydrosaurus amboinensis*, family Agamidae	**6**	Sumatra nose-horned lizard *Harpesaurus beccarii*, family Agamidae

7	Indo-Chinese forest lizard *Calotes mystaceus*, family Agamidae
8	Common green forest lizard *Calotes calotes*, family Agamidae
9	Tropical forest dragon *Gonocephalus liogaster*, family Agamidae

Clutch size Geckos (top), regardless of size or nutrient condition, produce two eggs per clutch. Some species can vary clutch size and egg size (centre). Large species (bottom) have large clutches of large eggs and the number and size of the eggs is proportionate to the size and physical condition of the female.

Gecko

Fence lizard

Komodo dragon

LIZARD REPRODUCTION

Reproductive patterns in lizards vary widely. Some lizard species mature rapidly, are short lived and are continuously producing an egg. Other species take several years to mature and then lay large clutches of large eggs for many years. Between these two extremes there are all possible variations of numbers of clutches per year and viviparity. Some species are egg layers at low altitudes but populations at high altitudes or latitudes are viviparous. The female acts as an incubator, moving with the developing embryos into optimum incubation temperatures. Equally amazing are some species that are stuck in evolutionary inertia and produce no more than two eggs per clutch regardless of their size or the amount of stored energy.

Continuous ovulation Anoles of all sizes only produce one egg per clutch; they have continuous ovulation, first from one ovary then the other.

Skink with eggs Many species of skinks and glass lizards brood their eggs. The female stays with them, helping to fend off attacks from insect predators, and protecting them from fungus and dehydration until they hatch. Some skinks even lick their young as they are hatching.

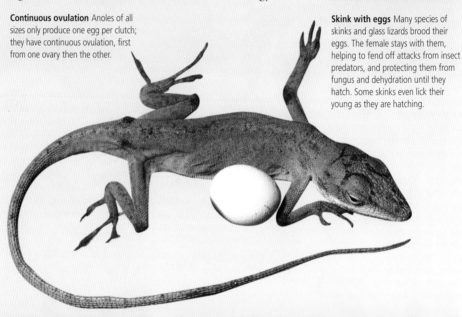

Sceloporus with eggs Fence lizards (Sceloporus) are able to vary the number and size of their eggs according to the time of year and their physical condition. They put their energy into large eggs for the first clutches and many smaller eggs for later clutches that will have less time to develop before the onset of winter.

Iguana with eggs Iguanas normally dig tunnels in sandy beaches and deposit between 25 and 40 eggs, depending on the size of the female. The eggs hatch in 3 months and the hatchlings seek out other iguanas in order to eat their faeces, thereby inoculating their guts with cellulose-digesting microbes.

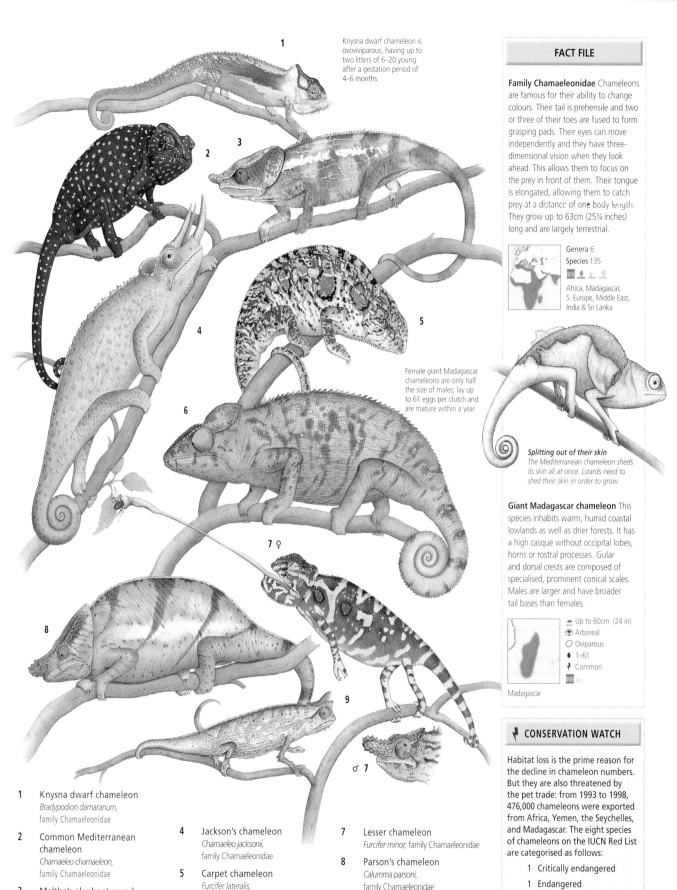

1

Knysna dwarf chameleon is ovoviviparous, having up to two litters of 6–20 young after a gestation period of 4–6 months

Female giant Madagascar chameleons are only half the size of males; lay up to 61 eggs per clutch and are mature within a year

2

3

4

5

6

7 ♀

8

9

♂ 7

FACT FILE

Family Chamaeleonidae Chameleons are famous for their ability to change colours. Their tail is prehensile and two or three of their toes are fused to form grasping pads. Their eyes can move independently and they have three-dimensional vision when they look ahead. This allows them to focus on the prey in front of them. Their tongue is elongated, allowing them to catch prey at a distance of one body length. They grow up to 63cm (25¼ inches) long and are largely terrestrial.

Genera 6
Species 135

Africa, Madagascar,
S. Europe, Middle East,
India & Sri Lanka

Splitting out of their skin
The Mediterranean chameleon sheds
its skin all at once. Lizards need to
shed their skin in order to grow.

Giant Madagascar chameleon This species inhabits warm, humid coastal lowlands as well as drier forests. It has a high casque without occipital lobes, horns or rostral processes. Gular and dorsal crests are composed of specialised, prominent conical scales. Males are larger and have broader tail bases than females.

Up to 60cm (24 in)
Arboreal
Oviparous
1–61
Common

Madagascar

⚡ CONSERVATION WATCH

Habitat loss is the prime reason for the decline in chameleon numbers. But they are also threatened by the pet trade: from 1993 to 1998, 476,000 chameleons were exported from Africa, Yemen, the Seychelles, and Madagascar. The eight species of chameleons on the IUCN Red List are categorised as follows:

1 Critically endangered
1 Endangered
4 Vulnerable
2 Near threatened

1 Knysna dwarf chameleon
Bradypodion damaranum,
family Chamaeleonidae

2 Common Mediterranean chameleon
Chamaeleo chamaeleon,
family Chamaeleonidae

3 Malthe's elephant-eared chameleon
Calumma malthe,
family Chamaeleonidae

4 Jackson's chameleon
Chamaeleo jacksonii,
family Chamaeleonidae

5 Carpet chameleon
Furcifer lateralis,
family Chamaeleonidae

6 Giant Madagascar chameleon
Furcifer oustaleti, family Chamaeleonidae

7 Lesser chameleon
Furcifer minor, family Chamaeleonidae

8 Parson's chameleon
Calumma parsoni,
family Chamaeleonidae

9 Horned leaf chameleon
Brookesia superciliaris,
family Chamaeleonidae

FACT FILE

Family Gekkonidae The geckos are the most speciose family of lizards, split into four subfamilies. Covered with small granular scales, they vary in size from 1.5–33cm (¾ inch to 3 inches). The tails are usually fragile and break easily.

Tongue washing
Most species of geckos do not have eyelids and use the tongue to clean the eye spectacles, as in Cogger's velvet gecko.

Genera 109
Species 970

Pan-tropical, S. North America, South America, Africa, S. Europe, S. Asia, Indo-Australia

Common leopard gecko Leopard geckos have moveable eyelids and lack toe pads. The sex is determined by incubation temperature.

✸ Up to 25cm (10 in)
◗ Terrestrial
○ Oviparous
● 2
♦ Common

Afghanistan, Pakistan, W. India, Iraq, Iran

Banded gecko This nocturnal gecko has large, moveable eyelids, no toe pads and pre-anal pores in a continuous row. Tails are easily lost.

✸ Up to 10cm (4 in)
◗ Terrestrial
○ Oviparous
● 2
♦ Common

S.W. USA to Mexico & Panama

ADAPTED FOR SAND

Fine free-flowing sand requires specialised feet to efficiently traverse the terrain. The African web-footed gecko (*Pallmatogecko rangeri*) uses its feet like snow shoes on the sand to keep it on the surface.

Sand shoes *Some lizards have fringes along the digits to allow them better traction on sand; others have paddle-like webbed feet.*

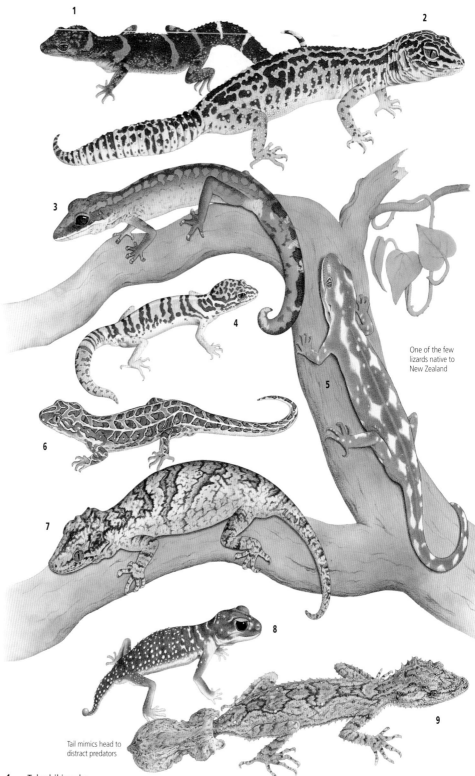

One of the few lizards native to New Zealand

Tail mimics head to distract predators

1   Tokashiki gecko
Goniurosaurus kuroiwae,
family Gekkonidae

2   Common leopard gecko
Eublepharis macularius,
family Gekkonidae

3   Prehensile tailed gecko
Aeluroscalabotes felinus,
family Gekkonidae

4   Banded gecko
Coleonyx variegatus, family Gekkonidae

5   Green tree gecko
Naultinus elegans, family Gekkonidae

6   Thomas's sticky-toed gecko
Hoplodactylus rakiurae,
family Gekkonidae

7   New Caledonia bumpy gecko
Rhacodactylus auriculatus,
family Gekkonidae

8   Stellate knob-tail
Nephrurus stellatus, family Gekkonidae

9   Northern leaf-tailed gecko
Saltuarius cornutus, family Gekkonidae

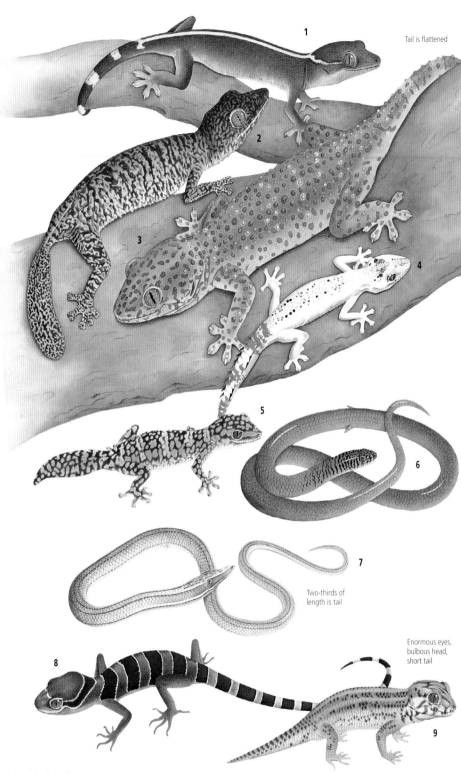

Tail is flattened

Two-thirds of length is tail

Enormous eyes, bulbous head, short tail

FACT FILE

Lined gecko This gekko has a distinct white dorsal stripe. The tail is cross-banded. They are nocturnal and have large distinct laminae on the toes for climbing. Males have a V-shaped row of enlarged pre-anal pores and hemi-penal bulges at the base of the tail.

❋ Up to 25cm (10 in)
◗ Terrestrial
○ Oviparous
● 2
🗡 Common

Indo-Australian archipelago

Gray's bow-fingered gecko This gecko has a flattened, compact body. The toes are long and thin, bending upward and at the ultimate phalange turning downwards, terminating with small lamellae. Granular dorsal scales become spine-like on the tail.

❋ Up to 20cm (8 in)
◗ Terrestrial
○ Oviparous
● 2
🗡 Common

Central Asia, S.E. Asia

Family Pygopodidae This family is closely related to the geckos. Forelimbs are lacking, and the hindlimbs are represented by a scaly flap just anterior to the cloaca. Their tails are fragile and easily broken. The eyes are snake-like, as they lack lids and are covered with an immovable spectacle. Some species have external ear openings. They breed in summer and most lay two eggs. The majority are insectivorous.

Rudimentary feet
The hindlimb of the Burton's snake lizard has been reduced to a flap-like scale, useful for traction in flowing sand.

Genera 8
Species 36

Australia except Tasmania, Aru Islands, New Guinea, New Briton

1   Lined gecko
Gekko vittatus, family Gekkonidae

2   Henkel's flat-tailed gecko
Uroplatus henkeli, family Gekkonidae

3   Tokay gecko
Gekko gecko, family Gekkonidae

4   Northern spiny-tailed gecko
Diplodactylus ciliaris, family Gekkonidae

5   Marbled velvet gecko
Oedura marmourata, family Gekkonidae

6   Marble-faced worm lizard
Delma australus, family Pygopodidae

7   Burton's snake-lizard
Lialis burtonis, family Pygopodidae

8   Grey's bow-fingered gecko
Cyrtodactylus pulchellus,
family Gekkonidae

9   Common wonder gecko
Teratoscincus scincus,
family Gekkonidae

🗡 CONSERVATION WATCH

The seven species of Pygopodidae listed on the IUCN Red List are categorised as follows:

   6   Vulnerable

   1   Near threatened

FACT FILE

Mourning gecko This arboreal gecko is covered with small scales. The tail is long and depressed with a lateral fringe of small, spinose scales.

✳ Up to 5cm (2 in)
✪ Arboreal
○ Oviparous
● 2
♦ Common

N.E. Australia, Malaysia to Oceania

Common wall gecko This gecko is strong and heavily built, with rows of keeled, tubercular scales. Males are territorial. The eggs take 10 weeks to hatch and the young 2 years to mature.

✳ Up to 15cm (6 in)
✪ Arboreal
○ Oviparous
● 2
♦ Common

Mediterranean & S. European coast

Kuhl's flying gecko This terrestrial species lays clutches of two eggs about 30 days apart. The eggs attach to bark or rocks and hatch in about 60 days.

✳ Up to 15cm (6 in)
✪ Arboreal
○ Oviparous
● 2
♦ Common

S.E. Asia

FLYING GECKO

At high speeds, the cutaneous flaps allow flying geckos to slow down and achieve shallower glide angles. The webbed feet function in gliding and their aerial locomotion is more similar to 'flying' tree frogs than to other reptilian gliders.

Parachuting
The skin flaps along the body and tail flare out in flight and allow the Kuhl's flying gecko to break its fall.

⚡ CONSERVATION WATCH

The 27 species of Geckonidae on the IUCN Red List are categorised as follows:

2 Extinct
1 Critically endangered
3 Endangered
8 Vulnerable
7 Near threatened
3 Data deficient
3 Least concern

Broad-tailed day gecko is native to Madagascar but is well established on Hawaii

1 **Madagascar day gecko**
Phelsuma madagascariensis,
family Gekkonidae

2 **Broad-tailed day gecko**
Phelsuma laticauda, family Gekkonidae

3 **Mourning gecko**
Lepidodactylus lugubris,
family Gekkonidae

4 **Common wall gecko**
Tarentola mauritanica,
family Gekkonidae

5 **Israeli fan-fingered gecko**
Ptyodactylus puiseuxi, family Gekkonidae

6 **Kuhl's flying gecko**
Ptychozoon kuhli, family Gekkonidae

7 **Anderson's short-fingered gecko**
Stenodactylus petrii, family Gekkonidae

8 **Ruppell's leaf-toed gecko**
Hemidactylus flaviviridis,
family Gekkonidae

9 **Cradock thick-toed gecko**
Pachydactylus geitje, family Gekkonidae

10 **Wiegmann's striped gecko**
Gonatodes vittatus, family Gekkonidae

Long-tail whip lizard is more than two-thirds tail; the tail will break off, if grasped by a predator, so that the lizard can escape

FACT FILE

Family Gerrhosauridae Plated lizards have large, symmetrical shields with bony plates, and the scales on the body are rectangular and overlapping. They are terrestrial and omnivorous, consuming insects and plants. Limbs are reduced in grassland species. Most species are viviparous. Clutches of between two and six eggs are laid.

Swimming through grass
The long-tail whip lizard is able to compress its legs against its body as it rapidly wriggles through grass stems to escape predators.

Genera 6
Species 32

S. Africa & Madagascar

Family Cordylidae Girdled lizards have large symmetrical scales with bony plates on the head. The rectangular, overlapping body scales are usually strongly keeled but are granular in flat lizards. Girdled lizards are terrestrial and produce live young.

Genera 4
Species 52

S. Africa

Rolled up in a ball
The armadillo girdled lizard (Cordylus cataphractus) bites its own tail to present an unswallowable form to predators.

🦎 CONSERVATION WATCH

The 11 species of Cordylidae on the IUCN Red List are categorised as follows:

1 Extinct
5 Vulnerable
5 Near threatened

---

1 Rough-scaled plated lizard
Gerrhosaurus major,
family Gerrhosauridae

2 Madagascar girdled lizard
Zonosaurus madagascariensis,
family Gerrhosauridae

3 Long-tail whip lizard
Tetradactylus tetradactylus,
family Gerrhosauridae

4 Lesser flat lizard
Platysaurus guttatus, family Cordylidae

5 Karoo girdled lizard
Cordylus polyzonus, family Cordylidae

6 Black crag lizard
Pseudocordylus melanotus,
family Cordylidae

7 Mole skink
Eumeces egregius, family Scincidae

8 Schneider's skink
Novoeumeces schneideri, family Scincidae

9 Sand fish
Scincus scincus, family Scincidae

FACT FILE

Family Scincidae Skinks are usually covered with overlapping smooth scales. The adults vary from 2.5–35cm (1–14 inches) in length. The body shape varies from robust species to species with no external limbs. Limbless species are usually burrowers and the rest are terrestrial or arboreal. Tails are long to moderately long. Tail autonomy is present in most species. Skinks are active foragers, using both visual and olfactory cues to find prey. Most species lay eggs, but viviparity evolved in the family at least 25 times.

Genera 116
Species 993

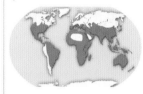

Cosmopolitan in most terrestrial habitats

Telltale tails *Territorial male five-lined skinks (Eumeces fasciatus) recognise females and juveniles by their bright blue tails and allow them access to their territories.*

Hosmer's spiny-tailed skink The base of this skink's tail lacks enlarged and expanded scales, and long, rugose ear lobules almost conceal the ear. This is a diurnal rock-dwelling lizard found in rock outcrops and stony hillsides, where it lives in crevices, under boulders and on tumbled rock slides.

✳ Up to 18cm (7 in)
🌣 Terrestrial
○ Oviparous
● 2
⚘ Common

N.E. Australia

Centralian blue-tongued lizard This lizard has a bright blue tongue, relatively short five-toed limbs, and a short tail. It thrives in stony areas in desert and semidesert areas where it feeds on insects and other invertebrates. The tail is about half the body length.

✳ Up to 30cm (12 in)
🌣 Terrestrial
⚲ Viviparous
● 10 live young
⚘ Common

N. & N.W. Australia

Solomon Island skink can grasp a branch and hang by its prehensile tail

1	**Solomon Island skink**	3	**Hosmer's spiny-tailed skink**	5	**Shingleback lizard**
	Corucia zebrata, family Scincidae		*Egernia hosmeri*, family Scincidae		*Tiliqua rugosa*, family Scincidae
2	**Emerald skink**	4	**Centralian blue-tongued lizard**	6	**Three-lined burrowing skink**
	Dasia smaragdina, family Scincidae		*Tiliqua multifasciata*, family Scincidae		*Androngo trivittatus*, family Scincidae
				7	**Otago skink**
					Oligosoma otagense, family Scincidae

1 Bridled mabuya
Mabuya vittata, family Scincidae

2 Christmas Island grass skink
Lygosoma bowringii, family Scincidae

3 Boulenger's legless skink
Typhlosaurus vermis, family Scincidae

4 Red-sided ctenotus
Ctenotus pulchellus, family Scincidae

5 Northwestern sandslider
Lerista bipes, family Scincidae

6 Cape York mulch skink
Glaphyromorphus crassicaudum, family Scincidae

7 Lined fire-tailed skink
Morethia ruficauda, family Scincidae

8 Juniper skink
Ablepharus kitaibelii, family Scincidae

9 Desert rainbow skink
Carlia triacantha, family Scincidae

10 Six-lined burrowing skink
Scelotes sexlineatus, family Scincidae

LIZARD COURTSHIP

Anole courtship displays Small, colourful arboreal lizards are most adapted to using visual communication for courtship. The males have species-specific, bright dewlap colours and head bobs, push-ups or other motions that attract females to them for copulation. Variation exists between individuals, so that females can select a male by the way he courts her. The male's vigour in courtship is the component most often used by females in their selection of a mate.

Bobbing rapidly The carpenter anole (Norops carpenteri) (above) has a simple display: the dewlap, which is uniformly orange-coloured, is extended and held open, while the head is bobbed at regular frequency. The male has a series of over a dozen rapid head bobs in his courtship display, while holding his dewlap extended the entire time.

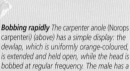

Variable bobbing The silky anole (N. sericeus) (above) has a compound display: the dewlap has a central colour that contrasts with the basal colour. When the dewlap is extended only partway, the spot does not show. The head bob pattern is independent of the dewlap extension rhythm. The male begins bobbing rapidly for the first five bobs, then bobs in slow motion for the remainder of the sequence; the dewlap is extended and retracted twice.

Slow bobbing The display of the lichen anole (N. pentaprion) (above) is complex. The dewlap has a red basal colour with blue lines: the number of blue lines exposed varies according to the extension of the dewlap. The slow bobbing sequence is synchronised with the extension of the dewlap – bob and extend, retract, bob and extend.

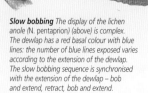

Courtship displays have evolved in lizards to ensure that gametes are not wasted on mating with the wrong species or inferior individuals. Males often maintain territories in resource-rich areas and will fight other males to maintain them. Females are allowed to enter males' territories and are encouraged to mate by energetic courtship displays. When there are many similar species or species in the same genus in the same habitat the courtship behavioural patterns are more complex. Courtship displays are most complex and have been most intensively studied in the family Polychrotidae. Courtship in monitor lizards (Varanidae) involves tongue flicks by males along different parts of the female's body during the initiation of courtship. Communication in skinks is primarily chemical.

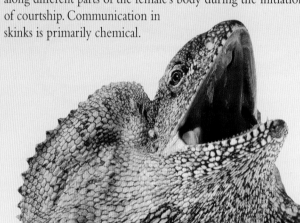

Larger than life
When the frill is extended fully, it can reach 35cm (14 inches) across, longer than its body length.

Rain-maker
Australian Aborigines will not hunt the frilled lizard because they believe that it calls the rain to come; without rain, the country falls into drought.

Pseudo-copulation In the whiptails (Cnemidophorus) of the southwestern deserts of the United States, females reproduce without males or their sperm (parthenogenetic reproduction). The genetic component of the female is identical to that of her offspring. Pseudo-copulation occurs in some species of these clones of all female lizards. One female behaves like a male and attempts to mount with another female. The courtship and pseudo-copulation stimulate ovulation.

Larger than life
By expanding its folded neck skin, the frilled dragon can appear much larger when threatening other males or attempting to attract females.

Expanding frill
Dominant male frilled lizards show off different display sequences during courtship of females or territoriality displays toward other males. Over 75 different sequences have been recorded, including head bobbing, push-ups, beard erection, colour changes, body inflations, head licking and jaw gaping. Apart from the changes in shape and size of the lizard, changes in colour and flashes of colour as they open the mouth are a major part of their repertoire.

FACT FILE

Family Lacertidae Adult lacertids are 4–25cm (1½–10 inches) in body length. The scales are variable, from large, overlapping smooth or keeled to small and granular. All species have limbs. Tails are long, sometimes over twice the body length. Most lacertids are terrestrial but some are arboreal. Most are oviparous, but some are viviparous and some populations are parthenogenetic. Almost all species are insectivorous and some eat seeds.

Genera 27
Species 220

🏛 🏔 ⚰ 🌿 🏘 ♨

Africa, Europe, Asia & N. East Indies

Giant Canary Island lizard Hatchlings take 3 years to reach maturity and live for about 12 years. Adults are primarily herbivorous and are important in seed dispersal. The disproportionately long hindlimbs of males allow them faster acceleration when escaping predators.

↔ Up to 27cm (10½ in)
⬡ Terrestrial
○ Oviparous
● 10
⚡ Common

Grand Canary Island (Canary Is.)

Tiger lizard These lizards actively hunt scorpions, which are dormant during the day and sparsely distributed, which makes them easy targets for predatory birds. Tiger lizards avoid predators by being active during the heat of the day at a body temperature of 39°C (102°F).

↔ Up to 20cm (8 in)
⬡ Terrestrial
○ Oviparous
● 3–8
⚡ Common

S. Namibia, S.W. Botswana, South Africa

⚡ CONSERVATION WATCH

The 13 species of Lacertidae on the IUCN Red List are categorised as follows:

1	Critically endangered
1	Endangered
5	Vulnerable
2	Near threatened
1	Data deficient
3	Least concern

1 **European green lizard**
   Ablepharus kitaibelii, family Lacertidae

2 **Giant Canary Island lizard**
   Gallotia stehlini, family Lacertidae

3 **Zagrosian lizard**
   Timon princeps, family Lacertidae

4 **Tiger lizard**
   Nucras tessellata, family Lacertidae

5 **Jeweled lizard**
   Timon lepidus, family Lacertidae

6 **Sand lizard**
   Lacerta agilis, family Lacertidae

7 **Gallot's lizard**
   Gallotia galloti, family Lacertidae

8 **Balkan emerald lizard**
   Lacerta trilineata, family Lacertidae

FACT FILE

Family Xantusiidae Even though Xantusiidae are called night lizards, many species are diurnal. They are small lizards, up to 10cm (4 inches) long, with small granular dorsal scales and large ventral scales. All species are viviparous. Most species feed on invertebrates, although one cave-dwellingspecies feeds on figs. Night lizards are terrestrial and arboreal. In Mexico, Lepidophyma, a species of night lizard, are called scorpions and are mistakenly thought to be venomous. Like many lizards, their tails will break off if grasped; a new tail will regenerate but will be of a uniform colour.

Liberated from males The yellow-spotted night lizard (Lepidophyma flavimaculata), is nocturnal and viviparous. Some populations are parthenogenetic.

Genera 3
Species 20

W. USA & E. Mexico, Central America & N. South America

Common wall lizard This is a colonial species. It is a good climber and basks on rocks. Wall lizards feed on invertebrates: beetles, flies, butterflies and spiders. They are prey items for raptors and snakes, particularly young horned vipers or large whip snakes.

✦ Up to10cm (4 in)
🌐 Terrestrial, arboreal
○ Oviparous
● 2–8
🍴 Common

Southern Europe & Balkans

⚡ CONSERVATION WATCH

Restricted range One species of Xantusiidae, the North American island night lizard (*Xantusia riversiana*), is listed on the IUCN Red List as vulnerable. The distribution of this lizard is restricted to San Clemente, Santa Barbara and the San Nicholas Islands off the coast of southern California, United States. They inhabit grasslands, cactus clumps, cliffs and rocky beaches. This lizard is vulnerable because of habitat destruction and development of its island habitats.

1	Italian wall lizard	**4**	Desert night lizard
	Podarcis sicula, family Lacertidae		*Xantusia vigilis*, family Xantusiidae
2	Common wall lizard	**5**	Granite night lizard
	Podarcis muralis, family Lacertidae		*Xantusia henshawi*, family Xantusiidae
3	Menorca wall lizard	**6**	Viviporus lizard
	Podarcis perspicillata, family Lacertidae		*Lacerta vivipara*, family Xantusiidae

7	Radd's rock lizard
	Lacerta raddei, family Xantusiidae
8	Uzzell's rock lizard
	Lacerta uzzeli, family Xantusiidae
9	Milo's wall lizard
	Podarcis milensis, family Xantusiidae

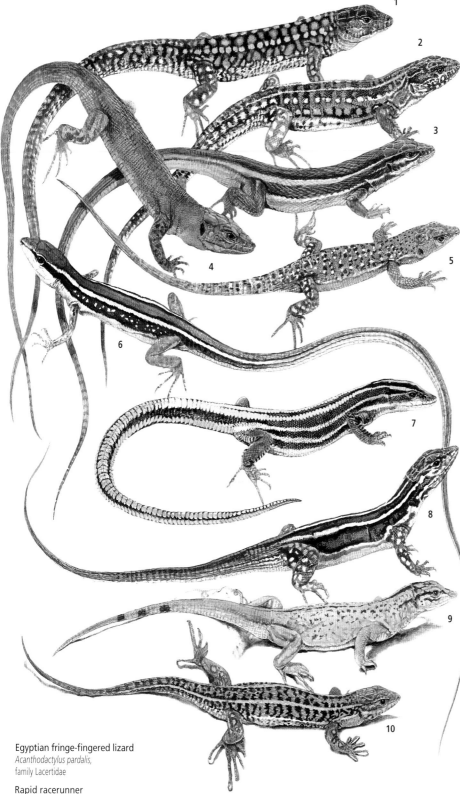

FACT FILE

Egyptian fringe-fingered lizard
The toes on these lizards have a fringe enabling better traction over windblown sand dunes. They also have shovel noses and countersunk lower jaws to allow them ease in plowing through sand. Ants make up most of their diet.

- ✶ Up to 20cm (8 in)
- ◓ Terrestrial
- ○ Oviparous
- ● 3–5
- ⚑ Common

Algeria, Egypt, Israel, Jordan & Libya

Blue-throated keeled-lizard These diurnal lizards are the smallest lacertids in Europe, and forage for insects in vineyards and buildings. They emerge from hibernation and breed in April; breeding males have a bright blue throat and orange-red ventral surface.

- ✶ Up to 20cm (8 in)
- ◓ Terrestrial, arboreal
- ○ Oviparous
- ● 2–3
- ⚑ Common

N.E. Italy to Gulf of Corinth & Ionian islands

Sawtail lizard Its flattened shape and striking colouration make this species unmistakable. This lizard uses its flat body and broad tail to glide through the air from tree to tree. They have long, stout trunks and tails and relatively strong hindlimbs.

Long jumper
The sawtail lizard jumps up to 10m (33 feet) from tree to tree, its flattened body and tail assisting the feat.

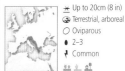

- ✶ Up to 12.5cm (5 in)
- ◓ Arboreal
- ○ Oviparous
- ● 2
- ⚑ Common

C., E. & W. Africa & Mozambique

Snake-eyed lizard This lizard gets its name from the large transparent disks that cover its eyes, so large that the eyelids no longer cover the eye. When escaping from a predator, they scamper from bush to bush and then pop up to look for the aggressor. They can also run short distances bipedally.

- ✶ Up to 5cm (2 in)
- ◓ Terrestrial
- ○ Oviparous
- ● 4–5
- ⚑ Common

N. Africa, S.E. Europe to Middle East & India

1 Egyptian fringe-fingered lizard
Acanthodactylus pardalis,
family Lacertidae

2 Rapid racerunner
Eremias velox, family Lacertidae

3 Algerian psammodromus
Psammodromus algirus,
family Lacertidae

4 Blue-throated keeled-lizard
Algyroides nigropunctatus,
family Lacertidae

5 Small-spotted lizard
Mesalina guttulata, family Lacertidae

6 Asian grass lizard
Takydromus sexlineatus,
family Lacertidae

7 Sawtail lizard
Holaspis guentheri, family Lacertidae

8 Mourning racerunner
Heliobolus lugubris, family Lacertidae

9 Slender sand lizard
Meroles anchietae, family Lacertidae

10 Snake-eyed lizard
Ophisops elegans, family Lacertidae

FACT FILE

Family Gymnophthalmidae The microtiids are small, oviparous lizards, up to 6cm (2½ inches) long, with a wide variation of scale patterns. Some species have reduced limbs. Tails are autonomous. Most of the lizards in this diverse family live within the forest-floor litter. A few species are semiaquatic. All species consume invertebrates.

Genera 36
Species 160

S. Central America &
N.W. South America

Family Teiidae Whiptail lizards and tegus, which are oviparous, vary in adult size from 5–40cm (2–16 inches) in snout–vent length. Dorsal and lateral scales are small and granular, while the ventral scales are larger, rectangular and in rows. The tails are long and autonomic. Smaller whiptails prefer deserts, grasslands and open areas in the forest where they prey on invertebrates. The larger tegus prefer open forests and are omnivorous.

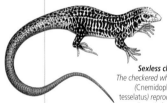

Sexless clones
*The checkered whiptail
(Cnemidophorus
tesselatus) reproduces
asexually; only females
are present in the
population.*

Genera 9
Species 118

N. USA to South America

Golden tegu This heavy-bodied lizard is one of the main predators of turtle eggs in the Amazon Basin. To protect their own eggs from predation, they lay them in arboreal termite nests.

✳ Up to 30cm (12 in)
◠ Terrestrial
○ Oviparous
● 4–32
⚡ Common

N. South America

Heliothermic species
that feeds on ants
and spiders in the
leaf litter

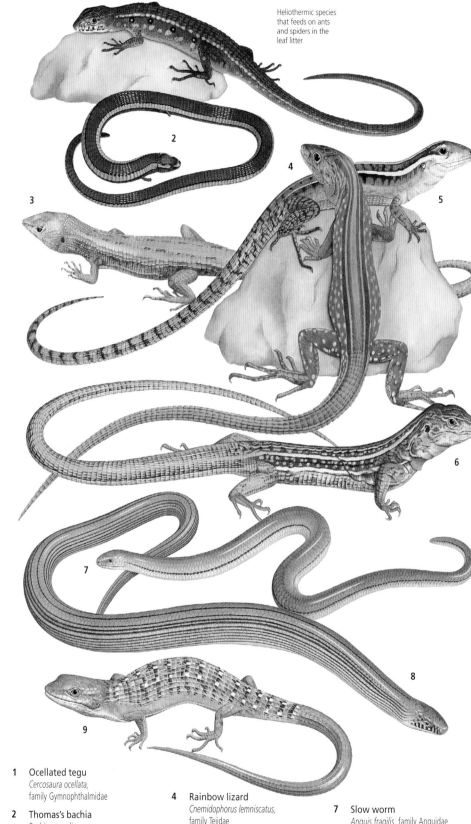

1   **Ocellated tegu**
Cercosaura ocellata,
family Gymnophthalmidae

2   **Thomas's bachia**
Bachia panoplia,
family Gymnophthalmidae

3   **Two-ridged neusticurus**
Neusticurus bicarinatus,
family Gymnophthalmidae

4   **Rainbow lizard**
Cnemidophorus lemniscatus,
family Teiidae

5   **Green calango**
Kentropyx calcarata, family Teiidae

6   **Four-toed tegu**
Teius teyou, family Teiidae

7   **Slow worm**
Anguis fragilis, family Anguidae

8   **Common worm lizard**
Ophiodes intermedius, family Anguidae

9   **Southern alligator lizard**
Elgaria multicarinata, family Anguidae

Lives in the low branches
of trees above the water;
the tail is high and flattened
dorso-laterally for swimming

1   Giant ameiva
Ameiva ameiva, family Teiidae

2   Banded galliwasp
Diploglossus fasciatus, family Anguidae

3   Chinese crocodile lizard
Shinisaurus crocodilurus,
family Xenosauridae

4   Golden tegu
Tupinambis teguixin, family Teiidae

5   European glass lizard
Pseudopus apodus, family Anguidae

6   Slender glass lizard
Ophisaurus attenuatus
family Anguidae

7   Crocodile tegu
Crocodilurus lacertinus, family Teiidae

8   Paraguay Caiman lizard
Dracaena paraguayensis, family Teiidae

FACT FILE

Family Helodermatidae The Gila monster and the Mexican beaded lizard are the only known venomous lizards. They have broad, flattened heads, and stocky bodies, strong limbs and thick tails that are used for fat storage. Both species are slow-moving, oviparous and diurnal. They feed on nestlings and lizard or birds' eggs.

Genera 2
Species 2

S.W. USA to Guatemala

Family Lanthanotidae These earless monitors have ptergoid teeth and lack a parietal eye. They are related to the Varanidae and Helodermatidae. The species is nocturnal and semi-aquatic, living along and in forest streams. Monitors forage in the water and on land for small vertebrates and invertebrates. They are oviparous with clutches of up to six eggs.

Genera 1
Species 1

Borneo

SHEDDING SKIN

The outer layer of a lizard's skin (the epidermis) is composed of keratin; scales are thickenings of this layer. As the lizard grows, the outer layer of keratin is shed in large flakes.

Splitting out
All lizards need to shed their skin periodically in order to grow.

⚡ CONSERVATION WATCH

Added protection Both species of Helodermatidae are listed on the IUCN Red List as vulnerable. The Gila monster is given complete protection in Arizona, United States, to keep it from wanton slaughter and being engulfed by the pet trade. Mexico lists both species, so the lizards cannot be legally sold on the international pet market and cannot be killed, stuffed and then sold as curios for the tourist trade.

Tail is round in
cross section, with no
evidence of a dorsal keel

1. **Mexican beaded lizard**
   Heloderma horridum,
   family Helodermatidae

2. **Spiny-tailed monitor**
   Varanus acanthurus, family Varanidae

3. **Roughneck monitor**
   Varanus rudicollis, family Varanidae

4. **Emerald monitor**
   Varanus prasinus,
   family Varanidae

5. **Gila monster**
   Heloderma suspectum,
   family Helodermatidae

6. **Borneo earless monitor**
   Lanthanotus borneensis,
   family Lanthanotidae

7. **Pygmy Mulga monitor**
   Varanus gilleni, family Varanidae

Komodo dragons have an extremely virulent symbiotic bacteria living in their mouths; within a few hours of being bitten, wounded prey will lose energy due to a fever caused by the bacteria, then drop to the ground. The dragon trails the animal and eats it when it is down

1 **Crocodile monitor**
Varanus salvadorii, family Varanidae

2 **Perentie**
Varanus giganteus, family Varanidae

3 **Grey's monitor**
Varanus olivaceus, family Varanidae

4 **Desert monitor**
Varanus griseus, family Varanidae

5 **Sand monitor**
Varanus gouldii, family Varanidae

6 **Nile monitor**
Varanus niloticus, family Varanidae

7 **Komodo dragon**
Varanus komodoensis, family Varanidae

FACT FILE

Family Varanidae Monitors are large, long-necked lizards with thick skin and many rows of small, rounded scales circling the body. Their tails are long and lack caudal autonomy. Their tongues are long and forked. The largest of the monitors is the komodo dragon.

Standing tall The sand monitor has an extremely thick tail, allowing it a firm tripod stance when searching for mates or prey.

Genera 1
Species 50

Africa, Asia, Australia & Pacific Is.

JACOBSON'S ORGAN

A large number of lizards sense the air around them with their tongues, picking up chemical cues regarding food, conspecifics, likely mates and predators. The Jacobson's organ has a pair of cavities lined with sensory cells on the roof of the mouth. The particles collected on the lizard's tongue are transported to ducts leading to these cavities by the tongue, explaining why the tongue is forked. The vomeronasal nerve then transmits the information collected to the brain for action.

Tongue testing Monitors and many other lizards pick up airborne scents on their forked tongues.

⚡ CONSERVATION WATCH

Monitoring monitors Many species of monitors are killed for their skins and meat. In Asia and Africa, they are exploited for traditional medicines; they also make up part of the diet of Australian indigenous people. More than a million Nile and other Asiatic monitors are killed annually for their skins, which are used in the manufacture of luxury shoes, belts, purses and accessories.

SNAKES

CLASS	Reptilia
ORDERS	Squamata
FAMILIES	17
GENERA	438
SPECIES	2,955

At nearly 3,000 species, the variety in snakes is enormous. They range from the tiny burrowing blind snakes of 10cm (4 inches) long to huge constrictors over 10m (33 feet) in length. Snakes have evolved special methods of locomotion, different ways of gathering environmental cues, and diverse venom delivery systems. Lizards appeared in the fossil record before snakes, and the presence of vestigial pelvic girdles and spurs in some primitive snakes indicates that snakes have evolved from them; the left lung is reduced or absent in snakes and legless lizards, but the right lung is reduced in amphisbaenians. Most of the organs of snakes are reduced in girth and elongated.

Tropic lovers Snakes are found on all continents except Antarctica, and ranges of some even pass above the Arctic circle. Some islands are also devoid of snakes, such as New Zealand, Ireland and Iceland, and sea snakes are absent from the Atlantic. Snake biodiversity is highest in the tropics.

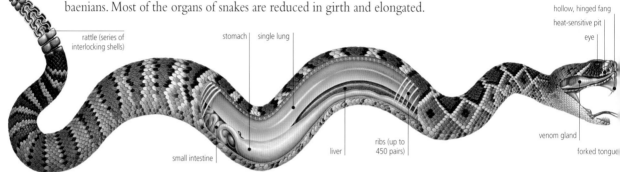

rattle (series of interlocking shells) — stomach — single lung — hollow, hinged fang — heat-sensitive pit — eye — venom gland — forked tongue — small intestine — liver — ribs (up to 450 pairs)

Snake anatomy As in the example of the Eastern diamondback rattlesnake (above), most snake organs have been reduced in diameter and have increased in length. Lungs in most species have been reduced to one, but males have two functional reproductive organs.

Defensive display Most species of cobras, such as the Cape cobra (Naja nivea) (right), have a hood that they can spread to look larger than life in order to frighten enemies or to transfix prey. The dorsal surface of the hood of some species is marked with large eye-like spots to suggest the eyes of a much larger animal.

Hidden fangs When pit vipers, including timber rattlesnakes (below), threaten with an open mouth they keep their fangs relaxed, so they do not obstruct the functioning of their pit organs. These scan for infrared signals from predators or prey.

AN EAR TO THE GROUND

Snakes are very close to their environment. In fact, their bellies are in contact with the substrate most of the time – only when they are gliding between trees, swimming or climbing trees are they free from this close contact with the ground. It is through this earthy contact that they pick up sound vibrations and follow the scent trails of prey and receptive females.

The shape of the snake determines where it will live and what it will do. Shovel-nosed snakes and worm snakes remain within the ground with modified snouts for burrowing and feeding on their subterranean prey. The slender, thin-necked, arboreal snakes are adapted for gliding through the branches and stretching out to reach the next branch only a nose away. They have small clutches of elongate eggs and eat thin, elongate prey, such as lizards or frogs. Short, thick-bodied snakes, like some vipers, are sit-and-wait predators and often gorge on a meal that weighs more than they do. Their awkward shape does not affect them, as they do not move much anyway, and many are venomous. Long-bodied, agile, fast-moving snakes are the athletes in the group, chasing down lizards and other snakes, and using their speed for escape. It is amazing how fast mambas and whip snakes can move

SNAKE SKIN TYPES

Snake skin is made up of scales, which are not separate items, but a thickened part of the skin connected to other scales by thinner areas of elastic skin. Fine, granular scales are common in boas, the smooth, glossy over-lapping scales are common in racers, and strongly keeled scales are characteristic of rattlesnakes.

Granular scales

Smooth scales

Keeled scales

Poised to strike
This young green tree python is coiled, half in the air, ready to strike.

Green constrictors The green tree python is an arboreal predator, feeding on birds, mammals and lizards. Grasping a bird or bat on the wing with its long teeth, it simultaneously throws a coil around the prey and constricts it. The hatchlings of the green tree python are 28–35cm (11–14 inches) long and are coloured differently from the adults. The bright juvenile colour pattern transforms to a vivid green in 6–8 months.

Infrared sensors
Green tree pythons have heat-sensing receptors embedded in the labial scales, which enable them to receive a visual image of light and heat.

venom duct

rear grooved fangs

Colubridae

venom duct

fixed front hollow fangs

Elapidae

venom duct

swinging front hollow fangs

Viperidae

Fang varieties Rear grooved fangs are associated with Duvernoy's gland secretions in Colubridae. Elapidae (cobras, coral snakes, sea snakes, and taipans) have fixed short front fangs. The vipers all have hinged front fangs.

Keen vision The king cobra has large, round pupils adapted for acute diurnal vision. They are designed for detecting the slightest motion of their preferred prey – other snakes – within the vegetation.

Hatchlings emerge Most pythons guard and incubate their eggs. However, once their first week outside the shell is over, the young shed their skins, leave the protective coil of the mother and disperse, like the young green tree python below.

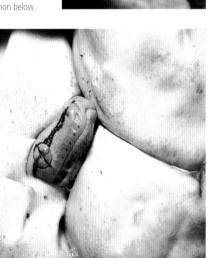

through the forest canopy: they do not slither, but flow like a stream of water. Sea snakes have modified their shape to have a paddle-like tail, useful for a pelagic life. Many species never touch land, but feed, breed and give birth at sea.

All male snakes have two hemipenes in the base of the tail; they are usually used alternately, each receiving sperm from only one of the testicles. This system perhaps evolved from the selective advantage of having a fast recovery time when participating in mass spring orgies following emergence from hiber-nation. Sperm can be stored for months or more than a year before it is utilised to fertilise eggs.

Females have evolved a range of modified behaviour patterns to enhance their genes. Most snakes lay eggs, but many of the more recent snakes have evolved viviparity and some parental care. Through muscle

contractions, pythons can raise their body temperatures when brooding their eggs. Female cobras guard their nest of eggs in a loose construction of leaves built over the nest.

Some of the most fantastic adaptations of modern snakes are the mechanisms they have developed for finding, capturing, killing and swallowing prey. Highly developed chemical receptors on the roof of the mouth help snakes to identify mates, enemies and prey. Infrared receptors possessed by pit vipers, boas and pythons allow them to visualise warm-blooded prey in terms of heat. The venom produced by Viperidae, Elapidae and Colubridae allow them to stop prey in its tracks and help in swallowing and digesting the meal. Obviously some snakes have evolved more than others, and many are now losing ground – humans are changing the environment faster than snakes can evolve.

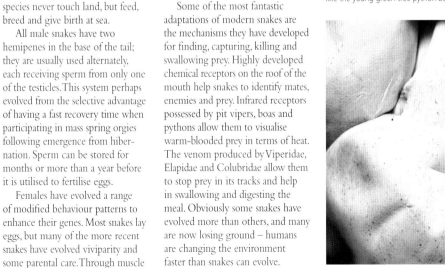

FACT FILE

Family Tropidophiidae These West Indian dwarf boas are small, about 1m (3¼ feet) in length. The island forms all appear to have diverged from a common mainland ancestor. They eat frogs, lizards, rodents and birds. When disturbed, these snakes bleed from the mouth and eyes and roll up into a tight ball as a defence mechanism.

Genera 2
Species 31

West Indies to Ecuador, S.E. Brazil, S.E. Asia

BOA AND PYTHON SKULLS

The kinetic jaws of snakes are designed to swallow objects up to five times their diameter. Teeth are curved so that by first moving one side and then the other, the food is pushed down the throat.

resting jaw

Full gape *The snake's lower jaw is free at the chin to move sideways. Flexible tendons allow the snake to drop its jaw both posteriorly and anteriorly.*

distended jaw

⚡ CONSERVATION WATCH

Round Island boas The now-extinct burrowing boa (*Bolyeria multocarinata*) was found only on Round Island in the Indian Ocean. Another species, the keel-scaled boa (*Casarea dusumieri*) is endangered due to the environmental damage on this island. Only 75 were known in the 1970s.

Male Mexican rosy boas have well-developed spurs; those of the female are smaller

Tatar sand boas are sold for high prices in central Asia for medicinal purposes

1 **Mexican rosy boa**
   Charina trivirgata, family Boidae

2 **Wood snake**
   Tropidophis melanurus,
   family Tropidophiidae

3 **New Guinea ground boa**
   Candoia aspera, family Boidae

4 **Calabar ground python**
   Calabaria reinhardtii, family Boidae

5 **Rubber boa**
   Charina bottae, family Boidae

6 **East African sand boa**
   Gongylophis colubrinu, family Boidae

7 **Schaefer's dwarf boa**
   Xenophidion schaeferi,
   family Tropidophiidae

8 **Isthmian dwarf boa**
   Ungaliophis continentalis,
   family Tropidophiidae

9 **Tatar sand boa**
   Eryx tataricus, family Boidae

10 **Feick's dwarf boa**
   Tropidophis feicki, family Tropidophiidae

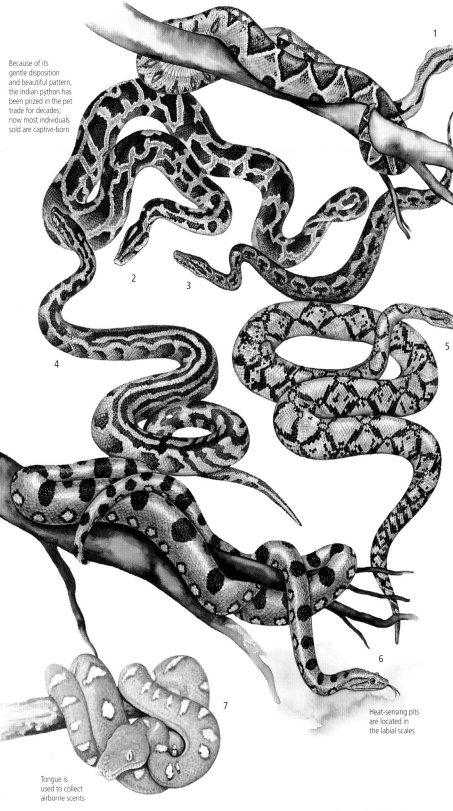

Because of its gentle disposition and beautiful pattern, the Indian python has been prized in the pet trade for decades; now most individuals sold are captive-born

Heat-sensing pits are located in the labial scales

Tongue is used to collect airborne scents

Family Boidae This family includes the boas, pythons and sand boas – the largest living snakes – but some species are less than 50cm (20 inches) long. The largest may reach 10m (33 feet) and feed on large mammals, capybaras, deer and caimans. Boas and sand boas are viviparous; pythons are oviparous.

Egg brooding
The children's python (Antaresia childreni) coils around its eggs to conceal and protect them. It increases body temperature by muscle contractions.

Genera 20
Species 74

Worldwide except Europe and Antarctica

Common boa constrictor Boas are heavy-bodied arboreal snakes that kill their prey by constriction. They have vestigial legs as spurs on either side of the cloaca, which suggests that they are of ancient origin.

➤ Up to 4.2m (14 ft)
⊛ Terrestrial, arboreal
⬮ Viviparous
● 30–50 live young
⬩ Common

S. Mexico to Argentina

Reticulated python One of the two largest snakes in the world, this python is more massive than the anaconda. Its prey includes large reptiles, such as lizards and crocodilians, and medium to large mammals, even humans.

➤ Up to 10m (33 ft)
⊛ Terrestrial
○ Oviparous
● 80–100
⬩ Common

S.E. Asia

The 10 species of Boidae on the IUCN Red List are categorised as follows:

1 Extinct
2 Endangered
4 Vulnerable
3 Near threatened

1 Common boa constrictor
Boa constrictor, family Boidae

2 Indian python
Python molarus, family Boidae

3 Madagascar ground boa
Acrantophis madagascariensis, family Boidae

4 African rock python
Python sebae, family Boidae

5 Reticulate python
Python reticulatus, family Boidae

6 Anaconda
Eunectes murinus, family Boidae

7 Emerald tree boa
Corallus caninus, family Boidae

FACT FILE

Green tree python This nocturnal constrictor feeds on mammals and birds. It is an example of parallel evolution: the emerald tree boa (*Corallus caninus*) of South America evolved in the same habitat and is similar in colour and form.

⚊ Up to 2m (6½ ft)
🌳 Arboreal
◯ Oviparous
● 12–18
🗡 Uncommon

N.E. Australia, New Guinea

Polymorphic colours
The young differ in colour from the bright-green adults; young are bright yellow to brick red when they hatch.

Cook's tree boa This boa feeds on small lizards when young, progressing to rodents and birds as it grows. Prey is ambushed: in one motion, the boa bites and wraps several coils of its body around its victim while suspended from a branch by its prehensile tail.

⚊ Up to 1.9m (6¼ ft)
🌳 Arboreal
🐍 Viviparous
● 30–80 live young
🗡 Common

Panama, N. South America, West Indies

Black-headed python This python is nocturnal in warmer months and diurnal in cooler months. Its diet consists of monitor lizards, frogs, birds, mammals and snakes – even death adders. Dingos are its main predator.

⚊ Up to 2.6m (8½ ft)
🌍 Terrestrial
◯ Oviparous
● 5–10
🗡 Common

N. Australia

Blood python Blood pythons are stocky, robust and semiaquatic, spending much time underwater in swamps or streams. They feed primarily on mammals and small birds. Blood python populations are diminishing due to the skin trade: the colourful skin is prized for the luxury leather market.

⚊ Up to 3m (10 ft)
🌍 Terrestrial, aquatic
◯ Oviparous
● 18–30
🗡 Common

S.E. Asia

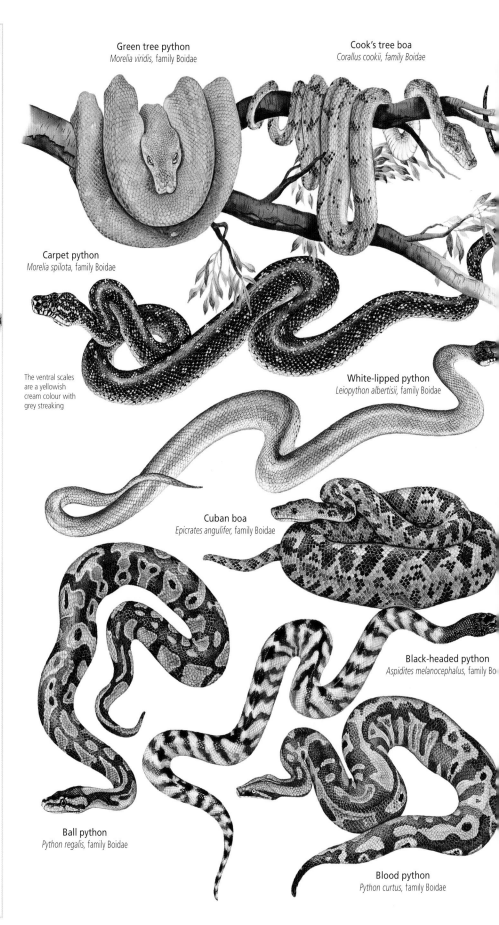

Green tree python
Morelia viridis, family Boidae

Cook's tree boa
Corallus cookii, family Boidae

Carpet python
Morelia spilota, family Boidae

The ventral scales are a yellowish cream colour with grey streaking

White-lipped python
Leiopython albertisii, family Boidae

Cuban boa
Epicrates angulifer, family Boidae

Black-headed python
Aspidites melanocephalus, family Bo

Ball python
Python regalis, family Boidae

Blood python
Python curtus, family Boidae

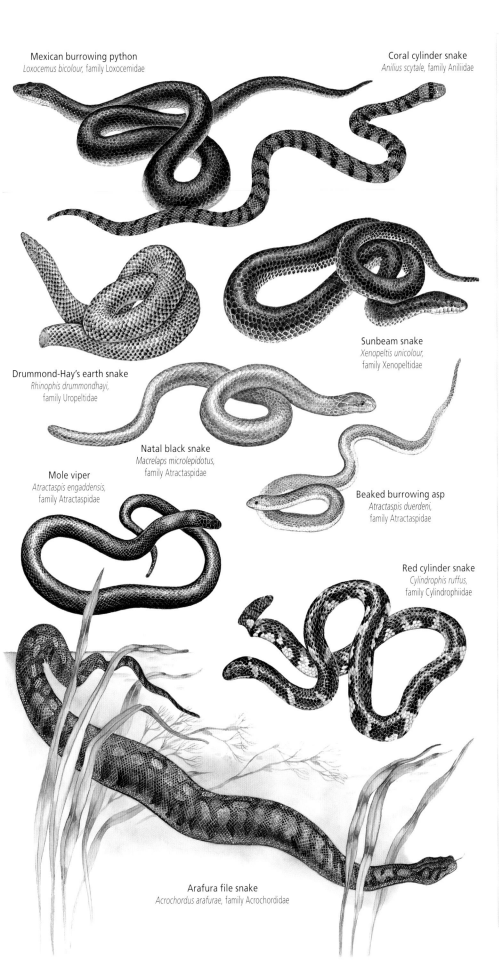

Mexican burrowing python
Loxocemus bicolour, family Loxocemidae

Coral cylinder snake
Anilius scytale, family Aniliidae

Sunbeam snake
Xenopeltis unicolour,
family Xenopeltidae

Drummond-Hay's earth snake
Rhinophis drummondhayi,
family Uropeltidae

Natal black snake
Macrelaps microlepidotus,
family Atractaspidae

Mole viper
Atractaspis engaddensis,
family Atractaspidae

Beaked burrowing asp
Atractaspis duerdeni,
family Atractaspidae

Red cylinder snake
Cylindrophis ruffus,
family Cylindrophiidae

Arafura file snake
Acrochordus arafurae, family Acrochordidae

FACT FILE

Mexican burrowing python This nocturnal python forages for small mammals and reptiles, and sea turtle and lizard eggs. Its pointed snout is useful for burrowing into reptile nests. The large plates on the head suggest those of more recent colubrid snakes, rather than the closely related boas.

⚟ Up to 1.4m (4¾ ft)
🌐 Terrestrial, burrowing
○ Oviparous
● 2–4
⚑ Rare

S. Mexico to Costa Rica

Family Atractaspidae These oviparous snakes are called stiletto vipers because they have a large semi-erect fang on each maxillary bone (upper jaw). They prey on burrowing rodents: the tight spaces mean it is impossible for them to gape their mouths to strike, so they wiggle alongside their prey, shift their jaw to the opposite side from the prey and expose their long fangs. They then proceed to envenomate their prey, stabbing it with a back-slash motion.

Genera 1
Species 18

Africa & Middle East

Family Aniliidae These brightly coloured coral-snake mimics live in leaf litter and feed on earthworms, caecilians, eels, amphisbaenians and snakes. They are on occasion found in the water, but are probably burrowers. When handled, they roll up into a ball.

Genera 1
Species 1

Amazonia (South America)

Family Acrochordidae These snakes have small, strongly keeled scales. File snakes are one of the most aquatic snakes, and are almost incapable of moving on land. They are nocturnal, and feed on fishes and crustaceans.

Genera 1
Species 3

India, S.E. Asia, Australia

Paddle tail
The laterally compressed tail of the little file snake (Acrochordus granulatus) is an adaptation for swimming.

SNAKE DEFENCE STRATEGIES

Looping in alarm The bandy-bandy (*Vermiculla annulata*) is a nocturnal, venomous elapid snake. It throws its body into loops off the ground when it is alarmed. It is possible that the snake is attempting to appear larger than it is by doing this, or that it is striking in a new direction to catch the predator off guard.

Snakes have many different strategies to avoid becoming a meal. Camouflage – utilising colour, pattern and shape – is the most common tactic. Many arboreal snakes have long, slender heads and necks like twigs so that they blend in with their favored habitat. Escape works if you are very fast, like the red racer (*Masticophis flagellum*), which is built for speed. Many defensive manoeuvres were designed to be effective against birds or mammals. The Indian cobra (*Naja naja*) raises half its body off the ground, spreads its hood and displays large eye spots so that it appears to be a much larger animal. The Arizona coral snake (*Micruroides euryxanthus*) raises its tail and pops its cloaca to distract predators from attacking its head. The prairie ringneck snake (*Diadophis punctatus*) is black dorsally; when threatened, it hides its head in its coils and raises a coiled tail which is bright orange ventrally to startle its attacker. Many snakes will hiss, thrash, bite and defecate to dissuade unwanted attention.

Rattling good tail When disturbed, a rattlesnake will vibrate its tail and make a loud rattling sound. The noise and the movement distract the potential prey or predators, who end up watching the tail and not the striking head. Many species of non-venomous snakes vibrate their tails as well.

Master of disguise The eyelash viper (*Bothriechis schlegelii*), an arboreal pit viper, is perfectly camouflaged. It chooses an appropriate perch on which to wait for passing mice or frogs. Its colour and shape blend in with the vegetation so that predatory birds are not alerted to its presence. The 'eyelashes' may help to protect its eyes from abrasion as it slips through the rainforest canopy.

Surprise under the sand Waiting for a meal to pass, the Peringuey's sidewinding adder (*Bitis peringueyi*) (below) becomes invisible as the shifting sand of the Namibian desert blows over it. The adder's pattern and colouration blend in with the golden sand; only its eyes and the black tip of its tail remain visible. Hiding is a good defence against canids and raptors.

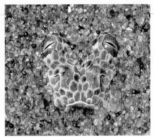

Mimicking danger Many non-venomous snakes have evolved colour patterns similar to those of venomous species in their region, to reap the benefit this warning colouration has on predators. This adaptation is called Batesian mimicry. The long-tailed false coral snake (*Pliocercus elapoides*) of the Yucatán peninsula, Mexico, is one of these imitators (far right). It closely resembles the Mayan coral snake (*Micrurus hippocrepis*) (right).

Feigning death When molested, the Eastern hognose snake (above) hisses and strikes with a closed mouth. If this fails to deter a predator, the snake writhes and contorts its body; its mouth is open, and it discharges fetid cloacal fluids. After a few minutes it will roll onto its back and lie limply with its mouth open as though dead. The impact is lost if you turn the snake over, as it will immediately roll onto its back again.

Aging rattles The rattle grows one button each time the snake sheds its skin. This can be four to six times a year.

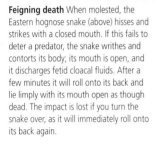

Snake in the grass When threatened, a bull snake (*Pituophis melanoleucus*) raises its head off the ground and expels air from its trachea; vibrating a cartilage at the tracheal opening creates a loud hissing sound. The tail is vibrated simultaneously, which produces a rattling sound in dry leaves or grasses. These effects combine to scare off most predators.

Threat display The venomous Florida cottonmouth (*Agkistrodon piscivorous*) opens its jaws to reveal a startlingly white mouth. This alerts predators to its presence and to the imminent danger. Sympatric nonvenomous water snakes have a similar colour pattern and mimic this behaviour for their defence.

FACT FILE

Family Colubridae About 63 per cent of all species of snakes are included in this family, which utilises all available reproductive styles and habitats. There are six loosely defined groups within the colubrids: Natricinae are small aquatic or terrestrial snakes; the largest group, Colubrinae, exploit all snake habitats except marine; the primarily oviparous Xenodontinae contains small, New World tropical and terrestrial species; Dipsadinae have diversified in Central and South America and occur in all available habitats; Homalopsinae contains 11 genera of diverse aquatic snakes occurring from northern Australia to Asia; and Aparallactinae are small snakes that range from sub-Saharan Africa to the Middle East.

Genera 320
Species 1,800

Worldwide, except Antarctica & polar regions

Snake trade
The brightly coloured corn snake (Elaphe guttata) has been sought after in the pet trade for over 50 years because of its attractive colours and mild disposition. Captive breeding colonies are now providing most pet snakes sold today.

COLUBRID VENOM

People often ignore the fact that most species of colubrids produce venom in the Duvernoy's gland. The venom is released and flows along grooved erect fangs in the back of the mouth. Since the venom is not forced through hollow fangs under pressure, as in front-fanged venom delivery (common to vipers and elapids), only about half enters the wound.

Duvernoy's gland

Non-lethal venom *When dispensed via a wound from the rear teeth, the venom from colubrids can be deadly. Herpetologists have died after under-estimating the venom's potency.*

Chinese rat snake
Ptyas karros, family Colubridae

Large whip snake
Coluber jugularis,
family Colubridae

Aesculapian snake
Elaphe longissima,
family Colubridae

Desert whip snake
Masticophis flagellum,
family Colubridae

Green whip snake
Coluber viridiflavus,
family Colubridae

Black-banded
trinket snake
Elaphe porphyracea,
family Colubridae

Red-tailed green ratsnake
Gonyosoma oxycephalum,
family Colubridae

Dahl's whip snake
Coluber najadum,
family Colubridae

Beauty snake
Elaphe taeniura,
family Colubridae

Tropical ratsnake
Spilotes pullatus,
family Colubridae

Indigo snake
Drymarchon corais,
family Colubridae

Spotted bush snake
Philothamnus semivariegatus,
family Colubridae

Chinese slug snake
Pareas chinensis,
family Colubridae

Milk snake
Lampropeltis triangulum,
family Colubridae

Grey-banded king snake
Lampropeltis alterna,
family Colubridae

Aesculapian false coral snake
Erythrolamprus aesculapii,
family Colubridae

Milk snake
(juvenile colour pattern)
Lampropeltis triangulum,
family Colubridae

Rhombic egg-eating snake
Dasypeltis scabra,
family Colubridae

Montpelier snake is rear-fanged
and has venom potentially
dangerous to humans

Schokari sand racer
Psammophis schokar,
family Colubridae

Montpelier snake
Malpolon monspessulanus,
family Colubridae

FACT FILE

Indigo snake This large diurnal snake is highly prized by the pet trade for its dark, blue-black colouration and docile temperament. Indigos feed on turtle eggs, reptiles, amphibians, birds, small mammals and snakes.

✦ Up to 2.7m (8¾ ft)
◯ Terrestrial
◯ Oviparous
● 15–26
✦ Uncommon

S.E. USA, Mexico to Paraguay

Milk snake This wide-ranging species is divided into 24 diverse subspecies. Milk snakes often mimic the colour pattern of coral snakes for defence.

✦ Up to 1.2m (4 ft)
◯ Terrestrial
◯ Oviparous
● 8–12
✦ Common

E. USA, Mexico to Venezuela & Ecuador

Schokari sand racer This slender, fast-moving, diurnal predator searches its desert habitat for prey. They have rear fangs and are mildly venomous.

✦ Up to 1.6m (5¼ ft)
◯ Terrestrial
◯ Oviparous
● 8–16
✦ Common

N.W. India, Afghanistan, Pakistan to N. Africa

SPECIALISED EGG-EATERS

African egg-eating snakes have evolved vertebrae with blunt spines that pierce the egg as it is forced down by muscle contraction. The contents are squeezed out and the eggshell regurgitated.

Egg room By not swallowing the eggshell, the snake has more space in its stomach for high-protein egg yolk.

⚑ CONSERVATION WATCH

Hobby farming In the 1970s in Texas, United States, the rare grey-banded king snake was protected, as it was popular with the pet trade. Hobbyists have since bred so many that wild populations have recovered and the species no longer needs protection.

FACT FILE

Western ground snake This snake is secretive, inhabiting areas with loose alluvial sand in dry washes, creosote bushes, desert flats and rocky hillsides. It prefers to hunt for prey at night and consumes centipedes, spiders, crickets, grasshoppers and insect larvae.

- ↔ Up to 50cm (20 in)
- Terrestrial
- ◯ Oviparous
- ● Unknown
- ⚑ Uncommon

S.W. USA & N.W. Mexico

Common bronze-back snake Bronze-backs are primarily arboreal in rain forest, coconut plantations and urban areas. Frogs and lizards, including flying lizards (Draco), are consumed.

- ↔ Up to 1m (3¼ ft)
- Terrestrial, arboreal
- ◯ Oviparous
- ● Unknown
- ⚑ Common

India, Burma, W. Malaysia, Indonesia, S. China

Ring-neck snake When attacked, these small woodland snakes hide their head and raise a coiled tail exposing the bright orange ventral surface. They feed on slugs, beetles, frogs, salamanders and small snakes.

- ↔ Up to 71cm (28 in)
- Terrestrial
- ◯ Oviparous
- ● 1–7
- ⚑ Common

S.E. Canada, USA, N. Mexico

GARTER SNAKE

In Canada, garter snakes (*Thamnophis sirtalis*) hibernate en masse in deep crevices below the frost line. In spring, thousands emerge simultaneously to bask and breed. Males trail receptive females by the scent trails they lay down; up to a hundred males can be in a ball courting the same female. After copulating, the male leaves a gelatinous sperm plug in the female, giving his sperm time to fertilise the embryos before other males' sperm can enter.

Different fathers DNA studies have shown that litters often have multiple paternities.

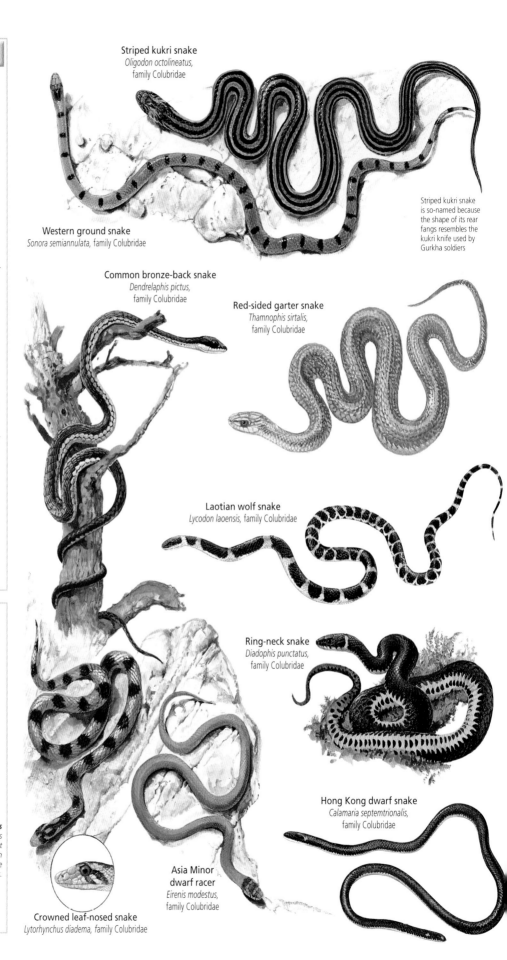

Striped kukri snake
Oligodon octolineatus,
family Colubridae

Western ground snake
Sonora semiannulata, family Colubridae

Striped kukri snake is so-named because the shape of its rear fangs resembles the kukri knife used by Gurkha soldiers

Common bronze-back snake
Dendrelaphis pictus,
family Colubridae

Red-sided garter snake
Thamnophis sirtalis,
family Colubridae

Laotian wolf snake
Lycodon laoensis, family Colubridae

Ring-neck snake
Diadophis punctatus,
family Colubridae

Hong Kong dwarf snake
Calamaria septemtrionalis,
family Colubridae

Asia Minor dwarf racer
Eirenis modestus,
family Colubridae

Crowned leaf-nosed snake
Lytorhynchus diadema, family Colubridae

New Guinea bockadam is tolerant of salt water

Rainbow water snake is important to the snake-skin leather industry

1 **Blue-necked keelback**
Macropisthodon rhodomelas,
family Colubridae

2 **Red-necked keelback**
Rhabdophis subminiatus,
family Colubridae

3 **European grass snake**
Natrix natrix, family Colubridae

4 **Northern water snake**
Nerodia sipedon, family Colubridae

5 **Queen snake**
Regina septemvittata, family Colubridae

6 **Masked water snake**
Homalopsis buccata, family Colubridae

7 **New Guinea bockadam**
Cerberus rynchops, family Colubridae

8 **Tentacle snake**
Erpeton tentaculatum,
family Colubridae

9 **Rainbow water snake**
Enhydris enhydris, family Colubridae

FACT FILE

European grass snake This is one of the few reptiles to live inside the arctic circle and above 7,000 feet (2,121 m). Frogs are one of their main dietary items. Declining frog populations mean grass snake numbers are falling.

Dead or alive?
When grass snakes are attacked, they inflate with air, hiss, bite, release a foul-smelling liquid from the cloaca, and writhe around with their mouth open before lying limp as if dead.

- Up to 6½ ft (2 m)
- Terrestrial, aquatic
- Oviparous
- 15–35
- Common

Europe, W. Asia, N.W. Africa

Queen snake The queen snake is endangered in parts of its range due to habitat destruction and pollution. This water snake inhabits cool, clear streams, where it forages for newly moulted crayfish under flat rocks.

- Up to 36½ in (93 cm)
- Aquatic
- Ovoviviparous
- 5–23 live young
- Status

S.E. Canada, E. USA

Masked water snake This nocturnal aquatic snake feeds on fishes and frogs. It has well-developed Duvernoy's glands and grooved, posterior maxillary teeth. Duvernoy's secretions are used to incapacitate prey animals, which makes them easier to eat.

- Up to 1.2m (4 ft)
- Aquatic
- Viviparous
- Unknown
- Common

S.E. Asia

Rainbow water snake This tropical water snake feeds primarily on fresh-water fish and is not tolerant of salt water. It is the main aquatic snake in most wetland habitats in Southeast Asia, but is at risk from the intrusion of salt water, associated with El Niño, into its habitats.

- Up to 32 in (81 cm)
- Aquatic
- Viviparous
- Unknown
- Common

S.E. Asia

FACT FILE

Mangrove snake This rear-fanged snake has mildly potent venom, and is capable of killing humans. They are semiarboreal, feeding on small mammals, tree shrews, birds and other snakes in mangrove swamps.

↔ Up to 2.5m (8¼ ft)
🌐 Aquatic, arboreal
○ Oviparous
● 7–14
♦ Common

S.E. Asia

Boomslang This venomous snake is the most dangerous colubrid. It is a rear-fanged snake, but its venom is more potent than that of cobras or vipers and causes internal bleeding. Boomslangs are active snakes that feed mainly on chameleons and other tree lizards, nestling birds and eggs.

↔ Up to 1.8m (6 ft)
🌲 Arboreal
○ Oviparous
● 10–25
♦ Common

Sub-Saharan Africa

Cape twig snake This is a venomous rear-fanged colubrid, capable of inflicting fatal bites on humans. The venom causes internal bleeding. The twig snake has special cartilage in the throat that allows it to puff its neck up greatly in a threat display.

↔ Up to 1.6m (5½ ft)
🌲 Arboreal
○ Oviparous
● 4–13
♦ Common

Sub-Saharan Africa

BROWN VINE SNAKE

These diurnal snakes forage in the lower branches of neotropical forests, where they easily strike and capture passing ground-dwelling lizards. They also feed on arboreal lizards, frogs, small birds and small mammals.

Look, no hands
The brown vine snake is a rear-fanged snake and kills its prey so that it is easier to manipulate and has less chance of dropping to the ground.

Rear-fanged nocturnal predator of lizards and birds; mildly venomous

1. **Mangrove snake**
   Boiga dendrophila, family Colubridae

2. **Brown vine snake**
   Oxybelis aeneus, family Colubridae

3. **Long-nosed tree snake**
   Ahaetulla nasuta, family Colubridae

4. **Boomslang**
   Dispholidus typus, family Colubridae

5. **Paradise flying snake**
   Chrysopelea paradisi, family Colubridae

6. **Cape twig snake**
   Thelotornis capensis, family Colubridae

7. **Mediterranean cat snake**
   Telescopus fallax, family Colubridae

8. **Forest flame snake**
   Oxyrhopus petola, family Colubridae

SNAKES AS PREDATORS

Heat vision Carpet pythons (Morelia spilota), with their labial heat-sensing pits, are able to detect and identify the size of a warm-blooded object before seeing it optically.

All snakes are carnivorous. The variety of prey sizes and taxa ranges from termites to crocodiles. Small snakes that feed on invertebrates search for their prey by sight or smell, often attacking them in their nests. Snakes use their tongues to collect scent data on where their prey has been and often trail them or wait for them to return; many of the large vipers and constricting snakes wait along rodent or game trails for prey to come to them. The large-eyed diurnal racers and whipsnakes are visual predators and chase down lizards and other snakes. The venom that vipers, elapids and some colubrids inject to kill their prey also helps in the digestion of the animal, since venom is an enzyme. Many large snakes eat a meal only a few times a year, but sometimes this meal has a greater mass than they do.

Strike force The eyelash viper (*Bothriechis schlegelii*) (above) is an arboreal sit-and-wait predator, ready to rapidly identify prey through visual, infrared and olfactory cues. It strikes on a moment's notice, as a bird, bat, lizard, frog, or in this case, rodent, passes by.

Snake-eaters Many species of snakes, including the king cobra (above), feed on other snakes such as coral snakes, king snakes, indigo snakes and mussuranas. Snakes are easy to swallow and the protein is easily digestible.

Gone fishing The mild venom of the Duvernoy's gland is sufficient to paralyse a fish. The grass snake (*Natrix natrix*) (above) can then more easily manipulate it for swallowing. All snakes swallow their prey whole.

Suffocation Many snakes, not just pythons, boas and anacondas, constrict their prey to kill it. The amethyst python (*Morelia amethistina*) (left) captures prey in its teeth and simultaneously wraps several coils around it. The coils get tighter as the animal exhales, and it dies from suffocation. Normally no bones are broken in this process.

Egg-eaters The egg-eater snake (*Dasypeltis scabra*) has a gland behind each eye that may supply extra fluids to the mouth to lubricate egg shells for swallowing. It can swallow an object about three times its diameter.

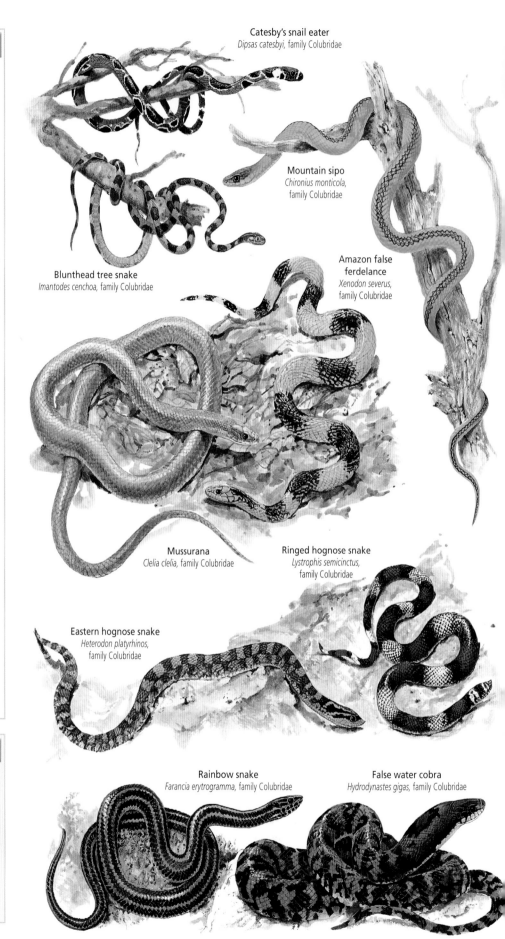

Catesby's snail eater
Dipsas catesbyi, family Colubridae

Mountain sipo
Chironius monticola, family Colubridae

Blunthead tree snake
Imantodes cenchoa, family Colubridae

Amazon false ferdelance
Xenodon severus, family Colubridae

Mussurana
Clelia clelia, family Colubridae

Ringed hognose snake
Lystrophis semicinctus, family Colubridae

Eastern hognose snake
Heterodon platyrhinos, family Colubridae

Rainbow snake
Farancia erytrogramma, family Colubridae

False water cobra
Hydrodynastes gigas, family Colubridae

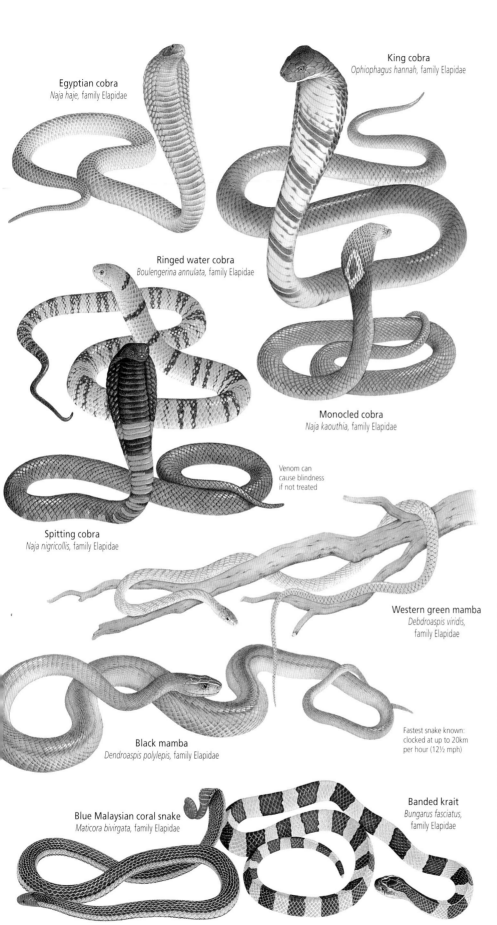

Egyptian cobra
Naja haje, family Elapidae

King cobra
Ophiophagus hannah, family Elapidae

Ringed water cobra
Boulengerina annulata, family Elapidae

Monocled cobra
Naja kaouthia, family Elapidae

Venom can
cause blindness
if not treated

Spitting cobra
Naja nigricollis, family Elapidae

Western green mamba
Debdroaspis viridis,
family Elapidae

Fastest snake known:
clocked at up to 20km
per hour (12½ mph)

Black mamba
Dendroaspis polylepis, family Elapidae

Blue Malaysian coral snake
Maticora bivirgata, family Elapidae

Banded krait
Bungarus fasciatus,
family Elapidae

FACT FILE

Family Elapidae This family comprises the cobras, kraits, seasnakes, coral snakes, death adders and allies. Elapids are venomous, with anterior erect fangs on each maxilla. Only the mambas and tree cobras are arboreal. Many are burrowing or leaf-litter snakes and have bright colouration. Most terrestrial species are oviparous or viviparous. All true sea snakes are viviparous, giving birth in the water. The sea kraits lay eggs on land.

Genera 62
Species 300

Worldwide except Antarctica & Atlantic

Spitting cobra Although this species usually does not bite, it can squirt its venom accurately up to 2.6m (9 feet), aiming for its attacker's eyes.

- Up to 2.2m (7¼ ft)
- Terrestrial
- Oviparous
- 10–22
- Common

Sub-Saharan Africa

Black mamba This large snake carries enough neuro-toxic venom to kill up to 10 adult humans. It is one of the fastest and most fearless snakes known. It can strike out to 40 per cent of its length (most snakes only manage 25 per cent).

- Up to 4.2m (14 ft)
- Terrestrial, arboreal
- Oviparous
- 12–14
- Common

África

SPITTING COBRA

Spitting cobras have an opening on the anterior surface of the fang above the tip. For better accuracy, the inside of the fangs have spiral grooves that put a spin on the projected venom.

Safe spitting
Spitting cobras avoid contact with potential predators by spitting venom in their eyes; this avoids injuries to their fangs and mouths.

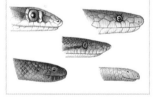
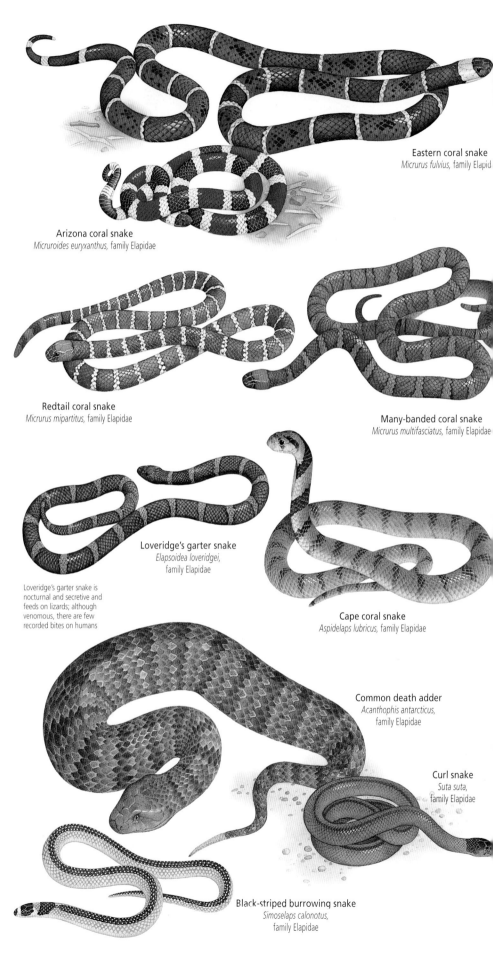

Eastern coral snake
Micrurus fulvius, family Elapid

Arizona coral snake
Micruroides euryxanthus, family Elapidae

Redtail coral snake
Micrurus mipartitus, family Elapidae

Many-banded coral snake
Micrurus multifasciatus, family Elapidae

Loveridge's garter snake
Elapsoidea loveridgei,
family Elapidae

Loveridge's garter snake is nocturnal and secretive and feeds on lizards; although venomous, there are few recorded bites on humans

Cape coral snake
Aspidelaps lubricus, family Elapidae

Common death adder
Acanthophis antarcticus,
family Elapidae

Curl snake
Suta suta,
family Elapidae

Black-striped burrowing snake
Simoselaps calonotus,
family Elapidae

Taipan
Oxyuranus scutellatus, family Elapidae

Black tiger snake
Notechis ater, family Elapidae

Mulga
Pseudechis australis, family Elapidae

Blue-lipped sea krait
Laticauda laticauda, family Elapidae

Western brown snake
Pseudonaja nuchalis, family Elapidae

Olive-brown sea snake
Aipysurus laevis, family Elapidae

Yellow-belly sea snake
Pelamis platurus, family Elapidae

Turtle-headed sea snake
Emydocephalus annulatus,
family Elapidae

Ornate reef snake
Hydrophis ornatus, family Elapidae

Scales at centre of
ornate reef snake's body
are hexagonal in shape

FACT FILE

Taipan The taipan is the world's deadliest snake, due to the toxicity of its venom. It inhabits wet tropical forests as well as dry forests and open savanna, and feeds on small mammals.

✺	Up to 2m (6½ ft)
◑	Terrestrial
○	Oviparous
●	3–20
▦	Common

S. New Guinea, Indonesia & Australia

Blue-lipped sea krait Unlike other sea snakes, sea kraits are oviparous and lay their eggs on land. They do not have reduced ventral scales or a well-developed paddle-like tail. They often come to shore to digest large meals, another point of difference with other sea snakes, and possess muscles that are well developed for moving on land.

✺	Up to 1m (3¼ ft)
◐	Aquatic
○	Oviparous
●	1–10
♦	Common

Indian & Pacific oceans

SEA SNAKES

Sea snakes were once grouped with Hydrophiidae, but are now part of the family Elapidae. They have many similar characteristics: all are venomous, and all except the sea krait (*Laticauda*) are viviparous and give birth at sea. All of these snakes have laterally compressed bodies, paddle-like tails, reduced ventral scales, and are incapable of moving well on land. There are 15 genera and 70 species distributed in Papua New Guinea, Australia, and tropical Pacific and Indian oceans.

No table Sea snakes evolved a very potent neuro-toxic venom so that they could stun fishes rapidly, and then easily manipulate them into their mouths without dropping them to the ocean floor.

⚑ CONSERVATION WATCH

The nine species of Elapidae on the IUCN Red List are categorised as follows:

7 Vulnerable

2 Near threatened

FACT FILE

Family Viperidae All vipers are venomous, and possess movable front fangs. The pit vipers (rattlesnakes and allies) have an external loreal pit for infrared detection. Adults range from 0.3–3.75m (1 12½ feet) in length. The vipers lack the loreal pit; adults range from (0.3–2m (1–6½ feet) in length. Most vipers have thick bodies and triangular-shaped heads. Young often eat amphibians, lizards or snakes and change to a diet of mammals and birds as adults.

Retractable fangs
Vipers are characterised by large retractable front fangs in the upper jaw, which are used to inject a potent venom to prey and predators alike.

Genera 32
Species 221

Central & South America, Africa, Europe, Asia

SIDEWINDER

The sidewinder (*Crotalus cerastes*) moves in loose sand by sidewinding. The head and neck are held off the sand and thrown sideways while the body remains in place. As soon as the head and neck hit the sand, the body and tail are hurled after it. As the tail touches the ground, the head and neck become airborne again, resulting in a continuous looping motion.

Sidewinding
Vipers in African deserts and sidewinder rattlesnakes in North American deserts evolved this skill separately for moving across windblown sand.

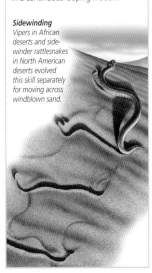

Lichtenstein's night adder
Causus lichtensteini,
family Viperidae

Adder
Vipera berus,
family Viperidae

Persian horned viper
Pseudocerastes persicus,
family Viperidae

Wagner's viper
Vipera wagneri,
family Viperidae

Green bush viper
Atheris squamigera,
family Viperidae

Saw-scaled viper
Echis carinatus,
family Viperidae

Russel's viper
Daboia russelii,
family Viperidae

Horned viper
Cerastes cerastes, family Viperidae

Fea viper
Azemiops faae,
family Viperidae

Levantine viper
Macrovipera lebetina, family Viperidae

Rhinoceros viper
Bitis nasicornis,
family Viperidae

Mauritanic viper
Macrovipera mauritanica,
family Viperidae

Tropical rattlesnake
Crotalus durissus,
family Viperidae

Gaboon adder
Bitis gabonica, family Viperidae

Pygmy rattlesnake
Sistrurus miliarius,
family Viperidae

Copperhead
Agkistrodon contortix,
family Viperidae

Banded rock
rattlesnake
Crotalus lepidus,
family Viperidae

Cantil
Agkistrodon bilineatus,
family Viperidae

Western
diamondback
rattlesnake
Crotalus atrox
family Viperidae

FACT FILE

Rhinoceros viper This heavy-bodied viper has two to three horns on the tip of its snout and is venomous but not aggressive. It is a sit-and-wait predator and mostly preys on mammals.

- Up to 1.2m (4 ft)
- Terrestrial
- Viviparous
- 6–35 live young
- Common

C. & W. Africa

Pygmy rattlesnake The genus *Sistrurus* is distinguished by having nine large scales on the dorsal surface of the head. Young pygmy rattlesnakes have a bright yellow tail tip, which they wiggle as a lure to attract small prey.

- Up to 80cm (31½ in)
- Terrestrial
- Viviparous
- 6–10 live young
- Common

S.E. USA

Western diamondback rattlesnake One of the most abundant rattlesnakes in the United States, it is responsible for more snake bites there than any other snake. Diet is primarily rodents, but the young prey on lizards.

- Up to 2.3m (7½ ft)
- Terrestrial
- Viviparous
- 4–25 live young
- Common

S.W. USA & N.W. Mexico

RATTLE

Rattlesnakes have a unique rattle at the end of their tails. It is made up of inter-locking segments of keratin; each time the snake sheds its skin, a new segment is added. When the tail is vibrating, the hollow segments bang against each other, making the anti-predator rattling sound.

⚡ CONSERVATION WATCH

The 20 species of Viperidae on the IUCN Red List are categorised as follows:

7	Critically endangered
4	Endangered
7	Vulnerable
1	Data deficient
1	Least concern

FACT FILE

Tiger rattlesnake This small nocturnal rattlesnake can often be found resting in pack rat (Neotoma) mounds in the daytime. At night it feeds on rodents and lizards. Although small, it has long fangs and potent venom.

✴ Up to 92cm (36 in)
◯ Terrestrial
🦎 Viviparous
● 2–5 live young
🐾 Common

Sonoran Desert (S.W. USA & N.W. Mexico)

Massasauga Massasauga means great river mouth in the Chippeawa language. The preferred habitat for this species is river-bottom forest in the floodplains of large rivers. They hibernate in cray-fish burrows after foraging for rodents and frogs during the summer. When vibrated, their small rattle sounds like the buzz of a cricket.

✴ Up to 76cm (30 in)
◯ Terrestrial
🦎 Viviparous
● 8–20 live young
🐾 Rare

S.E. Canada, N.E. USA to N.W. USA, N. Mexico

Black-tailed rattlesnake In the spring, males follow the chemical trails of females to court them. Courtship and mating often last several days. Females give birth in August and stay with their young until they have shed for the first time. They find prey by following animal scent trails to burrows or nests and waiting for their chosen prey to return.

✴ Up to 1.3m (4¼ft)
◯ Terrestrial
🦎 Viviparous
● 3–13 live young
🐾 Common

S.W. USA & N.W. Mexico

Timber rattlesnake These rattlesnakes have communal dens in rock out-croppings, usually on the south side of hills or mountains. Breeding usually takes place in the spring at the dens before the snakes disperse. The young follow the scent trails of the adults to reach the dens in the fall. Although this species is primarily terrestrial, young have been found in the lower branches of trees and recent studies have found adults in the treetops hunting squirrels.

✴ Up to 1.5m (5 ft)
◯ Terrestrial
🦎 Viviparous
● 6–15 live young
🐾 Common

N.E. USA

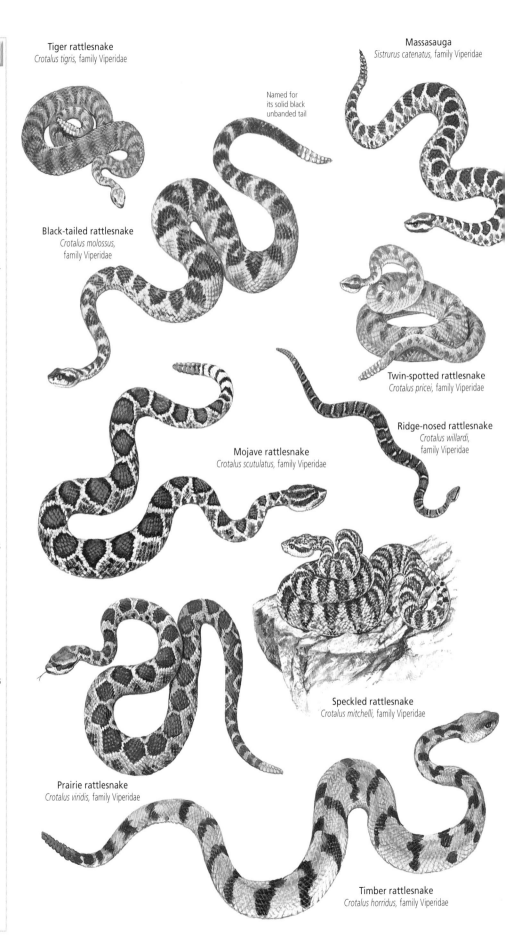

Tiger rattlesnake
Crotalus tigris, family Viperidae

Massasauga
Sistrurus catenatus, family Viperidae

Named for its solid black unbanded tail

Black-tailed rattlesnake
Crotalus molossus, family Viperidae

Twin-spotted rattlesnake
Crotalus pricei, family Viperidae

Mojave rattlesnake
Crotalus scutulatus, family Viperidae

Ridge-nosed rattlesnake
Crotalus willardi, family Viperidae

Speckled rattlesnake
Crotalus mitchelli, family Viperidae

Prairie rattlesnake
Crotalus viridis, family Viperidae

Timber rattlesnake
Crotalus horridus, family Viperidae

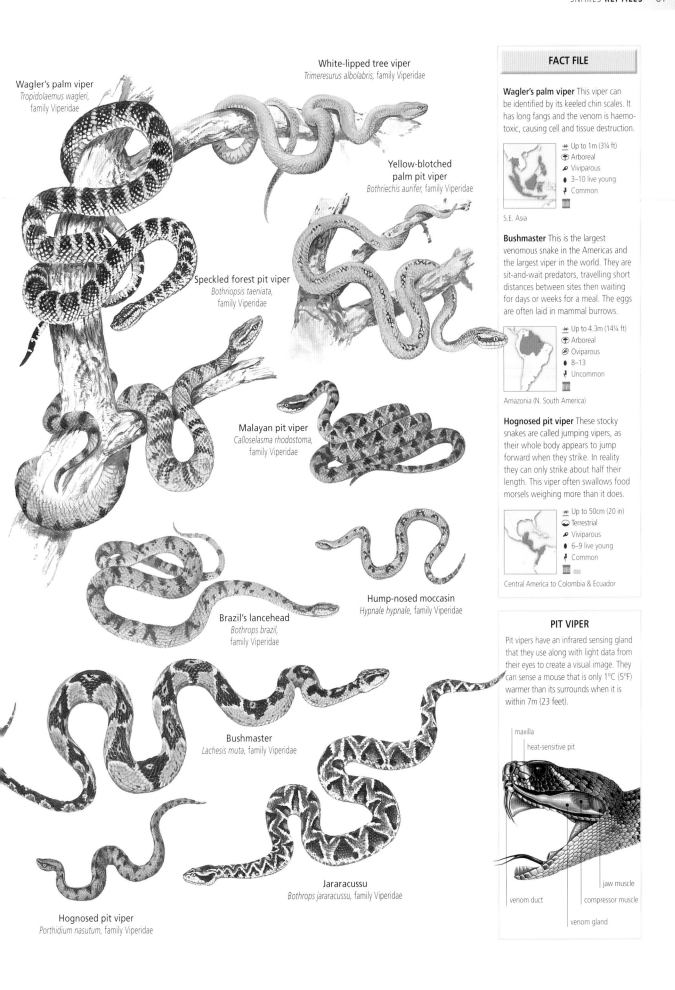

Wagler's palm viper
Tropidolaemus wagleri,
family Viperidae

White-lipped tree viper
Trimeresurus albolabris, family Viperidae

Yellow-blotched
palm pit viper
Bothriechis aurifer, family Viperidae

Speckled forest pit viper
Bothriopsis taeniata,
family Viperidae

Malayan pit viper
Calloselasma rhodostoma,
family Viperidae

Hump-nosed moccasin
Hypnale hypnale, family Viperidae

Brazil's lancehead
Bothrops brazil,
family Viperidae

Bushmaster
Lachesis muta, family Viperidae

Jararacussu
Bothrops jararacussu, family Viperidae

Hognosed pit viper
Porthidium nasutum, family Viperidae

FACT FILE

Wagler's palm viper This viper can be identified by its keeled chin scales. It has long fangs and the venom is haemo-toxic, causing cell and tissue destruction.

- Up to 1m (3¼ ft)
- Arboreal
- Viviparous
- 3–10 live young
- Common

S.E. Asia

Bushmaster This is the largest venomous snake in the Americas and the largest viper in the world. They are sit-and-wait predators, travelling short distances between sites then waiting for days or weeks for a meal. The eggs are often laid in mammal burrows.

- Up to 4.3m (14¼ ft)
- Arboreal
- Oviparous
- 8–13
- Uncommon

Amazonia (N. South America)

Hognosed pit viper These stocky snakes are called jumping vipers, as their whole body appears to jump forward when they strike. In reality they can only strike about half their length. This viper often swallows food morsels weighing more than it does.

- Up to 50cm (20 in)
- Terrestrial
- Viviparous
- 6–9 live young
- Common

Central America to Colombia & Ecuador

PIT VIPER

Pit vipers have an infrared sensing gland that they use along with light data from their eyes to create a visual image. They can sense a mouse that is only 1°C (5°F) warmer than its surrounds when it is within 7m (23 feet).

maxilla

heat-sensitive pit

jaw muscle

venom duct

compressor muscle

venom gland

AMPHIBIANS

AMPHIBIANS

PHYLUM	Chordata
CLASS	Amphibia
ORDERS	3
FAMILIES	44
GENERA	434
SPECIES	5,400

Amphibians arose from early lobe-finned fishes about 360 million years ago to become the first vertebrates established on land. There are three main modern groups. The earthworm-like caecilians have bullet-shaped heads, tails and no limbs. Salamanders have cylindrical bodies, long tails, distinct heads and necks and well-developed limbs. Anurans – frogs and toads – differ from all other vertebrates in having stout, tail-less bodies with a continuous head and body and well-developed limbs. All amphibians are ectothermic and none has scales or claws. Anurans and salamanders lay eggs, while some caecilians give birth to live young.

TERRESTRIAL LIFE

Features that have allowed amphibians to exploit terrestrial environments include a tongue, to help moisten and move food in the mouth; eyelids and associated glands to protect the cornea and keep it damp; an outer dead skin-cell layer that is regularly shed; external ear drums; a larynx in the throat for sound production; and the chemosensory Jacobson's organ in the roof of the mouth, for taste and smell.

Amphibian skin plays an active role in water-balance control. In frogs, for example, the skin's permeability changes according to their activity. When foraging on land, it increases for better water absorption. In water, permeability is greatly reduced. Some terrestrial frogs have a pelvic skin patch richly supplied with blood vessels that can absorb water from any moist area. When frogs hibernate in an aquatic environment, they must alter skin permeability and the ionic balance in their body fluids to reduce water absorption. Some desert toads retain urea in their urine to create an osmotic gradient across the skin that allows water to be absorbed from seemingly dry soil.

All adult amphibians are carnivorous, although a few frog species reportedly eat certain fruits. Most larval amphibians are also carnivorous, feeding on invertebrates, tadpoles and small fish. The tadpoles of most frog species are herbivorous. In this way, they are not competing with the adults for food. The digestive system of the tadpole must change as it is transforming to the adult stage.

Burrowing forms The ringed caecilian (*Siphonops annulatus*) is typical of an animal built for subterranean life. It has no limbs, but a fortified, bullet-shaped head and muscular segmented body designed for adept tunneling. Eyes, being of little use in a dark environment, are greatly reduced. Some salamanders also spend most of their lives foraging underground.

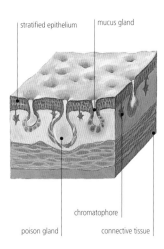

stratified epithelium | mucus gland

chromatophore

poison gland | connective tissue

Remarkable organ Amphibian skin does much more than provide physical protection for internal organs and tissues. Kept moist by glandular mucous secretions, it maintains water balance and often allows respiration. Potent antiviral, antifungal and antibacterial secretions are common. Some amphibians – usually those with bright warning colouration – also secrete poisons that are distasteful or even toxic to predators.

Regenerative powers Newts, such as the warty newt (larval form above), can regenerate body parts lost in tussles with predators or through other means. This capability is more pronounced in the hind part of the body and in younger individuals.

Frog view Like those of other land vertebrates, amphibian eyes have a cornea, iris, lens and retina. Most amphibians have an immovable upper eyelid and a movable lower eyelid, of which the upper part – known as the nictitating membrane – is usually transparent. Anurans have true colour vision. In addition to their role in visual perception, frogs blink their eyes to help push food from their mouths down their throats.

AMPHIBIANS THROUGH THE AGES

Evolutionary biologists cannot be sure which early fish or fishes gave rise to the amphibians. The most likely candidates were among the lobe-finned rhipidistians, a freshwater group common during the Devonian period (408–360 million years ago). The relationship is indicated by several key common features not evident in other fish groups. Labyrinthidonts are the earliest known amphibians, the oldest fossils of which come from Greenland, from around the end of the Devonian. These had a fish-like tail and the remnants of a bony gill-cover in the cheek region. Among the labyrinthidonts were the reptiliomorphs and the batrachomorphs. The former included the ancestor of reptiles, birds and mammals; the latter gave rise to the modern amphibians.

ANCIENT FORMS

None of the modern amphibians bears much physical resemblance to their earliest ancestors. The links are often gleaned from small skeletal details, such as features of the skull relating to the structure of the middle ear.

It is believed all three living orders arose from the long-extinct batrachomorph order Temnospondyli. One ancient representative was *Dendrerpeton*, a predominantly terrestrial amphibian thought to have been able to hear seismic, but not airborne, vibrations. Another was *Eryops*, a fierce swamp-dwelling predator that could swim better than run and which, at 1.5m (5 feet) in length, was the biggest land animal known from the Permian (290–248 million years ago). During the next 40 million years, the seas inundated the northern continents and many amphibians grew to astonishing sizes. In *Metoposaurus* and *Cyclotosaurus*, the skull alone was 1m (3¼ feet) long. These kinds of large creatures were evolutionary dead ends.

The earliest frogs are known from about 245 million years ago; salamanders appear in the fossil record from about 150 million years ago; and caecilians appear from about 65 million years ago.

Ancient frog *Messelobatrachus* (above) was an aquatic frog that survived during the early Eocene when Earth's climate was largely tropical. It is known from a fossil found in a rich deposit in the sediments of a lake in Grube Messel, in Germany, which dried up about 50 million years ago. The fossil does not reveal colour or pattern details.

Transitional life *Eusthenopteron*, an ancient lobe-finned fish (below), was probably similar to ancestors of the first amphibians. Having lungs as well as gills, it could breathe air when necessary. Its fins were like those from which tetrapod limbs evolved – paired and supported by muscular lobes with bony elements.

CLASSIFICATION

Lissamphibia, the living amphibians, includes three orders: the frogs and toads (Anura); the salamanders, newts and sirens (Caudata); and the caecilians (Gymnophiona). Amphibians are monophyletic – they are all derived from the same common ancestor. Smooth skin without scales is their main common feature. Biological classifications inevitably change as scientists gather more information and discover new species. The Malayan horned frog (right), for example, has been assigned six different scientific names since first described in 1858. At various times, the two species in the genus *Megophrys*, which look very similar, have been mistakenly considered the same species.

KINGDOM
Animalia
Malayan horned frog; tiger, coral, sponge, lizard, shark

PHYLUM
Chordata
Malayan horned frog, domestic cat, grizzly bear, human

CLASS
Amphibia
Malayan horned frog, all frogs, all toads, salamanders, newts, caecilians

ORDER
Anura
Malayan horned frog, all frogs, all toads

FAMILY
Megophryidae
Malayan horned frog, shaping frog, Karin hills frog, Asian toad

GENUS
Megophrys
Malayan horned frog; Asian spadefoot toad

SPECIES
Megophrys nasuta
Malayan horned frog

AMPHIBIANS

Class Amphibia

Order Caudata
Salamanders and newts

Order Gymnophiona
Caecilians

Order Anura
Frogs and toads

Order Anura, page 100

BIOLOGY AND BEHAVIOUR

Most amphibians are nocturnal and active only in moist environmental conditions. Some, however, exhibit water-conserving behaviour and even behaviour to regulate body temperature. Day-active frogs living in cool climates often bask in the Sun to raise their body temperature before foraging. Some periodically enter water to acquire moisture and lower their temperature. The North American bullfrog regulates its temperature by changing position in relation to the Sun's rays, and by evaporative cooling through mucous secretions and periodic rewetting of the skin. Grey tree frogs (*Hyla versicolour*) change their body colour from dark brown or grey when they want to be warmer, to light green when they are warm enough and want to reflect, rather than absorb, light.

STAYING SAFE

Feigning death is a widespread anti-predator response among amphibians, particularly frogs. Toads commonly inflate the body to appear bigger while raising themselves up, sometimes tilting their paratoid glands at predators and even squirting mild venom from these glands.

Some South American leptodactylid frogs have groin glands resembling 'eyespots', suggestive of a bigger animal. Large frogs may leap and snap at predators. Many emit loud screams when grasped, to frighten predators and warn other frogs.

Salamanders with poison glands on the tail lash it at predators; others, with cephalic glands, butt with their heads. Many exhibit caudal autonomy – a tail portion breaks in a predator's grasp and the salamander can escape while the predator is distracted by the piece of wriggling tail.

Independent offspring Tadpoles are not always at the mercy of predators and the environment as they seem to be. Many exhibit some control over body temperature by moving into shallow water on sunny days. Some are also toxic to potential predators, a fact advertised by bright warning colouration. Others school in big groups, appearing to be a larger animal to avoid predation.

Frog pharmacy The bright colouration of green and black poison dart frogs, from Central and South America, warns of toxic skin secretions. Medical researchers are investigating a substance from this frog's skin as a potential painkiller for humans, up to 200 times more potent than morphine, without side-effects.

Fountain of youth Larvae of the barred tiger salamander usually become adults within five months of hatching. This species is neotenic – under certain conditions, individuals will retain gills and other larval features throughout life. Although they reproduce, they never complete metamorphosis to a terrestrial existence. This allows them to live permanently in water.

PERNICIOUS PREDATORS

Most amphibians are opportunistic sit-and-wait predators that react to potential prey when it comes within reach. Some heavy-bodied frogs, such as the South American horned frogs, lure agile prey by waving the long toes on their hind feet. Other diurnal frogs, especially the small poison frogs of tropical America, actively forage for insects using visual cues.

Changing names Common names are often inconsistent. The frogs at left, for example, are called mission golden-eyed tree frogs, Amazon milk frogs and blue milk frogs. There is no ambiguity about the scientific name – *Phrynohyas resinifistrix*.

MATING SONGS

Males of most frog species have a unique mating call recognised by other individuals of the same species. Many frogs in seasonal environments have short breeding periods during which males move to temporary ponds and produce simple calls intended to attract females. Those active year-round, in tropical and subtropical regions, typically have more complex calls with courtship and territorial components.

Although some salamanders bark and squeak, they are not known to use vocalisations during sexual behaviour. Some mark territories with scent trails, recognised by members of the same species, and courtship is often elaborate and well developed. Male redbacked salamanders have a mental gland on their chin that is used to release hormones directly into the brain of females to stimulate them to mate. The only frogs with elaborate courtship are among the aquatic tongueless frogs.

NURSERY CARE

Some terrestrial frogs and toads actively care for their young. Female South American marsupial frogs, for example, transport eggs on their backs or in a dorsal pouch. Male Darwin's frogs, from Chile, gather hatchling tadpoles from their egg clutches to carry them in a vocal sac until development is complete. Likewise, male hip-pocket frogs, from Australia, transport tadpoles in flank pockets. Female Australian gastric-brooding frogs swallow fertilised eggs. Tadpoles complete development in the stomach, which shuts down digestion during brooding. The tadpoles of South American pond frogs often move in schools. Their mothers protect them by leaping aggressively at potential predators. Some tropical rainforest frogs nourish free-living tadpoles in tree holes or bromeliads with unfertilised eggs. The females of many terrestrial salamanders protect their eggs until they hatch.

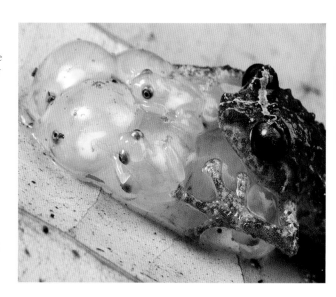

Egg brooders Most amphibians that deposit their eggs in water immediately abandon them to develop at the whims of the surrounding environment. It is common in species that deposit their eggs on land, however, for a parent to stay with them to prevent their theft by predators.

Male display This male crested newt (below) is in breeding condition. Usually, the sexes look very similar, but during breeding season the male's dorsal and tail crests increase in size. After courtship in the water, the eggs are fertilised internally and deposited singly on vegetation.

HABITATS AND ADAPTATIONS

Because amphibians are ectothermic and their body temperature is largely at the mercy of environmental conditions, few manage to be active in cold surroundings. They do not occur naturally in Antarctica or the extreme northern parts of Europe, Asia and North America. Amphibians are also noticeably absent from most oceanic islands: their need for fresh water does not make them good candidates for rafting across expanses of salt water, which is the way island fauna often begins. Caecilians are found throughout the tropics although they are absent from Madagascar, New Guinea and Australia. Salamanders are widely distributed in the temperate regions of the northern hemisphere. Even though they are small, their biomass can exceed that of mammals in some northern temperate forests. One family – the lungless salamanders – reaches its highest diversity in tropical Central and northern South America. In contrast, frogs have a worldwide distribution, with species diversity greatest in the tropics. Some Amazonian rain forests boast higher numbers of amphibian species than the entire United States.

HABITAT VARIETY

Most salamanders, caecilians and about half of the frog species are terrestrial. Some, especially the caecilians, spend most of their time below ground and are highly adapted to a subterranean lifestyle. One eel-like South American subfamily (*Typhlonectinae*) is strictly aquatic, living in lakes and rivers. Many frogs and a few salamanders live in trees.

Practically all adult frogs can swim. But members of two frog families are particularly specialised. South America's paradox frogs have extremely powerful hindlimbs and huge, fully webbed feet. These are active near the surface of ponds and their eyes protrude dorsally. Africa's clawed frogs and the Surinam toad and its relatives in South America also have fully webbed feet, but they have slightly flattened bodies and relatively small eyes. They rest and feed on the bottom of ponds, coming to the surface periodically to gulp air. If ponds dry up, these frogs burrow into the mud where they stay until the ponds fill with water again. The *Eleutherodactylus* frogs are free from standing water. They lay small clutches of large, yolked eggs in humid soil in shallow nests. Males guard the eggs until they hatch directly into miniature froglets – they have no tadpole stage. Often, a male will guard more than one nest from different females in the area.

AQUATIC AMPHIBIANS

Four salamander families in North America – mudpuppies, giant salamanders and hellbenders, Congo eels and sirens – are strictly aquatic. So are the giant salamanders of China and Japan, and the olm in south-eastern Europe. The olm and some North American aquatic salamanders are neotenic – never completely transforming into adults, but retaining the larval form. These include some of the largest salamanders. They breathe by means of gills and have larval tail fins.

The sirens and Congo eels are limbless, or nearly so, and swim like snakes. In contrast, mudpuppies, giant salamanders and hellbenders have somewhat flattened bodies and normal limbs. They crawl about on the bottom of lakes or rivers and are more sedentary in their habits.

Most of the so-called pond frogs of the genus *Rana* have powerful hind legs and fully webbed feet, well adapted for leaping from land into water and swimming. Toads from the genus *Bufo* have small hindlimbs modified for short hopping on land. They do not have fully webbed toes and are not well adapted for swimming. One subfamily of caecilians (*Typhonectinae*) in South America is strictly aquatic.

Treetop breeders Many frogs attach eggs to leaves or branches from which tadpoles later drop into water below. Others deposit eggs in water-filled tree holes or bromeliads. In this way, adults do not need to leave trees to reproduce.

Juvenile form The red-spotted newt (below) is aquatic for its first few months. It then develops lungs and loses its gills, to become a red-skinned terrestrial form called an eft. Two years later it metamorphoses again, returning to the water to breed.

ARBOREAL AMPHIBIANS

The ends of the fingers and toes of many tree frogs are expanded into specialised pads that help them cling to vertical surfaces. Their long, slender bodies and long limbs are adapted to perching on and leaping from leaves and branches. In the genus *Phyllomedusa,* found in the American tropics, the innermost fingers and toes are elongated and, like primate thumbs, are opposable to the outer digits. This allows these frogs to climb by grasping branches. Some tree frogs in Southeast Asia have huge, fully webbed hands and feet as well as fringes of extra skin along the limbs. These modifications provide an extensive surface area when the limbs are extended and the fingers and toes spread. By gliding on these wing-like structures, the tree frogs are able to travel considerable distances between tree branches, or even glide from tree to tree.

Some of the American tropic's casque-headed tree frogs have hard skin on the head that is firmly attached to underlying bones. They have a greatly reduced blood supply to this skin. To reduce water loss during dry seasons, these frogs back into holes or bromeliad plants containing small amounts of water, flexing their heads at right angles to secure themselves in place.

Frogs have responded to the challenge of reproduction in the trees with a range of effective adaptations. Perhaps the ultimate for arboreal reproduction occurs in some of the South American marsupial frogs in which fertilised eggs develop into miniature froglets in a pouch on the mother's back. In this way generations pass without any individuals leaving the trees.

There are small poison frogs in the family *Dendrobatidae* which forage on the forest floor in Central and South America. The males guard the eggs until they hatch in terrestrial nests. They then carry the tadpoles on their backs up trees and deposit them in water-filled tree holes to finish development. The reverse happens as well; many tree frogs (*Hylidae*) forage in the trees but descend to temporary terrestrial ponds in order to breed.

Safe flashing Species in the genus *Bombina* are gregarious aquatic toads. When alarmed, they arch the back and flash their bright underbelly to confuse predators. Eggs are laid on pond surfaces as the Sun's warmth accelerates development.

Push and pull Caecilians propel themselves through soil by concertina locomotion. Part of the body remains in static contact with the earth while adjacent sections are pushed or pulled forward at the same time.

BURROWING AMPHIBIANS

Of all the amphibians, caecilians are most adept at burrowing. Worm-like and limbless, they have muscular bodies and compact skulls. With eyes covered by skin or bone, caecilians are blind but detect prey, such as earthworms, using a protrusible, chemosensory head tentacle.

Many groups of frogs have a large, keratinised, spade-like tubercle on the inner edge of each hind foot. They use this to bury themselves quickly in soft dirt or mud. Other burrowing frogs use calloused or pointed snouts, and tunnel head-first. Some bury themselves for daytime retreat. Others do so for longer periods, existing in a kind of suspended animation during dry seasons. They fill their urinary bladder with water before burrowing to avoid desiccation. Some further reduce the risk by secreting mucus, which hardens around them to form a cocoon. Australian desert species are known to have remained alive underground for over a year between rainy seasons.

AMPHIBIANS IN DANGER

Since 1980, it is believed that at least 122 amphibian species have gone extinct. One-third – just over 1,850 in number – are now facing the same fate according to IUCN figures. The fate of a further 113 remains uncertain because they have not been studied in sufficient detail to know their status in the wild today. While the figures on amphibian decline are worrying enough for the group itself, they have set alarm bells ringing in wider scientific and environmental communities because of what they mean for all life forms. The highly permeable skin of amphibians makes them extremely sensitive to environmental shifts, particularly pollution and temperature change. This means they are excellent biological indicators of habitat health. Current figures detailing amphibian losses confirm fears that Earth is experiencing a period of significant environmental decline. There are more herpetologists studying frogs now, however, than ever before so what we are documenting may be natural fluctuations in frog populations.

ALARMING DECLINES

There are several possible reasons for the amphibian losses observed around the world since the mid-1970s. Some of these are linked, and the impact of each varies from country to country. For example, the infectious fungal disease known as chytridiomycosis is thought to have been a major cause of decline among the amphibian fauna of Australia, the Caribbean and the Americas; there have also been smaller outbreaks in Asia, Africa and Europe. The disease is caused by the chytrid fungus. It interferes with the skin's permeability, and death by suffocation is the inevitable outcome. Recently, this fungus has been shown to have arisen in Africa in the 1930s. It was perhaps spread around the world by the use of the African clawed frog (*Xenopus laevus*) in pregnancy tests and the aquarium pet trade.

Habitat loss and modification, and collection for the international pet trade – particularly of some of the more colourful or physically spectacular frog and salamander species – are other serious problems.

Rising temperatures that are linked to global climate change; increased UV exposure due to declining levels of ozone in Earth's atmosphere; and herbicide and pesticide pollution have also played critical roles in the decline of amphibians. Developing nations in tropical areas, particularly those in Central and South America, are reporting the worst losses.

Small, isolated populations are more likely to be eradicated by disease or natural disaster than large ones. Because some disappearing species exist only in what appear to be pristine environments, it is not entirely clear whether or not all losses are caused by human activity.

Medical argument Skin secretions of toads and frogs, such as Australia's green and golden bell frog (above), are receiving increasing attention as potential sources of new medications for humans. This is a compelling reason to preserve amphibian biodiversity, but too many species are disappearing before researchers can investigate their potential.

Mysterious losses Golden toads, (below) are inhabitants of Central American high mountain cloud forest. They congregate in the breeding season to mate at small ponds and streams. During the 1980s, this was one of many highland species worldwide that suffered a catastrophic and largely unexplained decline, in many cases to apparent extinction.

SALAMANDERS AND NEWTS

CLASS	Amphibia
ORDER	Caudata
FAMILIES	10
GENERA	60
SPECIES	472

Salamanders, newts, mudpuppies, waterdogs and sirens belong to the order Caudata. All have tails and most have four legs. Most species are very secretive, living terrestrially in leaf litter or rotting logs, underground, in arboreal bromeliads or underwater. Some live terrestrially but return to the water to reproduce. Although seldom seen, they are not uncommon; astoundingly, in some deciduous forests in North America, the biomass of salamander populations is greater than that of the birds and mammals. All salamanders and their larvae are carnivorous, and they in turn become prey for many larger carnivores, such as snakes, birds and mammals.

Distribution Salamanders are widely distributed in North and Central America, northern South America, Europe, northern Africa and Asia.

Warning colours The red salamander (*Pseudotriton ruber*) is semiaquatic, living in or under moss or flat rocks in or near springs or spring creeks. It prefers cool, clear water that flows through woods or meadows. Many species of salamanders are brightly coloured to warn their principal predators – birds – that they are distasteful.

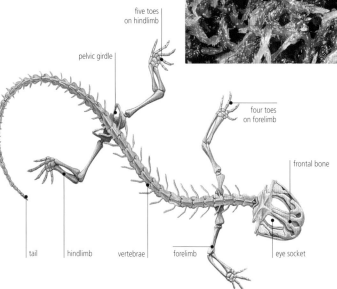

Four-toed salamander *Hemidactylium scutatm* lays up to 24 eggs under logs or in moss near clear-water creeks. The female guards them until they hatch; then the larvae enter the water to finish development.

Salamander skeleton A salamander's vertebral column is rigid to support the head, pelvic and pectoral girdles, and viscera, but is also flexible, permitting lateral and dorsoventral movements. Salamanders have 10–60 presacral vertebrae and a variable number of postsacral vertebrae: 2–4 precaudals and a number of caudal vertebrae.

five toes on hindlimb
pelvic girdle
four toes on forelimb
frontal bone
tail
hindlimb
vertebrae
forelimb
eye socket

SILENT CARNIVORES

Salamanders evolved to live on land, with four legs and a tail. Some species have secondarily returned to live permanently in the water and have reduced limbs; these are known as sirens.

Salamanders more closely resemble early fossil amphibians than do frogs and toads. Unlike frogs, they do not emphasise vocal communications during breeding. The skin of salamanders is generally smooth, moist, and flexible, with oxygen exchange taking place through the skin. Many species have lungs as well, but some families lack lungs and respire entirely cutaneously. As the salamander grows, the skin is regularly shed. Because it is made up of the salamander's own cells and is easy to digest, the animal usually devours its own skin as it is sloughed.

Salamanders and their larvae are completely carnivorous. Adults consume insects, spiders, snails, slugs, worms and other invertebrates. The larvae devour mosquito larvae and other insects. As they grow, they eat larger prey, including tadpoles and the larvae of the dragonfly that was once their feared predator. Some species of salamanders are able to extend their tongues rapidly for half the length of their body to capture prey.

Salamanders have moist, slippery skin, while newts, both in their aquatic and terrestrial phases, have rough, dry skin. Some species of newts live on land as adults, coming to the water only to breed, while the adults of some species are aquatic. Red-spotted newts are equally at home in the water or on land. The aquatic larvae metamorphose into a terrestrial red eft, and after 1–2 years on land return to the water to breed.

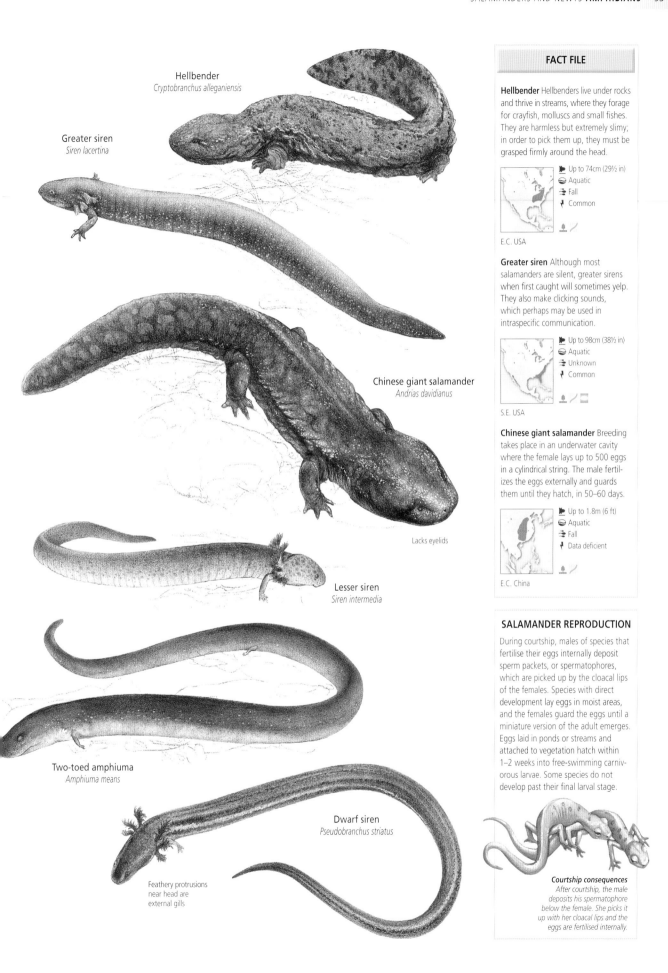

Hellbender
Cryptobranchus alleganiensis

Greater siren
Siren lacertina

Chinese giant salamander
Andrias davidianus

Lacks eyelids

Lesser siren
Siren intermedia

Two-toed amphiuma
Amphiuma means

Dwarf siren
Pseudobranchus striatus

Feathery protrusions
near head are
external gills

FACT FILE

Hellbender Hellbenders live under rocks and thrive in streams, where they forage for crayfish, molluscs and small fishes. They are harmless but extremely slimy; in order to pick them up, they must be grasped firmly around the head.

- Up to 74cm (29½ in)
- Aquatic
- Fall
- Common

E.C. USA

Greater siren Although most salamanders are silent, greater sirens when first caught will sometimes yelp. They also make clicking sounds, which perhaps may be used in intraspecific communication.

- Up to 98cm (38½ in)
- Aquatic
- Unknown
- Common

S.E. USA

Chinese giant salamander Breeding takes place in an underwater cavity where the female lays up to 500 eggs in a cylindrical string. The male fertilizes the eggs externally and guards them until they hatch, in 50–60 days.

- Up to 1.8m (6 ft)
- Aquatic
- Fall
- Data deficient

E.C. China

SALAMANDER REPRODUCTION

During courtship, males of species that fertilise their eggs internally deposit sperm packets, or spermatophores, which are picked up by the cloacal lips of the females. Species with direct development lay eggs in moist areas, and the females guard the eggs until a miniature version of the adult emerges. Eggs laid in ponds or streams and attached to vegetation hatch within 1–2 weeks into free-swimming carniv-orous larvae. Some species do not develop past their final larval stage.

Courtship consequences
After courtship, the male deposits his spermatophore below the female. She picks it up with her cloacal lips and the eggs are fertilised internally.

FACT FILE

Mudpuppy These neotenic salamanders are characterised by their large, red external gills. They feed nocturnally on crustaceans, insect larvae, fishes, worms, molluscs and other amphibians. Females guard and aerate their eggs.

- Up to 48cm (19 in)
- Aquatic
- Fall
- Common

N.C. USA

Olm Olms live in flooded underground caves and are blind, with only vestigial eyes occurring beneath the pigmentless skin. They are neotenic. They lay up to 70 eggs, or may retain eggs and produce fewer living young.

- Up to 30cm (12 in)
- Aquatic
- Spring
- Vulnerable

Adriatic seaboard & N.E. Italy

Chinese salamander This terrestrial salamander with short limbs migrates to streams or ponds for breeding. Males are attracted to females by chemical and visual cues.

- Up to10cm (4 in)
- Terrestrial
- Spring
- Common

Hubei Province (S. China)

⚡ CONSERVATION WATCH

Going, going... Three species of salamander are listed on the IUCN Red List as critically endangered. The Lake Lerma salamander (*Ambystoma lermaense*) has not been seen for years and is now presumed to be extinct. It was endemic to Lake Lerma, Mexico, which was affected by dam construction and pollution.

The Sardinian brook salamander (*Europroctus platycephalus*) is the most threatened salamander in Europe, due to pesticide (DDT) treatment of water bodies in the battle against malaria; the introduction of trout, which feed on and compete with the salamanders for food; and the reduction of water levels due to agriculture.

The desert slender salamander (*Batrachoseps major aridus*) only lives in one canyon in Riverside County, California, United States. As the water table lowers, this species' habitat is slowly vanishing.

Mudpuppy
Necturus maculosus

Extremely slimy skin

Olm
Proteus anguinus

Vestigial eyes

⚡ Siberian salamander
Ranodon sibiricus

Fischer's clawed salamander
Onychodactylus fischeri

Dybowski's salamander
Salamandrella keyserlingii

Sichuan salamander
Liua shihi

Chinese salamander
Hynobius chinensis

⚡ Paghman mountain salamander
Batrachuperus mustersi

Luschan's salamander
Mertensiella luschani

European fire salamander
Salamandra salamandra

Olympic torrent salamander
Rhyacotriton olympicus

Golden striped salamander
Chioglossa lusitanica

Pyrenees mountain salamander
Euproctus asper

Californian giant salamander
Dicamptodon ensatus

Red-spotted newt
Notophthalmus viridescens

Common newt
Triturus vulgaris

Male in breeding
condition

Luristan newt
Neurergus kaiseri

Banded newt
Triturus vittatus

FACT FILE

European fire salamander This oviparous salamander breeds on land. Once the embryos are mature, the female releases 20–30 membranous eggs into the water, where they hatch immediately. The larvae take between 2 and 6 months to metamorphose into the terrestrial form.

▶ Up to 25cm (10 in)
🌐 Terrest., aquatic larvae
🌱 Spring
🔸 Common

Europe & W. Asia

Californian giant salamander Females guard their 50 or more eggs for up to 6 months in streams beneath rocks. Terrestrial adults often climb into low shrubs up to 2.4m (8 feet) above the ground. The males make a low rattling sound when disturbed.

▶ Up to 36cm (14 in)
🌐 Terrestrial, aquatic
🌱 Spring
🔸 Common

N.W. USA

Common newt Males are smaller than females. During the breeding season, males develop a wavy crest from head to tail, as well as a fringe on the hind toes. They remain in the breeding ponds from March to July, after which they are terrestrial.

▶ Up to 11.5cm (4½ in)
🌐 Terrestrial, aquatic
🌱 Spring
🔸 Data deficient

Europe & W. Asia

NEOTENY

Neoteny is the developmental state where the aquatic larval form with gills is maintained throughout adulthood. This usually occurs in species which live in oxygen-deficient water. Some species are permanently neotenic. The Mexican axolotl is neotenic if iodine is absent in the environment.

Fire salamander
'Salamander' is from the Greek word for 'fire lizard', because they were seen crawling out of logs that had been thrown onto campfires.

FACT FILE

Ringed salamander This species has narrow crossbands, a slate-coloured belly and a light-grey stripe along the sides of its thin body, unlike the marbled and tiger salamanders.

- Up to 23cm (9 in)
- Aquatic, burrowing
- Fall
- Common

S.C. USA

Tiger salamander These salamanders are fossorial for most of the year, only emerging to breed once the early spring rains begin. After breeding in ponds or marshes, the adults retreat underground.

- Up to 33cm (13 in)
- Aquatic, burrowing
- Early spring
- Common

S. Canada to Mexico

Marbled salamander This species congregates to lay up to 230 eggs in dry depressions from September to December. Females remain wrapped around the eggs, protecting them from predation and desiccation, until fall rains fill the pools.

- Up to 13cm (5 in)
- Terrestrial, aquatic
- Fall
- Common

S.E. USA

Japanese firebelly newt Males of this species differ from females by having swollen cloacas. The tails of breeding males develop a bluish iridescent sheen and a small filament at the tip.

- Up to 13.2cm (5¼ in)
- Aquatic
- Spring
- Common

Japan

Vietnam warty newt This is the largest species of the genus. It is characterised by a distinct belly pattern of orange-yellow or reddish blotches, each with black or dark brown mottling.

- Up to 20cm (8 in)
- Aquatic
- Spring
- Vulnerable

N. Vietnam

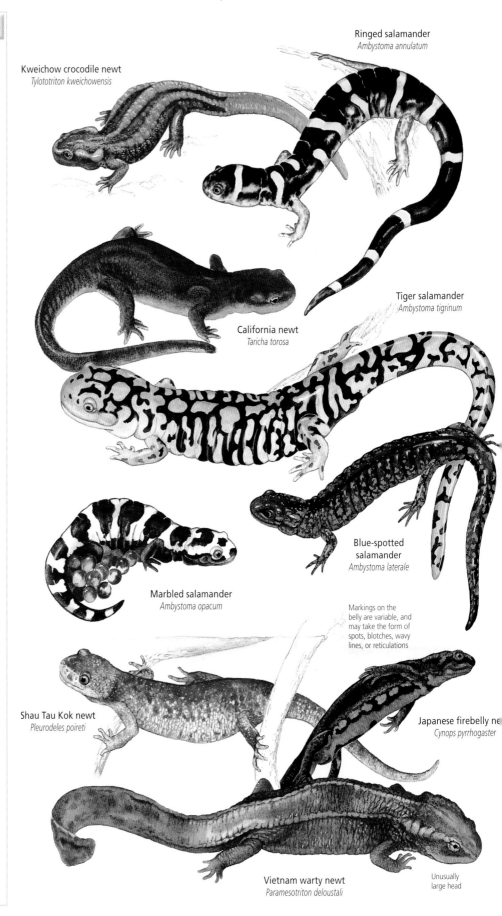

Kweichow crocodile newt
Tylototriton kweichowensis

Ringed salamander
Ambystoma annulatum

California newt
Taricha torosa

Tiger salamander
Ambystoma tigrinum

Blue-spotted salamander
Ambystoma laterale

Marbled salamander
Ambystoma opacum

Markings on the belly are variable, and may take the form of spots, blotches, wavy lines, or reticulations

Shau Tau Kok newt
Pleurodeles poireti

Japanese firebelly ne
Cynops pyrrhogaster

Vietnam warty newt
Paramesotriton deloustali

Unusually large head

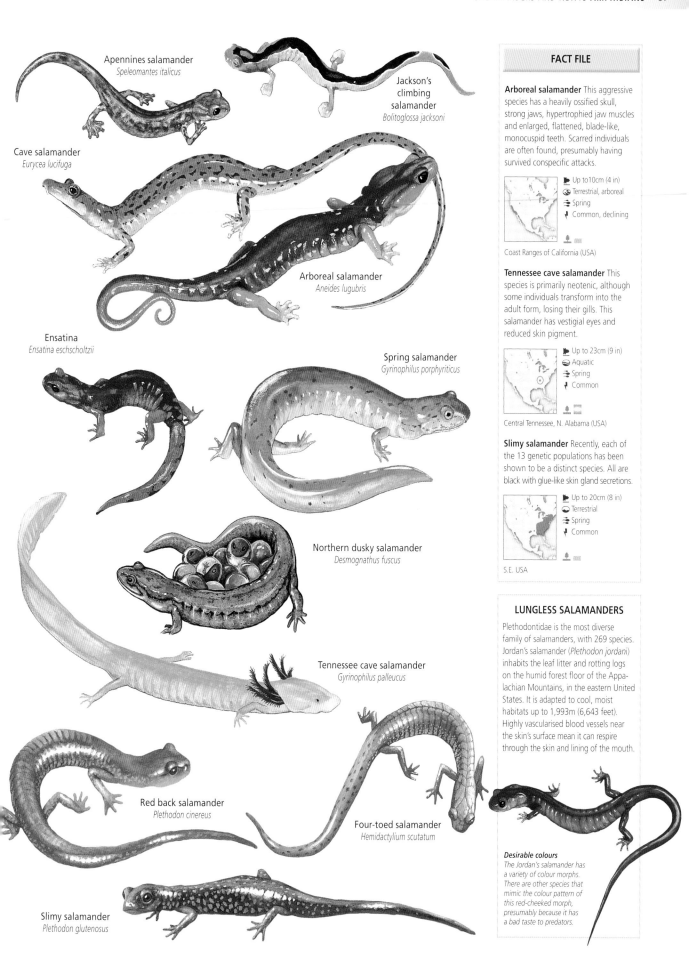

Apennines salamander
Speleomantes italicus

Jackson's climbing salamander
Bolitoglossa jacksoni

Cave salamander
Eurycea lucifuga

Arboreal salamander
Aneides lugubris

Ensatina
Ensatina eschscholtzii

Spring salamander
Gyrinophilus porphyriticus

Northern dusky salamander
Desmognathus fuscus

Tennessee cave salamander
Gyrinophilus palleucus

Red back salamander
Plethodon cinereus

Four-toed salamander
Hemidactylium scutatum

Slimy salamander
Plethodon glutenosus

FACT FILE

Arboreal salamander This aggressive species has a heavily ossified skull, strong jaws, hypertrophied jaw muscles and enlarged, flattened, blade-like, monocuspid teeth. Scarred individuals are often found, presumably having survived conspecific attacks.

- Up to 10cm (4 in)
- Terrestrial, arboreal
- Spring
- Common, declining

Coast Ranges of California (USA)

Tennessee cave salamander This species is primarily neotenic, although some individuals transform into the adult form, losing their gills. This salamander has vestigial eyes and reduced skin pigment.

- Up to 23cm (9 in)
- Aquatic
- Spring
- Common

Central Tennessee, N. Alabama (USA)

Slimy salamander Recently, each of the 13 genetic populations has been shown to be a distinct species. All are black with glue-like skin gland secretions.

- Up to 20cm (8 in)
- Terrestrial
- Spring
- Common

S.E. USA

LUNGLESS SALAMANDERS

Plethodontidae is the most diverse family of salamanders, with 269 species. Jordan's salamander (*Plethodon jordani*) inhabits the leaf litter and rotting logs on the humid forest floor of the Appalachian Mountains, in the eastern United States. It is adapted to cool, moist habitats up to 1,993m (6,643 feet). Highly vascularised blood vessels near the skin's surface mean it can respire through the skin and lining of the mouth.

Desirable colours
The Jordan's salamander has a variety of colour morphs. There are other species that mimic the colour pattern of this red-cheeked morph, presumably because it has a bad taste to predators.

AMPHIBIAN LIFE CYCLES

Most amphibians have a dual life cycle involving a court-ship ritual, the deposition of sperm and eggs, external fertilisation, an aquatic larval stage and transformation into the adult life form. Modifications made to this cycle involve internal fertilisation, direct development, viviparity, neoteny or parental care. There is a trade-off between multitudes of small eggs with no parental care and a few large eggs with parental care.

Swollen egg sacs The egg sac of the Jefferson salamander (*Ambystoma jeffersonianum*) is much larger than the adult after the eggs have absorbed water. This species does not brood or guard its eggs.

Salamander life cycle Pheromones stimulate courtship behaviour in sala-manders. Males then deposit sperm as spermatophores on the substrate below the female. She retrieves the spermatophores with her cloacal lips, fertilising the eggs internally as she deposits them in water or in a moist substrate. Aquatic larvae hatch from the eggs in the water or direct develop-ment may occur in terrestrial eggs.

terrestrial adult

larva with fully developed limbs and gills

egg

larva with gill buds

larva with developing gills and forelimbs, and hindlimb buds

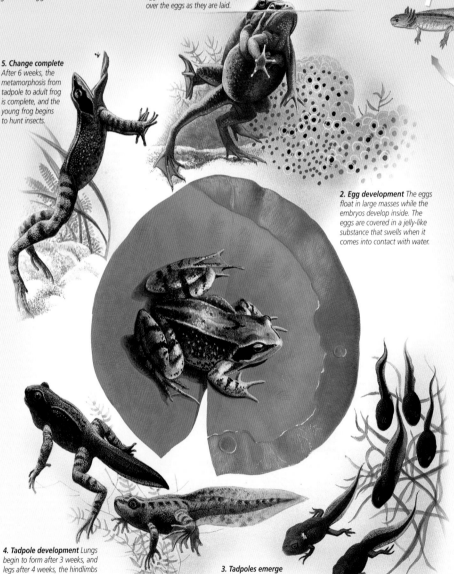

1. Mating The male clasps the female around the middle. The female carries the male until she is ready to lay her eggs. The male then sheds his sperm over the eggs as they are laid.

5. Change complete After 6 weeks, the metamorphosis from tadpole to adult frog is complete, and the young frog begins to hunt insects.

2. Egg development The eggs float in large masses while the embryos develop inside. The eggs are covered in a jelly-like substance that swells when it comes into contact with water.

Safe development Marsupial frogs (*Gastrotheca*) have one or two pouches, similiar to those of marsupials, which open dorsally to the cloaca. Eggs are placed in the pouch as the male fertilises them. Thus the eggs develop in a moist and safe environment. The young emerge as tadpoles or froglets, depending on the species.

Frog life cycle Frogs and toads have a complex life cycle. Males call to attact females, and shed sperm over the eggs as the female deposits them in a selected site. The eggs absorb water and in a few days develop into free-swimming tadpoles, which are normally herbivorous. After a few weeks, months or years (depending on the species) the tadpoles meta-morphose into identical small replicas of the adults. It then takes months or years of a carnivorous diet before sexual maturity is reached.

4. Tadpole development Lungs begin to form after 3 weeks, and legs after 4 weeks, the hindlimbs developing first. The tadpole's tail shrinks and its gills are reabsorbed.

3. Tadpoles emerge After 2 weeks, the eggs hatch into tadpoles. When the mouth develops, the tadpoles feed on algae. They breathe through external gills.

CAECILIANS

ss Amphibia
ER Gymnophiona
MILIES 6
JERA 33
CIES 149

Caecilians have radiated to a variety of aquatic and terrestrial habitats, with specialised characteristics for a fossorial life not present in any other vertebrates – chemo-sensing tentacles, an extra set of jaw-closing muscles, and skin that is ossified to the skull. Adults range in size from just under 7cm (3 inches) to 1.6m (5¼ feet). Fertilisation is internal. Some species are oviparous; others have direct development; and about half of the known species are viviparous. They feed on earthworms, beetle larvae, termites and crickets.

Distribution Caecilians have a limited pantropical distribution in India, southern China, Malaysia, the Philippines, Africa, Central America and South America. No species are known from Europe, Australia or Antarctica.

Caecilian skull Caecilians are built for burrowing, with massive, bullet-shaped skulls. They are streamlined, but reinforced for burrowing through soil or protruding into the substrate in search of invertebrate prey. They move through the soil by undulating the body: the muscles move in a wave from the head to the tail. The body curves resist the soil or water, and forward motion is achieved.

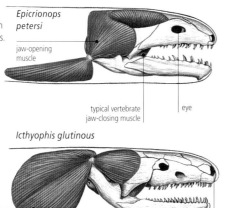

Epicrionops petersi

jaw-opening muscle

typical vertebrate jaw-closing muscle

eye

Icthyophis glutinous

strong jaw-closing muscles

nostril

Gymnophis multiplicate All species in the family Caeciliidae are chacterised by distinct annuli, which have caused some people to confuse them with earthworms. Caecilians have a retractable tentacle on each side of the head, which helps them to search for prey by transmitting chemical clues to the nasal cavity.

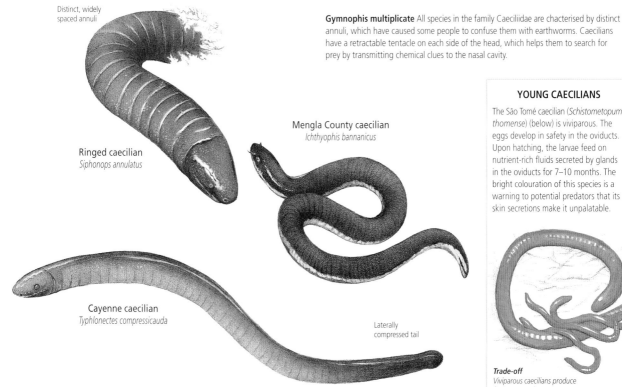

Distinct, widely spaced annuli

Ringed caecilian
Siphonops annulatus

Mengla County caecilian
Ichthyophis bannanicus

Cayenne caecilian
Typhlonectes compressicauda

Laterally compressed tail

YOUNG CAECILIANS

The São Tomé caecilian (*Schistometopum thomense*) (below) is viviparous. The eggs develop in safety in the oviducts. Upon hatching, the larvae feed on nutrient-rich fluids secreted by glands in the oviducts for 7–10 months. The bright colouration of this species is a warning to potential predators that its skin secretions make it unpalatable.

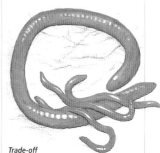

Trade-off
Viviparous caecilians produce fewer young than oviparous species but provide better care.

FROGS AND TOADS

CLASS	Amphibia
ORDER	Anura
FAMILIES	28
GENERA	338
SPECIES	4,937

Anuran is the collective term for this group of tailless amphibians. This is the largest order of amphibians, with nearly 5,000 known species. Anurans come in all shapes and sizes, from the tiny Brazilian Izecksohn's toad (*Psyllophryne didactyla*), which is less than 1cm (less than half an inch) long, to the African goliath frog (*Conraua goliath*), which is 30cm (12 inches) long and weighs 3.3kg (7$^{1}/_{3}$ pounds). Frogs and toads are easily identified by their long hind legs, short trunk, moist skin and lack of tail. Anurans are the only amphibians that are extremely vocal when breeding. The largest genus of frogs – *Eleutherodactylus* (rain frogs) – is also the largest genus of all vertebrates.

Distribution Frogs and toads occur on all continents except Antarctica. More than 80 per cent of species are tropical; at one site alone, 67 species have been recorded. Two species extend north of the Arctic Circle.

Flying frogs The Java flying frog (*Rhacophorus reinwardtii*) has broad webs of skin between its toes, allowing it to parachute between trees or guiding it in a controlled fall to another branch. This adaptation is important for life in the rainforest canopy.

SINGING FOR THEIR LIVES

A notable feature of frogs and toads is the voices of the males calling for mates. These calls herald spring in the temperate zone and the onset of the rainy season in the tropics. Each species of frog has a specific call that distinguishes it from all other species. Females can assess the size of the male, and thus his fitness, by the tone of his call. Only males call, and females come to the calling male to mate. These calls also have the disadvantage of attracting some predators, notably bats.

In some species, calling sites are at a premium and males defend them against other calling males. To avoid confrontations, satellite males wait silently near the calling male in hopes of intercepting a gravid female before she reaches him. This lessens their chance of being eaten by a bat, and reduces the energy lost by calling or by fighting with the dominant male.

The above are characteristics of frogs with long breeding seasons. Many other species are explosive breeders, coming to the breeding ponds with the first heavy rains, breeding by the thousands for 2–3 days, and then retreating until the following year. These species

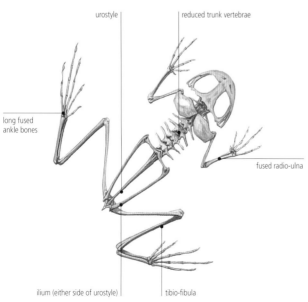

urostyle | reduced trunk vertebrae

long fused ankle bones

fused radio-ulna

ilium (either side of urostyle) | tibio-fibula

Tongue lashing Frogs and toads have long, sticky tongues, like the Japanese toad (*Bufo japonicus*) (above), which they use to capture prey. Once the insect is inside the mouth, the toad blinks its eyes and the eyes push the food out of the mouth and down the throat. Males also use their tongues in combat, lashing them into the eyes of other males in territorial battles or in bouts over access to a female.

Frog skeleton Anurans have a shortened vertebral column of nine or fewer vertebrae. The epipodial elements of both fore and hindlimbs are fused; also, the ankle is elongated and made up of two fused elements. The postsacral vertebrae are uniquely fused into a rod-shaped urostyle. The long hindlimbs give frogs the propulsive force to propel themselves forward. A short, compact body is easier to move forward. The reinforced pectoral girdle and forelimbs are built to absorb the shock of landing.

Calling for a mate During the breeding season, male frogs and toads call to attract the females to mate. Each species has a distinct attraction call. This natterjack toad (*Bufo calamita*) (above) has his gular sac inflated and is making a trilling sound.

Energy transfers The northern leopard frog (*Rana pipiens*) (right) leaps to escape a predator. Frogs and tadpoles transform the energy in their food (algae, detritus and insects) into larger packets of energy that are then available to bigger predators.

usually have loud, carrying calls and lay thousands of small eggs. To avoid predation of their eggs by aquatic predators, many species of tree frogs (*Hylidae*) lay their eggs in vegetation overhanging their breeding ponds. When the eggs hatch, the tadpoles fall into the water, where they complete their development. Other species of casque-headed tree frogs (*Osteocephalus*) lay a few large fertilised eggs in tree holes. The female returns regularly to deposit unfertilised eggs in the nest to feed her tadpoles. Many species of poison frogs (*Dendrobatidae*) guard their eggs in terrestrial nests and, upon hatching, carry their tadpoles to the water, or in some cases up trees and into bromeliads. Many species of *Eleutherodactylus* lay 15–25 large yolked eggs in terrestrial nests, the eggs having direct development. Midwife toads, Surinam toads and gastric-brooding frog females carry the eggs with them until they hatch into small frogs. Other *Leptodactylid* and *Rhacophorid* frogs build foam nests to deposit their eggs and rear their tadpoles.

Frogs are indicators of environmental pollution. Since the 1970s, there has been growing worldwide evidence that frog populations are declining on a massive scale and that many species are going extinct, even though their populations appear to be within pristine areas. The decline may be the result of a number of factors, including pollution, pesticides (such as DDT), herbicides (such as Atrizine), road salts, UV radiation, global warming, lower rainfall or lower humidity. At present, the fungus *chytridiomycosis* seems to be the greatest threat. The fungus, which probably originated in Africa, invades the skin and lowers the frogs' immune system so they are more susceptible to diseases.

CONSERVATION WATCH

The 342 species of anurans on the IUCN Red List are categorised as follows:

7	Extinct
27	Critically endangered
27	Endangered
64	Vulnerable
1	Conservation dependent
15	Near threatened
67	Data deficient
134	Least concern

FACT FILE

Brown New Zealand frog Males of this species do not have a prominent breeding call. Call notes are made by resonance frequencies in the head and body, not by the vibration frequency of the vocal cords.

🐸 Up to 5cm (2 in)
◯ Terrestrial
🔁 Spring
🏃 Vulnerable

Stephens & Maud Islands (New Zealand)

Oriental firebelly toad This toad is one of the most common in its range, constituting up to a third of the total anurans at some localities. The density at breeding sites can reach nine toads per square metre (three toads per sq. ft).

🐸 Up to 6cm (2½ in)
◯ Terrestrial
🔁 Summer
🏃 Common

Russia, Korea, China

Tailed frog This frog has no breeding call. Its 'tail' – used for internal fertilisation in fast-moving streams – is unique among anurans. Eggs are deposited in strings under rocks in streams. Tadpoles take 1–4 years to metamorphose to juveniles, and then 7–8 years to first breeding.

🐸 Up to 5cm (2 in)
◯ Terrestrial, aquatic
🔁 Summer
🏃 Common

N.W. USA

ANURAN FERTILISATION

Fertilisation of the eggs usually occurs while the frogs are in amplexus. As the female deposits her eggs, males release sperm above them in the water. The coqui and some other terrestrial species achieve internal fertilisation by cloacal apposition; only the tailed frog has an intermittent organ.

Frogs in amplexus
The female carries the male to an appropriate spot to deposit the eggs.

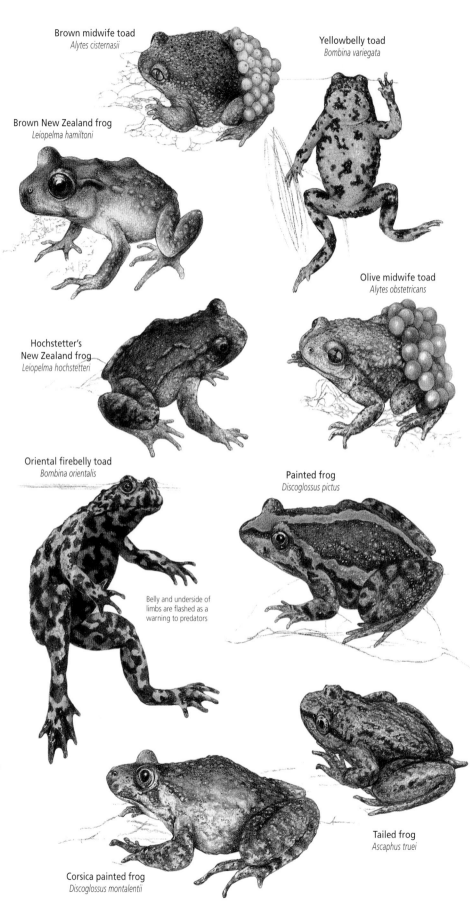

Brown midwife toad
Alytes cisternasii

Yellowbelly toad
Bombina variegata

Brown New Zealand frog
Leiopelma hamiltoni

Olive midwife toad
Alytes obstetricans

Hochstetter's
New Zealand frog
Leiopelma hochstetteri

Oriental firebelly toad
Bombina orientalis

Painted frog
Discoglossus pictus

Belly and underside of limbs are flashed as a warning to predators

Tailed frog
Ascaphus truei

Corsica painted frog
Discoglossus montalentii

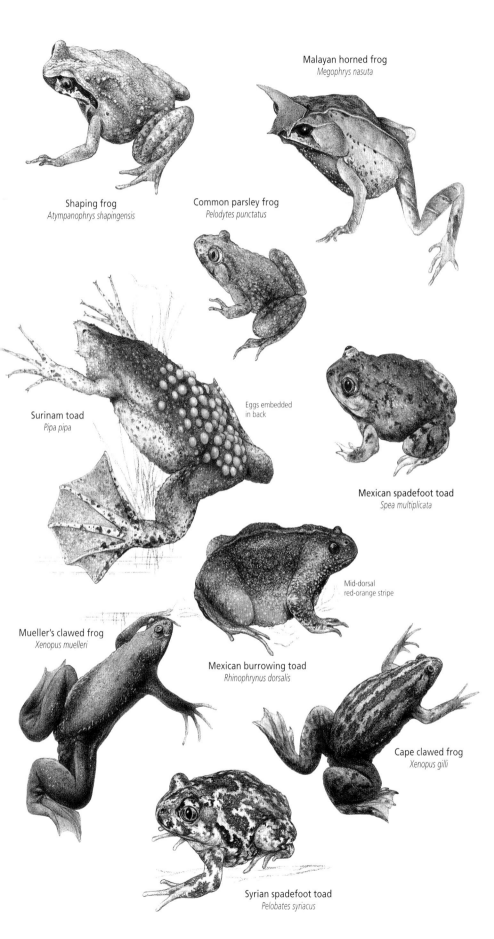

Shaping frog
Atympanophrys shapingensis

Malayan horned frog
Megophrys nasuta

Common parsley frog
Pelodytes punctatus

Surinam toad
Pipa pipa

Eggs embedded
in back

Mexican spadefoot toad
Spea multiplicata

Mid-dorsal
red-orange stripe

Mueller's clawed frog
Xenopus muelleri

Mexican burrowing toad
Rhinophrynus dorsalis

Cape clawed frog
Xenopus gilli

Syrian spadefoot toad
Pelobates syriacus

FACT FILE

Common parsley frog Male parsley frogs can be heard calling from below the surface of the water. The tadpoles are larger than the adult frogs, at up to 6cm (2½ in) in length. The eggs are laid in strings across aquatic plants.

> Up to 5cm (2 in)
> Terrestrial, aquatic
> Spring
> Common

Iberia, France, W. Belgium, N.W. Italy

Surinam toad During amplexus, the female releases eggs one at a time. The male fertilises and embeds each egg in the skin of her back, where the eggs sink in and form a honeycomb of pockets. After 3–4 months, froglets emerge from her back.

> Up to 20cm (8 in)
> Aquatic
> Spring
> Common

N. South America

Mexican spadefoot toad Spadefoots are nocturnal during the summer rainy season, when they are breeding. The rest of the year, they occupy burrows that they dig in the soft earth.

> Up to 5cm (2 in)
> Terrestrial
> Summer
> Common

S.C. USA, N. Mexico

Cape clawed frog Modification of the acid, black-water ponds inhabited by this species allowed the invasion of the common clawed frog (*Xenopus laevis*). The two are interbreeding, producing sterile hybrids and further driving this species toward extinction.

> Up to 5cm (2 in)
> Aquatic
> Winter
> Vulnerable

S.W. South Africa

Mexican burrowing toad This toad spends most of its life underground, only emerging to breed after heavy rains. Males' bodies are so inflated when calling that they resemble balloons.

> Up to 9cm (3½ in)
> Terrestrial
> Summer
> Common

Texas (USA) to Costa Rica

FACT FILE

Turtle frog This frog burrows head-first with its strong forelimbs, often into termite nests to eat the inhabitants. Males call from the soil surface or with only their heads uncovered. Up to 40 large eggs are laid underground.

- Up to 6cm (2½ in)
- Terrestrial, burrowing
- Rainy season
- Uncommon

S.W. Australia

Crucifix toad This fossorial toad spends most of its life underground and only emerges to breed after heavy rains in temporary pools. Males call while floating on the surface. Small eggs are deposited in the water.

- Up to 5.5cm (2¼ in)
- Terrestrial, burrowing
- Rainy season
- Common

S.E. Australia

Giant banjo frog Adults spend day-light hours and drier months buried beneath the surface. Males call while floating on vegetation or concealed in burrows at the water's edge. Oviposition take place in flooded burrows.

- Up to 9cm (3½ in)
- Aquatic
- Spring, summer
- Uncommon

S.E. Australia

GASTRIC BROODERS

Fertilised eggs or larvae are swallowed by the female gastric-brooding frog (*Rheobatrachus silus*) and develop in her stomach. The production of hydro-chloric acid in the female's stomach ceases during this time. Tadpoles develop from the nutrients in the egg yolk, so the labial teeth are absent.

Up they come *The young crawl out into the world after developing in their mother's stomach for 6–7 weeks.*

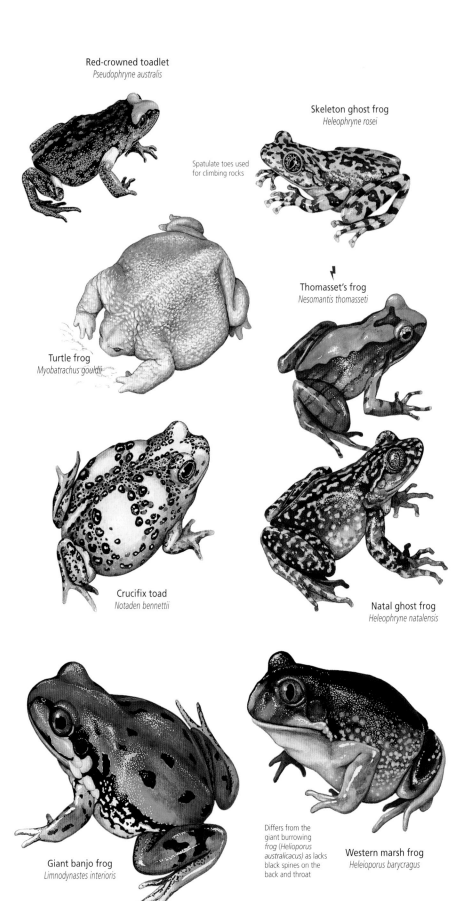

Red-crowned toadlet
Pseudophryne australis

Skeleton ghost frog
Heleophryne rosei

Spatulate toes used for climbing rocks

Turtle frog
Myobatrachus gouldii

Thomasset's frog
Nesomantis thomasseti

Crucifix toad
Notaden bennettii

Natal ghost frog
Heleophryne natalensis

Giant banjo frog
Limnodynastes interioris

Differs from the giant burrowing frog (*Helioporus australicacus*) as lacks black spines on the back and throat

Western marsh frog
Heleioporus barycragus

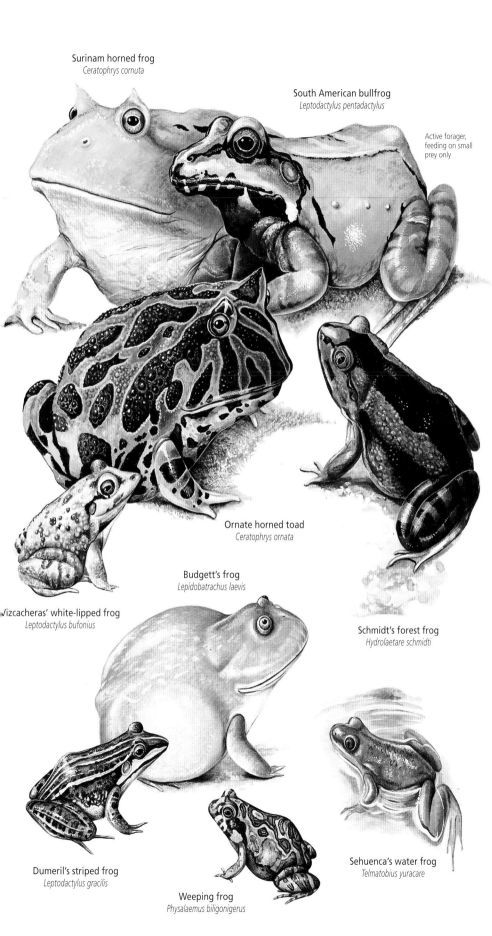

Surinam horned frog
Ceratophrys cornuta

South American bullfrog
Leptodactylus pentadactylus

Active forager, feeding on small prey only

Ornate horned toad
Ceratophrys ornata

Budgett's frog
Lepidobatrachus laevis

Schmidt's forest frog
Hydrolaetare schmidti

Vizcacheras' white-lipped frog
Leptodactylus bufonius

Dumeril's striped frog
Leptodactylus gracilis

Weeping frog
Physalaemus biligonigerus

Sehuenca's water frog
Telmatobius yuracare

DROUGHT RESISTANCE

During the dry winter months, ornate horned toads are inactive underground, encased in a hard shell composed of layers of unshed skin. This 'cocoon' protects the animal from excessive water loss and allows it to survive until the rains arrive. These signal the beginning of the wet summer months in South America, which last from October to February. The heavy rains flood the Gran Chaco and create transient pools for foraging and breeding.

Digging in Ornate horned toads will remain buried until rains signal the beginning of the wet summer months.

FACT FILE

Coqui This species gets its name from its high-pitched chirp, which sounds like *co qui*. Eggs are laid on land with direct development in the egg. Coquis have been introduced into Florida and Hawaii, United States.

- Up to 5.5cm (2¼ in)
- Terrestrial, arboreal
- Year round
- Common

Puerto Rico (Caribbean)

Barking frog The breeding call of this species sounds like a dog barking when heard at a distance; close up, it is a guttural 'whurr'. Females make a screech when grasped. When captured, their bodies puff up immensely.

- Up to 9.5cm (3¾ in)
- Terrestrial
- Spring
- Common

S.W. USA to C.W. Mexico

Peru robber frog This species has direct development. The eggs are deposited in moist areas in the leaf litter. The males, which are considerably smaller than the females, call day and night from the forest floor.

- Up to 3cm (1¼ in)
- Terrestrial
- Fall rainy season
- Common

W. Amazonia (Brazil, Bolivia, Peru, Ecuador)

Lowland tropical frog Females deposit up to 20 unpigmented eggs in a foam nest. The tadpoles developing in the nest subsist entirely on the egg yolk. Males call from mudflats.

- Up to 3cm (1¼ in)
- Terrestrial
- Spring
- Common

Amazonia (N. South America)

Gold-striped frog The flash colouration – bright red spots in the groin and on the rear of the thighs – is displayed when the frog moves. Its colouration mimics that of the spotted-thighed poison frog (*Epipedobates femoralis*). Eggs are deposited in foam nests.

- Up to 5cm (2 in)
- Terrestrial
- Winter
- Common

N. South America

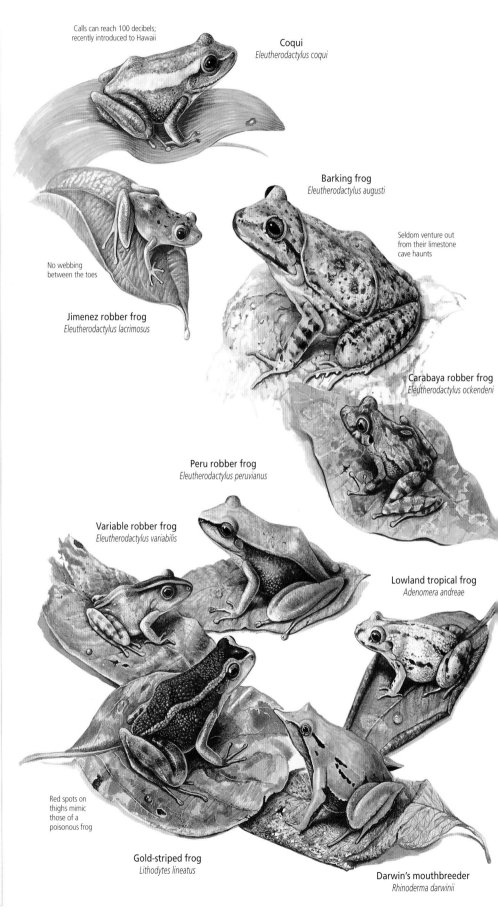

Calls can reach 100 decibels; recently introduced to Hawaii

Coqui
Eleutherodactylus coqui

Barking frog
Eleutherodactylus augusti

Seldom venture out from their limestone cave haunts

No webbing between the toes

Jimenez robber frog
Eleutherodactylus lacrimosus

Carabaya robber frog
Eleutherodactylus ockendeni

Peru robber frog
Eleutherodactylus peruvianus

Variable robber frog
Eleutherodactylus variabilis

Lowland tropical frog
Adenomera andreae

Red spots on thighs mimic those of a poisonous frog

Gold-striped frog
Lithodytes lineatus

Darwin's mouthbreeder
Rhinoderma darwinii

ADVANCE OF THE CANE TOAD

Successful stories of the cane toad (*Bufo marinos*) (also known as the marine toad) being introduced into the sugarcane fields of Puerto Rico to control insect pests convinced the sugarcane growers in Queensland, Australia, to import and breed 100 adult toads. In 1935, they released 62,000 subadults in Queensland to control the greyback cane beetle (*Dermolepida albohirtum*). Since the neotropical cane toad has no natural predators in Australia, populations have reached plague proportions. The toads adapted well to feeding on all animals smaller than themselves, even competing with dogs for the rations in their bowls. Studies in Brazil are yet to come up with a solution.

paratoid gland

Toad nightmare The cane fields did not have proper daytime cover so the introduced toads dispersed into the countryside. They are now so abundant that gardens become a moving mass of toads at night and the roads are slippery with splattered bodies.

Cane toad poison When cane toads are threatened, they inflate their bodies and begin sweating a milky, latex-like liquid from the paratoid glands. In extreme cases, the secretions can be projected up to 92cm (3 feet) toward the aggressive attacker, but are not toxic unless ingested. The poison has been used as a hallucinogenic drug.

Breeding The cane toad breeds year-round in Australia in temporary pools, stock tanks, lakes, and streams. The prolific toads are capable of producing up to 13,000 eggs at a time. Their tadpoles transform rapidly and have minimal habitat requirements: algae and water. Although cane toads take several years to mature, they can live for over 20 years. Calling cane toads interfere with the breeding choruses of native frogs.

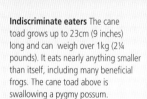

Indiscriminate eaters The cane toad grows up to 23cm (9 inches) long and can weigh over 1kg (2¼ pounds). It eats nearly anything smaller than itself, including many beneficial frogs. The cane toad above is swallowing a pygmy possum.

Fatal meal The cane toad's paratoid glands contain a secretion that is fatal to some animals. The cane toad pictured right has angled its paratoid glands toward the approaching snake. Populations of Australian snakes that normally consume native anurans are diminishing because they die from swallowing cane toads. This is also a problem for other indigenous animals. Birds, dingos, monitor lizards and other anurans see the cane toad as possible prey. Fishes die from ingesting the toxic tadpoles. And the problem is not restricted to areas into which it has been introduced: in South America, a group of Peruvian Indians is believed to have perished after eating a soup made from cane toad eggs.

FACT FILE

Colourado river toad The skin glands of these toads produce a toxin that can cause intoxication and hallucination in humans, and is a controlled substance in the United States, where people have been arrested for milking toads.

- Up to 20cm (8 in)
- Terrestrial
- Summer
- Common

S.W. USA & N.W. Mexico

Common Asian toad Once common, this species is declining due to habitat alteration and loss, caused by drought, deforestation, drainage of habitat, pesticides, fertilisers and pollutants.

- Up to 15cm (6 in)
- Terrestrial
- Summer
- Declining

S.E. Asia

AMPHIBIAN EGG

Amphibian embryos have gelatinous membranes around them, but lack the protective amnion present in reptiles. Since eggs also lack shells, they must be protected from desiccation. Eggs contain nutrients for the tadpoles to develop into free-swimming larvae. Eggs of some species have enough yolk to nourish the embryos until they hatch as miniature adults.

Tadpole developing in egg
Anurans must either deposit their eggs in water or in moist places to avoid desiccation.

⚡ CONSERVATION WATCH

The 18 species of Bufonidae on the IUCN Red List are categorised as follows:

- 1 Critically endangered
- 6 Endangered
- 6 Vulnerable
- 2 Near threatened
- 3 Data deficient

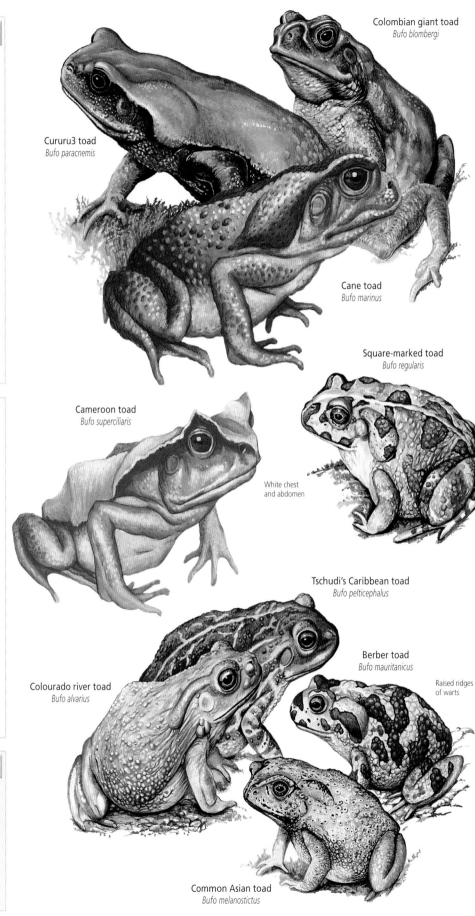

Colombian giant toad
Bufo blombergi

Cururu3 toad
Bufo paracnemis

Cane toad
Bufo marinus

Square-marked toad
Bufo regularis

Cameroon toad
Bufo superciliaris

White chest and abdomen

Tschudi's Caribbean toad
Bufo pelticephalus

Berber toad
Bufo mauritanicus

Raised ridges of warts

Colourado river toad
Bufo alvarius

Common Asian toad
Bufo melanostictus

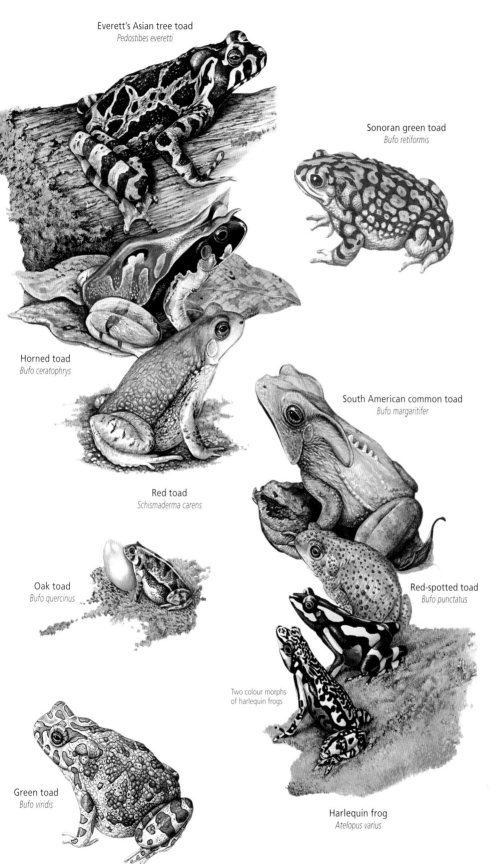

Everett's Asian tree toad
Pedostibes everetti

Sonoran green toad
Bufo retiformis

Horned toad
Bufo ceratophrys

South American common toad
Bufo margaritifer

Red toad
Schismaderma carens

Oak toad
Bufo quercinus

Red-spotted toad
Bufo punctatus

Two colour morphs
of harlequin frogs

Green toad
Bufo viridis

Harlequin frog
Atelopus varius

FACT FILE

Horned toad This diurnal toad lives
on the forest floor where it forages for
termites and breeds in forest streams.

	Up to (8.2cm (3¼ in)
	Terrestrial
	Unknown
	Common

N.W. Amazonia (South America)

Green toad Green toads form dense
populations in areas altered by people,
and these are often much higher than
in adjacent natural habitats. They
prefer burrows and live in the burrows
of rodents. Abundance can reach more
than 100 individuals per 100 square
metres 1,075 square feet).

	Up to 12cm (4¾ in)
	Terrestrial
	Spring
	Common

Europe to Asia

Harlequin frog No courtship has been
reported for this species. Amplexus is
prolonged; females carry males on their
backs from a few days to over a month
until about 20 eggs are laid in water.

	Up to 5cm (2 in)
	Terrestrial, aquatic
	Fall
	Declining

S. Costa Rica, Panama, N. Colombia

TOADS VERSUS FROGS

In Europe and North America, toads
(family *Bufonidae*) have short legs
for hopping, dry warty skin, and are
terrestrial. Frogs (family *Ranidae*) have
long, slender legs for leaping great
distances, moist skin, and are aquatic.
However, the use of the terms 'frog'
and 'toad' depends on the region
of the world you are in. In Africa, the
smooth and moist-skinned aquatic
Cape clawed frog (*Xenopus gilli*) is
called a clawed toad.

To kiss a toad
*Even though South Africans call Bufo
pardalis (above) the leopard frog, it
belongs to the toad family Bufonidae.*

FACT FILE

Australian lace-lid frog This frog has huge eyes with vertically elliptical pupils and a lower eyelid with a golden reticulation. It is found on rocks and vegetation in fast-flowing rocky streams in rain forest up to 1,200m (3,900 feet).

- Up to 6cm (2½ in)
- Arboreal
- Spring, summer
- Endangered

N.E. Australia

Southern bell frog Males call while floating on the water. The call is a low growl lasting about a second. The eggs are deposited in a floating jelly that later sinks. They feed on other frogs and even their own species.

- Up to10cm (4 in)
- Terrestrial, aquatic
- Summer
- Locally common

S.E. Australia & Tasmania

Short-footed frog This is a robust, burrowing frog with striking and highly variable markings. The back is dark brown with silver-brown blotches. The frog usually also has a silver-brown stripe down the back and a white belly.

- Up to 5cm (2 in)
- Terrestrial, burrowing
- Unknown
- Common

N.E. Australia

Paradox frog This frog has large webbed feet and extremely slippery skin. The tadpoles are three times as large as the adults, up to 25cm (10 inches) in length.

- Up to 7.5cm (3 in)
- Aquatic
- Rainy season
- Common

Amazonia (South America) to N. Argentina

Water-holding frog This species spends the long dry periods, which can be up to several years long, in burrows deep underground. It surrounds itself with a cocoon-like chamber, formed with sloughed dead layers of its skin.

- Up to 6cm (2½ in)
- Terrestrial, burrowing
- Variable
- Common

Central Australia

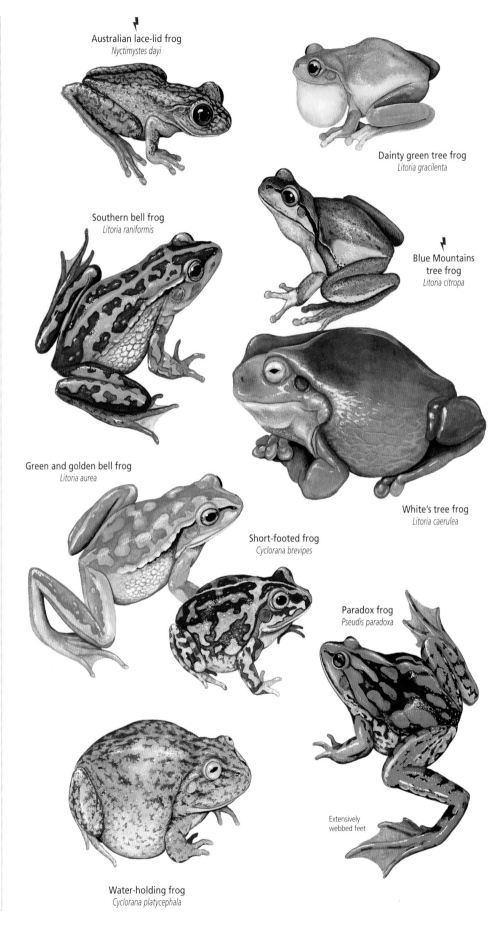

Australian lace-lid frog
Nyctimystes dayi

Dainty green tree frog
Litoria gracilenta

Southern bell frog
Litoria raniformis

Blue Mountains tree frog
Litoria citropa

Green and golden bell frog
Litoria aurea

Short-footed frog
Cyclorana brevipes

White's tree frog
Litoria caerulea

Paradox frog
Pseudis paradoxa

Extensively webbed feet

Water-holding frog
Cyclorana platycephala

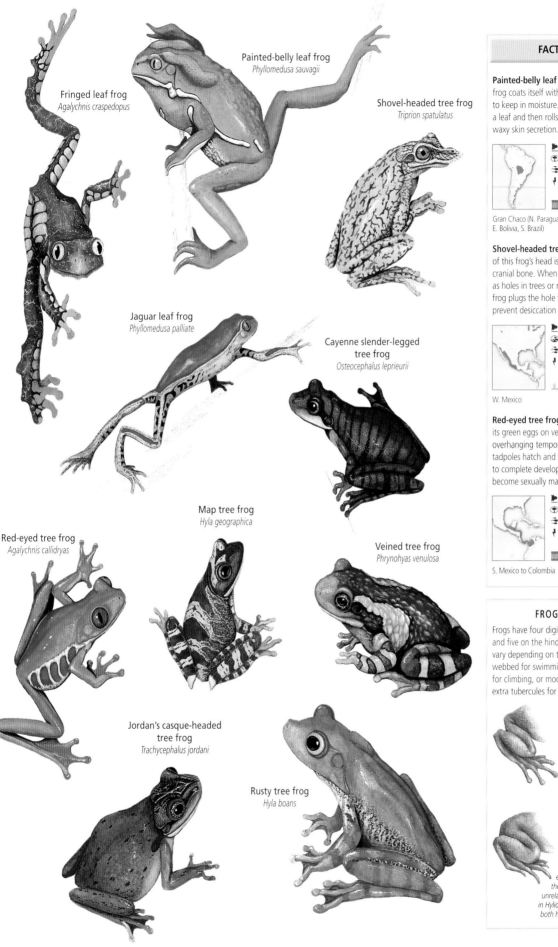

Fringed leaf frog
Agalychnis craspedopus

Painted-belly leaf frog
Phyllomedusa sauvagii

Shovel-headed tree frog
Triprion spatulatus

Jaguar leaf frog
Phyllomedusa palliate

Cayenne slender-legged
tree frog
Osteocephalus leprieurii

Map tree frog
Hyla geographica

Red-eyed tree frog
Agalychnis callidryas

Veined tree frog
Phrynohyas venulosa

Jordan's casque-headed
tree frog
Trachycephalus jordani

Rusty tree frog
Hyla boans

FACT FILE

Painted-belly leaf frog This tree frog coats itself with a waxy secretion to keep in moisture. It lays eggs on a leaf and then rolls it up with this waxy skin secretion.

📏 Up to 8.5cm (3¼ in)
🌳 Arboreal
🌧 Rainy season
✦ Common

Gran Chaco (N. Paraguay, N. Argentina, E. Bolivia, S. Brazil)

Shovel-headed tree frog The skin of this frog's head is fused to the cranial bone. When in retreats, such as holes in trees or rock crevices, the frog plugs the hole with its head to prevent desiccation and predation.

📏 Up to7.5cm (3 in)
🌍 Terrestrial, arboreal
🌧 Summer
✦ Common

W. Mexico

Red-eyed tree frog This species lays its green eggs on vegetation or rocks overhanging temporary ponds. The tadpoles hatch and fall into the water to complete development. The males become sexually mature after a year.

📏 Up to 7.5cm (3 in)
🌳 Arboreal
🌧 Summer
✦ Common

S. Mexico to Colombia

FROG FEET

Frogs have four digits on the forelimbs and five on the hindlimbs. The shapes vary depending on their habits: fully webbed for swimming, or toe pads for climbing, or modified claws with extra tubercules for digging.

Frog toes *Parallel evolution has produced the same types of toes in unrelated families: tree frogs in Hylidae and Rhacophoridae both have rounded toe pads.*

FACT FILE

Nicaragua giant glass frog This species calls – using a three-note series of high-pitched 'ticks' – from above streams. It attaches eggs to leaves that overhang the streams. Tadpoles attach to rocks with their suction mouth.

▸ Up to 2.5cm (1 in)
✪ Arboreal
➔ Summer
♪ Common

N. Nicaragua to Colombia & Ecuador

Barking tree frog This frog gets its name from its loud raucous call of nine or ten notes from high in the treetops, possibly a territorial call. Its breeding call is a simple 'doonk' or 'toonk'. The female deposits eggs singly on the bottom of the breeding pond.

▸ Up to 7cm (2¾ in)
✪ Terrestrial, arboreal
➔ Spring, summer
♪ Common

S.E. USA

European tree frog This tree frog is declining in western and central Europe due to loss of habitat, habitat isolation, pollution and climate change.

▸ Up to 5cm (2 in)
✪ Terrestrial, arboreal
➔ Spring
♪ Common

Europe, W. Asia, N.W. Africa

Marsupial frog During amplexus, the male pushes the fertilised eggs into a pouch on the back of the female. Direct development takes place in the pouch without a tadpole stage.

▸ Up to 2¾ in (7 cm)
✪ Terrestrial, arboreal
➔ Spring, summer
♪ Common

Amazonia (Peru, Bolivia)

⚡ CONSERVATION WATCH

The 72 species of Hylidae on the IUCN Red List are categorised as follows:

  6 Critically endangered
  5 Endangered
  5 Vulnerable
  5 Near threatened
  8 Data deficient
 43 Least concern

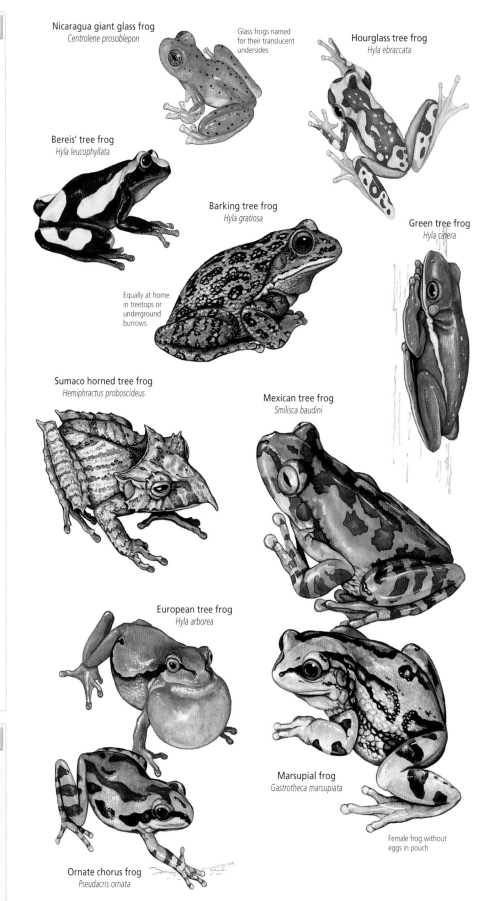

Nicaragua giant glass frog
Centrolene prosoblepon

Glass frogs named for their translucent undersides

Hourglass tree frog
Hyla ebraccata

Bereis' tree frog
Hyla leucophyllata

Barking tree frog
Hyla gratiosa

Green tree frog
Hyla cinera

Equally at home in treetops or underground burrows

Sumaco horned tree frog
Hemiphractus proboscideus

Mexican tree frog
Smilisca baudini

European tree frog
Hyla arborea

Marsupial frog
Gastrotheca marsupiata

Female frog without eggs in pouch

Ornate chorus frog
Pseudacris ornata

TREE FROGS

The family *Hylidae* – tree frogs – comprises 855 species in 42 genera, distributed primarily in North America, South America and Australia, and to a lesser extent in Europe and Asia. Tree frogs range in size from the 12mm (half-inch) adult javelin frog (*Litoria microbelos*) to the 14cm (5½ inch) Hispaniola tree frog (*Hyla vasta*). Most hylids are arboreal, but some are terrestrial, aquatic or burrowing. Most possess adhesive toe pads, which allow them to cling to any surface. Almost all are very flattened and streamlined, with long legs that are useful for leaping from branch to branch. Tree frogs have horizontally elliptical pupils, with the exception of the *Phyllomedusids*, which have vertical pupils.

Striking skin The Bereis' tree frog has a variable colour pattern resembling the markings of a giraffe; other tree frogs are less striking. Large toe pads and loose belly skin allow this frog to stick to leaves and other smooth surfaces when climbing and searching for prey.

Burrowing habits The burrowing tree frog (*Pternohyla fodiens*) is found in many habitats subject to seasonal inundation. They are well adapted for burrowing and spend the dry season in a dormant state beneath the surface. They will only breed after heavy rain.

Harlequin flying tree frog
The harlequin flying tree frog (*Rhacophorus pardalis*) is found from 200–1,700m (650–5,575 feet) and has a 6.5cm (2½ inch) snout–vent length. They lay up to 50 eggs in a foamy mass on leaves suspended in the trees above ponds between March and May and can be found in the Philippines, Borneo and Sumatra.

Safe hands The brown-belly leaf frog (*Phyllomedusa tarsius*) is nocturnal and arboreal in primary and secondary rainforests in the Amazon. The first digit on the front foot is opposable, so these frogs can grasp small branches like a primate as they crawl slowly through the canopy oblivious to wind and rain. They have rounded paratoid glands extending at least to mid-body.

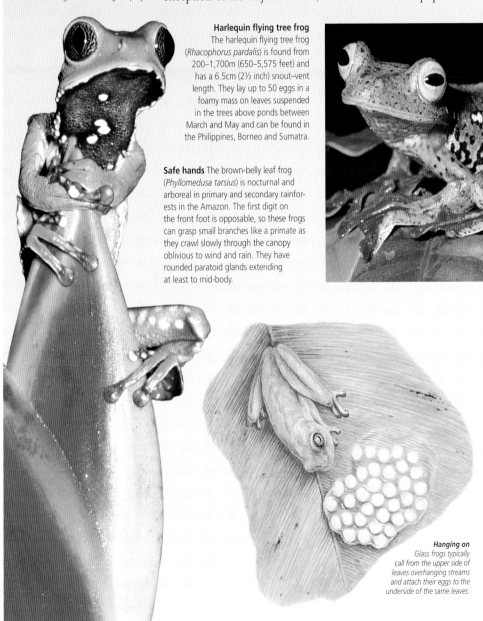

Hanging on
Glass frogs typically call from the upper side of leaves overhanging streams and attach their eggs to the underside of the same leaves.

Reproduction in the trees Males have species-specific vocalisations that they use to attract gravid females. Amplexus stimulates the females to deposit eggs, usually in water, where they hatch into free-swimming tadpoles. Many species deposit their eggs in overhanging vegetation; when the eggs hatch, the tadpoles fall into the water to finish their development. Some species deposit thir eggs in bromeliads and the tadpoles develop there. Casqueheaded tree frogs (*Osteocephalus oophagus*) have parental care. After fertilising the eggs laid in bromeliads or tree holes, males guard their progeny from predators. Females join in by laying yolked unfertilised eggs at regular intervals in these nests to feed their tadpoles.

FACT FILE

Nosy Be giant tree frog This species' call is a single whistling note that lasts for only 55–65 milliseconds. The call is repeated over a hundred times a minute. Their hands lack webbing and the feet are barely webbed.

- ▶ Up to 3cm (1¼ in)
- ◉ Terrestrial, arboreal
- ⇌ Unknown
- ↟ Common

N.W. Madagascar

Dotted humming frog This frog exists mutualistically with tarantulas in their burrows, feeding on ants that prey on tarantula eggs. At night, the frogs sit between the legs of the spiders at the mouths of their burrows.

- ▶ Up to 2.5cm (1 in)
- ◔ Terrestrial
- ⇌ Summer
- ↟ Common

E. Ecuador, S.E. Peru, N.W. Bolivia

Tomato frog The bright red colouration of this frog acts as a clear warning to potential predators that it is a toxic meal. A white, sticky fluid secreted from the skin deters snakes and can produce an allergic reaction in humans.

- ▶ Up to 10cm (4 in)
- ◉ Terrestrial, aquatic
- ⇌ Summer
- ↟ Vulnerable

N.E. Madagascar

RAIN FROGS OF AFRICA

Rain frogs (genus *Breviceps*) have short heads and stout bodies. They appear above ground only during torrential rain. Males have loud, bellowing calls that can be heard from great distances, and sticky skin secretions that attach them to the females during amplexus. They lay their eggs underground, and the young frogs develop without any need for water.

Puffed up like a balloon
Desert rain frog males (Breviceps maacrops) *inflate their bodies enormously when calling for mates.*

Ornate rice frog
Microhyla ornata

Nosy Be giant tree frog
Platypelis milloti

Red rain frog
Scaphiophryne gottlebei

Dotted humming frog
Chiasmocleis ventrimaculata

Red-banded frog
Phrynomantis bifasciata

Muller's termite frog
Dermatonotus muelleri

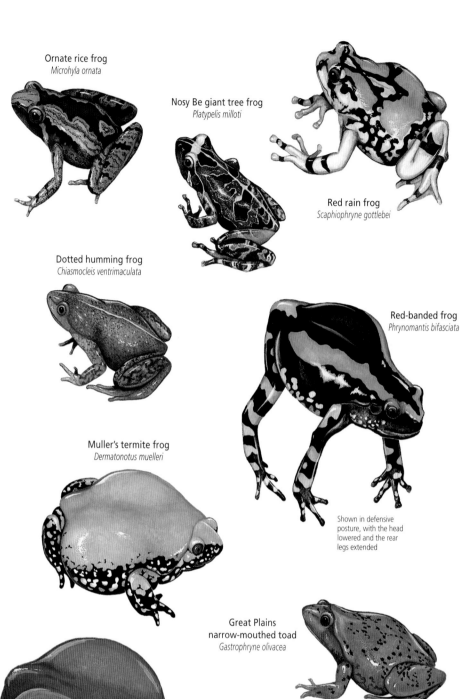

Shown in defensive posture, with the head lowered and the rear legs extended

Great Plains narrow-mouthed toad
Gastrophryne olivacea

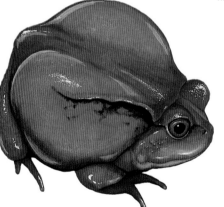

Tomato frog
Dyscophus antongilii

Malaysian narrow-mouthed toad
Kaloula pulchra

Males are patterned like females, but are slightly smaller in size

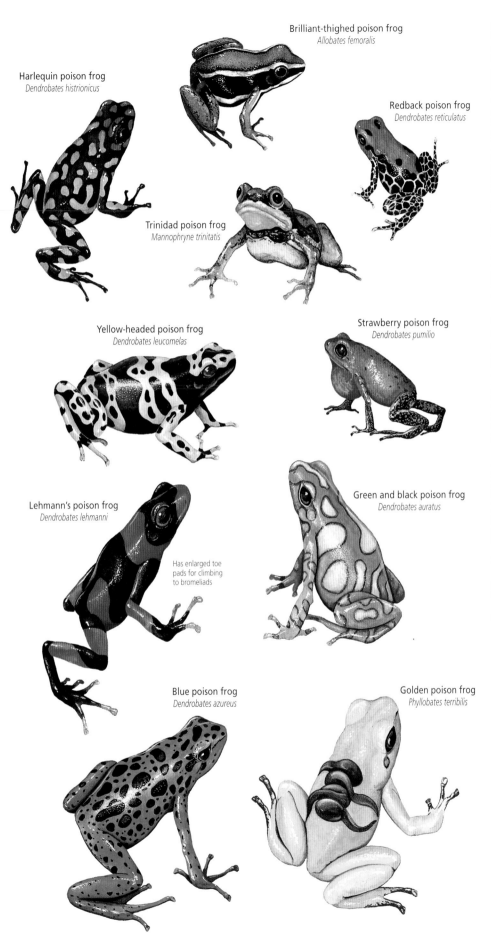

Brilliant-thighed poison frog
Allobates femoralis

Harlequin poison frog
Dendrobates histrionicus

Redback poison frog
Dendrobates reticulatus

Trinidad poison frog
Mannophryne trinitatis

Yellow-headed poison frog
Dendrobates leucomelas

Strawberry poison frog
Dendrobates pumilio

Lehmann's poison frog
Dendrobates lehmanni

Has enlarged toe
pads for climbing
to bromeliads

Green and black poison frog
Dendrobates auratus

Blue poison frog
Dendrobates azureus

Golden poison frog
Phyllobates terribilis

FACT FILE

Harlequin poison frog The male calls from branches up to 92cm (3 feet) high. The male often sits on the back of the female on the way to the oviposition site. Their complex courtship ritual, which lasts for 2–3 hours, involves a sequence of sitting, bowing, crouching, touching, and circling behaviour patterns.

🦶 Up to 4cm (1½ in)
🌐 Terrestrial, arboreal
🔄 Rainy season
🏹 Common

Colombia, Ecuador

Redback poison frog Females lay either two or three eggs, 2mm (⅛ inch) in diameter. Although they are primarily found on the forest floor, males hop up tree trunks carrying one or two tadpoles to deposit in bromeliads.

🦶 Up to 2cm (¾ in)
🌐 Terrestrial, arboreal
🔄 Rainy season
🏹 Common

N.E. Peru, W. Brazil

Blue poison frog Females lay eggs in water for the males to fertilise. The males usually guard the eggs until the tadpoles develop after about 12 days. At 12 weeks, the tadpoles metamorphose into grown frogs.

🦶 Up to 5cm (2 in)
◯ Terrestrial
🔄 Rainy season
🏹 Uncommon

Suriname

POISON-ARROW FROGS

Indigenous tribes coat their dart tips with the secretions of dendrobatids, or poison-arrow frogs. This toxin blocks neural transmission at the acetylcholine receptor of the neuro-muscular junction, which causes paralysis or even death. To produce these skin toxins, the frogs need to consume ants that produce formic acid.

FACT FILE

Madagascar reed frog These frogs are common in dunes, savanna and deforested habitats of the east coast of Madagascar. They are active at night in the vegetation above, or at the edge of, shallow ponds and swamps. During the day they take refuge near pools, submerging when disturbed by a potential predator. Eggs are laid in the water.

▶ Up to 4cm (1½ in)
◯ Terrestrial
🗘 Year round
⚑ Common

Madagascar

Tulear golden frog The species was described from a series of specimens obtained via the pet trade, for which it is currently subject to intense collecting at the beginning of the rainy season (October to December). During the first rains, these frogs, which breed explosively, come out from their refuges and are very easy to capture.

▶ Up to 3.2cm (1¼ in)
◯ Terrestrial
🗘 Rainy season
⚑ Uncommon

Madagascar

Weal's running frog Males call from elevated positions in vegetation, on the banks of, or partly submerged among, plants in a pond. The voice is a coarse, loud rattle, similar to the creak of a cork being removed from a wine bottle. One call, lasting about half a second, is emitted every 3–5 seconds.

▶ Up to 4.4cm (1¾ in)
◯ Terrestrial
🗘 Rainy season
⚑ Common

E. & S.E. South Africa

⚑ CONSERVATION WATCH

In danger At least 27 species of anurans are listed on the IUCN Red List as critically endangered, many because of direct encroachment of humans, habitat destruction, water pollution and use of herbicides and pesticides. But even populations of the golden toad (*Bufo periglenes*), which lives in protected reserves on mountain tops, have recently plummeted. This may be due to global warming and forest cutting, which affect the rainfall patterns that maintain the misty environment in montane cloud forests.

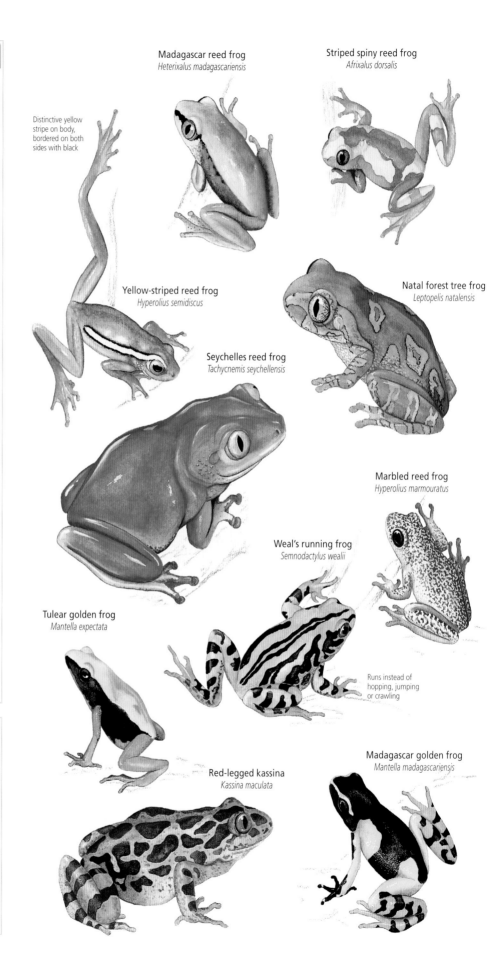

Madagascar reed frog
Heterixalus madagascariensis

Striped spiny reed frog
Afrixalus dorsalis

Distinctive yellow stripe on body, bordered on both sides with black

Yellow-striped reed frog
Hyperolius semidiscus

Natal forest tree frog
Leptopelis natalensis

Seychelles reed frog
Tachycnemis seychellensis

Marbled reed frog
Hyperolius marmouratus

Weal's running frog
Semnodactylus wealii

Tulear golden frog
Mantella expectata

Runs instead of hopping, jumping or crawling

Madagascar golden frog
Mantella madagascariensis

Red-legged kassina
Kassina maculata

Red-eared frog
Rana erythraea

African bullfrog
Pyxicephalus adspersus

European common frog
Rana temporaria

Malaysian frog
Rana luctuosa

Marsh frog
Rana ridibunda

Pickerel frog
Rana palustris

Pig frog
Rana grylio

Dorsum has two rows of
square chocolate-coloured
blotches, while the leopard
frog, for which it has been
mistaken, usually has
round blotches

Amazon river frog
Rana palmipes

Bullfrog
Rana catesbeiana

FACT FILE

Pickerel frog These frogs produce toxic skin secretions that irritate human skin and can be fatal to small animals, especially other amphibians. Many frog-eating snakes avoid these frogs. Leopard frogs (*Rana pipiens*) mimic the colour pattern of pickerel frogs in areas of sympatry to avoid snake predation.

- Up to 7.5cm (3 in)
- Terrestrial, aquatic
- Spring
- Common

E. USA

Amazon river frog This aquatic species forages day and night along the edges of rivers, permanent ponds and lakes. They consume invertebrates and vertebrates, such as insects, fishes, other frogs, and small birds, both in and out of the water.

- Up to 11.5cm (4½ in)
- Aquatic
- Rainy season
- Common

Central America to Peru & Brazil

Bullfrog This large frog eats anything that moves that it can swallow. This species was introduced into the western United States, where it reduced or extirpated local species of amphibians and reptiles. Tadpoles take 2 years to develop and the adults several years to mature.

- Up to 20cm (8 in)
- Aquatic
- Summer
- Common

E. USA

MASS SPAWNING

The European common frog mates en masse in 3 days in spring, each laying about 400 black eggs in gelatinous clusters. The eggs absorb UV radiation, which increases the water temperature and thus the eggs' developmental rate.

Group sex
Mass breeding reduces the chance of predation by swamping predators with more than they could possibly eat.

FACT FILE

Singapore wart frog In the field, this frog can be distinguished from Blyth's giant frog (*Limnonectes blythii*) by the sharp angle of the dark line behind the eye, and by the clearly defined black patch on the upper tympanum.

- Up to 10cm (4 in)
- Terrestrial
- Unknown
- Common

W. Malaysia, Singapore, Sumatra, Borneo, Java

Cape dainty frog This frog lives in inundated grasslands and depressions in dunes and on cultivated lands on poorly drained clays.

- Up to 4cm (1½ in)
- Terrestrial
- Winter
- Near threatened

South Africa

ANURAN DEFORMITIES

Like the canaries in the coal mines, frogs are whistling a warning about chemical pollution in the environment when they begin appearing with grossly deformed bodies. Part of the chemical pollution is hormonal from the progesterone used in birth control pills not being filtered out at sewage-treatment plants.

Multi-legged frog
Notice how chemical pollution in the breeding ponds caused this frog to develop with extra legs.

⚡ CONSERVATION WATCH

The 49 species of Ranidae on the IUCN Red List are categorised as follows:

- 3 Extinct
- 7 Critically endangered
- 6 Endangered
- 15 Vulnerable
- 4 Near threatened
- 12 Data deficient
- 2 Least concern

Dahaoping sucker frog
Amolops viridimaculatus

Borneo splash frog
Staurois tuberilinguis

Banded stream frog
Strongylopus bonaspei

Mascarene Ridge frog
Ptychadena mascareniensis

Cape dainty frog
Cacosternum capense

Bulbous glands on the back and sides

Striped sand frog
Tomopterna cryptotis

Singapore wart frog
Limnonectes malesianus

African ornate frog
Hildebrandtia ornata

Spotted snout-burrower
Hemisus guttatus

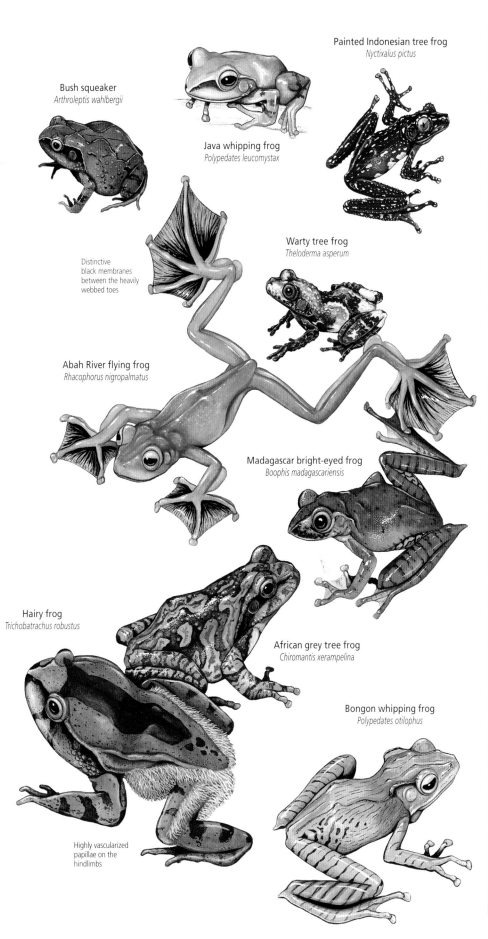

Bush squeaker
Arthroleptis wahlbergii

Painted Indonesian tree frog
Nyctixalus pictus

Java whipping frog
Polypedates leucomystax

Distinctive
black membranes
between the heavily
webbed toes

Warty tree frog
Theloderma asperum

Abah River flying frog
Rhacophorus nigropalmatus

Madagascar bright-eyed frog
Boophis madagascariensis

Hairy frog
Trichobatrachus robustus

African grey tree frog
Chiromantis xerampelina

Bongon whipping frog
Polypedates otilophus

Highly vascularized
papillae on the
hindlimbs

CONTROLLED FALLING

Frogs possessing expanded webs of the feet are able to fall in a controlled fashion to avoid predation or move about. They can adjust the impact and control the direction of their fall.

Expanded webbing The Java flying frog (Rhacophorus reinwardtii) uses its expanded webbed feet to guide its leaps from tree to tree.

INVERTEBRATES

INVERTEBRATES

INVERTEBRATES	
PHYLA	> 30
CLASSES	> 90
ORDERS	> 370
SPECIES	> 1.3 million

Constituting more than 95 per cent of all known animal species, invertebrates are not distinguished by any single positive characteristic. Instead, this group is characterised by what its members lack: they have no backbone, no bones and no cartilage. Although the term invertebrate is in common use, it has little scientific validity. It is, in fact, a contrived category that arose in the 19th century to account for all the animal groups not clearly or seemingly directly related to the human species. Unlike vertebrates, which belong to a single phylum, invertebrates are a collection of more than 30 phyla.

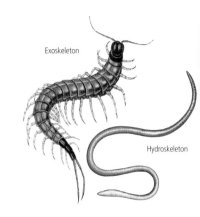

Exoskeleton

Hydroskeleton

DIVERSITY OF FORM

Invertebrates encompass such diverse forms as porous sponges, floating jellyfish, parasitic flatworms, jet-propelled squids, hard-cased crabs, venomous spiders and fluttering butterflies. They arose in the oceans and that is where their greatest diversity still occurs. But invertebrates are now found in virtually all land and water habitats, from air currents passing over Mount Everest to deep-sea thermal vents.

Most species are small and some are microscopic. However, a few invertebrates reach staggering proportions. The elusive giant squid – the stuff of sea monster legends – can grow up to 18m (59 feet) in length and attain weights of up to 900kg (1,980 pounds).

There are two basic invertebrate body plans. Species with radial symmetry, such as jellyfish and sea anemones, have a circular body and a central mouth. Others, such as insects and worms, have bilateral symmetry with a distinct head and right and left sides.

Invertebrates lack bones but all are supported by some sort of skeleton. While many appear soft, they are held together by protein fibres, a feature of all animals. Many worms have a hydrostatic skeleton, with fluid held under pressure inside the body cavity. Sponges and echinoderms have endoskeletons, with hard elements made of substances such as silica and calcium carbonate providing support inside their tissues. Most molluscs and all arthropods have an exoskeleton, a tough external casing. A mollusc's exoskeleton is a hard shell, while an arthropod's tough external skeleton is jointed and flexible.

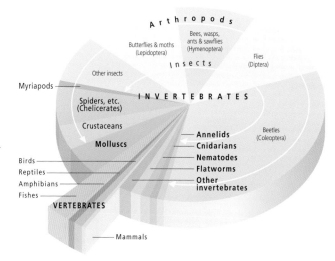

Arthropods

Butterflies & moths
(Lepidoptera)

Bees, wasps,
ants & sawflies
(Hymenoptera)

Flies
(Diptera)

Insects

Other insects

Myriapods

INVERTEBRATES

Spiders, etc.
(Chelicerates)

Crustaceans

Beetles
(Coleoptera)

Molluscs

Annelids
Cnidarians
Nematodes
Flatworms
Other
invertebrates

Birds
Reptiles
Amphibians
Fishes

VERTEBRATES

Mammals

Most invertebrates reproduce sexually, releasing vast numbers of fertilised eggs that are usually left to hatch on their own. Some species, however, develop from unfertilised eggs, and others reproduce by fragmenting or budding, with parts of their own body becoming the offspring. While the young of some invertebrates are similar in body form to their parents, others produce offspring, called larvae, that are quite unlike them. These must go through a major transformation to become adults. This metamorphosis, as it is known, is a characteristic feature of many groups of insects.

Travel modes Portuguese men-of-war can cover great distances floating at the whim of oceanic currents and winds. Their close relatives, the sea anemones, do not move so easily. As adults they usually remain fixed in one spot and wave their tentacles. However, during the larval stage of their life cycle they are dispersed by drifting with the currents.

Body support Invertebrate skeletons are not constructed from bones. An internal fluid-filled hydroskeleton supports the bodies of creatures such as worms, but is viable only in moist environments. An external skeleton (exoskeleton) helped arthropods, such as centipedes, colonise land.

Species scores Invertebrates (see chart at left) account for the overwhelming majority of animal species. So far, scientists have described about 1.75 million species of life-forms. But they estimate they have between 5 and 100 million still to discover. Most will be invertebrates, particularly insects. One million are already described but there may be as many as 30 million more that we are yet to find.

INVERTEBRATES THROUGH THE AGES

Tracks and burrows in ancient rocks indicate that the first invertebrate-like life had appeared on Earth by 1 billion years ago. The first body fossils of ancient multicellular life come from about 600 million years ago, toward the end of the Precambrian period. They belong to a group of soft-bodied marine organisms known as the Ediacaran fauna, the first evidence of which was found in ancient rocks in the Ediacara Hills, in South Australia's Flinders Ranges, in the 1940s. Since then, similar fossils have been found on all continents except Antarctica. They include some bizarre forms unlike anything known from other times. Others are reminiscent of modern invertebrates such as worms, jellyfish and arthropods. Their relationship to modern animals remains mysterious and is a subject of ongoing scientific debate.

CAMBRIAN EXPLOSION

During the Cambrian period, between 570 and 530 million years ago, life underwent an abrupt and massive rise in diversity, the scale of which has never been seen since. Ancestors of almost all major living invertebrate phyla – which account for the majority of modern animal species – appear in the fossil record for the first time in the Cambrian during a period spanning just 40 million years.

Of particular significance is the earliest evidence of hard shells and exoskeletons. Long-extinct trilobites, early arthropods with unusually well-developed eyes, proliferated. So too did sponges. Echinoderms were also plentiful and were represented by several large classes. Only one from that time, however, Class Crinoidea, survives. Both gastropod and cephalopod molluscs occurred in the Cambrian, but these groups did not reach their heyday until later. The earliest chordates, distant ancestors of our own species and all other vertebrates, appeared as well. There were also many strange life-forms that do not seem directly allied to any known group and may, perhaps, represent invertebrate evolutionary dead-ends.

Dominant creatures Trilobites (below) dominated the Cambrian seas but became extinct 250 million years ago. Their bodies consisted of three sections: a shield-like head with paired eyes and antennae, a hinged trunk, and a tail of fused segments.

Evolution in action Rapid life cycles and high reproductive rates seem to expedite invertebrate evolution. The best-known example is the peppered moth (above), which became darker with successive generations to maintain camouflage in an increasingly dirty industrial environment.

Lichida   Agnostida   Proetida

Living fossils At 3.5 billion years of age, stromatolites are the world's oldest fossils. These ancient reef-building structures were formed mainly by colonial cyanobacteria, known also as blue-green algae, believed to have been Earth's dominant life-form for about 2 billion years. Oxygen, released as these organisms photosynthesised, built up in the atmosphere until there were sufficient amounts for the ancestors of the first recognisable invertebrates. Stromatolites survive in Shark Bay, Western Australia.

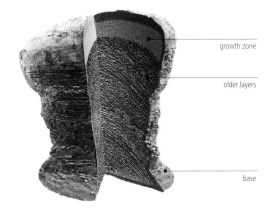

growth zone

older layers

base

CLASSIFICATION

Over 95 per cent of all animals are invertebrates. They are characterised by a structure that they all lack: a backbone or vertebral column. Invertebrates are divided into about 30 phyla, each displaying a distinct body form. Features that define phyla include the organisation of the body as a loose association of cells (Porifera), through tissue formation (Cnidaria) to the development of organs (Platyhelminthes). The acquisition of a fluid-filled body cavity was a defining point in animal evolution that allowed animals, such as Nematoda, Annelida and many other phyla of worms, to move about by an hydraulic system driven by fluid pressure. The origin and form of these body cavities characterise different phyla. While these phyla are soft-bodied, others are protected and supported by various types of skeletons, such as shells in Mollusca and a jointed exoskeleton in Arthropoda.

KINGDOM
Animalia
red widow spider, seastar, dragonfly, sponge, kangaroo

PHYLUM
Arthropoda
red widow spider, butterfly, crab, scorpion, millipede

CLASS
Arachnida
red widow spider, black widow spider, harvestman, scorpion, tick

ORDER
Araneae
red widow spider, black widow spider, funnel-web spider, wolf spider

FAMILY
Theridiidae
red widow spider, black widow spider, tentweb spider, button spider

GENUS
Latrodectus
red widow spider, black widow spider

SPECIES
Latrodectus bishopi
red widow spider

Stinging phylum Anemones were originally classified as 'zoophytes' or animal plants, in reference to their flower-like appearance. Modern classification groups anemones, corals, jellyfish, and hydroids as the phylum Cnidaria. This phylum refers to microscopic stinging cells that members of this group use to harpoon and immobilise prey.

Widow family Known commonly as the red widow, this spider (top right) is a close relative of the notoriously deadly black widow. Widow spiders, in which females allegedly consume males, are included in the genus *Latrodectus*. This genus, in turn, is included in the family Theridiidae, known as comb-footed spiders due to small hairs on their hind feet.

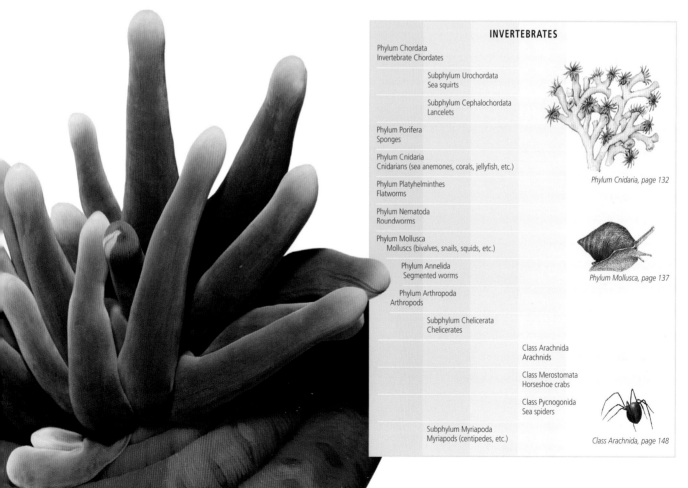

INVERTEBRATES

Phylum Chordata
Invertebrate Chordates

    Subphylum Urochordata
    Sea squirts

    Subphylum Cephalochordata
    Lancelets

Phylum Porifera
Sponges

Phylum Cnidaria
Cnidarians (sea anemones, corals, jellyfish, etc.)

Phylum Platyhelminthes
Flatworms

Phylum Nematoda
Roundworms

Phylum Mollusca
  Molluscs (bivalves, snails, squids, etc.)

  Phylum Annelida
  Segmented worms

  Phylum Arthropoda
  Arthropods

    Subphylum Chelicerata
    Chelicerates

      Class Arachnida
      Arachnids

      Class Merostomata
      Horseshoe crabs

      Class Pycnogonida
      Sea spiders

    Subphylum Myriapoda
    Myriapods (centipedes, etc.)

Phylum Cnidaria, page 132

Phylum Mollusca, page 137

Class Arachnida, page 148

Subphylum Crustacea
Crustaceans

Subphylum Hexapoda
Hexapods

Class Insecta
Insects

Order Odonata, page 166

Order Odonata
Dragonflies and damselflies

Order Mantodea
Mantids

Order Blattodea
Cockroaches

Order Isoptera
Termites

Order Orthoptera
Crickets and grasshoppers

Order Hemiptera
Bugs

Order Coleoptera
Beetles

Order Diptera
Flies

Order Coleoptera, page 175

Order Lepidoptera
Butterflies and moths

Order Hymenoptera
Bees, wasps, ants and sawflies

Order Embioptera
Web-spinners

Order Dermaptera
Earwigs

Order Thysanura
Silverfish

Order Phasmatodea
Stick and leaf insects

Order Archaeognatha
Bristletails

Order Raphidioptera
Snakeflies

Order Ephemeroptera
Mayflies

Order Lepidoptera, page 182

Order Megaloptera
Dobsonflies and alderflies

Order Phthiraptera
Parasitic lice

Order Psocoptera
Book lice and bark lice

Order Siphonaptera
Fleas

Order Thysanoptera
Thrips

Order Neuroptera
Lacewings, ant lions and allies

Order Mecoptera
Scorpionflies

Order Plecoptera
Stoneflies

Order Trichoptera
Caddisflies

Order Zoraptera
Angel insects

Order Grylloblattodea
Rock crawlers

Order Siphonaptera, page 192

Order Strepsiptera
Strepsipterans

Class Collembola
Springtails

Class Protura
Proturans

Class Diplura
Diplurans

Phylum Echinodermata
Echinoderms (sea stars, sea urchins, sea cucumbers, etc.)

Phylum Nemertea
Ribbon worms

Phylum Entoprocta
Goblet worms

Phylum Tardigrada
Water bears

Phylum Ctenophora
Comb jellies

Phylum Rotifera
Rotifers (wheel animals)

Phylum Hemichordata
Hemichordates (acorn worms)

Phylum Chaetognatha
Arrow worms

Phylum Echinodermata, page 195

Phylum Gastrotricha
Gastrotrichs

Phylum Kinorhyncha
Spiny-crown worms

Phylum Phoronida
Horseshoe worms

Phylum Onychophora
Velvet worms

Phylum Brachiopoda
Brachiopods (lamp shells)

Phylum Bryozoa
Bryozoans (lace animals)

Phylum Sipuncula
Peanut worms

Phylum Echiura
Spoon worms

Phylum Loricifera
Brushheads

Phylum Priapulida
Phallus worms

Phylum Nematomorpha
Horsehair worms

Phylum Acanthocephala
Spiny-headed worms

Phylum Pogonophora
Beard worms

Phylum Gnathostomulida
Sand worms

Phylum Cycliophora
Cycliophorans

Phylum Placozoa
Placozoans

Phylum Orthonectida
Orthonectids

Phylum Rhombozoa
Rhombozoans

Phylum Gastrotricha, page 198

Phylum Onychophora, page 199

BIOLOGY AND BEHAVIOUR

Most invertebrate behaviour is highly instinctive and usually relates to gathering food, avoiding predators and reproducing the species. Some of these innate behavioural responses are very complex, such as the social organisation of honeybees. Many invertebrates are also capable of extensive behavioural modification. Octopus, for example, change their behaviour by learning from previous experiences. Invertebrates have a diversity of sensory structures to facilitate sight, smell, taste, touch and hearing. Many adopt a cryptic approach to life, hidden among vegetation, within leaf-litter or buried in sediment and soil. Some exhibit exquisite forms of camouflage, such as spiders that look and even smell like bird droppings or stick and leaf insects that mimic the vegetation on which they browse.

Communicating odours Like most moths, the African moon moth communicates with its own species using chemicals known as pheromones. Females release pheromones to attract males from afar while males do so only when close by, to sexually stimulate females.

Silk trappings Tarantulas do not spin the sorts of webs traditionally associated with spiders. This species – the Arizona blond tarantula – is a long-lived nocturnal ground hunter that dwells in a subterranean burrow. It uses its silk to plug the burrow in winter, when it survives on fat reserves.

Toxic warning Some invertebrates have poisons in their flesh or body parts to deter predators. Most, such as this nudibranch (below) – a sea slug that accumulates toxin by consuming other poisonous invertebrates – are brightly coloured to warn would-be attackers.

EAT OR BE EATEN

Invertebrates play a crucial role in most food chains, which makes them essential to the health of ecosystems. Zooplankton feeding on phytoplankton in the oceans and invertebrates feeding on terrestrial plants provide the first link between the primary producers (plants) and the consumers (animals).

Invertebrates are also among the most active consumers of the dead bodies of plants and animals. Many invertabrates are parasites, feeding on the blood or other tissues of their animal hosts. In turn, invertebrates make up the diet of many species of vertebrates. The flesh of a number of invertebrates, including oysters, squid, prawns, crabs and lobsters, is considered a delicacy by humans.

HABITATS AND ADAPTATIONS

Each generation of a species results in a slightly different range of genetic combinations. For this reason, animals with rapid reproductive rates – such as most invertebrates – are better equipped than less prolific breeders to deal with changing environments. This partly explains why invertebrates have managed to adapt to and exploit virtually every available habitat, from the deepest oceans to the highest mountains, polar ice caps, hot springs, and hypersaline lakes.

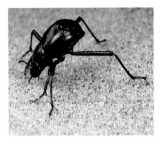

Fog catcher Early morning fog rolling in from the coast is the only regular moisture in Africa's Namib Desert. The darkling beetle (left) points its rear upward, the fog condenses on its back, and the water droplets trickle down dorsal grooves to its mouth.

Invertebrate builders Hard coral reefs are built by tiny invertebrates called polyps. Although sedentary, their larvae drift in oceanic currents before eventually settling out of the water column to form new reefs or re-seed old ones.

OCEANIC BEGINNINGS

Invertebrates are critical components of some of the planet's most productive habitats. All reef systems in the world are ultimately based on invertebrate life-forms. Animal life arose in the oceans and it is here that the greatest diversity of invertebrates is found. Many groups of invertebrates are predominately or exclusively marine, such as sponges, cnidarians and echinoderms. Sponges, found in the fossil record from the Cambrian to the present, have barely changed during their 600 million years of existence. When found alongside other fossils in preserved reefs, sponge fossils enable scientists to piece together entire ancient ecosystems.

Arthropods were the first animals to emerge from the sea to lead a terrestrial existence and their extraordinary success on land has been due largely to their tough, waxy exoskeleton. Scorpions had ventured onto the land by about 350 million years ago and were soon followed by terrestrial insects. Now ubiquitous in land habitats, insects have also invaded fresh water but they are rare in oceans.

Underlying the success of insects is their life cycle, which involves an extreme metamorphosis into adulthood. This ensures that juveniles and adults of a particular species are able to exploit different environments and do not have to compete for the same resources such as food or shelter.

AQUATIC INVERTEBRATES

Aquatic habitats include oceans, estuaries, rivers, streams and freshwater and hypersaline lakes. Each is characterised by a particular salinity level. At the base of the food chain are single-celled algae, the phytoplankton, which are fed upon by small to microscopic zooplankton. Most invertebrate phyla have representatives that spend at least part of their life cycle as zooplankton. Larger invertebrates also feed by filtering out the plankton. Others graze or browse on larger plants, prey upon each other or scavenge in the sediments for decaying remains. Sunlight, and its abscence, has a direct impact on aquatic life.

DESERT INVERTEBRATES

The majority of the invertebrates in deserts are insects. They are among the most dominant of desert animals. Behavioural adaptations are as important as physiological specialisations to desert survival. Invertebrates are rarely seen in deserts because most tend to be active only at night or in the milder conditions of early morning or late afternoon. During the day they shelter in small burrows in the sand. The tough, waterproofed external skeleton of arthropods is a particularly useful desert adaptation. It reduces evaporative water loss, allowing insects, spiders, centipedes and scorpions to survive in arid habitats.

MANGROVE INVERTEBRATES

Mangroves stabilise shorelines in wave-protected river deltas, estuaries and other vulnerable coastal areas. Almost three-quarters of tropical coastlines are narrowly fringed by this valuable habitat, once widely and mistakenly dismissed as unproductive and smelly. The dominant trees and shrubs in mangroves are salt-tolerant and shallow-rooted.

Because of their high nutrients and the protected havens they form for larvae and juveniles, mangroves are exploited by animals as nursery grounds. Nevertheless, they remain the domain of adult invertebrates. Crustaceans, worms and molluscs occur in enormous numbers in these waters. Some burrow in the sediments, extracting nutrients in the way earthworms extract them from soil. Others come to the surface to feed on the algal film covering the sediment or on dead plants and animals stranded by the low tide. The mangrove invertebrates are themselves fed upon by fishes during the high tides and by wading birds that forage on the flats at low tide.

PARASITIC INVERTEBRATES

Animal parasites are exclusively invertebrate and range from worms, such as flukes, tapeworms and round worms, to blood-sucking arthropods, such as fleas and lice. Parasites can feed on the skin or live within the body, feeding on the digested food or tissues of the host. To offset the hazards of locating a host, parasites have an enormous reproductive capacity that often includes both sexual and asexual strategies. Some remain dormant as resistant eggs or encysted stages, waiting to be accidentally ingested, while others actively seek a host and penetrate its skin. Still others use the bodies of other animals as intermediate hosts in which further bouts of reproduction may occur. Using this strategy, some parasites can pass from one host to another in the food chain.

POLAR INVERTEBRATES

Antarctica is the coldest, windiest, driest continent and the Arctic is

Grisly nursery Parasitic wasps often lay their eggs directly into still-living caterpillars that they have paralysed with their stings. In this way, the grub-like larvae will have a source of fresh food readily available to them when they hatch.

almost as inhospitable. There is, however, a surprisingly high level of invertebrate life, mostly underwater, at the poles. It includes giant sponges, sea anemones and a range of worms, many of which have a form of antifreeze in their body fluids. Tiny crustaceans known as krill occur in truly huge numbers at the poles and form the basis of critical food chains, including some that support commercially valuable fisheries.

Vertical life Sediments around the roots of mangroves lack oxygen. Extensions (called pneumatophores) grow beyond the surface to convey oxygen to the roots below. These provide habitats for a variety of invertebrates, such as this mangrove crab.

FOREST INVERTEBRATES

Invertebrates, particularly insects, are important to the health of all forests. Insects undoubtedly eat far more leaves, bark, sap and fruits than large herbivorous mammals. A vast amount of dead vegetation is also consumed by invertebrates such as insects, millipedes and burrowing earthworms. Insect larvae also play a significant role in the recycling of dead animals. Scavengers are critical to forests. Their actions eventually result in the release of minerals and nutrients by fungi and bacteria, making them available to plants. Many temperate-forest invertebrates lead a distinctly seasonal existence, bursting into a flurry of activity that coincides with springtime growth after spending cold winter months hidden away in a form of torpor.

Web builders Spiny spiders of the genus *Gasteracantha* (above) are renowned spinners of vertical orb-webs in forest environments worldwide. Bushwalkers invariably stumble into their tough, sticky webs that often look like the perfectly crafted wheels of a horse-drawn carriage.

Under ice Sea floor-dwelling species such as sea anemones and sponges (left) are able to survive and flourish in relatively tranquil, unfrozen polar waters.

INVERTEBRATES IN DANGER

There are two main problems in assessing the conservation status of invertebrates. First, many biologists have estimated that we have described only a fraction of the total number of species. How can we assess invertebrates that have not even been identified? Second, because invertebrates are usually small and cryptic, estimates of their population density can be very difficult to measure. Consequently, invertebrates are significantly underrepresented in the IUCN Red List of Threatened Species, with only 600 species listed as endangered or critically endangered. The conservation status of most of the invertebrate world remains unknown. Extrapolation of data obtained from those invertebrates whose endangered status has been evaluated is sobering. Analysts predict that three-quarters of the roughly 1 million insect species so far described, 86 per cent of crustaceans, and almost half of all known mollusc species are, in fact, endangered.

Big threat The giant clam (above and below), native to the Pacific and Indian oceans, is the world's largest bivalve mollusc, reaching lengths of more than 1.2m (4 feet) and weights of around 227kg (500 pounds). The species is listed as vulnerable due to extensive collecting for food, their shells, and the aquarium trade. They have been severely over-harvested across their range. Ilegal collecting continues to be a threat to the species.

DISAPPEARING TREASURES

Many people can look at the exquisite forms and adaptations of mammals such as the cheetah, blue whale or polar bear and feel passionate about securing them a future place on the planet. Unfortunately, far fewer people feel the same way about invertebrate animals. Arguments of altruism and responsible stewardship aside, there are two very good reasons why we should be as alarmed about invertebrate losses as we are about the decline of vertebrates.

First, Earth's invertebrate fauna harbours many unique genes, which means many unique substances, some of which may turn out to be safe and simple cures for human disease. There is particular interest among the world's pharmaceutical companies in marine invertebrates such as sponges, worms and molluscs. Second, invertebrates are often highly sensitive to environmental change created by pollution, habitat clearing and climate shifts. As a result, they can be excellent biological markers of the health of an ecosystem.

The current rate of invertebrate losses could be a warning about the tenuous hold we have on our own future as a species. It is not likely that the extinction of just one invertebrate species from an ecosystem would ever have as big an effect as that of a mammal or other large vertebrate. But invertebrates are being lost from the planet at a truly alarming rate and it is rare that just one invertebrate species disappears from a habitat. More often they topple like dominoes, so that several species disappear at once. It is then we see whole ecosystems suffering.

So what can we do? We must take responsibility for conserving habitats by preventing processes that threaten them, such as clearing land, draining wetlands and polluting natural environments.

Collectable beauty The Rajah Brooke's birdwing butterfly (left) is regarded as one of the most beautiful of all butterflies. That, however, could become its downfall. Birdwings are highly sought after by collectors and the trade has already forced several species onto the IUCN Red List of Threatened Species, although this species is still secure, for the moment.

INVERTEBRATE CHORDATES

PHYLUM	Chordata
SUBPHYLA	2
CLASSES	4
ORDERS	9
FAMILIES	47
SPECIES	> 2,000

The phylum Chordata is made up of three subphyla. The largest of these is Vertebrata, which includes all the vertebrates (mammals, birds, reptiles, amphibians and fishes). The other two subphyla are marine invertebrate groups: Urochordata, which contains about 2,000 species of sea squirts and their relatives, and Cephalochordata, which has about 30 species of lancelets. These invertebrate chordates do not have a backbone made of vertebrae, but they do have a flexible skeletal rod known as a notochord. The notochord is present in vertebrate embryos, but is resorbed and replaced by the backbone. This strongly suggests that vertebrates have evolved from invertebrate chordates.

From the deep The predatory tunicate (*Megalodicopia hians*) lives on the floor of deep oceans. After a small animal such as a krill floats into its mouth-like hood, the hood quickly closes to capture the prey.

Colonies This photo shows several colonies of magnificent ascidians (*Botrylloides magnicoecum*). The dark spots represent individual inhalant openings; the sieve-like plates are communal exhalant openings.

FIXED AND FREE

Also known as tunicates, sea squirts hatch from eggs as a tadpole-shaped larva with a notochord in their tails. After dispersing to a new location, the tadpole usually attaches itself to the sea floor, resorbs the tail and notochord and moves its mouth to its free end. This sessile sea squirt is a bag-like creature. Water enters through an inhalant opening and leaves via an exhalant opening. On the way, the water passes through a perforated pharynx (throat), which uses mucus to filter out particles of food. Sea squirts can be solitary or colonial. Most are fixed as adults, but a small number remain free-living throughout their lives. They are almost all hermaphrodites that release eggs and sperm into the water to produce their young.

Superficially resembling little eels, lancelets (or amphioxus) can swim well, but usually stay partly buried in sand or gravel in shallow waters, with only the head protruding. They filter-feed using the same method as sea squirts, with water entering one opening, passing through the pharnx and exiting via a second opening. The sexes are separate and the eggs are fertilised externally.

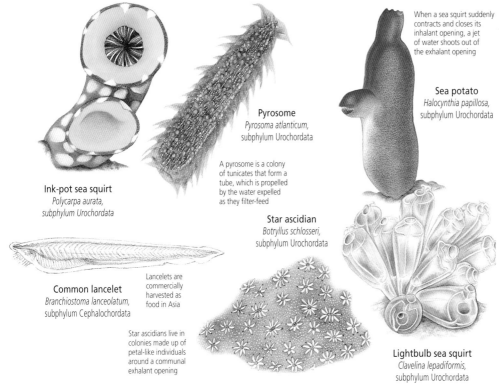

Ink-pot sea squirt
Polycarpa aurata,
subphylum Urochordata

Pyrosome
Pyrosoma atlanticum,
subphylum Urochordata

A pyrosome is a colony of tunicates that form a tube, which is propelled by the water expelled as they filter-feed

When a sea squirt suddenly contracts and closes its inhalant opening, a jet of water shoots out of the exhalant opening

Sea potato
Halocynthia papillosa,
subphylum Urochordata

Common lancelet
Branchiostoma lanceolatum,
subphylum Cephalochordata

Lancelets are commercially harvested as food in Asia

Star ascidian
Botryllus schlosseri,
subphylum Urochordata

Star ascidians live in colonies made up of petal-like individuals around a communal exhalant opening

Lightbulb sea squirt
Clavelina lepadiformis,
subphylum Urochordata

SPONGES

YLUM Porifera
ASSES 3
RDERS 18
MILIES 80
ECIES about 9,000

More than 2,000 years ago, Aristotle considered sponges to be animals, but his claim remained without proof until 1765. In the interim, most scientists believed sponges, with their lack of movement and often branching form, to be plants. Sponges are unique in the animal kingdom. They do not possess a nervous system, muscles or stomach. Their cells do not form tissues or organs, but are specialised for particular functions, such as food collection, digestion, defence or skeleton formation. Able to migrate throughout a sponge, the cells can transform from one type to another, which allows the sponge to completely regenerate from a fragment or even from individual cells.

Electric sponge Although they lack nerves, glass sponges (class Hexactinellida) react to disturbances by sending electrical impulses through their body, which prompt their food-filtering system to shut down.

Supportive spicules A sponge's skeleton is made of units known as spicules, which can be scattered throughout the sponge or combined into fibres. This magnified view shows the needle-like and star-like spicules of a sponge at 100 times their actual size.

Budding young While most sponges reproduce sexually, many also use asexual reproduction. Some species fragment, while others grow buds (far right), which break away to become new sponges. Sponges may also expel collections of cells and food granules called gemmules which remain in a dormant state, growing into a sponge only when conditions are favourable.

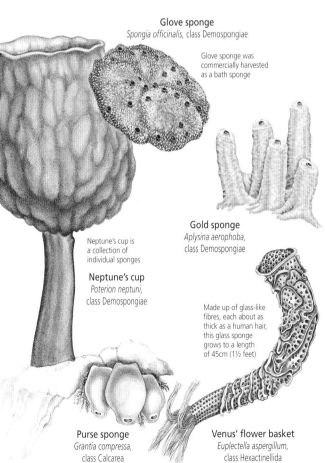

Glove sponge
Spongia officinalis, class Demospongiae

Glove sponge was commercially harvested as a bath sponge

Neptune's cup is a collection of individual sponges

Neptune's cup
Poterion neptuni,
class Demospongiae

Gold sponge
Aplysina aerophoba,
class Demospongiae

Made up of glass-like fibres, each about as thick as a human hair, this glass sponge grows to a length of 45cm (1½ feet)

Purse sponge
Grantia compressa,
class Calcarea

Venus' flower basket
Euplectella aspergillum,
class Hexactinellida

POROUS FILTER-FEEDERS
Ranging in length from less than 1cm–2m (½ inch to 6½ feet), sponges may be shaped like trees, bushes, vases, barrels, balls, cushions or carpets, or they may simply form a shapeless mass. They are found in every marine habitat, from the shallows to the depths, and a small number of species have colonised freshwater lakes and rivers.

The skeletons of sponges are made of minerals, protein or both. Species in the class Calcarea have skeletons of calcium carbonate and tend to be small and drab. Those in the class Hexactinellida are known as glass sponges and have skeletons made of silica. More than 90 per cent of sponge species belong to the class

Demospongiae. They have skeletons of silica and/or protein.

Sponges usually feed by filtering microorganisms from the water. After entering via tiny pores called ostia, the water travels through a system of canals, and is expelled via a large opening called the osculum. The collar cells that line the sponge's interior beat their whip-like flagella to maintain a constant current. A few carnivorous sponges use hook-like filaments to capture crustaceans.

Most sponges are hermaphrodites. Sperm are released into the water and carried to other sponges to fertilise their eggs. The larvae are free-swimming for a short period before attaching to a surface and developing into an adult sponge.

CNIDARIANS

PHYLUM	Cnidaria
CLASSES	4
ORDERS	27
FAMILIES	236
SPECIES	about 9,000

The phylum Cnidaria is a diverse assortment of mostly marine invertebrates, including sea anemones, corals, jellyfish and hydroids. All members are carnivores and use cells containing stinging nematocysts to subdue prey and deter predators. The cnidarian body is organised around a gastrovascular cavity that digests food and acts as a hydroskeleton. Food enters and waste leaves via a single opening, the mouth, which is often surrounded by tentacles. Cnidarians occur in two forms: polyp and medusa. Polyps are cylindrical and attached to a surface, with the mouth and tentacles at the free end. Medusae are free-swimming and umbrella-shaped, with the mouth and tentacles hanging down.

Fixed in position The jewel anemone (*Corynactis viridis*) has up to 100 tentacles arranged in three rings around its mouth. Attached to the substrate by a sucker-like disk, sea anemones rarely move but some are able to glide very slowly.

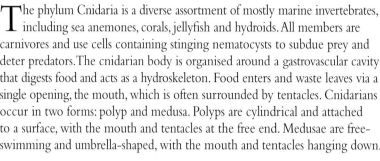

polyp   medusa

Jelly sandwich Between a cnidarian's two cell layers, the outer ectoderm and the inner endoderm, there is a jelly-like layer known as the mesoglea (shown as orange). In polyps, the mesoglea is thin, but in medusae, it forms the bulk of the animal.

Floating home At up to 45cm (1½ feet) wide, the purple jellyfish (*Pelagia panopyra*) offers a temporary haven to fish and young crabs. Like other jellyfish, it has only weak jet propulsion and relies mainly on ocean currents for transport.

POLYPS AND MEDUSAE

A small number of cnidarians live in fresh water, but most are marine, occupying all latitudes and levels of the ocean and reaching their greatest numbers in shallow tropical waters. They feed primarily on the fishes and crustaceans that swim past. Found mainly on the tentacles, a cnidarian's nematocysts (stingers) hold a coiled, barbed thread that can be ejected to spear and paralyse the prey. The tentacles then move the food to the mouth.

While corals and sea anemones exist only as polyps, many other cnidarians alternate between polyp and medusa during their life cycle. Usually, the polyps asexually produce medusae, and the medusae sexually produce larvae that become polyps. Polyps and some medusae may grow buds or divide to create more of their own kind asexually. If the offspring detach from the parent they become clones, but if they remain attached they form colonies, such as the vast colonies that make up coral reefs. In some colonies, each member has a particular role and form, and may be specialised for feeding, defence, reproduction or locomotion, for example.

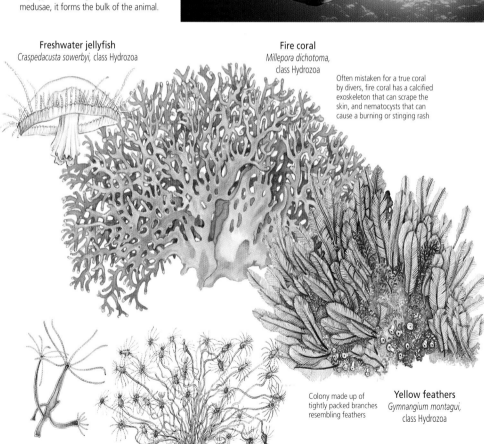

Freshwater jellyfish
Craspedacusta sowerbyi, class Hydrozoa

Fire coral
Millepora dichotoma, class Hydrozoa

Often mistaken for a true coral by divers, fire coral has a calcified exoskeleton that can scrape the skin, and nematocysts that can cause a burning or stinging rash

Colony made up of tightly packed branches resembling feathers

Yellow feathers
Gymnangium montagui, class Hydrozoa

Green hydra
Chlorohydra viridis, class Hydrozoa

Oaten pipes hydroid
Tubularia indivisa, class Hydrozoa

Upside-down jellyfish
Cassiopeia andromeda,
class Scyphozoa

Attaches to sandy
ocean floor

**Portuguese
man-of-war**
Physalia physalis,
class Hydrozoa

The Portuguese man-of-war is a free-
floating colony, with a modified medusa
forming the gas-filled float, and some
polyps delivering a potent sting, some
digesting food, and others reproducing

Hula skirt siphonophore
Physophora hydrostatica,
class Hydrozoa

Lion's mane jellyfish
Cyanea arctica,
class Scyphozoa

Dead man's fingers
Alcyonium digitatum, class Anthozoa

Sea wasp
Chironex fleckeri,
class Cubozoa

A sea wasp
contains enough
venom to kill
60 people

By-the-wind sailor
Velella velella, class Hydrozoa

Phosphorescent sea pen
Pennatula phosphorea,
class Anthozoa

The stalked jellyfish
exists as a polyp
attached to algae
and does not occur
as a medusa

Stalked jellyfish
Haliclystus auricula, class Scyphozoa

Formosan soft coral
Sarcophyton glaucum, class Anthozoa

Organ-pipe coral
Tubipora musica, class Anthozoa

FACT FILE

Class Scyphozoa True jellyfish belong to
the class Scyphozoa. Generally, they spend
most of their lives as medusae,
but these medusae produce larvae that
settle on the seabed as minute polyps.
The polyps then divide horizontally
and break off to become medusae.
Most jellyfish are free-swimming. By
pulsating their bell, they squirt out jets
of water that provide weak propulsion.

Species 200

Worldwide; marine

Common jelly
*Found worldwide
in coastal waters,
the moon jellyfish
(Aurelia aurita) is
often seen washed
up onto beaches.*

Class Hydrozoa This class contains
species that have both polyps and
medusae in the life cycle, but the
medusae are often reduced to buds
on the polyp's surface. Many species
are colonial, often with the individuals
specialised for different functions.

Species 3,300

Worldwide

Freshwater hydra
*The brown hydra
(Pelmatohydra oligactis)
is found in lakes and
ponds. Its tentacles
can reach lengths of
25cm (10 inches).*

Class Cubozoa Viewed from above,
the box jellies in this class have a square
shape, which distinguishes them from
true jellyfish. They are also faster and
more agile swimmers, and include
some of the ocean's deadliest species.

Species 36

Worldwide; tropical & temperate seas

YOUNG CNIDARIANS

When cnidarians sexually reproduce,
they produce a microscopic planula
larva, which either swims using its
beating cilia (tiny hairs) or crawls along
the bottom. After a time, the planula
transforms into a polyp by attaching its
front end to a surface and developing
tentacles at its free end. For corals and
sea anemones, which do not become
medusae, the larval stage is the only
chance for the species to disperse.

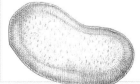

FACT FILE

Class Anthozoa Anthozoans spend their adult lives as attached polyps and most are colonial. They include the reef-building true corals, the naked sea anemones, the leathery soft corals, the many-branched sea fans and red corals, the sea pens and the black corals. True corals secrete an exoskeleton, while the others have an endoskeleton.

Species 6,500

Worldwide; marine

Different shapes The tube anemone (Cerianthus lloydi) (below) and the sea pen (Pennatula grisea) (right) indicate the diversity of forms in Anthozoa.

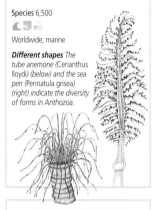

GREAT BARRIER REEF

Stretching more than 2,240km (1,400 miles) along the northeastern coast of Australia, the Great Barrier Reef is a collection of coral reefs that together form the largest natural feature on Earth. It was created over millions of years from the calcium carbonate exoskeletons of true corals. Symbiotic algae live inside the coral polyps, supplying most of the corals' energy. The corals are restricted to clear, shallow waters where the algae can photosynthesise.

Teeming with life With 400 species of coral, 1,500 species of fish and 4,000 species of mollusc, the Great Barrier Reef's biodiversity rivals that of tropical rain forests.

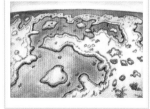

🜲 CONSERVATION WATCH

Dying reefs Corals are extremely sensitive to environmental stress and can die from even small changes in the temperature, salinity or nitrogen levels of the water. Consequently, they are particularly vulnerable to ocean pollution and global warming. Mass tourism, over-collecting and introduced species have also taken their toll, and half of all the world's reefs could die in the next 50 years.

Red brain coral
Lobophyllia hemprichii, class Anthozoa

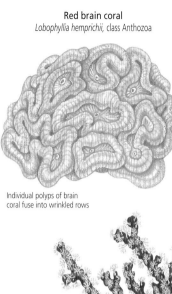

Individual polyps of brain coral fuse into wrinkled rows

Clubbed finger coral
Porites porites, class Anthozoa

Bubble coral
Plerogyra sinuosa,
class Anthozoa

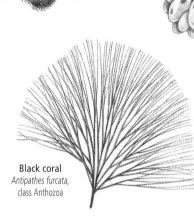

Red coral forms tree-like colonies

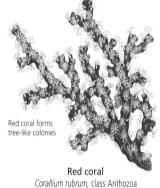

Red coral
Corallium rubrum, class Anthozoa

Black coral
Antipathes furcata,
class Anthozoa

The tentacles of beadlet anemones retract when the tide goes out

Beadlet anemone
Actinia equina,
class Anthozoa

Lophelia pertusa,
class Anthozoa

Lophelia pertusa is a deep-water coral that forms reefs in the cold North Atlantic

West Indian sea fan
Gorgonia flabellum,
class Anthozoa

Stalk is inserted into deep crevices or buried in mud or sand

Daisy anemone
Cereus pedunculatus,
class Anthozoa

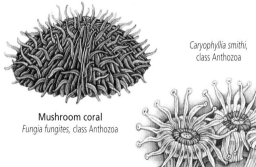

Mushroom coral
Fungia fungites, class Anthozoa

Caryophyllia smithi,
class Anthozoa

FLATWORMS

YLUM Platyhelminthes	
ASSES 4	
DERS 35	
MILIES 360	
ECIES 13,000	

The flatworms that make up the phylum Platyhelminthes range from microscopic free-living species, to tapeworms up to 30m (100 feet) long that live inside humans and other vertebrates. The simplest animals possessing bilateral symmetry, flatworms have no body cavity and lack respiratory and circulatory systems. A few parasitic species also do without a digestive system. In most species, the gut has a single opening to take in food and expel waste. The indistinct head contains a brain and many of the sense organs, including ocelli (simple eyes) that can perceive light and dark, and receptors that can detect chemicals, balance, gravity and water movement.

A long colony A parasite of rats, the tapeworm *Hymenolepis diminuta* is shown here at 50 times its actual size and with its colour enhanced, revealing its individual proglottids and the suckers at its tip.

A PARASITIC LIFE

While the flukes of Monogenea have a single host in their lifetime, most parasitic flatworms make use of different hosts at different stages in their life cycle.

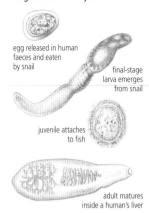

egg released in human faeces and eaten by snail

final-stage larva emerges from snail

juvenile attaches to fish

adult matures inside a human's liver

Eggs of the Chinese liver fluke Opisthorchis sinensis *(class Trematoda) eggs are eaten by aquatic snails. The final-stage larvae emerge to attach to fish, which are eaten by humans. Once the flukes mature into adults, their eggs are passed out in the human host's faeces.*

Crawling leaf Although some small species are cylindrical, most flatworms are flattened. Many marine species, such as Pseudoceros *dimidiatus*, are leaf-like.

DIFFERENT LIFESTYLES

Flatworms are divided into four classes. The first of these, Turbelleria, is predominantly free-living. Most species are marine, but many are found in lakes, ponds and rivers, and a few can even tolerate both fresh and salt water. There are also a number of species that live on land in moist habitats. Turbellarians usually prey on invertebrates. They move along slime trails produced by special glands, beating cilia (tiny hairs) to propel themselves.

The other three flatworm classes are all parasitic during at least part of their often complex life cycle. Members of Monogenea are small flukes. At the rear end, they have an opisthaptor, a bulb bearing suckers and/or hooks that attach to a fish's gills or a frog's bladder. Most flukes, however, belong to Trematoda. The adults are parasites of vertebrates, using suckers to attach to the gut and other organs. The class Cestoda contains the tapeworms, internal parasites that are long, flat colonies made up of individuals called proglottids. Almost all flatworms are hermaphrodites, and tapeworms have a set of male and female sex organs in each proglottid.

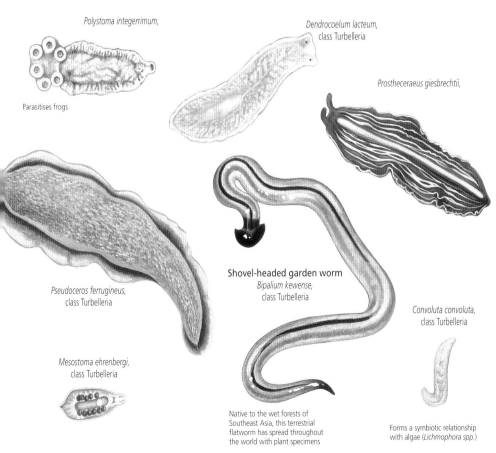

Polystoma integerrimum,

Parasitises frogs

Dendrocoelum lacteum, class Turbelleria

Prostheceraeus giesbrechtii,

Pseudoceros ferrugineus, class Turbelleria

Shovel-headed garden worm
Bipalium kewense, class Turbelleria

Convoluta convoluta, class Turbelleria

Mesostoma ehrenbergi, class Turbelleria

Native to the wet forests of Southeast Asia, this terrestrial flatworm has spread throughout the world with plant specimens

Forms a symbiotic relationship with algae (*Lichmophora spp.*)

ROUNDWORMS

PHYLUM	Nematoda
CLASSES	4
ORDERS	20
FAMILIES	185
SPECIES	> 20,000

Although a species of roundworm that parasitises sperm whales can grow to a length of 13m (43 feet), most members of the phylum Nematoda are microscopic. Also known as nematodes, roundworms are among the most abundant of all animals – one rotting apple was found to contain about 90,000 individual roundworms. Free-living roundworms occur in virtually every aquatic and terrestrial habitat, and those living in soil play a crucial role in recycling detritus. Parasitic roundworms are found in most groups of plants and animals. Common roundworms, hookworms, pinworms, threadworms and other roundworms infest more than half the world's human population.

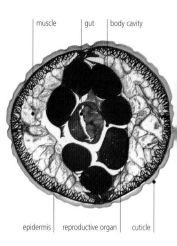

Uncomplicated design The simple body plan of a roundworm, shown here in a magnified cross section, is not necessarily a sign of primitiveness, as it may have been derived from a more complex ancestor.

Growing up After hatching, this juvenile parasitic roundworm possesses all the features of an adult except for a mature reproductive system. It will moult four times before reaching adulthood.

Adaptable worms Free-living roundworms may be marine (right), freshwater or terrestrial. Species occur in ice, hot springs and even in acids, such as vinegar.

SIMPLE AND RESILIENT

Roundworms have long, slender, cylindrical bodies and often resemble tiny threads, a shape that allows them to live in tiny spaces between grains of soil, for example. They are bilaterally symmetrical and often tapered at both ends. The epidermis (skin) secretes a tough but flexible outer cuticle. As in arthropods such as insects, roundworms must moult as they grow. Most shed the cuticle four times before reaching maturity.

When a roundworm moves, it may appear to be thrashing aimlessly back and forth. Between the gut and the body wall, a body cavity known as a pseudocoel contains fluid under pressure. As the worm contracts its muscles, which run only lengthways down its body, this pressure causes the body to flex from side to side – a method of locomotion that works well against soil particles or in water films.

After food enters a roundworm's mouth, it is pumped through the simple gut by a muscular pharynx (throat). Waste is released through an anus at the rear of the worm.

If they encounter unfavourable conditions, such as extreme heat or cold or drought, roundworms can enter a death-like state, known cryptobiosis, for months or even years. When conditions improve, they resume their life processes.

Although some roundworms are hermaphrodites, the sexes are more often separate. During copulation, the male holds onto the female with his hooked rear end. The young resemble miniature adults.

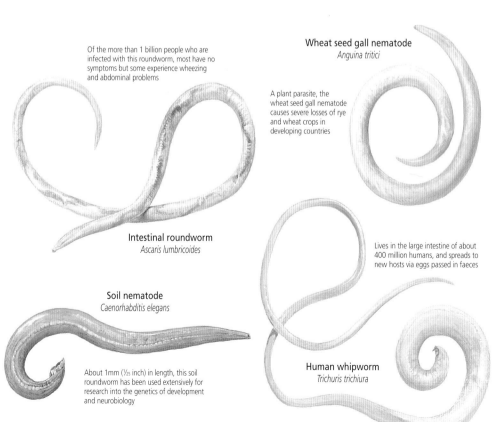

Of the more than 1 billion people who are infected with this roundworm, most have no symptoms but some experience wheezing and abdominal problems

Wheat seed gall nematode
Anguina tritici

A plant parasite, the wheat seed gall nematode causes severe losses of rye and wheat crops in developing countries

Intestinal roundworm
Ascaris lumbricoides

Lives in the large intestine of about 400 million humans, and spreads to new hosts via eggs passed in faeces

Soil nematode
Caenorhabditis elegans

About 1mm (½s inch) in length, this soil roundworm has been used extensively for research into the genetics of development and neurobiology

Human whipworm
Trichuris trichiura

MOLLUSCS

YLUM Mollusca
ASSES 8
DERS 35
MILIES 232
CIES 75,000

Abundant and adaptable, molluscs have diversified to fill most ecological niches. They are predominantly marine and are found in every level of the ocean, but have also colonised fresh water and land throughout the world. The diversity of their habitats is reflected in an immense variety of forms, from jet-propelled squid to creeping snails and fixed clams. Features shared by most molluscs include a well-developed head; a body cavity containing the internal organs; a specialised skin called the mantle that covers the body and secretes a shell of calcium carbonate; an intucking of the mantle to form a mantle cavity that houses the gills; and a muscular, often mucus-secreting foot.

Giants of the sea While many molluscs are small or even minute, some species reach great sizes. The largest bivalve, the giant clam (below), can measure almost 1.5m (5 feet) across. It is dwarfed, however, by the giant squid, which grows to the astounding length of 18m (59 feet).

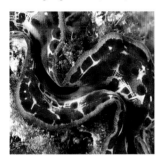

Bottom-dweller Also known as sea slugs, nudibranchs are shell-less gastropods with external, feathery gills. *Chromodouris bullocki* is shown here feeding on coral.

Changing display Many cephalopods can change their colours and patterns, often for camouflage but also for communication. In a ritualised competition, male Caribbean reef squids (*Sepioteuthis sepioidea*) both try a zebra display to win the right to mate.

VARIED DESIGN

Molluscs are split into eight classes. The Aplacophora is a small class of worm-like molluscs that lack a shell. About 20 species that possess a low, rounded shell constitute the Monoplacophora. The chitons of Polyplacophora are protected by eight plates and creep on a sucker-like foot. Scaphopoda contains the burrowing tusk shells. The clams, oysters, mussels and other bivalves of the class Bivalvia have a hinged, two-part shell and a tiny head. Gastropods such as snails and slugs (Gastropoda) sometimes have a spiral shell, but many have no shell at all. Octopuses, squids and other cephalopods (Cephalopoda) have mobile arms and often lack a shell. They include the largest and most intelligent of all invertebrates.

Feeding habits among molluscs are varied. Species may feed on detritus, scrape algae from rocks, eat leaves, filter tiny organisms from the water or actively pursue prey such as crustaceans and fishes. Food is taken in through the mouth, often with the help of a rasping, toothed organ called a radula, then passes through a complex digestive system terminating in an anus.

Most molluscs have separate sexes; some release eggs and sperm into the sea, while others copulate. Larvae tend to be free-swimming.

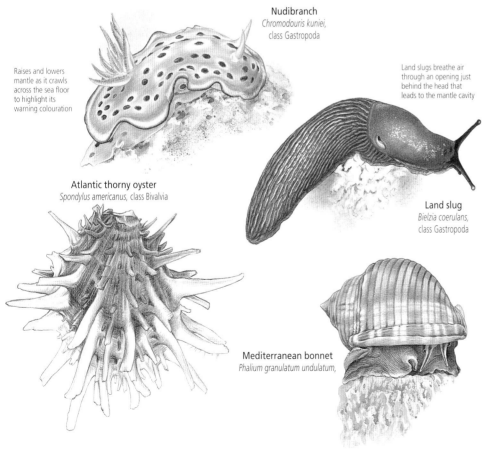

Nudibranch
Chromodouris kuniei,
class Gastropoda

Raises and lowers mantle as it crawls across the sea floor to highlight its warning colouration

Land slugs breathe air through an opening just behind the head that leads to the mantle cavity

Atlantic thorny oyster
Spondylus americanus, class Bivalvia

Land slug
Bielzia coerulans,
class Gastropoda

Mediterranean bonnet
Phalium granulatum undulatum,

FACT FILE

Class Monoplacophora Known only from fossil shells until 1952, this rare class is made up of small, limpet-like molluscs living at great depths, from roughly 200m (660 feet) to ocean trenches at 7,000m (23,000 feet). They are distinguished by the repetition of body parts: there are five or six pairs of gills, six pairs of kidneys and eight pairs of retractor muscles.

Species 20

Atlantic, Pacific, Indian Ocean; on sea floor

Deep crawler
Monoplacophorans, such as Neopilina galatheae, are about 2.5cm (1 inch) long and have a cap-like shell. They use a large flat foot to crawl across the sea floor.

Class Polyplacophora Ranging from 3mm–40cm (1/10 inch–16 inches) in length, the chitons in this class are long and flat and have a shell of eight overlapping plates. They creep slowly on their broad, flat foot, often using their long radula to scrape algae from rocks or shells. If disturbed, they will clamp down to create a vacuum that makes them very difficult to dislodge.

Species 500

Worldwide; intertidal zone to deeper sea floor

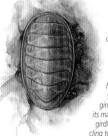

Shell clinger
As in other chitons, the shell of the common eastern chiton Chaetopleura apiculata of North America is surrounded by a girdle formed from its mantle. It uses this girdle and its foot to cling to rocks or shells.

Class Scaphopoda This class contains the tusk shells, burrowing molluscs with long, tubular shells that are open at both ends. A muscular foot and a small head bearing sticky, thread-like tentacles protrude from the large end of the shell. Tusk shells feed on tiny organisms that are collected by the tentacles and broken up by the radula.

Species 500

Worldwide; sandy or muddy sea floor

Burrowing foot
Scaphopods, such as this Entalina sp., use their well-developed foot to burrow into sand or mud on the sea floor.

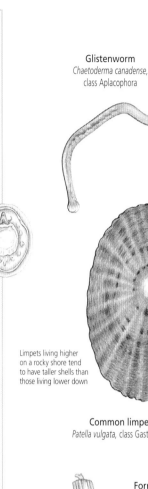

Glistenworm
Chaetoderma canadense,
class Aplacophora

Browses on sedentary invertebrates such as sponges and bryozoans

Mottled red chiton
Tonicella marmourea,
class Polyplacophora

Stenochiton longicymba,
class Polyplacophora

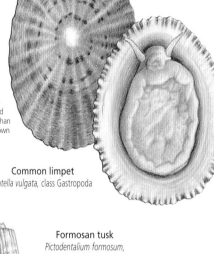

Limpets living higher on a rocky shore tend to have taller shells than those living lower down

Common limpet
Patella vulgata, class Gastropoda

Formosan tusk
Pictodentalium formosum,
class Scaphopoda

Chiton olivaceus,
class Polyplacophora

Elephant tusk
Dentalium elephantinum,
class Scaphopoda

Unlike the jade-green *Dentalium elephantinum,* most tusk shells are white or yelllowish

Antalis tarentinum,
class Scaphopoda

Tusk shells range from 4mm–15 cm (3/16 inch to 6 inches) in length

West Indian green chiton
Chiton tuberculatus,
class Polyplacophora

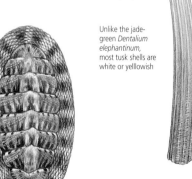

One of the most common chitons in the Caribbean

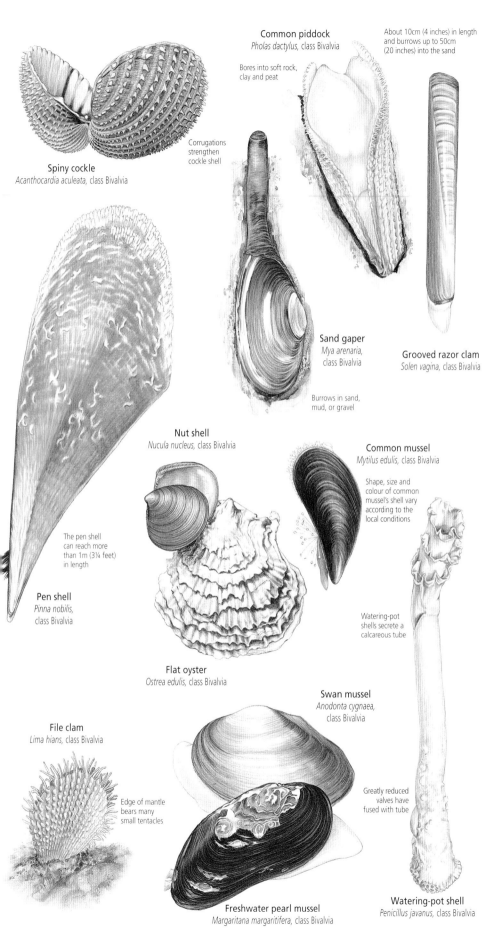

Spiny cockle
Acanthocardia aculeata, class Bivalvia

Corrugations strengthen cockle shell

Common piddock
Pholas dactylus, class Bivalvia

Bores into soft rock, clay and peat

About 10cm (4 inches) in length and burrows up to 50cm (20 inches) into the sand

Sand gaper
Mya arenaria, class Bivalvia

Burrows in sand, mud, or gravel

Grooved razor clam
Solen vagina, class Bivalvia

The pen shell can reach more than 1m (3¼ feet) in length

Pen shell
Pinna nobilis, class Bivalvia

Nut shell
Nucula nucleus, class Bivalvia

Common mussel
Mytilus edulis, class Bivalvia

Shape, size and colour of common mussel's shell vary according to the local conditions

Flat oyster
Ostrea edulis, class Bivalvia

Watering-pot shells secrete a calcareous tube

Swan mussel
Anodonta cygnaea, class Bivalvia

File clam
Lima hians, class Bivalvia

Edge of mantle bears many small tentacles

Greatly reduced valves have fused with tube

Freshwater pearl mussel
Margaritana margaritifera, class Bivalvia

Watering-pot shell
Penicillus javanus, class Bivalvia

FACT FILE

Class Bivalvia Clams, oysters, mussels and other bivalves live inside a hinged two-valve shell. Most are burrowers, but some cement one valve to a firm surface or attach themselves with a byssus, sticky fibres secreted by the foot. Other bivalves live free on the sediment or in the water.

Species 10,000

Worldwide

Brooder The greater European pea clam (*Pisidium amnicum*) broods its eggs inside its shell and releases young that resemble miniature adults.

GIANT CLAM

The largest bivalve of all lives on the tropical coral reefs of the Indian and Pacific oceans. Weighing up to 320kg (700 pounds), giant clams (*Tridacna gigas*) remain embedded in the sediment, filtering plankton from the water. The bulk of their nutrition, however, comes from the algae that they host in the exposed thick lips of the mantle.

INSIDE A BIVALVE

A bivalve's mantle forms a sheet of tissue lining the two valves. The adductor muscles are used to close the shell, and the blade-like foot is often used for burrowing. Bivalves use their gills to filter particles from the water and their palps to sort them by size.

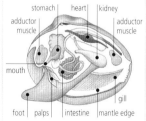

stomach | heart | kidney
adductor muscle | | adductor muscle
mouth
foot | palps | intestine | mantle edge | gill

🏴 CONSERVATION WATCH

Unwelcome mussels First noticed in the Great Lakes in the 1980s, the European zebra mussels (*Dreissena* sp.) have now invaded many of the United States' major rivers and lakes. By filtering vast amounts of phytoplankton from the water, they are having a dramatic effect on aquatic food webs and endangering native molluscs and other species.

FACT FILE

Class Gastropoda This is the largest class of molluscs and includes snails, slugs, limpets, and nudibranchs. Some gastropods have lost their shells, but most have a spiral shell that contains a twisted body mass. Gastropods usually have a distinct head with eyes and tentacles. The mantle cavity lies over the head, allowing the head to retract into the shell. The muscular foot is used for creeping, swimming, or burrowing.

Species 60,000

Worldwide

Gastropod cannibal The banded tulip (Fasciolaria hunteria) can be very aggressive and will eat other members of its species.

RADULAS

A mollusc's mouth usually includes a tongue-like structure known as a radula. In some species, such as deep-sea limpets (*Neomphalus* sp.), a covering of hardened teeth makes the radula a rasping tool, able to scrape algae from rocks. In others, such as the slit shell mollusc (*Scissurella* sp.), the surface of the radula is feathery and is used to sweep detritus from sand. In a few carnivorous species, such as cone shells (*Conus* sp.), the radula has become a sharp, venom-injecting tooth.

THE GASTROPOD SHELL

While gastropod shells display immense variety in their details, the typical shell is a conical spire. The mantle adds new material to the inner and outer lips of the shell at slightly different rates, resulting in the spiral form.

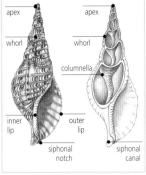

apex

whorl

inner lip

outer lip

siphonal notch

apex

whorl

columnella

outer lip

siphonal canal

Plain marginella
Marginella cornea,
class Gastropoda

Purple bubble-raft snail
Janthina janthina, class Gastropoda

Floats at the ocean's surface, buoyed by mucus-covered bubbles

Phyllidia ocellata,
class Gastropoda

Colour of *Phyllidia* ocellata is variable, but it can be identified by its knobby tubercles and white-ringed black spots

Crown conch
Melongena corona, class Gastropoda

European edible abalone
Haliotis tuberculata,
class Gastropoda

The mucus of *Murex brandarius* was used by the ancient Greeks to produce a dye called Tyrian purple, which was so rare that it was used only for the clothes of royalty

Purple-dye murex
Murex brandarius, class Gastropoda

Trumpet triton
Charonia tritonis,
class Gastropoda

Ruffled flaps of tissue (parapodia) resemble lettuce leaves

Lettuce sea slug
Elysia crispata,
class Gastropoda

Tiger cowry
Cypraea tigris, class Gastropoda

Floats upside down and feeds on Portuguese man-of-war, ingesting the host's nematocysts (stingers) to use in its own defence

Blue sea slug
Glaucus atlanticus, class Gastropoda

Common egg cowrie
Ovula ovum, class Gastropoda

Queen conch
Strombus gigas, class Gastropoda

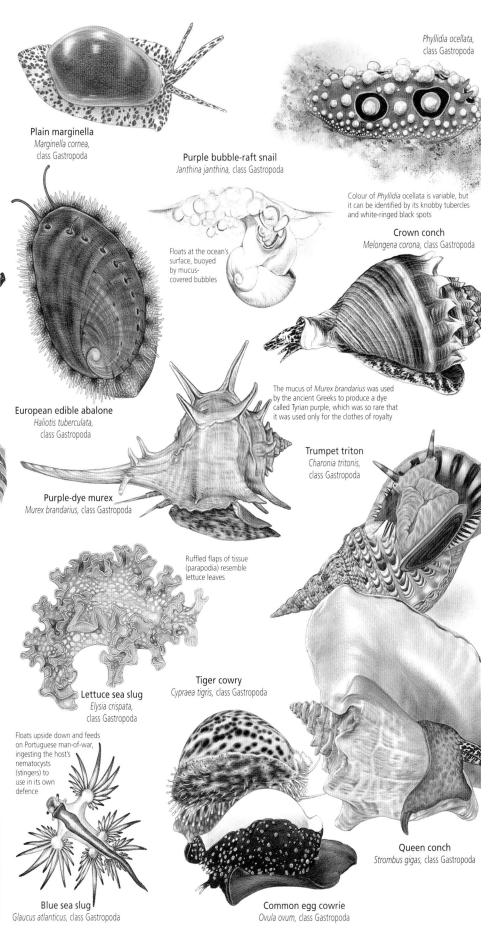

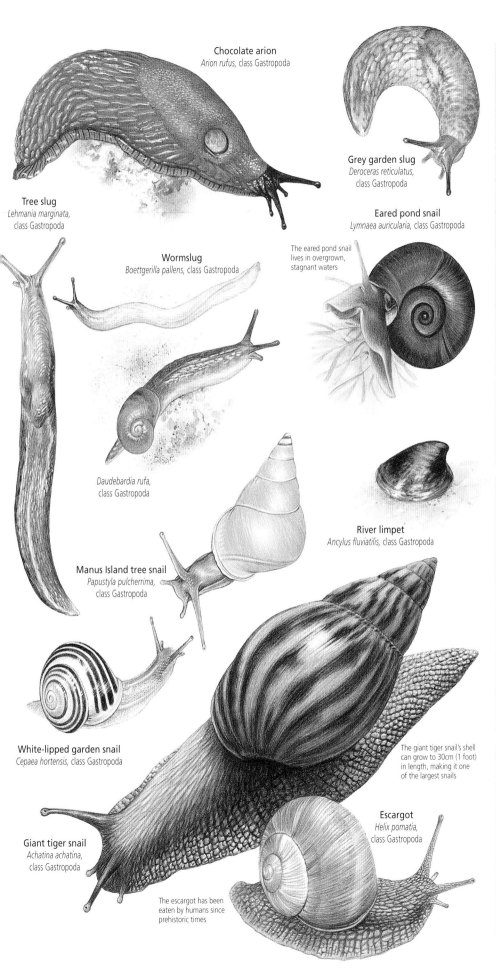

Chocolate arion
Arion rufus, class Gastropoda

Grey garden slug
Deroceras reticulatus,
class Gastropoda

Tree slug
Lehmania marginata,
class Gastropoda

Eared pond snail
Lymnaea auricularia, class Gastropoda

Wormslug
Boettgerilla pallens, class Gastropoda

The eared pond snail
lives in overgrown,
stagnant waters

Daudebardia rufa,
class Gastropoda

River limpet
Ancylus fluviatilis, class Gastropoda

Manus Island tree snail
Papustyla pulcherrima,
class Gastropoda

White-lipped garden snail
Cepaea hortensis, class Gastropoda

The giant tiger snail's shell
can grow to 30cm (1 foot)
in length, making it one
of the largest snails

Escargot
Helix pomatia,
class Gastropoda

Giant tiger snail
Achatina achatina,
class Gastropoda

The escargot has been
eaten by humans since
prehistoric times

LIFE ON LAND

Several times during the course of evolution, gastropods have adapted to life on land. There are now roughly 20,000 land snail species. In most, gills have been lost and replaced by a lung. Some species, however, have both a gill chamber and a lung. Out of water, the shell has become lightweight and now protects against desiccation as well as against predators. The mantle and the mucus that cover the body also help to keep the snail moist. If conditions become too dry, a snail will attach itself to a plant or other surface and become dormant. Land slugs, which have lost the shell, live largely in crevices.

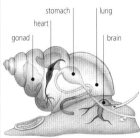

stomach | lung
heart |
gonad | brain

Air breather *Most land snails lack gills. Instead, the mantle wall has become filled with blood vessels and acts as a lung.*

MATING HERMAPHRODITES

Land snails are hermaphrodites but do not self-fertilise. Before mating, two snails will usually circle each other, touch tentacles, intertwine bodies and bite each other. In the copulation that follows, sperm are exchanged so that the eggs of both snails can be fertilised.

Love darts *The courtship of some land snails, such as Helix sp., is bizarre. When the snails are intertwined, one will shoot a chalky dart from its body into its mate. The dart appears to carry a chemical that helps the sperm reach the storage area in the female reproductive system.*

⚑ CONSERVATION WATCH

Mollusc losses Non-marine molluscs appear to be the most threatened of all animal groups. In the last 300 years, 284 species of non-marine mollusc are known to have become extinct – far more than in mammals (74 extinctions) or birds (129 extinctions). Although the oceans are by no means pristine, terrestrial and freshwater habitats have been drastically modified by human activities and their mollusc populations have suffered as a result.

FACT FILE

Class Cephalopoda The cephalopod foot lies close to the head and has been modified to form arms, tentacles and a funnel. Nautiluses retain a large external shell; in squids and cuttlefishes the shell has been reduced and covered by tissue; and octopuses have lost their shell altogether. With the most developed brains of any invertebrates, cephalopods display complex behaviour and are able to learn.

Species 600

Worldwide; marine

Predator *Like all cephalopods, the European common squid* (Loligo subulata) *is carnivorous. It captures prey with its tentacles and arms and breaks it up with its beak and radula.*

THE CHAMBERED NAUTILUS

The most primitive of the cephalopods, chambered nautiluses live in the last chamber of their large shell. The other chambers are filled with gas, and the nautilus controls its buoyancy by adding fluid to or removing fluid from them.

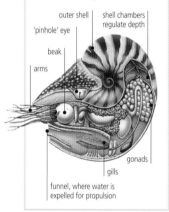

outer shell
'pinhole' eye
beak
arms
shell chambers regulate depth
gonads
gills
funnel, where water is expelled for propulsion

CEPHALOPOD SIGHT

Most cephalopods have excellent vision. Like the eyes of vertebrates, their eyes have a cornea, iris, lens and retina. While humans bring objects into focus by changing the shape of the lens, cephalopods move the entire lens closer to or farther from the retina. Guided by the cephalopod's statocysts (balance organs), the slit-shaped pupils maintain a horizontal position no matter what the angle of the head.

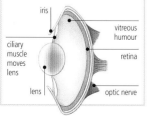

iris
vitreous humour
ciliary muscle moves lens
retina
lens
optic nerve

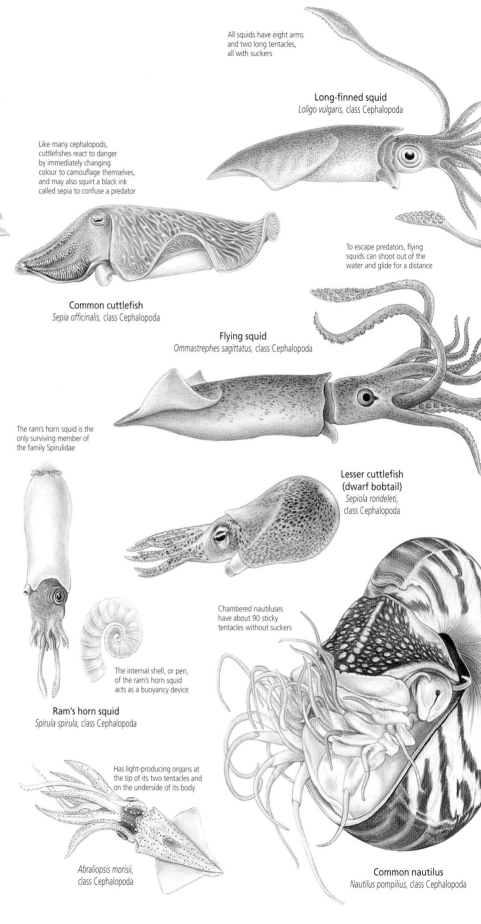

All squids have eight arms and two long tentacles, all with suckers

Long-finned squid
Loligo vulgaris, class Cephalopoda

Like many cephalopods, cuttlefishes react to danger by immediately changing colour to camouflage themselves, and may also squirt a black ink called sepia to confuse a predator

To escape predators, flying squids can shoot out of the water and glide for a distance

Common cuttlefish
Sepia officinalis, class Cephalopoda

Flying squid
Ommastrephes sagittatus, class Cephalopoda

The ram's horn squid is the only surviving member of the family Spirulidae

Lesser cuttlefish (dwarf bobtail)
Sepiola rondeleti, class Cephalopoda

The internal shell, or pen, of the ram's horn squid acts as a buoyancy device

Chambered nautiluses have about 90 sticky tentacles without suckers

Ram's horn squid
Spirula spirula, class Cephalopoda

Has light-producing organs at the tip of its two tentacles and on the underside of its body

Abraliopsis morisii, class Cephalopoda

Common nautilus
Nautilus pompilius, class Cephalopoda

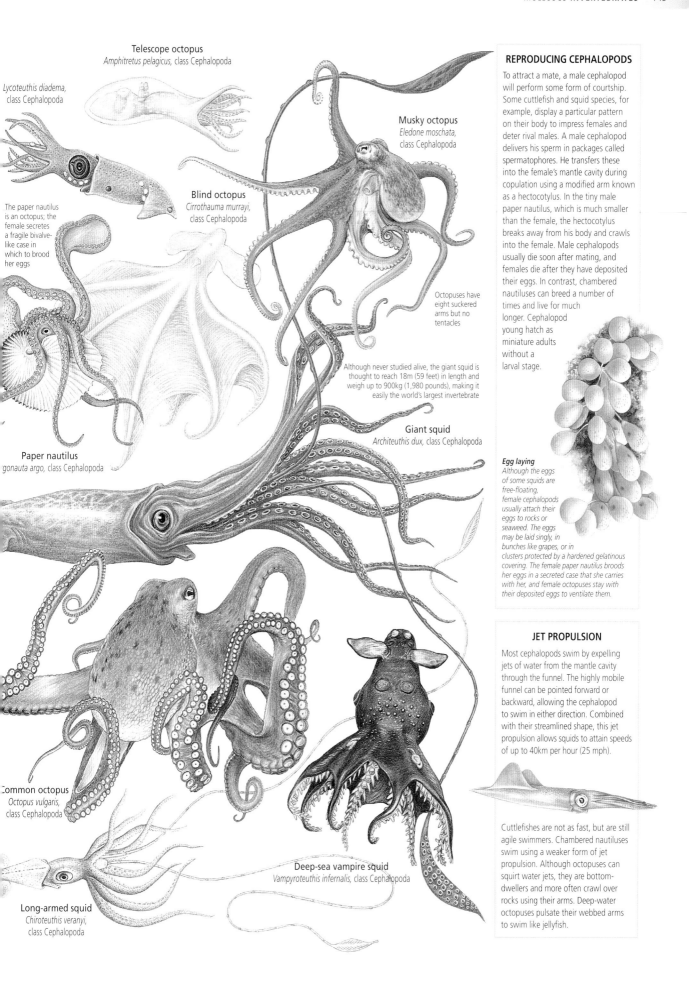

Telescope octopus
Amphitretus pelagicus, class Cephalopoda

Lycoteuthis diadema,
class Cephalopoda

The paper nautilus
is an octopus; the
female secretes
a fragile bivalve-
like case in
which to brood
her eggs

Blind octopus
Cirrothauma murrayi,
class Cephalopoda

Musky octopus
Eledone moschata,
class Cephalopoda

Octopuses have
eight suckered
arms but no
tentacles

Paper nautilus
gonauta argo, class Cephalopoda

Although never studied alive, the giant squid is
thought to reach 18m (59 feet) in length and
weigh up to 900kg (1,980 pounds), making it
easily the world's largest invertebrate

Giant squid
Architeuthis dux, class Cephalopoda

Common octopus
Octopus vulgaris,
class Cephalopoda

Long-armed squid
Chiroteuthis veranyi,
class Cephalopoda

Deep-sea vampire squid
Vampyroteuthis infernalis, class Cephalopoda

REPRODUCING CEPHALOPODS

To attract a mate, a male cephalopod
will perform some form of courtship.
Some cuttlefish and squid species, for
example, display a particular pattern
on their body to impress females and
deter rival males. A male cephalopod
delivers his sperm in packages called
spermatophores. He transfers these
into the female's mantle cavity during
copulation using a modified arm known
as a hectocotylus. In the tiny male
paper nautilus, which is much smaller
than the female, the hectocotylus
breaks away from his body and crawls
into the female. Male cephalopods
usually die soon after mating, and
females die after they have deposited
their eggs. In contrast, chambered
nautiluses can breed a number of
times and live for much
longer. Cephalopod
young hatch as
miniature adults
without a
larval stage.

Egg laying
Although the eggs
of some squids are
free-floating,
female cephalopods
usually attach their
eggs to rocks or
seaweed. The eggs
may be laid singly, in
bunches like grapes, or in
clusters protected by a hardened gelatinous
covering. The female paper nautilus broods
her eggs in a secreted case that she carries
with her, and female octopuses stay with
their deposited eggs to ventilate them.

JET PROPULSION

Most cephalopods swim by expelling
jets of water from the mantle cavity
through the funnel. The highly mobile
funnel can be pointed forward or
backward, allowing the cephalopod
to swim in either direction. Combined
with their streamlined shape, this jet
propulsion allows squids to attain speeds
of up to 40km per hour (25 mph).

Cuttlefishes are not as fast, but are still
agile swimmers. Chambered nautiluses
swim using a weaker form of jet
propulsion. Although octopuses can
squirt water jets, they are bottom-
dwellers and more often crawl over
rocks using their arms. Deep-water
octopuses pulsate their webbed arms
to swim like jellyfish.

SEGMENTED WORMS

PHYLUM Annelida	
CLASSES 2	
ORDERS 21	
FAMILIES 130	
SPECIES 12,000	

Also known as annelids, segmented worms have a head and a long body made up of segments that look like rings from the outside. Each segment has its own fluid-filled body cavity that acts as a hydroskeleton and contains a separate set of excretory, locomotory and respiratory organs. The segments are united, however, by common digestive, circulatory and nervous systems. Segmented worms crawl or swim by wriggling from side to side, or burrow by waves of contractions that pass down the length of the body. Stiff bristles known as chetae protrude from each segment and provide traction. While many species are highly active, others live in burrows or tubes.

In the soil Long and thin with a small head, earthworms are shaped for burrowing. With up to 800 per square metre (650 individuals per sq. yd.), earthworms play a crucial role in aerating and fertilising the soil.

Food-filtering fans
Fanworms are annelids that live attached to the sea floor. Most of their body is hidden inside a tube that they have secreted or built from sediment. A crown of fine tentacles, each covered in tiny beating hairs called cilia, filters particles of food from the water.

IN WATER AND ON LAND

Segmented worms are found in all levels of the ocean, in freshwater lakes and rivers, and on land. They include filter-feeders, predators and blood-suckers, as well as deposit-feeders such as earthworms, which eat sediment to extract nutrients.

Commonly called bristleworms, the species in the class Polychaeta are almost entirely marine and usually swim or crawl using paddle-like appendages known as parapodia. The parapodia are often lost in tube-living forms, which have a modified head region for food-gathering. Typically, the sexes are separate and release eggs and sperm into the water for fertilisation.

The class Clitellata includes many terrestrial and freshwater species such as earthworms and leeches, as well as some marine species. Most are hermaphrodites that exchange sperm by copulation. They all bear a clitellum, a ring of glandular skin that secretes a cocoon for the eggs.

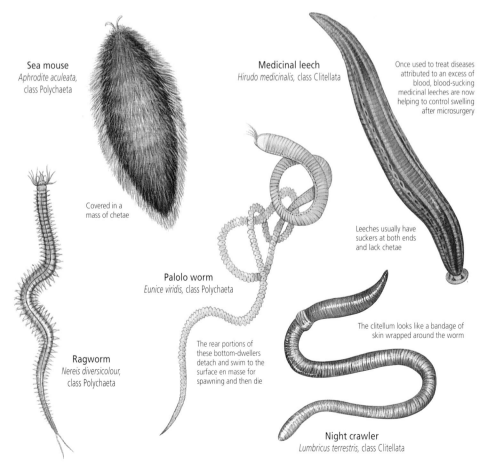

Sea mouse
Aphrodite aculeata,
class Polychaeta

Covered in a mass of chetae

Medicinal leech
Hirudo medicinalis, class Clitellata

Once used to treat diseases attributed to an excess of blood, blood-sucking medicinal leeches are now helping to control swelling after microsurgery

Leeches usually have suckers at both ends and lack chetae

Palolo worm
Eunice viridis, class Polychaeta

The rear portions of these bottom-dwellers detach and swim to the surface en masse for spawning and then die

The clitellum looks like a bandage of skin wrapped around the worm

Ragworm
Nereis diversicolour,
class Polychaeta

Night crawler
Lumbricus terrestris, class Clitellata

Instantly withdraws its feathery crown if disturbed

Red feather duster
Spirographis spallanzanii,
class Polychaeta

METAMORPHOSIS

While some newly hatched invertebrates resemble little adults, most look quite distinct from their parents and have a very different lifestyle. To become adults, these young must go through a transformation known as metamorphosis. Corals, clams, many crustaceans and most other invertebrates metamorphose into adults after a brief larval stage. For most insects, the larval stage is prolonged. In some insect groups, such as crickets and bugs, metamorphosis is incomplete. The hatched form, called a nymph, is structured like the adult, but lacks wings and full sex organs until it emerges from the final moult. Other insects, such as butterflies and bees, have complete metamorphosis. The young, called larvae, differ so much from their parents that they must go through a pupal stage, in which their bodies break down and are built up again as adults.

Veliger larva Marine gastropods such as sea snails have a free-swimming veliger larva, which feeds and propels itself using tiny hairs known as cilia. The larva gradually develops a shell, mantle cavity and foot (above), then metamorphoses into an adult (below).

Zoea larva Decapods such as squat lobsters often hatch as a zoea, a free-swimming, spiny larva (above). The zoea metamorphoses into a postlarval megalopa, with adult appendages. This sinks to the sea floor and becomes a bottom-dwelling adult (below).

Egg to nymph to adult A dragonfly develops through incomplete metamorphosis. **1.** Male and female mate. **2.** Female lays eggs in water or in stem of water plant. **3.** Aquatic nymph hatches. **4.** Nymph feeds on tadpoles and worms and grows through a series of moults. **5.** Nymph emerges from the water for its final moult. **6.** Adult bursts from the nymphal skin. **7.** Adult rests while its wings dry out. **8.** Feeding on flying insects, adult flies to a new location to find a mate.

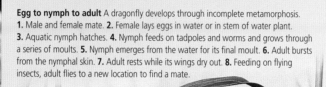

ARTHROPODS

| PHYLUM Arthropoda |
| CLASSES 22 |
| ORDERS 110 |
| FAMILIES 2,120 |
| SPECIES > 1.1 million |

The insects, spiders, crustaceans, centipedes and other invertebrates in the phylum Arthropoda account for three-quarters of all known animal species, and millions more remain to be discovered. Arthropods have adapted to fill virtually every ecological niche on land, in fresh water and in the oceans. Consequently, their anatomy and lifestyles are extraordinarily diverse, but they share a number of defining features. The name arthropod means 'jointed feet', and arthropods do have jointed appendages and segmented bodies. They are distinguished from other invertebrates by their tough but flexible exoskeleton, which provides both protection and support.

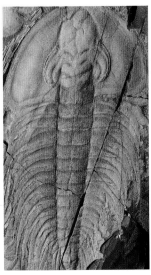

Fossilized marine class Arthropods called trilobites dominate marine fossil beds from about 500 million years ago, and include more than 15,000 known species. They disappeared about 250 million years ago.

Insects everywhere Insects account for about 90 per cent of all arthropod species. Ubiquitous on land and in fresh water, but rare in the ocean, insects include predators such as the praying mantis, and nectar-feeders such as the swallowtail butterfly.

EARLY ARRIVALS

The first arthropods appeared in the oceans about 530 million years ago and included crustaceans; ancestors of horseshoe crabs; and the now-extinct trilobites. These early species tended to have numerous body segments, each bearing a similar pair of appendages. Over time, the appendages became specialised for particular tasks, such as locomotion, food collection, sensory perception and copulation. Furthermore, the segments became arranged into distinct regions of the body called tagma, such as the head, thorax and abdomen of insects.

Arthropods were the first animals to leave the sea and the first to take to the sky. Scorpions had ventured onto land by 350 million years ago and were soon followed by the first terrestrial insects. Before long, winged insects had emerged. The success of arthropods on land rests in part on their waxy exoskeleton, which stops them from drying out. Jointed legs also make arthropods highly mobile, thus enhancing their ability to find food and mates, evade predators, and colonise new places. In insects, the development of wings increases the advantage.

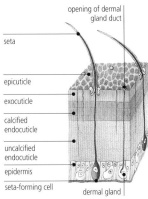

opening of dermal gland duct

seta

epicuticle

exocuticle

calcified endocuticle

uncalcified endocuticle

epidermis

seta-forming cell

dermal gland

Arthropod armour Secreted by epidermal cells, the arthropod exoskeleton has thin layers of wax and protein, known as the epicuticle, overlying various layers of chitin and protein. Tanning of proteins in the exocuticle, and often calcification in the endocuticle, hardens exoskeleton. This coral crab (*Hoplophrys oatesii*) (right) discards its old exoskeleton as it grows.

Legs and bodies Tarantulas (left) and other spiders have eight legs and a body divided into two parts: the cephalothorax (fused head and thorax) and the abdomen. Insects have six legs and a three-part body made up of a head, thorax and abdomen.

Deadly bites While some arthropods are venomous, few deliver a bite that is fatal to humans. Far more deadly are the diseases transmitted by blood-sucking arthropods such as mosquitoes (below), which transfer malaria and other illnesses from one vertebrate host to another.

WAYS OF BREATHING

The arthropod exoskeleton offers great protection, but it is also usually too impermeable to allow gas exchange. While some tiny arthropods can breathe directly through the body wall, most have developed specialised structures. Aquatic arthropods tend to have gills. Derived from gills are book lungs, found in many arachnids. Terrestrial arthropods often rely on minute air ducts known as tracheae, which deliver air to all parts of the body.

Gills Oxygen is absorbed from water by the gills (above), which also help to maintain salt balance. In crustaceans, the gills are external and often positioned on the legs, but are protected by the exoskeleton. Horseshoe crabs have unique structures called book gills, with flaps like the pages of a book.

Limbs in motion By modifying their jointed limbs for walking, running, leaping, pushing, burrowing and swimming, arthropods have been able to occupy diverse habitats. In some, such as grasshoppers (right), the legs also hold their hearing organs.

While many arthropods are themselves predators, almost all are prey to vertebrates or to other invertebrates. The compound eyes found on many arthropod species are made up of multiple lenses and are extremely effective at detecting motion. Simple eyes, with a single lens, detect light intensity. Hairs (known as setae), projections, and slits on the antennae, mouthparts and legs detect subtle vibrations. A cerebral ganglion (brain) connects via a nerve cord to ganglia (clusters of nerve cells) in each body segment. In arthropods' open circulatory system, a heart pumps hemolymph (blood) to bathe the organs.

The sexes are separate in most arthropod species, and reproduction usually involves the male's sperm fertilising the female's eggs. Often, the sperm is transferred in packages known as spermatophores, which the female can use when she is ready. The life stages of arthropods vary greatly. Some species are like small adults when they hatch, while others add segments as they grow. Many insect larvae look nothing like their parents and must go through a pupal stage to transform into a winged adult.

Book lungs Most likely derived from the book gills attached to the under surface of the abdomen of horseshoe crabs, book lungs have become internalised within the abdominal cavity. A small opening allows air to flow into the cavity of the book lung, whose 'pages' form the respiratory surface. Book lungs are found in many arachnids either as the only respiratory organ, such as in scorpions, or in combination with tracheae, as in most spiders. Oxygen from the air diffuses across the respiratory surface and is taken into the blood for distribution to the tissues. Carbon dioxide diffuses in the opposite direction.

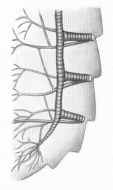

Tracheae Found in insects, arachnids, and centipedes and millipedes, tracheae (above) are tubes that collect air through minute openings in the exoskeleton called spiracles, and transport it to the tissues or blood. The spiracles can be closed to minimise moisture loss.

ARACHNIDS

PHYLUM	Arthropoda
SUBPHYLUM	Chelicerata
CLASS	Arachnida
ORDERS	17
FAMILIES	450
SPECIES	80,000

Including some of the most feared and fascinating of all invertebrates, the class Arachnida encompasses spiders, scorpions, harvestmen (or daddy-longlegs) and mites and ticks, along with several lesser known groups. Apart from some families of aquatic mites and a few species of water spiders, all arachnids are terrestrial, and the majority are predators of other invertebrates. Many spiders use silk webs to snare prey, and both scorpions and spiders inject their prey with venom to paralyse or kill it. Most arachnids are unable to swallow solid food and must squirt digestive enzymes into the prey and then suck the liquefied meal into their mouth.

Diurnal vision Most arachnid species are nocturnal and their simple eyes detect only variations in light. In daytime hunters, such as jumping spiders (family Salticidae), the two primary simple eyes provide very sharp vision at close range.

Arachnid anatomy A spider displays many of the typical arachnid features, including a two-part body, eight jointed legs, a pair of chelicerae, a pair of pedipalps and a number of simple eyes. It also has venom glands in its chelicerae, and silk glands at its rear, both of which play an important role in hunting and defence.

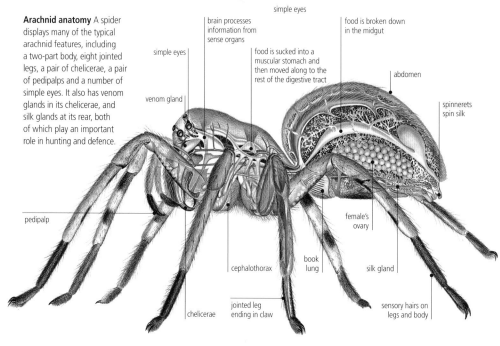

simple eyes

brain processes information from sense organs

food is broken down in the midgut

simple eyes

food is sucked into a muscular stomach and then moved along to the rest of the digestive tract

abdomen

venom gland

spinnerets spin silk

pedipalp

female's ovary

cephalothorax

book lung

silk gland

chelicerae

jointed leg ending in claw

sensory hairs on legs and body

EIGHT-LEGGED PREDATORS

Like other arthropods, arachnids have a segmented body, a tough but flexible exoskeleton and jointed limbs. Mites and ticks have rounded bodies made up of a single region, but other arachnids have two-part bodies, with a cephalothorax holding the eyes, mouthparts and limbs, and an abdomen containing many of the internal organs.

Arachnids have eight legs, unlike insects, which have six. They also have two pairs of appendages near the mouth. The first pair, known as chelicerae, may be pincer-like or can form fangs that inject venom. They are used for subduing prey. The second pair, the pedipalps, are often used like antennae to sense the surroundings. Scorpions and some other arachnids use pedipalps to seize prey, while male spiders use them to transfer sperm to females.

To find prey and avoid danger, arachnids rely on the fine sensory hairs on their body and legs. They also have a number of simple eyes. Fine slits in the cuticle may detect odours, gravity or vibrations.

Arachnids breathe using book lungs or a tracheal system, or both. Book lungs probably developed from gills and are made up of stacked leaves of tissue. The tracheal system takes air in through tiny pores called spiracles and distributes it to tissues via a network of tubes.

Development of arachnids is direct, with the young hatching as small versions of their parents and growing through a series of moults. Most arachnids are solitary.

Blood-sucking parasite While most arachnids hunt live prey, ticks and some mites are parasites. A tick uses its hooked mouthparts to pierce the skin of a mammal, then feed on its blood. Once engorged, the tick drops off the host and moults.

Stinging defence While arachnids such as spiders and scorpions are widely feared, only a tiny minority of species deliver a bite or sting that can be fatal to humans. The giant desert hairy scorpion (*Hadrurus arizonensis*) has a painful sting, but the effect of its venom on humans is mild.

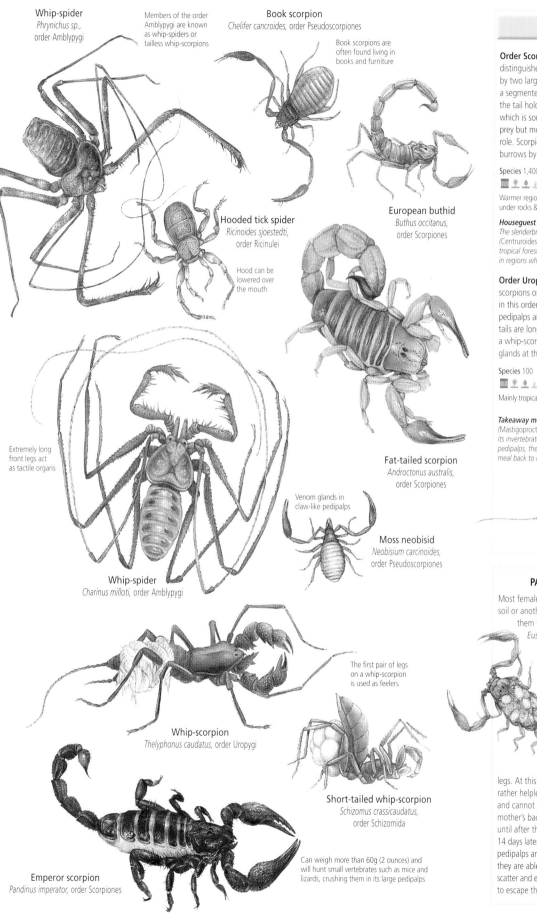

Whip-spider
Phrynichus sp.,
order Amblypygi

Members of the order
Amblypygi are known
as whip-spiders or
tailless whip-scorpions

Book scorpion
Chelifer cancroides, order Pseudoscorpiones

Book scorpions are
often found living in
books and furniture

Hooded tick spider
Ricinoides sjoestedti,
order Ricinulei

Hood can be
lowered over
the mouth

European buthid
Buthus occitanus,
order Scorpiones

Extremely long
front legs act
as tactile organs

Fat-tailed scorpion
Androctonus australis,
order Scorpiones

Venom glands in
claw-like pedipalps

Moss neobisid
Neobisium carcinoides,
order Pseudoscorpiones

Whip-spider
Charinus milloti, order Amblypygi

The first pair of legs
on a whip-scorpion
is used as feelers

Whip-scorpion
Thelyphonus caudatus, order Uropygi

Short-tailed whip-scorpion
Schizomus crassicaudatus,
order Schizomida

Can weigh more than 60g (2 ounces) and
will hunt small vertebrates such as mice and
lizards, crushing them in its large pedipalps

Emperor scorpion
Pandinus imperator, order Scorpiones

FACT FILE

Order Scorpiones Scorpions are
distinguished from other arachnids
by two large clawed pedipalps and
a segmented abdomen. The tip of
the tail holds a prominent stinger,
which is sometimes used to subdue
prey but more often plays a defensive
role. Scorpions shelter in crevices or
burrows by day, and hunt by night.

Species 1,400

Warmer regions;
under rocks & bark

Houseguest
The slenderbrown scorpion
(Centuroides gracilis) usually lives in
tropical forests, but may dwell in houses
in regions where it has been introduced.

Order Uropygi Known as whip-
scorpions or vinegaroons, the arachnids
in this order resemble scorpions but their
pedipalps are stouter, and their
tails are long and thin. If threatened,
a whip-scorpion will spray acid from
glands at the base of its whip-like tail.

Species 100

Mainly tropical regions; under rocks

Takeaway meals The giant whip-scorpion
(Mastigoproctus giganteus) seizes and crushes
its invertebrate prey with its
pedipalps, then carries the
meal back to its burrow.

PARENTAL CARE

Most female arachnids lay their eggs in
soil or another safe location and leave
them to hatch on their own. In
Euscorpius carpathicus (left)
and other scorpions,
however, the
fertilised eggs
develop
inside the
mother and
she produces
live young. The
mother catches
them in her first or
first and second pairs of
legs. At this stage, the larval young are
rather helpless as they lack pedipalps
and cannot sting. They crawl onto the
mother's back and are carried around
until after their first moult, about 3 to
14 days later. Now equipped with their
pedipalps and a functioning stinger,
they are able to hunt. They quickly
scatter and establish their own territories
to escape their mother eating them.

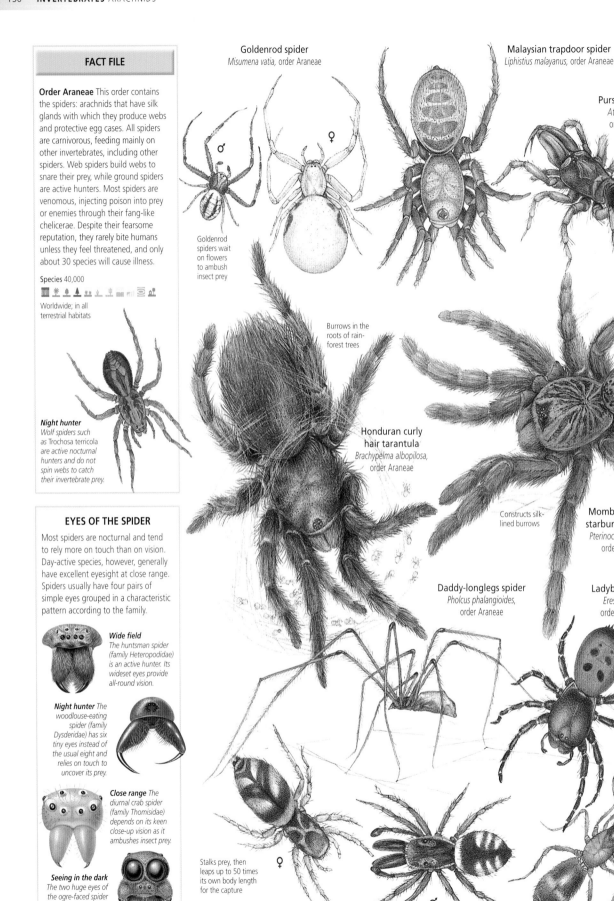

Order Araneae This order contains the spiders: arachnids that have silk glands with which they produce webs and protective egg cases. All spiders are carnivorous, feeding mainly on other invertebrates, including other spiders. Web spiders build webs to snare their prey, while ground spiders are active hunters. Most spiders are venomous, injecting poison into prey or enemies through their fang-like chelicerae. Despite their fearsome reputation, they rarely bite humans unless they feel threatened, and only about 30 species will cause illness.

Species 40,000

Worldwide; in all terrestrial habitats

Night hunter
Wolf spiders such as Trochosa terricola are active nocturnal hunters and do not spin webs to catch their invertebrate prey.

EYES OF THE SPIDER

Most spiders are nocturnal and tend to rely more on touch than on vision. Day-active species, however, generally have excellent eyesight at close range. Spiders usually have four pairs of simple eyes grouped in a characteristic pattern according to the family.

Wide field
The huntsman spider (family Heteropodidae) is an active hunter. Its wideset eyes provide all-round vision.

Night hunter *The woodlouse-eating spider (family Dysderidae) has six tiny eyes instead of the usual eight and relies on touch to uncover its prey.*

Close range *The diurnal crab spider (family Thomisidae) depends on its keen close-up vision as it ambushes insect prey.*

Seeing in the dark
The two huge eyes of the ogre-faced spider (family Deinopidae) enable it to see prey in near-total darkness.

Goldenrod spider
Misumena vatia, order Araneae

Goldenrod spiders wait on flowers to ambush insect prey

Malaysian trapdoor spider
Liphistius malayanus, order Araneae

Purseweb spider
Atypus muralis, order Araneae

Burrows in the roots of rainforest trees

Honduran curly hair tarantula
Brachypelma albopilosa, order Araneae

Constructs silk-lined burrows

Mombasa golden starburst tarantula
Pterinochilus murinus, order Araneae

Daddy-longlegs spider
Pholcus phalangioides, order Araneae

Ladybird spider
Eresus niger, order Araneae

Stalks prey, then leaps up to 50 times its own body length for the capture

Zebra jumping spider
Salticus scenicus, order Araneae

Ground spider
Micaria formicaria, order Araneae

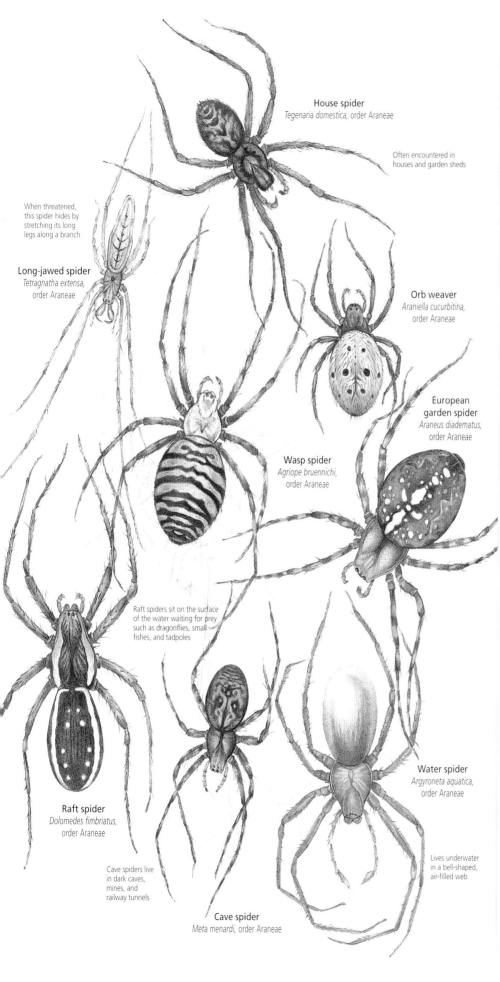

House spider
Tegenaria domestica, order Araneae

Often encountered in houses and garden sheds

When threatened, this spider hides by stretching its long legs along a branch

Long-jawed spider
Tetragnatha extensa, order Araneae

Orb weaver
Araniella cucurbitina, order Araneae

European garden spider
Araneus diadematus, order Araneae

Wasp spider
Agriope bruennichi, order Araneae

Raft spiders sit on the surface of the water waiting for prey such as dragonflies, small fishes, and tadpoles

Raft spider
Dolomedes fimbriatus, order Araneae

Cave spiders live in dark caves, mines, and railway tunnels

Cave spider
Meta menardi, order Araneae

Water spider
Argyroneta aquatica, order Araneae

Lives underwater in a bell-shaped, air-filled web

CAPTURE METHODS

Not all spiders sit waiting for prey to fall into their webs. The spitting spider (*Scytodes thoracica*) has an enlarged cephalothorax that houses linked venom and silk glands. It hunts its prey by night, stealthily approaching until it is within spitting distance. The spider then ejects two poisonous silk threads, covering the prey in a zig-zag pattern. The prey is glued to the ground by the silk and paralysed by the venom.

Spitting spider *With only six small eyes, the spitting spider has poor vision and uses the sensory hairs on its front legs to find prey such as flies and moths.*

Bolas spiders belong to the orb-weaver family, Araneidae, but they do not build orb webs. Instead, they 'fish' for their prey, suspending a single strand of silk tipped with a sticky globule known as a bolas. The bolas seems to be laced with pheromones that mimic those of particular female noctuid moths. When male moths are attracted to the bolas and become stuck, the spider reels them in.

Bolas spider *When it senses a moth approaching, a bolas spider will start swinging its fishing line in a circle.*

Spiders in various families have adapted their anatomy to convincingly mimic ants. They are even thought to produce pheromones that allow them to infiltrate ant colonies. Some ant-mimics use their disguise to prey on the unsuspecting ants. Others may merely be protecting themselves from predators such as wasps and birds that avoid ants because of the formic acid ants produce when threatened.

Brazilian ant-mimicking spider *Like other ant-mimics, Aphantochilus rogersi has a long waist and the abdomen is partially divided into segments to give the impression of an insect body. The first pair of legs is held in front like antennae.*

SILK AND WEBS

While only some species build webs, almost all spiders produce silk. Made of the protein fibroin, spider silk is as strong as nylon thread but has greater elasticity. A spider may have up to eight silk glands in its abdomen, each yielding a different kind of silk. One kind of silk is used for the dragline a spider usually spins after itself like a mountain climber's safety line. Other types are used for cocooning fertilised eggs or wrapping up captured prey. Male spiders may use silk to hold their packages of sperm. Some spiderlings use threads of silk like balloons to carry them aloft so they can disperse. The best known use of silk is among the webspinning spiders, which build a remarkable variety of webs to snare their prey.

Captured prey A net-casting spider (*Deinopus* sp.) prepares a little snare net each night and holds it in its legs as it awaits prey. When a potential victim passes by, the spider flings the net over it, quickly wraps the catch in extra silk and then bites it.

Scaffold web A scaffold web has stretched traplines with sticky ends attached to the ground. If a crawling insect walks into a trapline, the line snaps back, with the victim dangling in the air.

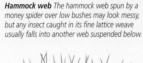

Hammock web The hammock web spun by a money spider over low bushes may look messy, but any insect caught in its fine lattice weave usually falls into another web suspended below.

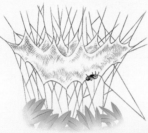

Triangle web A spider holds a triangular web in its front legs while anchored by a thread of silk to the twig behind it. When an insect hits the web, the spider releases its grip and the web collapses, entangling the prey.

Orb web The most elaborate of all webs, the orb web covers a large area using a minimum of silk. An outer framework supports a continuous spiral and a series of spokes. The web is suspended between tree branches to capture flying insects.

Lace-sheet web The trap spun by a lace-web weaver is made of fine, woolly silk. It may not be sticky, but insects soon get tangled up in its many fibres, and remain trapped until the spider is ready for food.

No sticky feet Spiders such as this orb weaver (*Argiope* sp.) (right) avoid getting trapped in their own webs because only some of the threads are sticky and they know where to tread.

Shared nest While most spiders are solitary, some share communal nests. Some species are truly colonial, and hunt and feed together. In others, such as *Cryptophora* sp., each spider guards its own orb web and feeds alone, but the webs share frame lines, creating a vast network of silk (below).

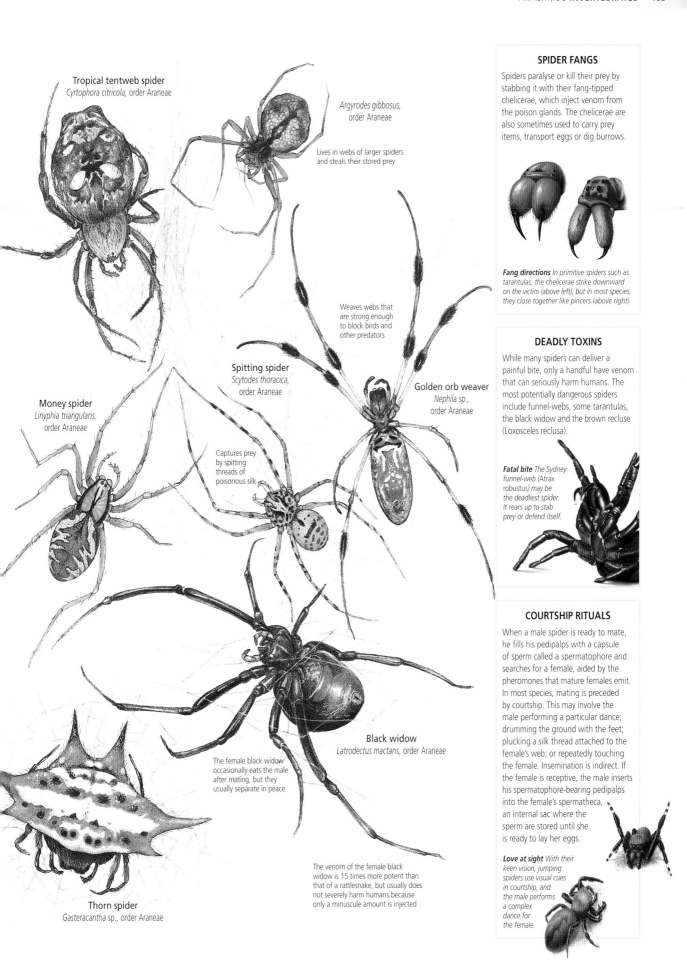

Tropical tentweb spider
Cyrtophora citricola, order Araneae

Argyrodes gibbosus,
order Araneae

Lives in webs of larger spiders
and steals their stored prey

Weaves webs that
are strong enough
to block birds and
other predators

Spitting spider
Scytodes thoracica,
order Araneae

Golden orb weaver
Nephila sp.,
order Araneae

Money spider
Linyphia triangularis,
order Araneae

Captures prey
by spitting
threads of
poisonous silk

The female black widow
occasionally eats the male
after mating, but they
usually separate in peace

Black widow
Latrodectus mactans, order Araneae

The venom of the female black
widow is 15 times more potent than
that of a rattlesnake, but usually does
not severely harm humans because
only a minuscule amount is injected

Thorn spider
Gasteracantha sp., order Araneae

SPIDER FANGS

Spiders paralyse or kill their prey by
stabbing it with their fang-tipped
chelicerae, which inject venom from
the poison glands. The chelicerae are
also sometimes used to carry prey
items, transport eggs or dig burrows.

Fang directions *In primitive spiders such as
tarantulas, the chelicerae strike downward
on the victim (above left), but in most species,
they close together like pincers (above right).*

DEADLY TOXINS

While many spiders can deliver a
painful bite, only a handful have venom
that can seriously harm humans. The
most potentially dangerous spiders
include funnel-webs, some tarantulas,
the black widow and the brown recluse
(*Loxosceles reclusa*).

Fatal bite *The Sydney
funnel-web (*Atrax
robustus*) may be
the deadliest spider.
It rears up to stab
prey or defend itself.*

COURTSHIP RITUALS

When a male spider is ready to mate,
he fills his pedipalps with a capsule
of sperm called a spermatophore and
searches for a female, aided by the
pheromones that mature females emit.
In most species, mating is preceded
by courtship. This may involve the
male performing a particular dance;
drumming the ground with the feet;
plucking a silk thread attached to the
female's web; or repeatedly touching
the female. Insemination is indirect. If
the female is receptive, the male inserts
his spermatophore-bearing pedipalps
into the female's spermatheca,
an internal sac where the
sperm are stored until she
is ready to lay her eggs.

Love at sight *With their
keen vision, jumping
spiders use visual cues
in courtship, and
the male performs
a complex
dance for
the female.*

FACT FILE

Order Opiliones The harvestmen, or daddy-longlegs, in this order differ from spiders in that they lack venom glands, silk glands and a waist. Most species have very long, fine legs. Unlike most other arthropods, fertilisation is direct, with the male using a penis to deposit sperm in the female.

Species 5,000

Worldwide; in leaf litter & under stones

Bringing in the harvest *The harvestman Phalangium opilio looks for small arthropods in the leaf litter. It is also common in crops, where it feeds on pests such as aphids.*

Subclass Acari Classified in seven orders in the subclass Acari, mites and ticks are the most varied and abundant arachnids. They flourish in almost every kind of habitat, from polar caps to deserts, thermal springs to ocean trenches. With some species small enough to live inside a human hair follicle, mites are so tiny that they are rarely noticed. Ticks tend to be larger, but rarely exceed 1cm (½ inch) in length. Mites and ticks have only six legs when they hatch as larvae and acquire an extra pair as nymphs before becoming adults.

Species 30,000

Worldwide

Dust to dust *Flour mites (Acarus siro) are found living in the dust of grain crops, in animal cages, and in food stores.*

DISEASE SPREADERS

While most members of Acari are free-living inhabitants of soil, leaf litter and water, some are parasites of other animals or plants. Those mites and ticks that feed on vertebrates often transmit bacteria that cause potentially fatal diseases in humans. Several species of ticks also commonly trigger acute paralysis in humans and domestic animals.

Sick tick
The European castor bean tick (Ixodes ricinus) infests livestock, dogs and humans, and can spread Lyme disease and other illnesses.

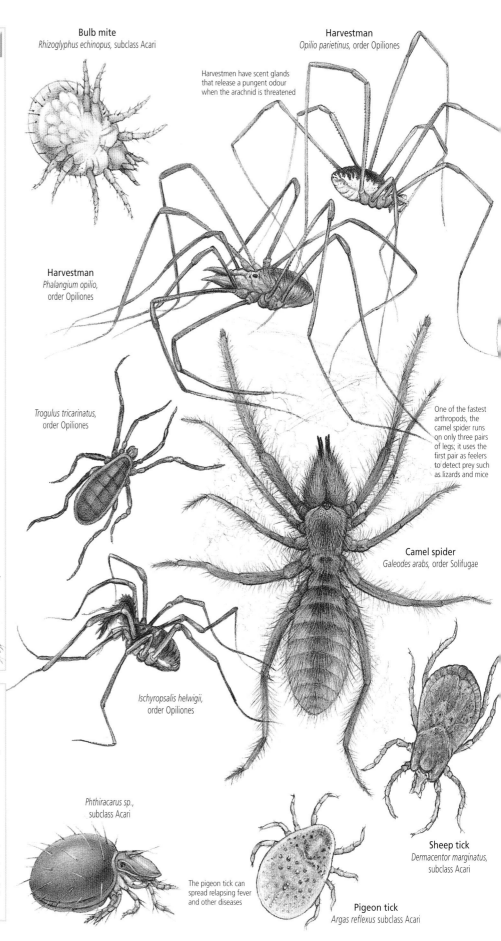

Bulb mite
Rhizoglyphus echinopus, subclass Acari

Harvestman
Opilio parietinus, order Opiliones

Harvestmen have scent glands that release a pungent odour when the arachnid is threatened

Harvestman
Phalangium opilio,
order Opiliones

Trogulus tricarinatus,
order Opiliones

One of the fastest arthropods, the camel spider runs on only three pairs of legs; it uses the first pair as feelers to detect prey such as lizards and mice

Camel spider
Galeodes arabs, order Solifugae

Ischyropsalis helwigii,
order Opiliones

Phthiracarus sp.,
subclass Acari

The pigeon tick can spread relapsing fever and other diseases

Sheep tick
Dermacentor marginatus,
subclass Acari

Pigeon tick
Argas reflexus subclass Acari

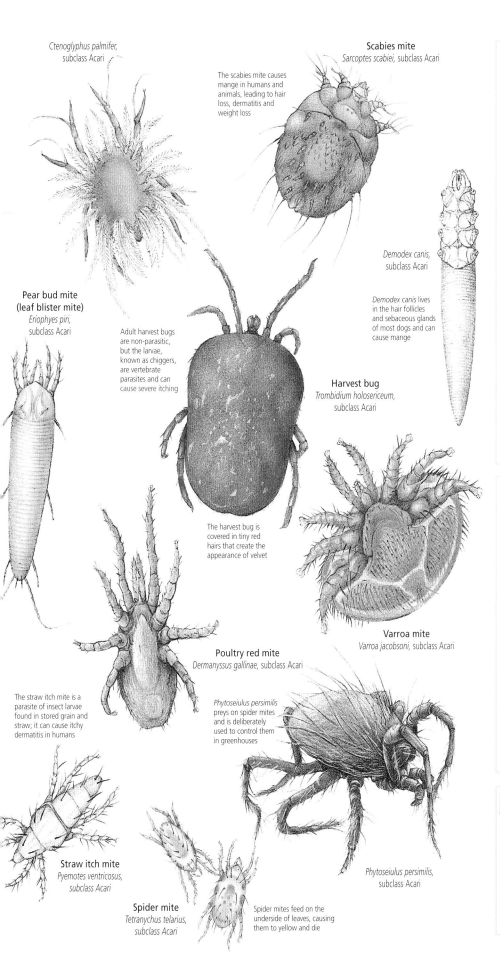

Ctenoglyphus palmifer,
subclass Acari

Scabies mite
Sarcoptes scabiei, subclass Acari

The scabies mite causes
mange in humans and
animals, leading to hair
loss, dermatitis and
weight loss

Demodex canis,
subclass Acari

Demodex canis lives
in the hair follicles
and sebaceous glands
of most dogs and can
cause mange

**Pear bud mite
(leaf blister mite)**
Eriophyes piri,
subclass Acari

Adult harvest bugs
are non-parasitic,
but the larvae,
known as chiggers,
are vertebrate
parasites and can
cause severe itching

Harvest bug
Trombidium holosericeum,
subclass Acari

The harvest bug is
covered in tiny red
hairs that create the
appearance of velvet

Varroa mite
Varroa jacobsoni, subclass Acari

The straw itch mite is a
parasite of insect larvae
found in stored grain and
straw; it can cause itchy
dermatitis in humans

Poultry red mite
Dermanyssus gallinae, subclass Acari

Phytoseiulus persimilis
preys on spider mites
and is deliberately
used to control them
in greenhouses

Straw itch mite
Pyemotes ventricosus,
subclass Acari

Phytoseiulus persimilis,
subclass Acari

Spider mite
Tetranychus telarius,
subclass Acari

Spider mites feed on the
underside of leaves, causing
them to yellow and die

AQUATIC MITES

Some mites have adapted to a life in
water. They are found in every kind
of freshwater habitat, from puddles to
deep lakes, hot springs to raging rivers.
Some have also colonised the ocean,
where they live on mudflats, coral
reefs, and the sea floor, absent only
from open waters. While semiaquatic
mites are found in many groups within
Acari, more than 40 families of fully
aquatic mites are gathered in the
subcohort Hydracarina. These mites lay
their eggs underwater on stones or
plants or in sponges or mussels. The
larvae are parasitic and quickly attach
themselves to an invertebrate host.
As the host is often a flying insect such
as a dragonfly, it not only provides the
mite larva with food, but also disperses
it to a new body of water. As nymphs
and adults, water mites are predators
and feed on other mites, aquatic
insects and crustaceans.

Bright warning
Water mites such as
Brachypoda versicolour
*often display bright
colours, possibly to
warn fishes and other
predators that they
are distasteful.*

HONEYBEE THREAT

A honeybee colony can be severely
harmed or even killed by the varroa
mite (*Varroa jacobsoni*). An adult
female mite moves into a honeybee's
brood cell to lay her eggs. Both the
mite and her hatched offspring then
feed on the bee larva as it matures.
The mite offspring mate while still in
the brood cell. The males then die,
but the females emerge attached to
the young adult bee. The female mites
then find another brood cell where
they can deposit their eggs.
Parasitised honeybee
pupae tend to emerge
as weak, deformed adults.

Snug fit *The varroa
mite usually inserts itself
between the honeybee's
body segments, making
it difficult to see.*

⚡ CONSERVATION WATCH

Arachnid alert The conservation
movement has paid little attention
to arachnids. Only 18 species have
been assessed by the IUCN, but all
of these are on the Red List. Further
research is needed, but arachnid
diversity is no doubt threatened
by habitat loss, pollution, pesticide
use and invasive exotic species.

HORSESHOE CRABS

PHYLUM	Arthropoda
SUBPHYLUM	Chelicerata
CLASS	Merostomata
ORDER	Xiphosura
FAMILY	Limulidae
SPECIES	4

More closely related to arachnids than to crustaceans, the horseshoe crabs of the class Merostomata have changed little in the past 200 million years. The four living species, found off the east coasts of North America and Asia, are marine. Their body is made up of a cephalothorax and abdomen, each protected by a hard shell. The horseshoe-shaped cephalothorax bears the pincer-like chelicerae, which are used for seizing worms and other prey from the muddy sea floor, and five pairs of legs, used for both walking and handling food. The formidable tail spine, or telson, does not act as a weapon but helps the horseshoe crab to right itself and to plow through mud.

Can grow 60cm
(2 feet) long

Horseshoe crab
Limulus polyphemus

Time to breed
Breeding horseshoe crabs gather on beaches in spring. The eggs are buried in the sand just below the high-tide mark, where they stay moist but are warmed by the sun.

SEA AND SHORE

Horseshoe crabs spend most of their time on the sea floor at depths of about 30m (100 feet), breathing through book gills on the abdomen. They push through mud, and can also swim on their back and walk.

In spring, horseshoe crabs come ashore to breed. A male will cling onto a female's back as she makes her way over the tidal zone. The female scoops out holes in the sand and lays up to 300 eggs in each, and the male then covers the eggs with sperm to fertilise them. The larvae reach adulthood after about 16 moults over 9 to 12 years.

SEA SPIDERS

PHYLUM	Arthropoda
SUBPHYLUM	Chelicerata
CLASS	Pycnogonida
ORDER	Pantopoda
FAMILIES	9
SPECIES	1,000

With their long legs, sea spiders bear a superficial resemblance to spiders, but they evolved separately and have many unique features. A sea spider's body is greatly reduced. The small head region, known as the cephalon, holds a long proboscis with the mouth; four simple eyes on a stalk; and, usually, two chelicerae (to grasp prey) and two pedipalps (used as sensors). It also bears the first pair of walking legs and a pair of appendages called ovigers, used for grooming and egg-carrying. A segmented trunk holds another three pairs of legs, and leads to a tiny abdomen at the rear. Because the abdomen is so small, the digestive and reproductive organs extend into the legs.

Antarctic forms Both the red sea spider (*Pycnogonum decalopoda*) and the smaller spider (*P. nymphon*) live under the sea ice.

BOTTOM-DWELLERS

Sea spiders live in every ocean, from warm, shallow waters to icy depths of 7,000m (23,000 feet). Most are small, but some deep-sea species have a leg-span of up to 70cm (28 inches). Although some sea spiders can swim, most are bottom-dwellers and feed on soft-bodied invertebrates such as sponges and corals.

To breed, a female sea spider releases her eggs into the water and the male covers them with sperm. The male then carries the fertilised eggs on his ovigers until they hatch.

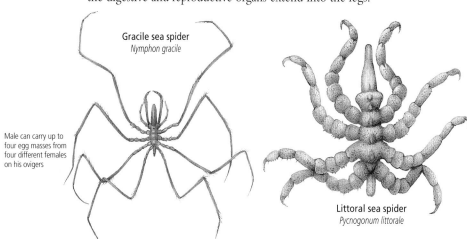

Gracile sea spider
Nymphon gracile

Male can carry up to four egg masses from four different females on his ovigers

Littoral sea spider
Pycnogonum littorale

MYRIAPODS

YLUM Arthropoda

BPHYLUM Myriapoda

ASSES 4

DERS 20

MILIES 140

ECIES 13,500

Centipedes (class Chilopoda), millipedes (class Diplopoda), symphylids (class Symphyla) and pauropods (class Pauropoda) are all myriapods with long, segmented bodies; simple eyes; a pair of jointed antennae; and numerous pairs of legs. Most centipedes are carnivores and hunt through leaf litter for other small invertebrates. They paralyse prey with a pair of venomous fangs on the underside of the head that can deliver a nasty bite even to humans. Millipedes are plant-feeders and do not bite, but many react to danger by curling into a coil and emitting a toxic substance. Resembling tiny centipedes, symphylids and pauropods live in leaf litter and soil and feed on decaying plant matter.

Tropical species Centipedes are most diverse in tropical forests. Their many legs can be short and hooked, or long and slender. The final pair may be antenna-like (as in the *Scutigera* sp. above) or pincer-like.

Coiled defence A forest log millipede (*Narceus americanus*) has curled into the typical millipede defensive posture that leaves only the tough, calcareous plates of its exoskeleton exposed. It may also squirt out a pungent, irritating liquid.

MANY LEGS

Centipedes have flattened, worm-like bodies, with one pair of legs attached to each body segment except the last. They have at least 15 and as many as 191 pairs of legs. The largest centipede, *Scolopendra gigantea* of the American tropics, can grow to 28cm (11 inches) long. It is strong enough to prey on mice, frogs and other small vertebrates.

A millipede's body is rounded and made up of doubled segments known as diplosomites, most of which bear double pairs of legs. Millipedes range from 2mm–28cm (½ inch–11 inches) long, and have up to 200 pairs of legs.

Measuring no more than 1cm (½ inch) in length, symphylids have 12 pairs of legs. Pauropods are even smaller, at less than ½ inch (2 mm) long, and bear nine pairs of legs.

Most myriapods are nocturnal, live in moist forests and tend to be hidden in leaf litter or soil or under rocks or logs. Some species, however, are found in grasslands or deserts. Millipedes usually lay their eggs in a soil nest, while some centipedes curl around their eggs and young to protect them.

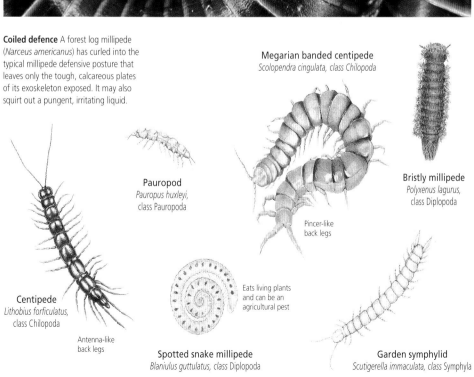

Pauropod
Pauropus huxleyi,
class Pauropoda

Megarian banded centipede
Scolopendra cingulata, class Chilopoda

Bristly millipede
Polyxenus lagurus,
class Diplopoda

Pincer-like
back legs

Centipede
Lithobius forficulatus,
class Chilopoda

Antenna-like
back legs

Eats living plants
and can be an
agricultural pest

Spotted snake millipede
Blaniulus guttulatus, class Diplopoda

Garden symphylid
Scutigerella immaculata, class Symphyla

CRUSTACEANS

PHYLUM	Arthropoda
SUBPHYLUM	Crustacea
CLASSES	11
ORDERS	37
FAMILIES	540
SPECIES	42,000

From water fleas less than 0.25mm (¹⁄₁₀₀ inch) long, to giant spider crabs with legs spanning 3.7m (12 feet), crustaceans are an extraordinarily diverse group. Although some species have adopted a terrestrial lifestyle, it is in aquatic environments that crustaceans have flourished, gradually evolving to exploit every marine and freshwater niche. Free-swimming planktonic species, such as krill, form the basis of vast aquatic food webs. Crabs and other bottom-dwellers may burrow into or crawl over the sediment. Barnacles remain cemented in place, filtering food from the water. There are also parasitic crustaceans, some of which exist in their adult form as a collection of cells inside the host.

LAND INVADERS

While crustaceans are abundant in water, only a minority have adapted to life on land. These tend to live in damp places and some return to water to breed. Sometimes known as pill bugs or sow bugs, the wood lice of family Oniscoidea are the most terrestrial crustaceans and even include a few desert species. Some wood lice curl into a tight ball when threatened (below). The limited exploitation by crustaceans of land habitats can be attributed to the lack of a waxy, water-tight cuticle and the reliance on gills for breathing.

Attractive claw In many crustaceans, the first pair of limbs has been modified to form claws known as chelipeds. As a male fiddler crab (*Uca* sp.) (above) matures, the right cheliped grows disproportionately, until it accounts for 65 per cent of the crab's total weight. The crab waves this huge claw to attract mates and intimidate rival males. It may also use it to make sounds that entice females into its burrow.

CRUSTACEAN ANATOMY

Like other arthropods, crustaceans have a segmented body, jointed legs and an exoskeleton, and grow by moulting. The exoskeleton can be thin and flexible, as in water fleas, or rigid and calcified, as in crabs. The body usually has three regions – head, thorax, and abdomen – but in many of the larger species, the head and thorax form a cephalothorax, which is protected by a shield-like carapace. The abdomen often has a tail-like extension called a telson.

A typical crustacean's head holds two pairs of antennae; a pair of compound eyes, often on stalks; and three pairs of biting mouthparts. The thorax and sometimes the abdomen carry the limbs, each of which usually has two branches. In many species, particular limbs have become specialised for walking, swimming, food collection, or defence. Crabs, for example, have modified their first pair into claws called chelipeds.

While some female crustaceans lay eggs in water, many brood eggs on their body. The eggs of some species hatch into free-swimming nauplius larvae, with two pairs of antennae, a pair of mandibles and a single simple eye. In most species, the eggs hatch at a more advanced stage or even as miniature adults.

Shrimp design Like most crustaceans, shrimps have two pairs of antennae, the second of which is highly mobile; a pair of compound eyes, each with as many as 30,000 lenses; and specialised limbs. A shrimp's blood is pumped by a heart, and it breathes through gills attached to its legs.

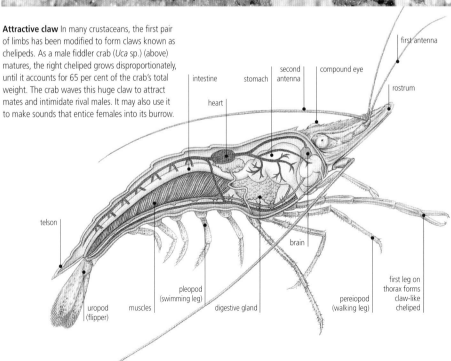

intestine · stomach · second antenna · compound eye · first antenna · rostrum · heart · brain · telson · uropod (flipper) · muscles · pleopod (swimming leg) · digestive gland · pereiopod (walking leg) · first leg on thorax forms claw-like cheliped

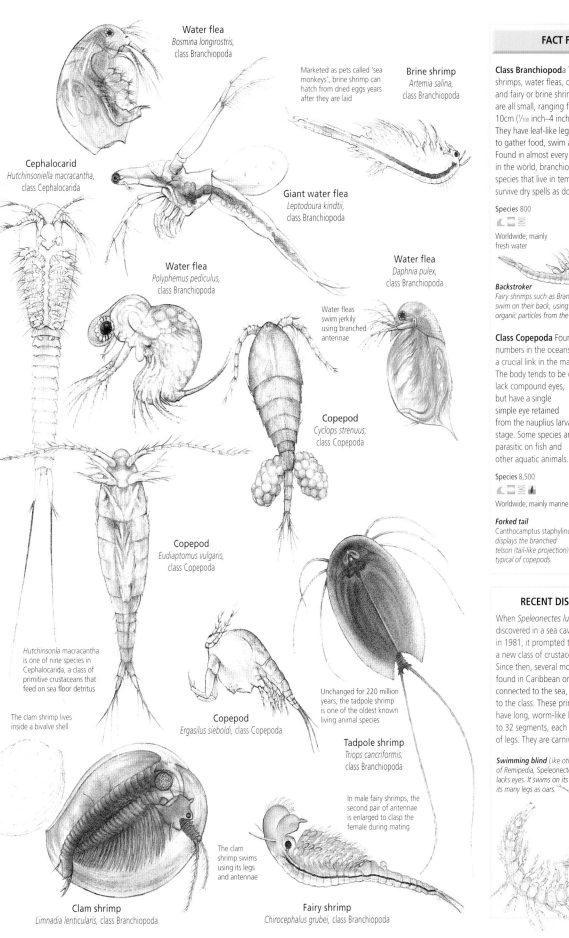

Water flea
Bosmina longirostris,
class Branchiopoda

Marketed as pets called 'sea monkeys', brine shrimp can hatch from dried eggs years after they are laid

Brine shrimp
Artemia salina,
class Branchiopoda

Cephalocarid
Hutchinsoniella macracantha,
class Cephalocarida

Giant water flea
Leptodoura kindtii,
class Branchiopoda

Water flea
Polyphemus pediculus,
class Branchiopoda

Water flea
Daphnia pulex,
class Branchiopoda

Water fleas swim jerkily using branched antennae

Copepod
Cyclops strenuus,
class Copepoda

Copepod
Eudiaptomus vulgaris,
class Copepoda

Hutchinsonia macracantha is one of nine species in Cephalocarida, a class of primitive crustaceans that feed on sea floor detritus

The clam shrimp lives inside a bivalve shell

Copepod
Ergasilus sieboldi, class Copepoda

Unchanged for 220 million years, the tadpole shrimp is one of the oldest known living animal species

Tadpole shrimp
Triops cancriformis,
class Branchiopoda

In male fairy shrimps, the second pair of antennae is enlarged to clasp the female during mating

The clam shrimp swims using its legs and antennae

Clam shrimp
Limnadia lenticularis, class Branchiopoda

Fairy shrimp
Chirocephalus grubei, class Branchiopoda

FACT FILE

Class Branchiopoda The tadpole shrimps, water fleas, clam shrimps, and fairy or brine shrimps in this class are all small, ranging from 0.25mm–10cm ($\frac{1}{100}$ inch–4 inches) in length. They have leaf-like legs, which they use to gather food, swim and breathe. Found in almost every freshwater body in the world, branchiopods include species that live in temporary pools and survive dry spells as dormant eggs.

Species 800

Worldwide; mainly fresh water

Backstroker
Fairy shrimps such as Branchipus stagnalis swim on their back, using their legs to filter organic particles from the water.

Class Copepoda Found in vast numbers in the oceans, copepods are a crucial link in the marine food web. The body tends to be cylindrical. They lack compound eyes, but have a single simple eye retained from the nauplius larval stage. Some species are parasitic on fish and other aquatic animals.

Species 8,500

Worldwide; mainly marine

Forked tail
Canthocamptus staphylinus *displays the branched telson (tail-like projection) typical of copepods.*

RECENT DISCOVERY

When *Speleonectes lucayensis* was discovered in a sea cave in the Bahamas in 1981, it prompted the description of a new class of crustacean, Remipedia. Since then, several more species, all found in Caribbean or Australian caves connected to the sea, have been added to the class. These primitive forms have long, worm-like bodies with up to 32 segments, each bearing a pair of legs. They are carnivorous.

Swimming blind Like other members of Remipedia, Speleonectes lucayensis lacks eyes. It swims on its back using its many legs as oars.

FACT FILE

Class Cirripedia The only sessile group of crustaceans, the barnacles that make up the class Cirripedia are entirely marine. Barnacles were believed to be molluscs until 1830, when it was discovered that they hatch from eggs as free-swimming nauplius larvae and therefore are crustaceans. The larvae mature and cement themselves head-down to rocks or boats or to hosts such as fish, turtles and whales. Most adult barnacles are protected by calcareous plates and collect food particles from the water with their long, feathery legs (cirri). Barnacles are hermaphrodites. They live in tightly packed communities and can internally fertilise one another.

Species 900

Worldwide; in marine waters

Class Ostracoda Known as mussel shrimps or seed shrimps, the members of this class are distinguished by their carapace, which takes the form of a hinged, bivalve shell. Only the antennae and end bristles of the legs emerge from the shell.

Species 6,000

Worldwide; in all types of water bodies

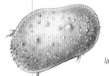

Self-reproducing
The ostracod Ilyocypris gibba can reproduce sexually but most often uses parthogenesis, with larvae developing from unfertilised eggs.

TOTAL INVASION

The parasite *Sacculina carcini* can only be recognised as a barnacle by its free-swimming nauplius larvae. When a female larva has matured, it invades a host, usually the green crab (*Carcinus maenas*). The larva metamorphoses into a needle-like form that injects cells into the host. The cells form a root-like system, called an interna, throughout the crab's body. The interna eventually develops a reproductive body, an externa, outside the crab. Male larvae attach to the externa, into which they release cells that develop into sperm. Fertilisation results in nauplius larvae.

Freshwater fish louse
Argulus foliaceus, class Branchiura

Adult fish lice parasitise freshwater fish, feeding on the skin or in the gills of the host and causing tissue damage

Ostracod
Cypris pubera, class Ostracoda

Like other members of the small class Mystacocarida, Derocheilocaris remanei lives among sand grains in the intertidal zone

Mystarocarid
Derocheilocaris remanei, class Mystacocarida

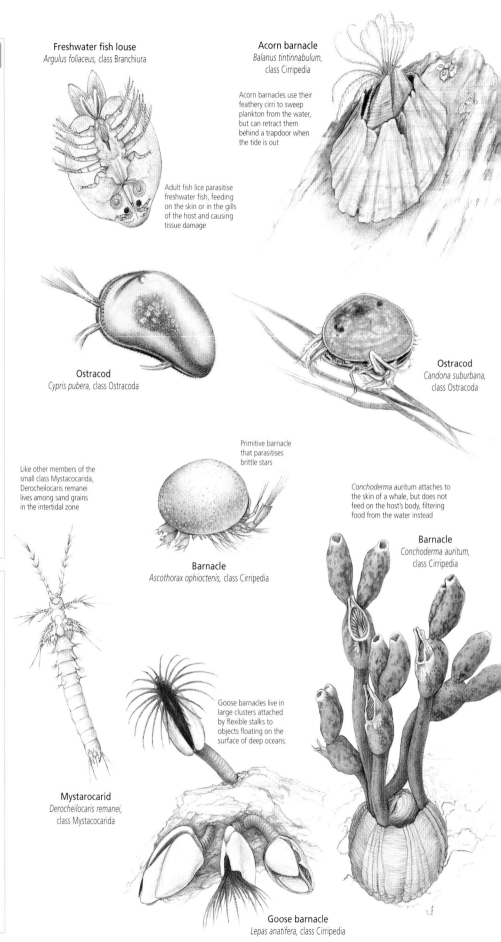

Acorn barnacle
Balanus tintinnabulum, class Cirripedia

Acorn barnacles use their feathery cirri to sweep plankton from the water, but can retract them behind a trapdoor when the tide is out

Ostracod
Candona suburbana, class Ostracoda

Primitive barnacle that parasitises brittle stars

Barnacle
Ascothorax ophioctenis, class Cirripedia

Conchoderma auritum attaches to the skin of a whale, but does not feed on the host's body, filtering food from the water instead

Barnacle
Conchoderma auritum, class Cirripedia

Goose barnacles live in large clusters attached by flexible stalks to objects floating on the surface of deep oceans.

Goose barnacle
Lepas anatifera, class Cirripedia

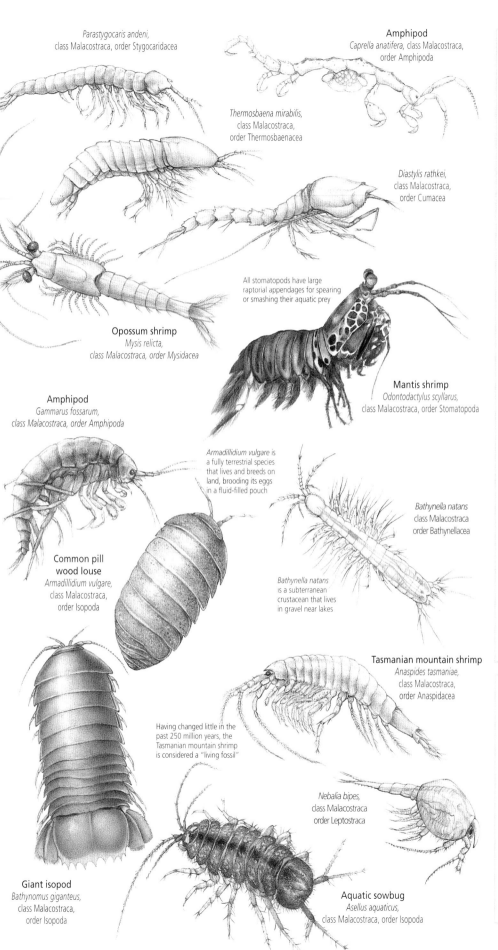

Parastygocaris andeni,
class Malacostraca, order Stygocaridacea

Amphipod
Caprella anatifera, class Malacostraca,
order Amphipoda

Thermosbaena mirabilis,
class Malacostraca,
order Thermosbaenacea

Diastylis rathkei,
class Malacostraca,
order Cumacea

All stomatopods have large
raptorial appendages for spearing
or smashing their aquatic prey

Opossum shrimp
Mysis relicta,
class Malacostraca, order Mysidacea

Mantis shrimp
Odontodactylus scyllarus,
class Malacostraca, order Stomatopoda

Amphipod
Gammarus fossarum,
class Malacostraca, order Amphipoda

Armadillidium vulgare is
a fully terrestrial species
that lives and breeds on
land, brooding its eggs
in a fluid-filled pouch

Bathynella natans
class Malacostraca
order Bathynellacea

**Common pill
wood louse**
Armadillidium vulgare,
class Malacostraca,
order Isopoda

Bathynella natans
is a subterranean
crustacean that lives
in gravel near lakes

Tasmanian mountain shrimp
Anaspides tasmaniae,
class Malacostraca,
order Anaspidacea

Having changed little in the
past 250 million years, the
Tasmanian mountain shrimp
is considered a "living fossil"

Nebalia bipes,
class Malacostraca
order Leptostraca

Giant isopod
Bathynomus giganteus,
class Malacostraca,
order Isopoda

Aquatic sowbug
Asellus aquaticus,
class Malacostraca, order Isopoda

FACT FILE

Class Malacostraca By far the largest
class of crustaceans, Malacostraca
contains 13 orders. Almost all species
have six head segments, eight thoracic
segments and six abdominal segments.
Except for the first head segment, each
segment usually bears two appendages.

Species 25,000

Worldwide; mainly aquatic

*Familiar crustaceans The
class Malacostraca includes
Daum's reef lobster (Enoplometopus
daumi), which joins other lobsters,
crabs, and shrimps in the order Decapoda.*

Order Amphipoda These small,
widespread members of the class
Malacostraca are found in marine,
freshwater and moist terrestrial
habitats. An amphipod's
body is usually flattened
laterally, often creating
a shrimp-like appearance.

Species 6,000

Worldwide; mainly aquatic

*Varied salinities The amphipod Corophium
volutator lives in U-shaped burrows in
saltwater, brackish and freshwater habitats.*

Order Isopoda Like amphipods,
isopods belong to Malacostraca. Their
bodies are flattened dorsoventrally
(from the back to the belly). They
include the truly terrestrial wood lice,
but most species crawl along the
bottom of aquatic habitats.

Species 4,000

Worldwide; mainly marine

*Aquatic isopod Like amphipods,
isopods such as Astacilla pusilla
lack a carapace. Most are
aquatic and can crawl and
swim. They tend to be omnivorous scavengers.*

PREDACIOUS EYES

The Stomatopoda is a highly specialised
order in the class Malacostraca. Known
as mantis shrimp, its members actively
prey on fish, crabs and molluscs. Their
success as predators depends not only
on their raptorial appendages, but also
on their complex compound eyes.

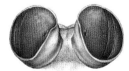

*Stomatopod vision Each compound eye is
divided by a band that provides colour vision
and also sees polarised light (contrast). The
rest of the eye provides monochromatic
vision and depth perception (perspective).*

FACT FILE

Order Decapoda Named after their five pairs of thoracic legs, decapods account for about one-quarter of all crustacean species. They can be divided into swimmers, which include shrimps, and crawlers, which include lobsters, crayfish and crabs. In many species, the first pair of legs, the chelipeds, form heavy pincers and are used to capture prey. Some species, however, are filte feeders, detritus-feeders or plant-feeders. Typically, decapods carry their fertilised eggs on their body. Most larvae hatch as a zoea, a tiny organism that is mostly head with appendages and a long spine out front.

Species 8,000

Worldwide; mainly marine

Noisy crab A male fiddler crab (Uca tangeri) can make a range of drumming, rasping and honking sounds by moving its oversized right cheliped against other parts of its body or the ground.

CRUCIAL KRILL

The small order Euphausiacea comprises about 85 species of krill, planktonic creatures with a shrimp-like body form. They are a crucial link in marine food webs, particularly in the Antarctic, where the southern krill (Euphausia superba) is the keystone species. Krill usually spend the day in the ocean depths, but gather in vast swarms at the surface to feed at night. Most species are filter-feeders and collect phytoplankton with their fringed legs. They may also prey on copepods. In turn, krill are the staple food of many fishes, squids, seabirds, baleen whales and seals. Many krill species have special light-producing organs. Their bioluminescence probably helps them form swarms and find mates.

Southern krill The biomass of Euphausia superba may be about 800 million tonnes (900 million tons) – more than that of Earth's human population. A southern krill is able to grow 6cm (2½ inches) long and lives for 5 to10 years.

Northern krill The dominant krill species in the North Atlantic is the northern krill (Meganyctiphanes norvegica).

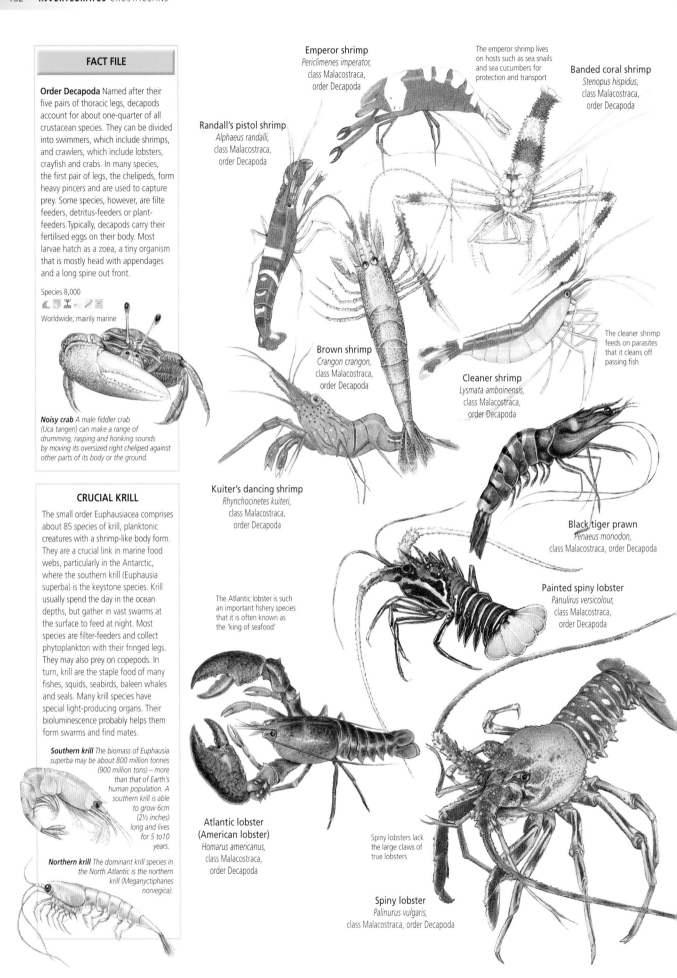

Emperor shrimp
Periclimenes imperator,
class Malacostraca,
order Decapoda

The emperor shrimp lives on hosts such as sea snails and sea cucumbers for protection and transport

Banded coral shrimp
Stenopus hispidus,
class Malacostraca,
order Decapoda

Randall's pistol shrimp
Alpheus randalli,
class Malacostraca,
order Decapoda

Brown shrimp
Crangon crangon,
class Malacostraca,
order Decapoda

The cleaner shrimp feeds on parasites that it cleans off passing fish

Cleaner shrimp
Lysmata amboinensis,
class Malacostraca,
order Decapoda

Kuiter's dancing shrimp
Rhynchocinetes kuiteri,
class Malacostraca,
order Decapoda

Black tiger prawn
Penaeus monodon,
class Malacostraca, order Decapoda

The Atlantic lobster is such an important fishery species that it is often known as the 'king of seafood'

Painted spiny lobster
Panulirus versicolour,
class Malacostraca,
order Decapoda

**Atlantic lobster
(American lobster)**
Homarus americanus,
class Malacostraca,
order Decapoda

Spiny lobsters lack the large claws of true lobsters

Spiny lobster
Palinurus vulgaris,
class Malacostraca, order Decapoda

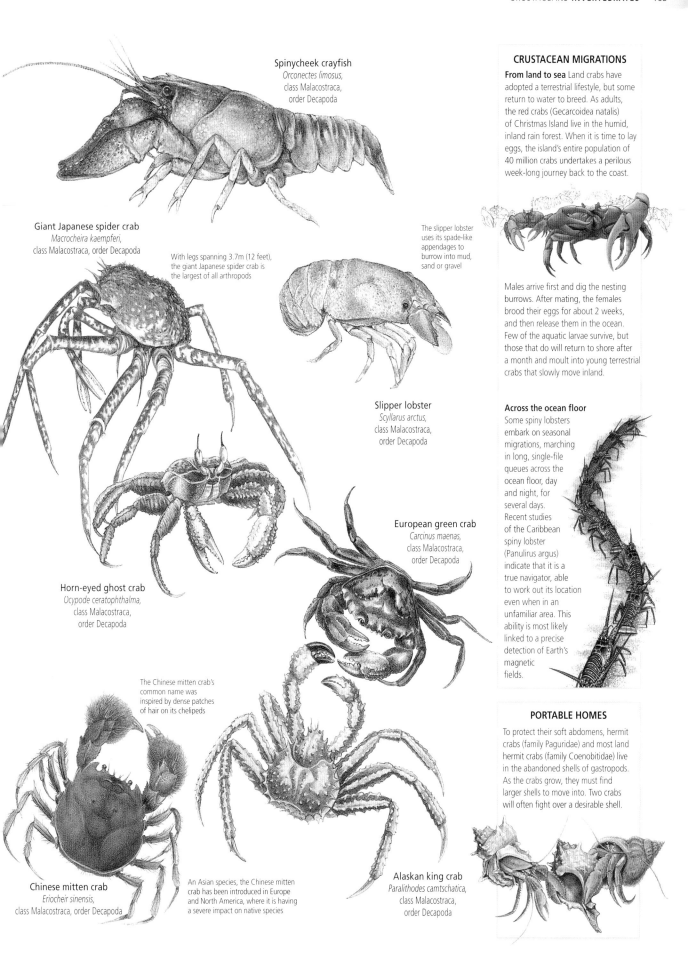

Spinycheek crayfish
Orconectes limosus,
class Malacostraca,
order Decapoda

Giant Japanese spider crab
Macrocheira kaempferi,
class Malacostraca, order Decapoda

With legs spanning 3.7m (12 feet),
the giant Japanese spider crab is
the largest of all arthropods

The slipper lobster
uses its spade-like
appendages to
burrow into mud,
sand or gravel

Slipper lobster
Scyllarus arctus,
class Malacostraca,
order Decapoda

Horn-eyed ghost crab
Ocypode ceratophthalma,
class Malacostraca,
order Decapoda

European green crab
Carcinus maenas,
class Malacostraca,
order Decapoda

The Chinese mitten crab's
common name was
inspired by dense patches
of hair on its chelipeds

Chinese mitten crab
Eriocheir sinensis,
class Malacostraca, order Decapoda

An Asian species, the Chinese mitten
crab has been introduced in Europe
and North America, where it is having
a severe impact on native species

Alaskan king crab
Paralithodes camtschatica,
class Malacostraca,
order Decapoda

CRUSTACEAN MIGRATIONS

From land to sea Land crabs have
adopted a terrestrial lifestyle, but some
return to water to breed. As adults,
the red crabs (Gecarcoidea natalis)
of Christmas Island live in the humid,
inland rain forest. When it is time to lay
eggs, the island's entire population of
40 million crabs undertakes a perilous
week-long journey back to the coast.

Males arrive first and dig the nesting
burrows. After mating, the females
brood their eggs for about 2 weeks,
and then release them in the ocean.
Few of the aquatic larvae survive, but
those that do will return to shore after
a month and moult into young terrestrial
crabs that slowly move inland.

Across the ocean floor
Some spiny lobsters
embark on seasonal
migrations, marching
in long, single-file
queues across the
ocean floor, day
and night, for
several days.
Recent studies
of the Caribbean
spiny lobster
(Panulirus argus)
indicate that it is a
true navigator, able
to work out its location
even when in an
unfamiliar area. This
ability is most likely
linked to a precise
detection of Earth's
magnetic
fields.

PORTABLE HOMES

To protect their soft abdomens, hermit
crabs (family Paguridae) and most land
hermit crabs (family Coenobitidae) live
in the abandoned shells of gastropods.
As the crabs grow, they must find
larger shells to move into. Two crabs
will often fight over a desirable shell.

INSECTS

PHYLUM	Arthropoda
SUBPHYLUM	Hexapoda
CLASS	Insecta
ORDERS	29
FAMILIES	949
SPECIES	>1 million

By most measures, insects are the most successful animals ever to have lived on Earth. With about a million described species, they account for more than half of all known animal species, and many more insects are still to be discovered, with estimates of the total number of insect species ranging from 2 million to 30 million. In terms of sheer numbers, insects overwhelm all other animal forms: some scientists believe that ants and termites alone make up 20 per cent of the world's animal biomass. Some form of insect has managed to colonise the hottest deserts and the coldest polar zones, as well as virtually every land and freshwater habitat in between, and a handful live in the sea.

Extreme habitats Brine flies (family Ephydridae) are found along the shores of California's salty Mono Lake, where their larvae feed on algae. Other insects have been found living in pools of crude oil, in hot springs, and in the ice of Antarctica.

Parental guard Most insects display little parental care, depositing large numbers of eggs and then leaving them to hatch by themselves. Some shield bugs, however, will guard their eggs and then stay with the nymphs until at least their first moult.

Pollinators Pollen sticks to a honeybee as it drinks nectar from a flower. When the bee visits the next flower, some pollen will be dislodged. Most flowering plants rely on insects for pollination and have evolved flowers with different shapes, colours, and odours to attract particular species and force them to collect pollen as they feed.

CONSERVATION WATCH

Of the 1 million known species of insects, only 768 have been assessed by the IUCN. Of these, 97 per cent are listed on the Red List, as follows:

70	Extinct, or extinct in wild
46	Critically endangered
118	Endangered
389	Vulnerable
3	Conservation dependent
76	Near threatened
42	Data deficient

SUCCESS STORY

Insects owe their incredible success to various aspects of their biology. Their tough, flexible exoskeleton provides protection without overly restricting movement. It is covered in a waxy coating that minimises moisture loss, enabling insects to survive in dry conditions.

As the first creatures and the only invertebrates ever to develop powered flight, insects were able to find both food and mates, evade their predators and colonise new areas with great efficiency. In most species, the wings can be folded over the body when at rest, so that the insect can exploit confined spaces inside bark, dung, leaf litter or soil, for example.

Insects breathe through spiracles, small openings in the sides of their body that can be closed to prevent moisture loss. Rather than being transported around the body in the blood, oxygen is distributed directly into the body tissues by a series of tiny pipes known as tracheae. This method of gas diffusion works well only over short distances, which may be the main reason insects have remained small. Most insects are no more than a few centimetres (an inch or two) long. Their small size allowed insects to take advantage of a wide range of microhabitats, a major factor in their great diversity.

Sensory organs are scattered over an insect's body. The head usually has two compound eyes as well as three simple eyes, or ocelli. The two antennae can detect scent, taste, touch and sound. Hearing organs

Spontaneous young Scarab beetles (family Scarabaeidae) use their sturdy front legs to roll dung into a large ball that may be taken underground as food, or used by the female as a nest for her eggs. Possibly because the young seemed to suddenly erupt from the dung, scarab beetles were revered by the ancient Egyptians.

INSECT FLIGHT

While some insects are wingless, the vast majority are winged as adults. Beetles and grasshoppers fly with a slow wing beat of 4–20 beats per second (bps) and limited manoeuvrability. Bees and true flies, with wing beats of about 190 bps, can hover and dart. Some midges have wing beats of 1,000 bps. The fastest sustained fliers are dragonflies, which can maintain speeds of 50km per hour (31 mph).

Folding wings
The hindwings of a mantis fold up like fans when not in use. This protects the wings and allows the mantis to squeeze into tight spaces.

Purpose-built mouthparts The highly varied feeding habits of insects are reflected by the shape of their mouthparts. A moth (above) has a long, coiled tube, or proboscis, that can be unfurled to collect nectar. Mosquitoes have beaks that can pierce the skin of prey and suck up the body fluids, while aphids have piercing mouthparts for gathering plant juices. The mandibles, or jaws, of carnivorous insects such as ground beetles are sharp for cutting, while those of herbivores such as grasshoppers are adapted for grinding.

Insect anatomy While insects display a staggering diversity of shapes and forms, they follow the same basic body plan. Like other arthropods, insects have segmented bodies made up of a head, thorax and abdomen; segmented limbs; and a tough exoskeleton. They are distinguished by having three pairs of legs and, usually, two sets of wings, a single pair of antennae and a pair of compound eyes.

three ocelli (simple eyes) detect light variations

head carries eyes, a pair of antennae and mouthparts

one pair of compound eyes, each made up of 100–30,000 lenses

two pairs of wings supported by thickened veins

abdomen contains digestive and reproductive organs

antennae help insect smell, taste, feel and hear

thorax carries wings and legs

three pairs of segmented legs

Stabilizers
True flies appear to have only one pair of wings. In fact, the second pair has been reduced to knob-like structures called halteres that provide stability in flight.

Plumed wings
In thrips and plume moths, the wings look like tiny feathers and are made up of fine hairs supported by a midrib.

Hooked wings
Connected by tiny hooks, a wasp's forewings and hindwings move up and down in unison.

can also be on the body or legs. Other sensors detect changes in air pressure, humidity and temperature.

The life cycles of many insects allow for very rapid reproduction, enabling populations to respond quickly to favourable conditions and recover from catastrophes. Most insects use internal fertilisation, but the female is able to store the male's sperm and use it over time. Some insects, such as aphids, can reproduce without fertilisation to rapidly increase their numbers, but also use sexual reproduction to ensure genetic diversity. Insect eggs are protected by a shell-like membrane called the chorion that prevents them from drying out, another factor in the successful

colonisation of dry habitats. While some insects resemble small versions of their parents when they hatch, most do not and must go through some form of metamorphosis. The juveniles and adults often occupy different ecological niches and eat different foods, which helps to avoid competition between them.

Because some species can cause human discomfort, spread disease and destroy food stores and crops, insects are often regarded as pests. This ignores the fact that the vast majority of insects cause little harm and play a crucial role in the world's environments. About three-quarters of all flowering plants rely on insects for pollination, and many animals depend on insects for food.

Giant insect About the size of a small rat, New Zealand's giant weta (*Deinacrida heteracantha*) can weigh up to 70g (2½ ounces), making it among the heaviest of all insect species. The smallest insect species is probably the parasitic wasp Dicopomorpha echmepterygis, at 0.14mm (1/200 inch) long.

Separate wings
A dragonfly's forewings and hindwings can beat in unison or independently. As in early flying insects, the wings do not fold back over the body.

Protective wings
In lady beetles and other beetles, the forewings have been modified to form protective cases known as elytra. The hindwings are used for flying.

DRAGONFLIES AND DAMSELFLIES

PHYLUM	Arthropoda
SUBPHYLUM	Hexapoda
CLASS	Insecta
ORDER	Odonata
FAMILIES	30
SPECIES	5,500

The first members of the order Odonata emerged more than 300 million years ago – 100 million years before dinosaurs appeared – and included the largest insect that has ever lived, a dragonfly with a wingspan of 70cm (28 inches). Today's dragonflies and damselflies are much smaller, with wingspans from 18mm to 19cm (¾ inch to 7½ inches). Often seen flying near water, these voracious aerial predators are most abundant in the tropics, but can be found worldwide except for the polar zones. Damselflies have a fluttery flight and usually rest with the wings near the body, while dragonflies are strong, agile flyers and always rest with the wings held out from the body.

Sharp sight A dragonfly's large compound eyes may be made up of 30,000 lenses, providing superb vision and a wide field of view. Strong, biting mouthparts indicate the insect's carnivorous diet.

Odonate aerobatics With two pairs of large, veined wings that can beat together or independently, a dragonfly has great manoeuvrability and can hover and fly backward. Some species reach speeds of 30km per hour (20 mph).

Mating position To mate, a male odonate grasps a female's head with claspers at the tip of his abdomen (below). The female will then bend her abdomen under the male to collect sperm from his sperm pouch.

AQUATIC BEGINNINGS

A dragonfly or damselfly spends most of its life as a wingless aquatic nymph. The nymph breathes via gills and feeds on other insect larvae, tadpoles and small fishes. It has a specialised lower mouthpart known as a mask that usually rests under its head but can shoot out to snatch prey in its pincers. Over a period of a few weeks to 8 years, depending on the species, the nymph may moult up to 17 times. For the final moult, it climbs out of the water and sheds its nymphal skin to reveal an adult with prominent eyes, sharp mouthparts, two pairs of transparent wings, a sloping thorax and a long, slender abdomen.

A newly emerged adult dragonfly or damselfly flies away from water and starts to feed, snatching flying insects on the wing. To find mates, dragonflies will gather along a body of water, and males may engage in aerial contests. After mating, the male usually guards the female as she lays her eggs in the water. Most adults live for only several weeks.

Beautiful demoiselle
Calopteryx virgo

Compound eyes set well apart

Females have golden-brown wings, while males have dark, iridescent wings

Legs set forward for seizing prey

Damselflies rest with wings together

Azure damselfly
Coenagrion puella

Enormous compound eyes set close together

Blue dasher
Pachydiplax longipennis

Dawn dropwing
Trithemis aurora

Dragonflies rest with wings spread

MANTIDS

YLUM Arthropoda
BPHYLUM Hexapoda
ASS Insecta
DER Mantodea
MILIES 8
ECIES 2,000

Waiting to ambush prey, a mantid will sit perfectly still, holding its large forelegs folded up before it – a posture that inspired the common name of praying mantis for some species. With lightning-quick reflexes, the raptorial forelegs will shoot out to snatch insect prey. Most mantids are medium-sized, measuring about 5cm (2 inches) long, but some tropical species reach lengths of 25cm (10 inches). These giant mantids may add small birds and reptiles to their primarily insectivorous diet. While the majority of mantids live in the tropics or subtropics, some are found in the warm temperate areas of southern Europe, North America, South Africa, and Australia.

Precision hunting With its forward-facing eyes supplying binocular vision, a praying mantis has used its spiky, hooked forelimbs to impale a passing wasp. The mantis's strong mandibles quickly devour the meal.

Foaming protection A female lays her eggs in a gummy fluid that she whips into a foam. When the foam hardens, it forms a case, or ootheca, that protects the eggs.

Cannibalistic mating In some mantid species, the transfer of sperm is more rapid if the female bites off the male's head. The male's self-sacrifice makes ecological sense as he is providing nourishment that will help his offspring survive.

First segment of thorax shaped like a violin

Wandering violin
Gongylus gongyloides

Common praying mantis
Mantis religiosa

A mantid's compound eyes provide excellent vision

Leathery forewings

Orchid mantis
Hymenopus coronatus

Resembles flower for camouflage

Wings mimic petals of orchid

Idolum diabolicum

SILENT HUNTERS

Mantids are masters at hiding from both predators and prey. They are the only insects that can turn their head without moving other parts of the body, allowing them to silently observe potential victims. Most species also have cryptic colouration that helps them blend in with the grass, leaves, twigs or flowers of their environment. An alarmed mantid will adopt a threat posture, raising and rustling its wings and rearing up to show off its vivid warning colouration. Mantids that are targeted by bats at night possess a single 'ear' on their thorax that can detect a bat's ultrasonic signals.

In some species, and especially in captivity, the female mantid will devour the male during copulation. Females mate only once, but from that single mating, they can produce up to 20 ootheca, or egg cases, each containing from 30 to 300 eggs. The young emerge from the ootheca as highly active nymphs, looking like miniature, wingless versions of their parents. Ready to hunt, they may even eat each other. The survivors disperse. After a series of moults, the nymphs mature and develop wings and adult colouration.

COCKROACHES

PHYLUM	Arthropoda
SUBPHYLUM	Hexapoda
CLASS	Insecta
ORDER	Blattodea
FAMILIES	6
SPECIES	4,000

As scavenging insects willing to feed on almost any plant or animal product, including stored food, trash, paper and clothing, some cockroaches thrive in human environments and are widely regarded as repulsive pests. In fact, less than 1 per cent of all cockroach species are pests – the remainder perform an important ecological role by recycling leaf litter and animal excrement in forests and other habitats. While most cockroaches are found in warm tropical zones, about 25 species have spread worldwide, accidentally transported on ships. Cockroaches are among the most primitive of all living insects, with an anatomy that has changed little in more than 300 million years.

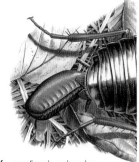

Safe eggs Female cockroaches deposit their eggs in an ootheca, or egg case. The nymphs emerge soft and white, but soon harden and turn brown. They eat the ootheca as their first food.

Maternal care Weighing up to 50g (1¾ ounces), the giant burrowing cockroach (Macropanesthia rhinoceros) of Australia is the heaviest of all cockroaches. As many as 30 young are born alive and are fed by the mother in her burrow for up to 9 months.

SENSITIVE INSECTS

A range of sensors helps cockroaches to detect minute changes in their surroundings. Their long antennae can find minuscule amounts of food and moisture. Sensors on the legs and abdomen can pick up tiny air movements, prompting the insect to flee danger in a split second. With its oval, flattened shape, a cockroach can scuttle into tiny crevices. Not all cockroaches have wings, but in those that do the forewings are usually hardened and opaque, and the hindwings are translucent.

Mating between cockroaches may be initiated when a female emits a pheromone to attract males. Females usually lay 14–32 eggs in a hardened case known as an ootheca. The ootheca may then be left to hatch alone; carried at the base of the mother's abdomen; or incubated inside the mother's body so that she produces live young. Nymphs moult up to 13 times before emerging as adults. A cockroach usually lives for 2–4 years.

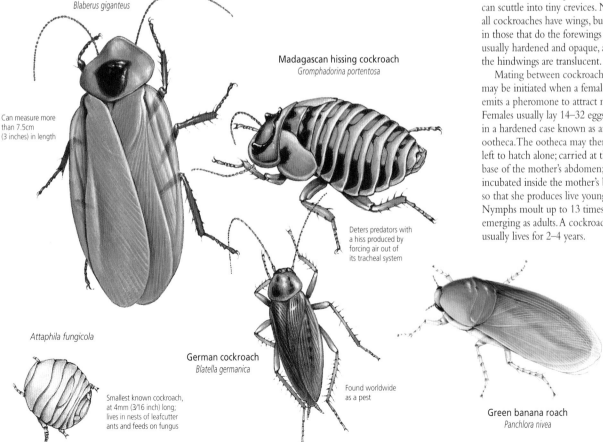

Giant cockroach
Blaberus giganteus

Can measure more than 7.5cm (3 inches) in length

Madagascan hissing cockroach
Gromphadorina portentosa

Deters predators with a hiss produced by forcing air out of its tracheal system

Attaphila fungicola

Smallest known cockroach, at 4mm (3/16 inch) long; lives in nests of leafcutter ants and feeds on fungus

German cockroach
Blatella germanica

Found worldwide as a pest

Green banana roach
Panchlora nivea

TERMITES

LUM	Arthropoda
PHYLUM	Hexapoda
SS	Insecta
ER	Isoptera
ILIES	7
IES	2,750

Termites may be the world's most monogamous animals. A king and queen mate for life, producing thousands or millions of offspring that operate together as a highly structured colony. These small insects are often referred to as white ants, but although their social system and anatomy resemble those of ants, they evolved independently and are most closely related to cockroaches. Found throughout much of the world, termites are most abundant in tropical rain forests, where there can be as many as 10,000 individuals per square kilometre (25,000 per sq. mile). By feeding on dead wood, they recycle nutrients in their natural habitats but can severely damage buildings in urban environments.

Wood-eaters With saw-toothed jaws that can shear through wood, termites cause costly damage to buildings. Infestations often involve introduced species that never found a niche in the natural environment.

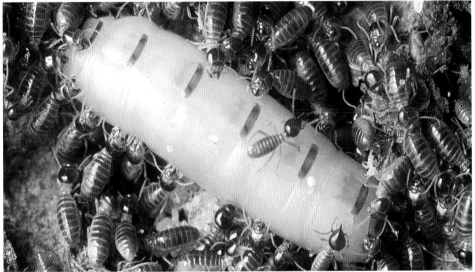

Egg-laying machine A termite queen, shown here attended by other colony members, can grow 11cm (4½ inches) long and produces 36,000 eggs a day from her enormous abdomen.

CASTE SOCIETY

A mature termite colony has three castes: reproductives, workers and soldiers. The main reproductives are the king and queen, who produce all the colony's other members and can live for 25 years. There may also be secondary reproductives ready to take over if the king or queen dies.

Workers and soldiers can be male or female. They are wingless, usually lack eyes and mature reproductive organs, and may live for 5 years. The pale and soft-bodied workers feed all other colony members and maintain the nest. Soldiers defend the colony, usually using powerful mandibles. Termite nymphs can develop into any caste, depending on the needs of the colony.

At a particular time each year, a swarm of winged males and females will emerge from a termite nest and disperse. They then shed their wings and form pairs, becoming the kings and queens of new colonies.

Male reproductive of *Macrotermes natalensis*

Nasutitermes triodiae soldier shoots a sticky liquid out of its long snout to entangle enemies

Spinifex termite
Nasutitermes triodiae

Macrotermes natalensis soldier has an enlarged head with hooked mandibles for attacking invaders

Large fungus-growing termite
Macrotermes natalensis

INSIDE A NEST

Termite nests create a stable, humid microclimate sealed from the elements. While some termites nest inside wood, most construct subterranean nests that may rise partly above ground as mounds. Worker termites use saliva or faeces to glue together particles of soil or wood, building a hard outer wall to protect the softer internal network of chambers.

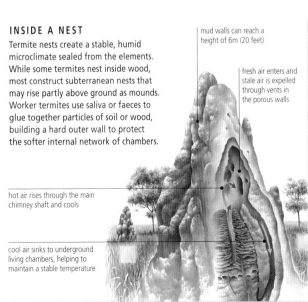

mud walls can reach a height of 6m (20 feet)

fresh air enters and stale air is expelled through vents in the porous walls

hot air rises through the main chimney shaft and cools

cool air sinks to underground living chambers, helping to maintain a stable temperature

CRICKETS AND GRASSHOPPERS

PHYLUM	Arthropoda
SUBPHYLUM	Hexapoda
CLASS	Insecta
ORDER	Orthoptera
FAMILIES	28
SPECIES	> 20,000

Renowned for their songs and leaping ability, the members of the order Orthoptera include grasshoppers, locusts, crickets, katydids (or bush crickets), and their kin. They are distinguished by elongated hind legs that allow them to jump. Most species are winged, with slender, toughened forewings protecting the membranous, fan-shaped hindwings. While most orthopterans are ground-dwellers in grasslands and forests, some are arboreal, burrowing or semiaquatic, and species can be found in deserts, caves, bogs and marshes, and seashores. Grasshoppers, groundhoppers and a few katydids are herbivores, while most other orthopterans are omnivorous.

Threat display Coloured to match the vegetation of its Amazon rainforest home, a spiky-headed katydid (*Copiphora* sp.) is covered in sharp spines and will rear up in a threat display to deter predators.

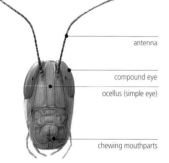

antenna

compound eye

ocellus (simple eye)

chewing mouthparts

Information collector An orthopteran's head features two fine, sensitive antennae, two large compound eyes and mouthparts adapted for chewing vegetation.

SINGING INSECTS

Most male orthopterans can make sounds by rubbing two parts of the body together, a technique known as stridulation. Crickets and longhorn grasshoppers move a scraper on one forewing along a row of teeth on the other forewing, while short-horned grasshoppers rub a ridged surface on the hindleg against a forewing. The sounds can be heard by tympanal organs located on the legs or abdomen.

There are three kinds of song: a calling song, to attract females from a distance; a courtship song, to entice a nearby female to mate; and a battle call, to deter rival males. The songs, some of which are too high-pitched to be heard by human ears, are unique to each species. Cricket songs tend to be affected by the weather, with the rate of chirps increasing with the temperature.

Warning colours While many crickets and grasshoppers have cryptic colouration that helps them blend in with the background, others, such as this rainforest grasshopper, are vividly coloured as a warning to potential predators that they are unpalatable.

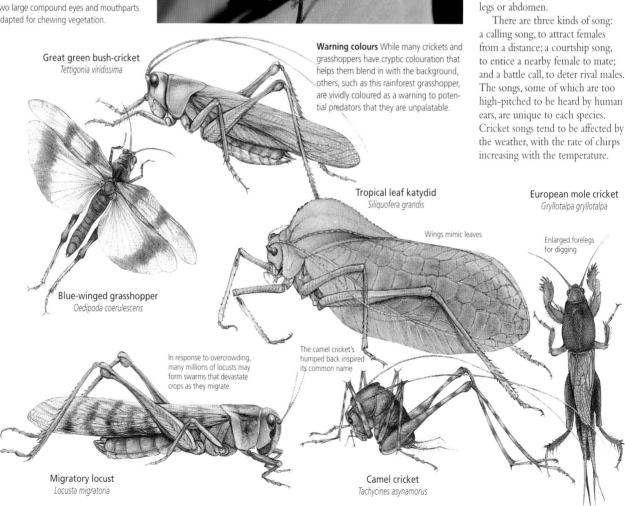

Great green bush-cricket
Tettigonia viridissima

Blue-winged grasshopper
Oedipoda coerulescens

Tropical leaf katydid
Siliquofera grandis

Wings mimic leaves

European mole cricket
Gryllotalpa gryllotalpa

Enlarged forelegs for digging

In response to overcrowding, many millions of locusts may form swarms that devastate crops as they migrate

The camel cricket's humped back inspired its common name

Migratory locust
Locusta migratoria

Camel cricket
Tachycines asynamorus

BUGS

LUM Arthropoda

PHYLUM Hexapoda

SS Insecta

DER Hemiptera

MILIES 134

CIES > 80,000

Ranging from minute wingless aphids to giant frog-catching water bugs, the members of the order Hemiptera are extremely diverse. The name *Hemiptera* means 'half wing', a reference to the fact that many, but not all, species have forewings that are leathery at the base and membranous at the tip. The one feature that all bugs have in common is their piercing and sucking mouthparts. With these, they pierce the surface of a plant or animal and inject saliva to start digesting the food, which they then suck into their mouth. Most bug species feed on plant sap, and some of these are significant agricultural pests. Other bugs suck the blood of vertebrates, or prey on other insects.

Malodourous defence The bright colours of many shield bugs serve to warn predators of the noxious odour produced when the insect is disturbed. Shield bugs are usually sap suckers, but a few are predatory.

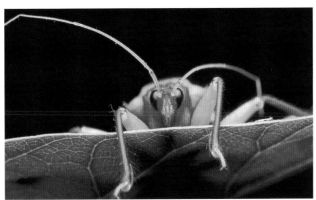

Mimicry In thornbugs, or treehoppers, the first plate of the thorax forms a thorn-shaped spine. This camouflages the insect as it sucks sap, and, even if an enemy does spot the insect, the spine deters an attack.

Predator bugs While many bugs use their sucking mouthparts to feed on plant juices, others employ them to snare live prey. This assassin bug lies in wait, ready to ambush an unwitting insect victim.

DIFFERENT BUGS

Distributed throughout the world, bugs can be found in almost all terrestrial habitats. Some species have specialised for an aquatic life – these include sea skaters (Halobates sp.), the only insects on the open ocean. Bugs range from 1mm–11cm (1/25 inch–4½ inches) in length. They undergo incomplete metamorphosis, with nymphs that usually resemble small, wingless versions of the adults. In cicadas and some other species, however, the burrowing nymphs and the adults look quite different.

The order Hemiptera is divided into three suborders. In the true bugs (suborder Heteroptera), the forewings are toughened at the base and sit flat, concealing membranous hindwings. True bugs can flex their head and mouthparts forward, and many have stink glands. Cicadas and hoppers (Auchenorrhyncha) hold their uniform forewings over the abdomen like a tent. The head and mouthparts point down and back. Aphids, scale insects, mealy bugs, whiteflies and their kin all belong to the suborder Sternorrhyncha. Most have soft bodies kept moist by a covering of wax or froth. Wings are often absent or reduced in adults.

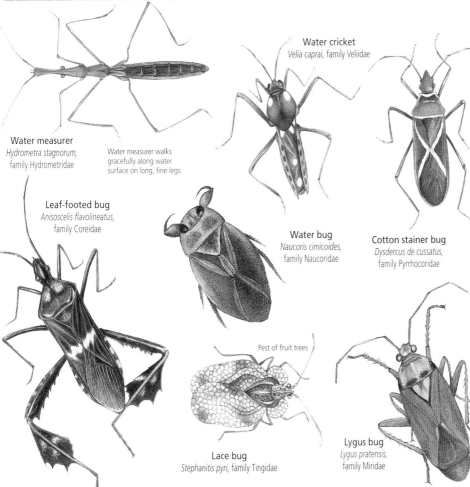

Water cricket
Velia caprai, family Veliidae

Water measurer
Hydrometra stagnorum,
family Hydrometridae

Water measurer walks gracefully along water surface on long, fine legs

Leaf-footed bug
Anisoscelis flavolineatus,
family Coreidae

Water bug
Naucoris cimicoides,
family Naucoridae

Cotton stainer bug
Dysdercus de cussatus,
family Pyrrhocoridae

Pest of fruit trees

Lace bug
Stephanitis pyri, family Tingidae

Lygus bug
Lygus pratensis,
family Miridae

FACT FILE

Family Pentatomidae Known as shield bugs because of their shield-shaped bodies, and as stink bugs because of the pungent odour produced by their thoracic glands, the members of this family have a distinctive large triangular plate on their back. Most species are plant suckers and many can be serious agricultural pests.

Species 5,500

Worldwide; on plants

Blending in *Like many stink bugs, the spined stink bug (Picromerus bidens) is brown to blend with its surroundings, but some species have vivid colours as a warning.*

Family Reduviidae This family contains the assassin bugs, predators that usually target other insects, but sometimes suck the blood of vertebrates. The bugs swing their curved proboscis forward to puncture the prey and inject paralysing saliva, then suck up the body fluids.

Species 6,000

Worldwide; on ground and plants

Kissing bug *The conenose bug (Triatroma sanguisuga) is a blood-sucker. It is also called the kissing bug because it sometimes bites sleeping humans near the mouth.*

PERIODICAL CICADAS

The noisiest insects in the world, male cicadas (family Cicadidae) produce their sound with structures on the abdomen known as tymbals. While many cicadas have a life cycle of up to 8 years, most of which is spent underground as a nymph, the periodical cicadas of the Magicicada genus are distinguished by their synchronized development. After up to 18 years underground, the entire population of an area will mature and emerge at the same time.

adult

Final moult *Periodical cicadas spend 13–18 years underground as nymphs, before emerging to moult into their adult form.*

emerging nymph

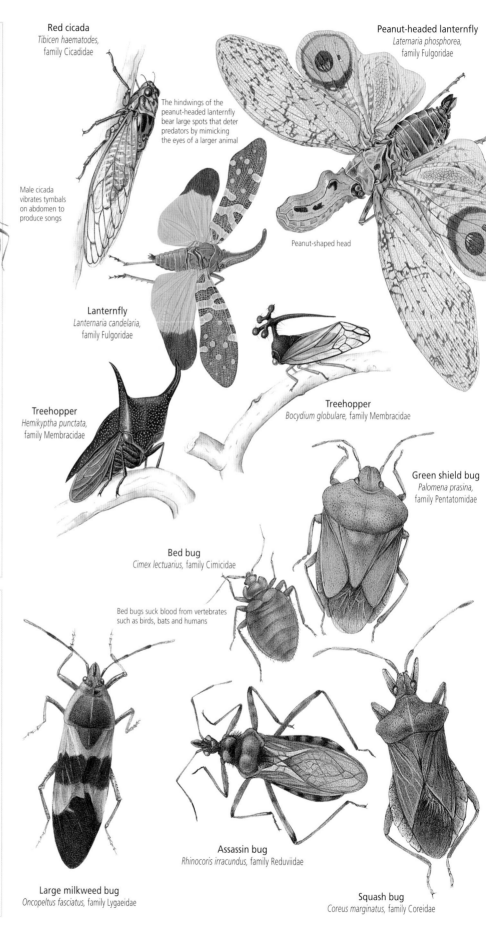

Red cicada
Tibicen haematodes,
family Cicadidae

Male cicada vibrates tymbals on abdomen to produce songs

Peanut-headed lanternfly
Laternaria phosphorea,
family Fulgoridae

The hindwings of the peanut-headed lanternfly bear large spots that deter predators by mimicking the eyes of a larger animal

Peanut-shaped head

Lanternfly
Lanternaria candelaria,
family Fulgoridae

Treehopper
Bocydium globulare, family Membracidae

Treehopper
Hemikyptha punctata,
family Membracidae

Green shield bug
Palomena prasina,
family Pentatomidae

Bed bug
Cimex lectuarius, family Cimicidae

Bed bugs suck blood from vertebrates such as birds, bats and humans

Assassin bug
Rhinocoris irracundus, family Reduviidae

Large milkweed bug
Oncopeltus fasciatus, family Lygaeidae

Squash bug
Coreus marginatus, family Coreidae

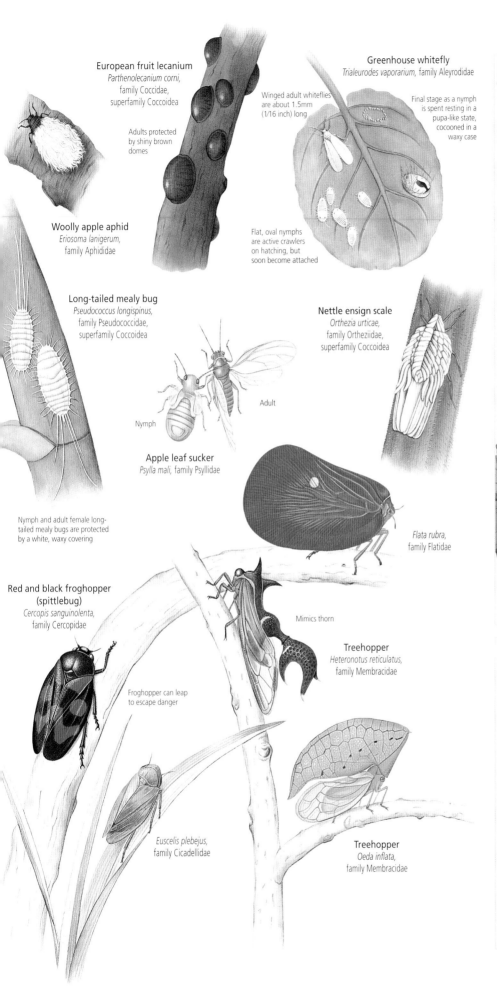

European fruit lecanium
Parthenolecanium corni,
family Coccidae,
superfamily Coccoidea

Adults protected
by shiny brown
domes

Woolly apple aphid
Eriosoma lanigerum,
family Aphididae

Greenhouse whitefly
Trialeurodes vaporarium, family Aleyrodidae

Winged adult whiteflies
are about 1.5mm
(1/16 inch) long

Final stage as a nymph
is spent resting in a
pupa-like state,
cocooned in a
waxy case

Flat, oval nymphs
are active crawlers
on hatching, but
soon become attached

Long-tailed mealy bug
Pseudococcus longispinus,
family Pseudococcidae,
superfamily Coccoidea

Nymph

Adult

Nettle ensign scale
Orthezia urticae,
family Ortheziidae,
superfamily Coccoidea

Apple leaf sucker
Psylla mali, family Psyllidae

Nymph and adult female long-
tailed mealy bugs are protected
by a white, waxy covering

Flata rubra,
family Flatidae

**Red and black froghopper
(spittlebug)**
Cercopis sanguinolenta,
family Cercopidae

Mimics thorn

Treehopper
Heteronotus reticulatus,
family Membracidae

Froghopper can leap
to escape danger

Euscelis plebejus,
family Cicadellidae

Treehopper
Oeda inflata,
family Membracidae

FACT FILE

Family Aphididae Aphids are tiny,
soft-bodied plant-suckers that cause
great damage to crops. They are able
to rapidly increase their numbers by
producing wingless or winged females
from unfertilised eggs. In autumn, the
winged females produce males and
females that mate. The fertilised eggs
lay dormant through winter and hatch
in spring as females to begin
the cycle again.

Species 2,250

Worldwide; on plants

Cabbage lover
Native to Europe,
the cabbage aphid
(Bravicoryne brassicae)
has spread to many
parts of the world. It
feeds on both wild and
cultivated plants, causing
particular damage to cabbage crops.

Superfamily Coccoidea Spending
most of their life protected by a waxy
secretion, the scale insects collected in
this superfamily barely resemble insects
at all. Adult females have sack-like,
wingless bodies and often lack
legs and eyes. Adult males
usually have wings and a
more defined head, thorax
and abdomen, but, lacking
mouthparts, they cannot
feed and are short-lived.

Species 7,300

Worldwide; on plants

Well protected
The oyster-shell scale
(Lepidosaphes ulmi) usually
overwinters as eggs.

APHIDS AS FOOD

Aphids provide food for many other
insects. They are prey for many lady
beetles (family Coccinellidae), hoverflies
(family Syrphidae) and lacewings
(order Neuroptera). They also have a
happier relationship with some species
of ants, which protect them from
predators and the elements. In return,
the ants stroke, or 'milk',
the aphids to feed on
honeydew, the sweet
waste product
of the aphids'
plant-sap diet.

Aphid predator
In its lifespan of
1–2 months, a lady
beetle can consume
more than 2,000 aphids.

WATER INSECTS

Only about 3 per cent, or 30,000, insect species are truly aquatic for at least part of their life cycle. Water insects have had to adapt to the low oxygen content of water, as well as to the difficulty of moving about in still water or staying put in flowing water. Some insects, such as water striders, live only on the surface. Many, such as backswimmers, breathe air but carry it with them when they swim underwater. Others, such as dragonfly nymphs, spend all their time submerged, using gills to absorb oxygen from the water. The vast majority of aquatic insects live in fresh water, and only 300 or so species live in saltwater habitats, possibly because crustaceans evolved in the sea first and offer too much competition.

Spinning swimmers Whirligig beetles (family Gyrinidae) swim in small circles on the surface, using their flattened hind legs like oars. They carry bubbles of air when they dive. Their eyes are split into two parts so they can see both above and below the water.

Bubble breather Predaceous diving beetles (family Dytiscidae) spend virtually their entire lives in water. The adults come to the surface to collect air, which they store in a bubble under their elytra (forewings). They swim using their hind legs, which are fringed in thick hairs.

Aquatic locomotion Aquatic insects have evolved various strategies for moving around. Water scorpions (family Nepidae) can swim but often crawl along the bottom of a pond and spend much of their time hanging from pond weeds, waiting to ambush prey. They breathe air through a tube that sticks out above the surface. Water boatmen (family Corixidae) have long, hairy hind legs that can 'row' powerfully through the water. Water striders (family Gerridae) have fine hairs on their feet that allow them to make small jumps along the surface.

Snorkelers Mosquito larvae hang from the surface and filter plant matter from the water. While most aquatic larvae breathe through gills, mosquito larvae breathe air through a snorkel-like tube. This allows them to survive in pools of stagnant, oxygen-poor water.

Aquatic predators While many water insects are omnivores or plant-feeders, some, such as the predaceous diving beetles, are highly carnivorous. Even as larvae, diving beetles will tackle tadpoles, small fishes and other prey larger than themselves. The adults use their powerful mandibles on substantial prey such as salamanders.

water scorpion hangs from pond weeds as it attacks a tadpole

water strider uses surface tension to 'walk' on water

water boatman swims by using its legs as oars

BEETLES

PHYLUM	Arthropoda
SUBPHYLUM	Hexapoda
CLASS	Insecta
ORDER	Coleoptera
FAMILIES	166
SPECIES	> 370,000

When asked what his study of the natural world had revealed about its creator, scientist J. B. S. Haldane replied, 'An inordinate fondness for beetles.' Of all known animal species, about one in four is a beetle. Members of the order Coleoptera have colonised almost all of Earth's habitats, from Arctic tundra and exposed mountaintops to deserts, grasslands, woodlands and lakes. They reach their greatest diversity, however, in the lush rain forests of the tropics. Most beetles are distinguished by their hardened, leathery forewings, known as elytra, which protect the membranous, flying hindwings and allow the insect to live in tight spaces under bark or in leaf litter.

Pollinating beetle Although considered pests by many gardeners, spotted cucumber beetles (Diabrotica undecimpunctata) and many other beetles that eat pollen and foliage play an important role in helping to pollinate the plants on which they feed.

Competing males The huge, branched mandibles of male stag beetles resemble a stag's antlers and perform a similar function, being used in competitions with rival males to win the right to mate. In some species, the mandibles are as long as the beetle.

DIVERSE FORMS

From lady beetles to diving beetles, scarab beetles to fireflies, the order Coleoptera encompasses enormous diversity. The feather-winged beetle (*Nanosella fungi*) is just 0.25mm (¹⁄₁₀₀ inch) long, while the South American longhorn beetle (*Titanus giganteus*) can exceed 16cm (6½ inches) in length. Adult beetles can be oval and flattened, long and slender, or squat and domed. While a few beetles are strong fliers, most are clumsy in flight, and some lack wings and cannot fly at all.

The mouthparts of beetles are all adapted for biting, but they have been put to many purposes. Plant-eating beetles may eat roots, stems, leaves, flowers, fruit, seeds or wood. Carnivorous beetles usually attack invertebrate prey. A key ecological role is filled by scavenging beetles, which recycle dead animals and plants, excrement and other waste.

Most beetles live on the ground, but some have specialised to live in trees, in water and underground – a few even make their home in the nests of ants and termites.

Beetles develop by complete metamorphosis, with larvae looking markedly different from the parents and going through a non-feeding, pupal stage before becoming adults.

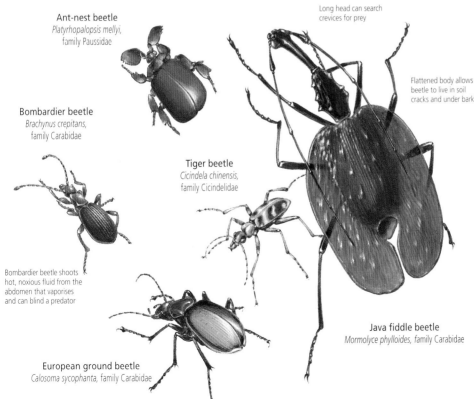

Ant-nest beetle
Platyrhopalopsis mellyi,
family Paussidae

Long head can search crevices for prey

Bombardier beetle
Brachynus crepitans,
family Carabidae

Tiger beetle
Cicindela chinensis,
family Cicindelidae

Flattened body allows beetle to live in soil cracks and under bark

Bombardier beetle shoots hot, noxious fluid from the abdomen that vaporises and can blind a predator

Java fiddle beetle
Mormolyce phylloides, family Carabidae

European ground beetle
Calosoma sycophanta, family Carabidae

FACT FILE

Family Buprestidae With spectacular colours and a metallic sheen, the jewel beetles in this family include some of the world's most attractive insects. They have a long oval body and are good fliers. Many adults feed on nectar, while larvae tend to be wood-borers.

Species 15,000

Worldwide; on plants

Decorative wings
The iridescent wings of South America's metallic wood-boring beetle (Euchroma gigantea) are used in jewellery by local people.

Family Coccinellidae Also called ladybirds or ladybugs, the lady beetles of this family are among the best known of all insects. They are usually brightly coloured and spotted, with a compact, rounded shape and short, clubbed antennae. Lady beetles are desired guests in gardens and farms. While a minority of species are plant-feeders, most lady beetles prey on aphids and other pests. A larva may eat 25 aphids a day, while an adult may eat as many as 50 aphids a day.

Species 5,200

Worldwide; on foliage

Lines and spots The convergent lady beetle (Hippodamia convergens) is named after the converging white lines on the first segment of its thorax. It usually has 13 spots.

Family Lampyridae This family is made up of fireflies. All firefly larvae glow, producing light via a chemical reaction while giving off little heat. Their luminescence may be a warning to predators of their unpleasant taste. The larvae themselves are predaceous, following slime trails to slugs and snails. Using organs on the abdomen, most adult fireflies also produce light, which they flash in a species-specific pattern to attract mates.

Species 2,000

Worldwide; on plants, in soil and under rocks

Aggressive mimic Some female fireflies mimic the flash patterns of other species in order to lure males as prey.

European splendor beetle
Anthaxia hungarica,
family Buprestidae

Vivid colour warns predators of lady beetle's foul taste

Seven-spotted lady beetle
Coccinella septempunctata,
family Coccinellidae

Larva of *Coccinella septempunctata*

Golden rove beetle
Emus hirtus,
family Staphylinidae

Golden rove beetle is covered in fine hairs

Flesh-eating beetle
Phosphuga atrata, family Silphidae

Common carpet beetle
Anthrenus scrophulariae,
family Dermestidae

Feeds on carpet, wool and other animal products

Glow worm
Lampyris noctiluca,
family Lampyridae

Water scavenger beetle
Sphaeridium scarabaeoides,
family Hydrophilidae

Winged male glow worms are attracted by the strong light emitted by wingless females

Larva of *Lampyris noctiluca*

European burying beetle
Necrophorus vespillo, family Silphidae

Buries corpses of small vertebrates as food for its young

Fuscous soldier beetle
Cantharis fusca, family Cantharidae

Beneficial insect that feeds on aphids and caterpillars

Bee beetle
Trichodes apiarius,
family Cleridae

Parasitises beehives

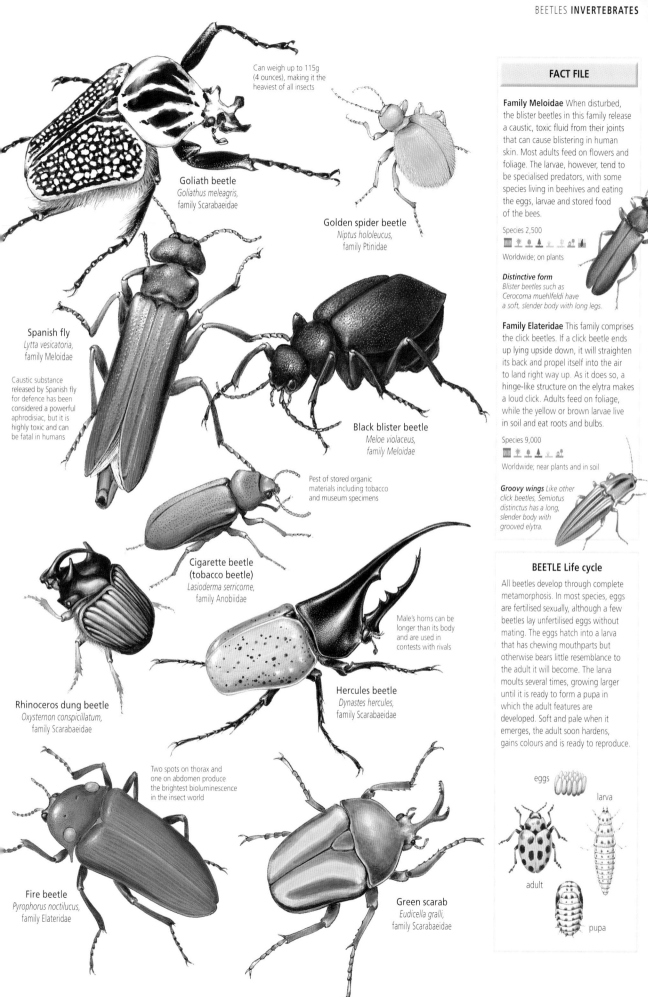

Goliath beetle
Goliathus meleagris,
family Scarabaeidae

Can weigh up to 115g
(4 ounces), making it the
heaviest of all insects

Golden spider beetle
Niptus hololeucus,
family Ptinidae

Spanish fly
Lytta vesicatoria,
family Meloidae

Caustic substance
released by Spanish fly
for defence has been
considered a powerful
aphrodisiac, but it is
highly toxic and can
be fatal in humans

Black blister beetle
Meloe violaceus,
family Meloidae

Pest of stored organic
materials including tobacco
and museum specimens

**Cigarette beetle
(tobacco beetle)**
Lasioderma serricorne,
family Anobiidae

Male's horns can be
longer than its body
and are used in
contests with rivals

Rhinoceros dung beetle
Oxysternon conspicillatum,
family Scarabaeidae

Hercules beetle
Dynastes hercules,
family Scarabaeidae

Two spots on thorax and
one on abdomen produce
the brightest bioluminescence
in the insect world

Fire beetle
Pyrophorus noctilucus,
family Elateridae

Green scarab
Eudicella gralli,
family Scarabaeidae

FACT FILE

Family Meloidae When disturbed, the blister beetles in this family release a caustic, toxic fluid from their joints that can cause blistering in human skin. Most adults feed on flowers and foliage. The larvae, however, tend to be specialised predators, with some species living in beehives and eating the eggs, larvae and stored food of the bees.

Species 2,500

Worldwide; on plants

Distinctive form
Blister beetles such as Cerocoma muehlfeldi have a soft, slender body with long legs.

Family Elateridae This family comprises the click beetles. If a click beetle ends up lying upside down, it will straighten its back and propel itself into the air to land right way up. As it does so, a hinge-like structure on the elytra makes a loud click. Adults feed on foliage, while the yellow or brown larvae live in soil and eat roots and bulbs.

Species 9,000

Worldwide; near plants and in soil

Groovy wings *Like other click beetles, Semiotus distinctus has a long, slender body with grooved elytra.*

BEETLE Life cycle

All beetles develop through complete metamorphosis. In most species, eggs are fertilised sexually, although a few beetles lay unfertilised eggs without mating. The eggs hatch into a larva that has chewing mouthparts but otherwise bears little resemblance to the adult it will become. The larva moults several times, growing larger until it is ready to form a pupa in which the adult features are developed. Soft and pale when it emerges, the adult soon hardens, gains colours and is ready to reproduce.

eggs
larva
adult
pupa

Family Lucanidae This family contains the stag beetles. Much larger than the females, male stag beetles are further distinguished by their huge mandibles. Rival males will use their mandibles in mating contests. Larvae feed on dead or rotting wood and may take several years to mature. Some adults eat leaves, but most feed on nectar.

Species 1,300

Worldwide; in trees

South American stag *Common in Chile and Argentina, Darwin's stag beetle (Chiasognathus grantii) often reaches 9cm (3½ inches) in length.*

Family Curculionidae Sometimes called snout beetles, weevils constitute Curculionidae, the largest of all families in the animal kingdom. A prominent snout carries biting mouthparts and is used for feeding on soft plants and boring holes in plants, seeds, fruit or soil for its eggs. Usually longest on females, the snout can be much longer than the body in some species. Some weevil species are serious agricultural pests.

Species 50,000

Worldwide; near plants

Shimmering weevil *The neotropical weevil Entimus splendidus has iridescent scales. The snout is less pronounced than in many other weevil species.*

Family Cerambycidae Known as longhorn or longicorn beetles, the members of this family have long, narrow bodies, which reach a length of 16cm (6½ inches) in the largest species. Their impressive antennae, however, can be many times as long as the body. The antennae are used for finding food such as pollen, nectar, sap or leaves. Larvae feed on living and dead trees.

Species 30,000

Worldwide; near flowers and sap

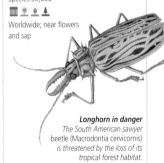

Longhorn in danger
The South American sawyer beetle (Macrodontia cervicornis) is threatened by the loss of its tropical forest habitat.

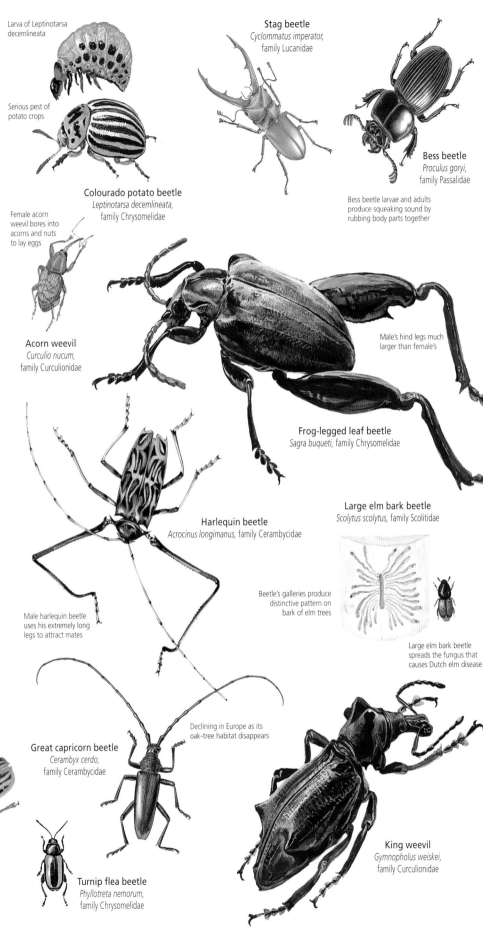

Larva of Leptinotarsa decemlineata

Serious pest of potato crops

Colourado potato beetle
Leptinotarsa decemlineata,
family Chrysomelidae

Female acorn weevil bores into acorns and nuts to lay eggs

Acorn weevil
Curculio nucum,
family Curculionidae

Stag beetle
Cyclommatus imperator,
family Lucanidae

Bess beetle
Proculus goryi,
family Passalidae

Bess beetle larvae and adults produce squeaking sound by rubbing body parts together

Male's hind legs much larger than female's

Frog-legged leaf beetle
Sagra buqueti, family Chrysomelidae

Large elm bark beetle
Scolytus scolytus, family Scolitidae

Harlequin beetle
Acrocinus longimanus, family Cerambycidae

Beetle's galleries produce distinctive pattern on bark of elm trees

Male harlequin beetle uses his extremely long legs to attract mates

Large elm bark beetle spreads the fungus that causes Dutch elm disease

Declining in Europe as its oak-tree habitat disappears

Great capricorn beetle
Cerambyx cerdo,
family Cerambycidae

Turnip flea beetle
Phyllotreta nemorum,
family Chrysomelidae

King weevil
Gymnopholus weiskei,
family Curculionidae

FLIES

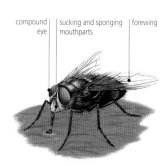

compound eye | sucking and sponging mouthparts | forewing

Eyes and wings Mostly active by day, flies rely on their large compound eyes, each with up to 4,000 lenses. The first segment of the thorax is enlarged to hold the huge muscles that propel the forewings.

PHYLUM	Arthropoda
SUBPHYLUM	Hexapoda
CLASS	Insecta
ORDER	Diptera
FAMILIES	130
SPECIES	120,000

Houseflies and mosquitoes are the most ubiquitous members of the order Diptera, which also includes gnats, midges, blowflies, fruit flies, crane flies, horseflies, hoverflies and other true flies. While most insects fly with four wings, dipterans are generally distinguished by their single pair of functional wings. The hindwings are reduced to halteres, tiny clubbed stalks that vibrate up and down in time with the forewings, helping the fly to balance during flight. Some species have lost their wings altogether and are flightless. Although often associated with moist environments and decaying matter, flies live almost everywhere in the world except Antarctica.

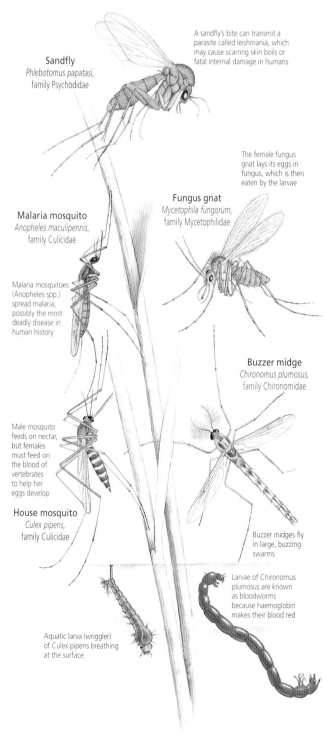

A sandfly's bite can transmit a parasite called leishmania, which may cause scarring skin boils or fatal internal damage in humans

Sandfly
Phlebotomus papatasi,
family Psychodidae

The female fungus gnat lays its eggs in fungus, which is then eaten by the larvae

Fungus gnat
Mycetophila fungorum,
family Mycetophilidae

Malaria mosquito
Anopheles maculipennis,
family Culicidae

Malaria mosquitoes (Anopheles spp.) spread malaria, possibly the most deadly disease in human history

Buzzer midge
Chironomus plumosus,
family Chironomidae

Male mosquito feeds on nectar, but females must feed on the blood of vertebrates to help her eggs develop

House mosquito
Culex pipens,
family Culicidae

Buzzer midges fly in large, buzzing swarms

Larvae of Chironomus plumosus are known as bloodworms because haemoglobin makes their blood red

Aquatic larva (wriggler) of Culex pipens breathing at the surface

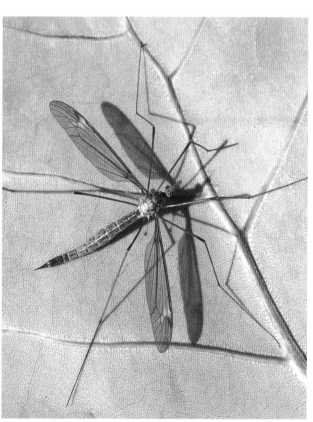

STICKY SUCKERS

Flies are small insects, ranging from midges 1mm (1⁄25 inch) in length, to robber flies about 7cm (3 inches) long. Their feet have sticky pads with tiny claws, allowing the insects to walk on smooth surfaces, even upside down along a ceiling.

With mouthparts designed for sucking, flies can consume only liquid food. Houseflies have fleshy pads on their mouth that can sponge up a meal. Mosquitoes have piercing mouthparts for feeding on nectar and blood. Robber flies use their mouthparts to stab insect prey.

Flies begin life as eggs, from which larvae hatch. Often known

Daddy long legs Crane flies make up Tipulidae, the largest family of flies. Adults have mosquito-like bodies with very long legs. They often feed on nectar in humid forests. Larvae live in moist soil or water.

as maggots, the larvae usually have pale, soft bodies and lack true legs. After several moults, they pupate into the adult form.

Their feeding habits, abundance and wide distribution have made flies responsible for the spread of deadly diseases such as malaria and sleeping sickness. They also play key ecological roles – as pollinators, as decomposers of organic matter and as links in the food chain.

FACT FILE

Family Syrphidae The hoverflies of this family will hover in one spot, then dart forward or sideways before hovering again. With their black and yellow abdomen and habit of feeding on nectar, they resemble bees or wasps, but do not bite or sting. The larvae of many hoverfly species are welcome in gardens because they eat aphids.

Species 6,000

Worldwide; on flowers

Pollinating pest
The narcissus fly (Merodon equestris) is considered a pest because its larvae eat plant bulbs, but, like the other hoverflies, the adults are important pollinators.

Family Tabanidae The stout flies in this family are known as horseflies or deerflies. While the males feed on nectar, honeydew and sap, the females are bloodsuckers because they need protein to develop their eggs. Females use their blade-like mouthparts to slice through the skin of mammals so they can suck up the blood.

Species 4,000

Worldwide; near mammals

Common names
Like other species in its genus, Chrysops caecutiens is usually known as a deerfly. Species in the genus Tabanus tend to be called horseflies.

FLIGHTLESS FLIES

In several families of flies, some species have lost their wings and do not fly. The family Tipulidae (crane flies) includes the flightless snow fly (*Chionea* sp.), which remains active throughout the winter in its snow-covered habitat. Able to tolerate temperatures of –6°C (20°F), it avoids the many predators that appear in warmer months. Since flight requires warmer muscles than possible in this environment, the snow fly has discarded its wings. The halteres, however, have been retained.

Wingless parasite *The bee louse (Braula caeca) from the family Chamaemyiidae is a wingless fly that lays its eggs in beehives so that the larvae can feed on the honey.*

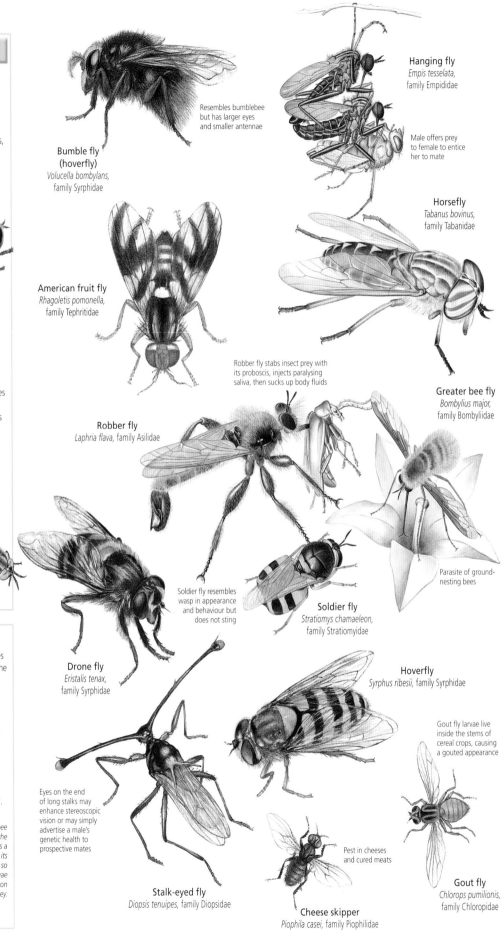

Resembles bumblebee but has larger eyes and smaller antennae

Bumble fly (hoverfly)
Volucella bombylans, family Syrphidae

Hanging fly
Empis tesselata, family Empididae

Male offers prey to female to entice her to mate

Horsefly
Tabanus bovinus, family Tabanidae

American fruit fly
Rhagoletis pomonella, family Tephritidae

Robber fly stabs insect prey with its proboscis, injects paralysing saliva, then sucks up body fluids

Greater bee fly
Bombylius major, family Bombyliidae

Robber fly
Laphria flava, family Asilidae

Parasite of ground-nesting bees

Soldier fly resembles wasp in appearance and behaviour but does not sting

Soldier fly
Stratiomys chamaeleon, family Stratiomyidae

Drone fly
Eristalis tenax, family Syrphidae

Hoverfly
Syrphus ribesii, family Syrphidae

Gout fly larvae live inside the stems of cereal crops, causing a gouted appearance

Eyes on the end of long stalks may enhance stereoscopic vision or may simply advertise a male's genetic health to prospective mates

Stalk-eyed fly
Diopsis tenuipes, family Diopsidae

Pest in cheeses and cured meats

Cheese skipper
Piophila casei, family Piophilidae

Gout fly
Chlorops pumilionis, family Chloropidae

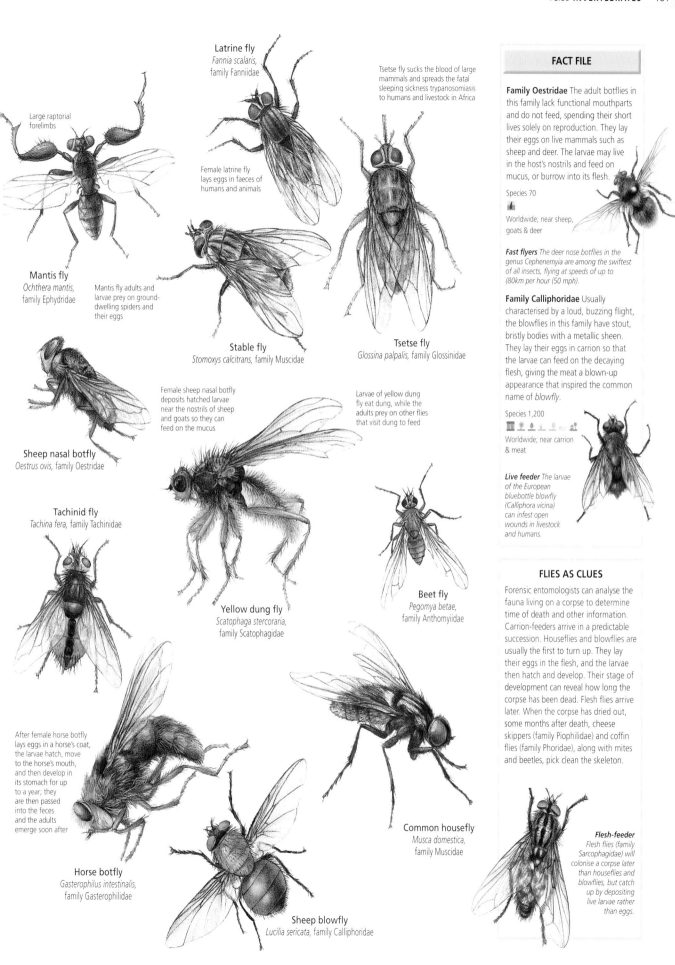

Large raptorial forelimbs

Mantis fly
Ochthera mantis,
family Ephydridae

Mantis fly adults and larvae prey on ground-dwelling spiders and their eggs

Latrine fly
Fannia scalaris,
family Fanniidae

Female latrine fly lays eggs in faeces of humans and animals

Tsetse fly sucks the blood of large mammals and spreads the fatal sleeping sickness trypanosomiasis to humans and livestock in Africa

Stable fly
Stomoxys calcitrans, family Muscidae

Tsetse fly
Glossina palpalis, family Glossinidae

Female sheep nasal botfly deposits hatched larvae near the nostrils of sheep and goats so they can feed on the mucus

Larvae of yellow dung fly eat dung, while the adults prey on other flies that visit dung to feed

Sheep nasal botfly
Oestrus ovis, family Oestridae

Tachinid fly
Tachina fera, family Tachinidae

Yellow dung fly
Scatophaga stercoraria,
family Scatophagidae

Beet fly
Pegomya betae,
family Anthomyiidae

After female horse botfly lays eggs in a horse's coat, the larvae hatch, move to the horse's mouth, and then develop in its stomach for up to a year; they are then passed into the feces and the adults emerge soon after

Horse botfly
Gasterophilus intestinalis,
family Gasterophilidae

Sheep blowfly
Lucilia sericata, family Calliphoridae

Common housefly
Musca domestica,
family Muscidae

FACT FILE

Family Oestridae The adult botflies in this family lack functional mouthparts and do not feed, spending their short lives solely on reproduction. They lay their eggs on live mammals such as sheep and deer. The larvae may live in the host's nostrils and feed on mucus, or burrow into its flesh.

Species 70

Worldwide; near sheep, goats & deer

Fast flyers The deer nose botflies in the genus Cephenemyia are among the swiftest of all insects, flying at speeds of up to (80km per hour (50 mph).

Family Calliphoridae Usually characterised by a loud, buzzing flight, the blowflies in this family have stout, bristly bodies with a metallic sheen. They lay their eggs in carrion so that the larvae can feed on the decaying flesh, giving the meat a blown-up appearance that inspired the common name of *blowfly*.

Species 1,200

Worldwide; near carrion & meat

Live feeder The larvae of the European bluebottle blowfly (Calliphora vicina) can infest open wounds in livestock and humans.

FLIES AS CLUES

Forensic entomologists can analyse the fauna living on a corpse to determine time of death and other information. Carrion-feeders arrive in a predictable succession. Houseflies and blowflies are usually the first to turn up. They lay their eggs in the flesh, and the larvae then hatch and develop. Their stage of development can reveal how long the corpse has been dead. Flesh flies arrive later. When the corpse has dried out, some months after death, cheese skippers (family Piophilidae) and coffin flies (family Phoridae), along with mites and beetles, pick clean the skeleton.

Flesh-feeder Flesh flies (family Sarcophagidae) will colonise a corpse later than houseflies and blowflies, but catch up by depositing live larvae rather than eggs.

BUTTERFLIES AND MOTHS

PHYLUM	Arthropoda
SUBPHYLUM	Hexapoda
CLASS	Insecta
ORDER	Lepidoptera
FAMILIES	131
SPECIES	165,000

With their delicate fluttering flight and often intricate wing patterns, butterflies and moths are the most studied and admired of all insects. They belong to the order Lepidoptera, which means 'scale wing' in Greek. Their four broad wings are covered by tiny, overlapping scales – hollow, flattened hairs that create the bright colours and iridescence of diurnal species. Almost all butterflies and moths are plant-feeders. Their larvae, known as caterpillars, have biting mouthparts for chewing plants, which can make them pests. Most adults have a long proboscis for sucking flower nectar and are important pollinators, though a few lack mouthparts and do not feed at all.

Nectar-feeder To drink nectar from flowers, butterflies and moths extend a long proboscis, which sits coiled like a watchspring when not in use. Many flowering plants evolved with colours and shapes to attract these pollinating insects.

Plant muncher A caterpillar is an eating machine, with biting mouthparts for munching through foliage or other plant food. Many species are brightly coloured to warn predators that they are unpalatable.

DAY AND NIGHT FLYERS

Absent only from the polar ice caps and the oceans, butterflies and moths are most abundant in the tropics but are found virtually anywhere that land plants grow. Most are highly specialised for feeding on particular flowering species.

As adults, butterflies and moths have slim bodies, broad wings, long antennae and two large compound eyes. Their wingspans range from about 4mm– 30cm (³⁄₁₆ inch–12 inches). More than 85 per cent of species in Lepidoptera are moths, most of which fly at night and have dull wings that are coupled by a spine-like structure known as a frenulum. Butterflies fly by day, display vibrant colours, have clubbed antennae and lack the frenulum. Some moth species, however, are also diurnal and brightly coloured.

Caterpillars are covered in hairs, and walk using three pairs of true legs and several false legs. When ready to pupate, they often enclose themselves in a cocoon using silk from modified salivary glands. The entire life cycle takes from a few weeks to a few years.

European pine shoot moth
Rhyacionia buoliana,
family Tortricidae

Larvae of European pine shoot moth feed on pine shoots, causing considerable damage in pine forests

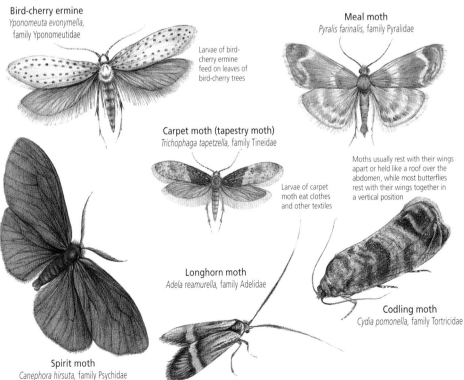

Bird-cherry ermine
Yponomeuta evonymella,
family Yponomeutidae

Larvae of bird-cherry ermine feed on leaves of bird-cherry trees

Meal moth
Pyralis farinalis, family Pyralidae

Carpet moth (tapestry moth)
Trichophaga tapetzella, family Tineidae

Larvae of carpet moth eat clothes and other textiles

Moths usually rest with their wings apart or held like a roof over the abdomen, while most butterflies rest with their wings together in a vertical position

Longhorn moth
Adela reamurella, family Adelidae

Codling moth
Cydia pomonella, family Tortricidae

Spirit moth
Canephora hirsuta, family Psychidae

⚡ CONSERVATION WATCH

Deadly trade Only 303 lepidopterids have been assessed by the IUCN, but of these, 94 per cent are on the Red List and 37 are extinct. Habitat loss is the major cause of the decline, but over-collecting has also had a major impact on attractive species such as the birdwing butterflies.

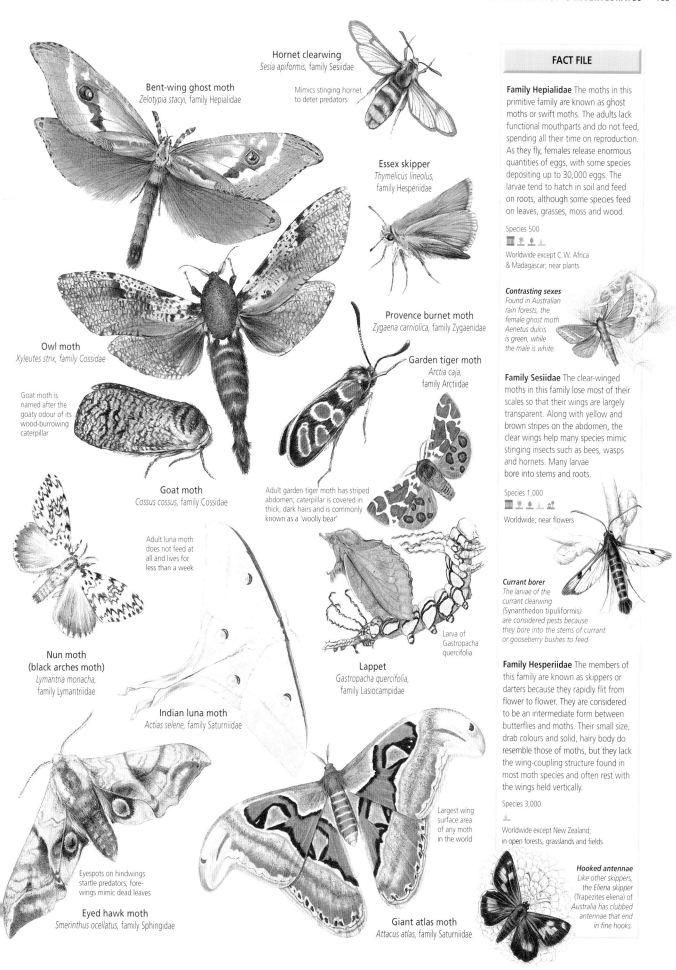

Bent-wing ghost moth
Zelotypia stacyi, family Hepialidae

Hornet clearwing
Sesia apiformis, family Sesiidae

Mimics stinging hornet
to deter predators

Essex skipper
Thymelicus lineolus,
family Hesperiidae

Provence burnet moth
Zygaena carniolica, family Zygaenidae

Owl moth
Xyleutes strix, family Cossidae

Goat moth is
named after the
goaty odour of its
wood-burrowing
caterpillar

Garden tiger moth
Arctia caja,
family Arctiidae

Goat moth
Cossus cossus, family Cossidae

Adult garden tiger moth has striped
abdomen; caterpillar is covered in
thick, dark hairs and is commonly
known as a 'woolly bear'

Adult luna moth
does not feed at
all and lives for
less than a week

Larva of
Gastropacha
quercifolia

Nun moth
(black arches moth)
Lymantria monacha,
family Lymantriidae

Lappet
Gastropacha quercifolia,
family Lasiocampidae

Indian luna moth
Actias selene, family Saturniidae

Largest wing
surface area
of any moth
in the world

Eyespots on hindwings
startle predators; fore-
wings mimic dead leaves

Eyed hawk moth
Smerinthus ocellatus, family Sphingidae

Giant atlas moth
Attacus atlas, family Saturniidae

FACT FILE

Family Hepialidae The moths in this primitive family are known as ghost moths or swift moths. The adults lack functional mouthparts and do not feed, spending all their time on reproduction. As they fly, females release enormous quantities of eggs, with some species depositing up to 30,000 eggs. The larvae tend to hatch in soil and feed on roots, although some species feed on leaves, grasses, moss and wood.

Species 500

Worldwide except C.W. Africa
& Madagascar; near plants

Contrasting sexes
*Found in Australian
rain forests, the
female ghost moth
Aenetus dulcis
is green, while
the male is white.*

Family Sesiidae The clear-winged moths in this family lose most of their scales so that their wings are largely transparent. Along with yellow and brown stripes on the abdomen, the clear wings help many species mimic stinging insects such as bees, wasps and hornets. Many larvae bore into stems and roots.

Species 1,000

Worldwide; near flowers

Currant borer
*The larvae of the
currant clearwing
(Synanthedon tipuliformis)
are considered pests because
they bore into the stems of currant
or gooseberry bushes to feed.*

Family Hesperiidae The members of this family are known as skippers or darters because they rapidly flit from flower to flower. They are considered to be an intermediate form between butterflies and moths. Their small size, drab colours and solid, hairy body do resemble those of moths, but they lack the wing-coupling structure found in most moth species and often rest with the wings held vertically.

Species 3,000

Worldwide except New Zealand;
in open forests, grasslands and fields

Hooked antennae
*Like other skippers,
the Eliena skipper
(Trapezites eliena) of
Australia has clubbed
antennae that end
in fine hooks.*

FACT FILE

Family Papilionidae Often large and brightly coloured, the swallowtails of this family are named after the tail-like extensions on the hindwings of most species. All swallowtail caterpillars have an osmetrium, a fork-shaped organ on their head that can release a foul odour to deter a predator. In some species, the caterpillars feed on poisonous plants, absorbing enough toxins to make both themselves and their adult form unpalatable.

Species 600

Worldwide; near flowers

Vivid warning
The bright wing markings of the crimson rose (Pachliopta hector) and many other swallow-tails warn predators that they have an unpleasant taste.

Family Noctuidae Noctuid or owlet moths make up the largest family in the order Lepidoptera. These night flyers have hearing organs on their thorax that can pick up echolocation signals emitted by bats, their main predators. Adults feed on nectar, sap, rotting fruit, tears or dung, while the larvae may eat foliage or seeds, or bore into stems and fruit, with some being serious crop pests.

Species 35,000

Worldwide; on plants

Background colours
Like many noctuid moths, Moma alpium has cryptic colouration, the mottled wings blending in with its woodland habitat.

Family Geometridae Known as geometer, looper or inchworm moths, the members of this family tend to be small with slender bodies. The larvae, which often resemble twigs when resting, lack at least one middle pair of false legs. They move by stretching out the front part of the body, then bringing the tail forward to meet it, creating a 'looping' or 'inching' gait.

Species 20,000

Worldwide; on foliage

Leaf mimic *The wings of the Southeast Asian geometer moth (Sarcinodes restitutaria) resemble leaves.*

Moth butterfly
Liphyra brassolis, family Lycaenidae

Caterpillars of moth butterfly feed on larvae of citrus ants and have tough skin that protects them from the ants' bites

African giant swallowtail
Papilio antimachus, family Papiolinidae

Orange-barred sulphur
Phoebis philea, family Pieridae

Cabbage butterfly
Pieris brassicae, family Pieridae

African giant swallowtail is the largest of all African butterflies, with a wingspan of 25cm (10 inches) or more

Scarce copper
Lycaena virgaureae, family Lycaenidae

Large blue
Maculinea arion, family Lycaenidae

Giant agrippa
Thysania agrippina, family Noctuidae

Union Jack butterfly
Delias mysis, family Pieridae

Giant agrippa has wingspan of up to 30cm (12 inches), the largest of any butterfly or moth

Bogong moth
Agrotis infusa, family Noctuidae

Bhutan glory butterfly
Bhutanitis lidderdalii, family Papilionidae

Newly emerged adult bogong moths avoid the summer heat by migrating to mountain caves and becoming dormant until autumn, when they return to the plains to breed

Apollo butterfly
Parnassius apollo, family Papilionidae

Only male mottled umbers fly; females are wingless

Red underwing moth
Catocala nupta, family Noctuidae

Mottled umber
Erannis defoliaria, family Geometridae

Large eyespot on hindwing deters predators

Adult owl butterfly feeds on rotting fruit

Owl butterfly
Caligo idomeneus,
family Nymphalidae

The postman
Heliconius melpomene,
family Nymphalidae

Helena butterfly
Morpho rhetenor, family Morphidae

All Helena butterflies have yellow-brown wings, but, on the males, air spaces between the scales scatter light and produce blue iridescence

Silver-washed fritillary
Argynnis paphia,
family Nymphalidae

Dead leaf butterfly
Kallima inachus,
family Nymphalidae

Patches on underside of wings mimic holes and other blemishes found on dead leaves

Kallima inachus in flight

Northern jungle queen butterfly
Stichophthalma camadeva,
family Nymphalidae

Female mimic is palatable but imitates the unpalatable African monarch to discourage predators

Mimic
Hypolimnas misippus,
family Nymphalidae

African monarch (lesser wanderer)
Danaus chrysippus,
family Nymphalidae

Male mimic waits on ground for females and is coloured to blend with the background

FACT FILE

Family Nymphalidae Known as brush-footed butterflies, the species in this family have very small and hairy forelegs, and walk using only the middle and back legs. The underside of the wings tends to be drab, while the upperside usually features strongly contrasting colours.

Species 5,200

Worldwide; near flowers

Seasonal variation *The map butterflies (Araschnia levana) that emerge in spring have orange-marked wings, while those that emerge in summer are black and white.*

COCOONS AND CHRYSALISES

When they are ready to transform into adults, caterpillars stop eating and find a safe spot. Some pupate underground without any further protection, but most moths spin a cocoon of silk, while almost all butterflies create a chrysalis, a hard shell formed from the caterpillar's skin and secured by silk to a branch.

Sticky cocoon *The larvae of bagworm moths (Thyridopteryx ephemeraeformis) live in cases of silk and plant debris, which harden into cocoons when they are ready to pupate.*

Transforming chrysalis *The pale green chrysalis of the monarch butterfly becomes transparent when the adult is ready to emerge.*

BUTTERFLY MIGRATION

A monarch butterfly (*Danaus plexippus*) may travel more than 2,900km (1,800 miles) in the 9 months of its life. Every autumn, millions of monarchs migrate south to their wintering sites in California and Mexico. Here, they shelter in great clusters on trees. In autumn, they begin the return journey north, during which they lay eggs and die. The new generation completes the trip to the summer feeding grounds.

BEES, WASPS, ANTS AND SAWFLIES

PHYLUM	Arthropoda
SUBPHYLUM	Hexapoda
CLASS	Insecta
ORDER	Hymenoptera
FAMILIES	91
SPECIES	198,000

The order Hymenoptera is named after the Greek words for 'membrane wing' and most of its species have two pairs of transparent wings. Although many bees, wasps and sawflies are solitary creatures, some species of bees and all species of ants live in highly structured societies, whose thousands or millions of members belong to different castes and perform specific tasks. Many of the world's most beneficial insects are hymenopterids. Bees and some wasps are the chief pollinators of both crops and wild plants, while many parasitic wasps play a crucial role in controlling the populations of other insects. Honeybees have been domesticated for their honey and wax.

Bite and sting Despite their formidable jaws, adult bull ants mainly eat nectar and plant juices, but they do capture insect prey to feed their young. They use an abdominal stinger to subdue prey and deter predators.

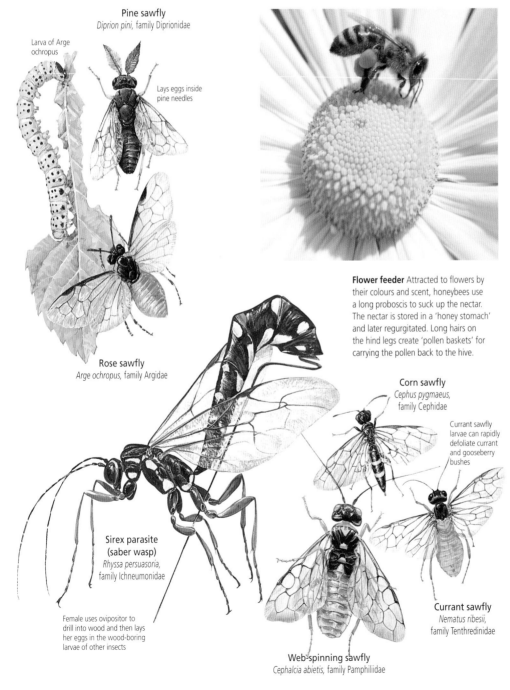

Pine sawfly
Diprion pini, family Diprionidae

Larva of Arge ochropus

Lays eggs inside pine needles

Rose sawfly
Arge ochropus, family Argidae

Flower feeder Attracted to flowers by their colours and scent, honeybees use a long proboscis to suck up the nectar. The nectar is stored in a 'honey stomach' and later regurgitated. Long hairs on the hind legs create 'pollen baskets' for carrying the pollen back to the hive.

Corn sawfly
Cephus pygmaeus, family Cephidae

Currant sawfly larvae can rapidly defoliate currant and gooseberry bushes

Sirex parasite (saber wasp)
Rhyssa persuasoria, family Ichneumonidae

Female uses ovipositor to drill into wood and then lays her eggs in the wood-boring larvae of other insects

Currant sawfly
Nematus ribesii, family Tenthredinidae

Web-spinning sawfly
Cephalcia abietis, family Pamphiliidae

ANATOMY AND LIFE CYCLE

Generally small to medium-sized, hymenopterans include the parasitic *Megaphragma caribea*, which, at just 0.17mm ($\frac{7}{1000}$ inch) long, is one of the smallest insects. Hymenopterids' hindwings are attached to the larger forewings by tiny hooks so that they beat together. The more primitive sawflies and their kin lack the slim waist that separates the thorax and abdomen of bees, wasps and ants.

Hymenopterans have mouthparts designed for biting or for biting and sucking. Sawflies, gall wasps, and some ants and bees are herbivorous, while most other species in the order are predatory or parasitic. In many species, the female's ovipositor (egg-laying organ) has become modified – sawflies use it for sawing into plant stems, where they lay their eggs; while bees, wasps and ants often use it for piercing or stinging predators or prey.

Female hymenopterans may lay their eggs in soil, in plants, in nests or hives, or in living insect hosts. In many species, the female determines whether the eggs are fertilised, with unfertilised eggs producing male larvae, and fertilised eggs producing females. In solitary species, the larvae hatch near a food source and develop independently, but in social species they rely on constant care from the adults. Development is by complete metamorphosis, and larvae usually pupate in a cocoon.

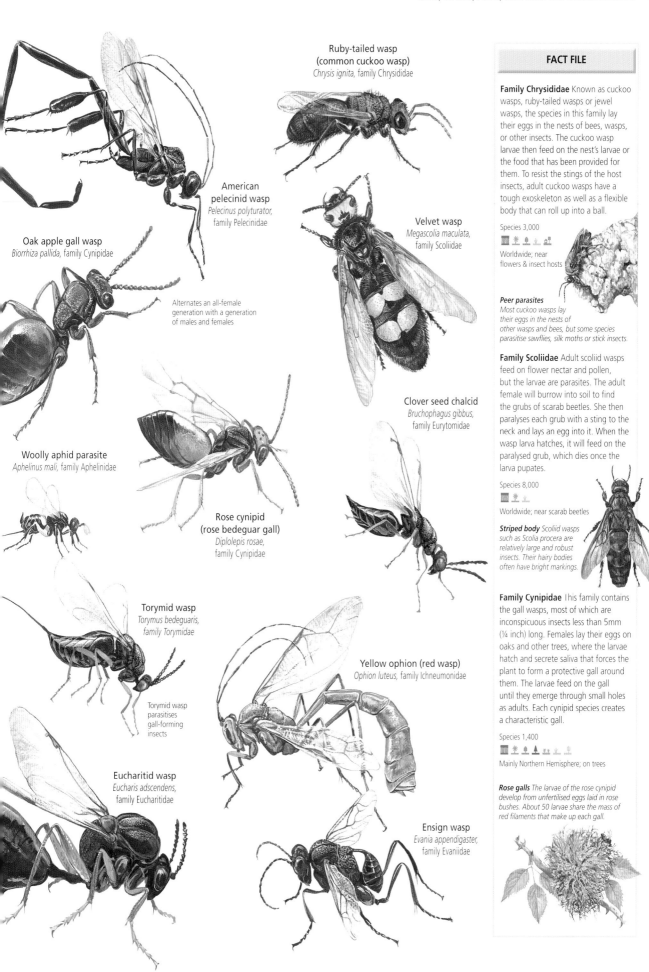

Ruby-tailed wasp (common cuckoo wasp)
Chrysis ignita, family Chrysididae

American pelecinid wasp
Pelecinus polyturator, family Pelecinidae

Oak apple gall wasp
Biorrhiza pallida, family Cynipidae

Alternates an all-female generation with a generation of males and females

Velvet wasp
Megascolia maculata, family Scoliidae

Woolly aphid parasite
Aphelinus mali, family Aphelinidae

Rose cynipid (rose bedeguar gall)
Diplolepis rosae, family Cynipidae

Clover seed chalcid
Bruchophagus gibbus, family Eurytomidae

Torymid wasp
Torymus bedeguaris, family Torymidae

Torymid wasp parasitises gall-forming insects

Yellow ophion (red wasp)
Ophion luteus, family Ichneumonidae

Eucharitid wasp
Eucharis adscendens, family Eucharitidae

Ensign wasp
Evania appendigaster, family Evaniidae

FACT FILE

Family Chrysididae Known as cuckoo wasps, ruby-tailed wasps or jewel wasps, the species in this family lay their eggs in the nests of bees, wasps, or other insects. The cuckoo wasp larvae then feed on the nest's larvae or the food that has been provided for them. To resist the stings of the host insects, adult cuckoo wasps have a tough exoskeleton as well as a flexible body that can roll up into a ball.

Species 3,000

Worldwide; near flowers & insect hosts

Peer parasites
Most cuckoo wasps lay their eggs in the nests of other wasps and bees, but some species parasitise sawflies, silk moths or stick insects.

Family Scoliidae Adult scoliid wasps feed on flower nectar and pollen, but the larvae are parasites. The adult female will burrow into soil to find the grubs of scarab beetles. She then paralyses each grub with a sting to the neck and lays an egg into it. When the wasp larva hatches, it will feed on the paralysed grub, which dies once the larva pupates.

Species 8,000

Worldwide; near scarab beetles

Striped body *Scoliid wasps such as Scolia procera are relatively large and robust insects. Their hairy bodies often have bright markings.*

Family Cynipidae This family contains the gall wasps, most of which are inconspicuous insects less than 5mm (¼ inch) long. Females lay their eggs on oaks and other trees, where the larvae hatch and secrete saliva that forces the plant to form a protective gall around them. The larvae feed on the gall until they emerge through small holes as adults. Each cynipid species creates a characteristic gall.

Species 1,400

Mainly Northern Hemisphere; on trees

Rose galls *The larvae of the rose cynipid develop from unfertilised eggs laid in rose bushes. About 50 larvae share the mass of red filaments that make up each gall.*

HIVE OF ACTIVITY

The social life of the honeybee (genus Apis) is among the most complex in the animal world. A queen bee can lay up to 1,500 eggs a day. Fertilised eggs develop into workers or queens, and unfertilised eggs become drones. The workers feed the hatched larvae before they are capped inside cells to pupate. When a hive reaches its optimum size, the old queen flies off to found a new colony, followed by thousands of workers. The first new queen to emerge will rule the old nest.

Close view This electron micrograph shows a honeybee's large compound eyes, each made up of more than 4,000 lenses. Two sensitive antennae emerge between the eyes.

Inside a beehive All the drones and workers in a hive (below) are the offspring of the queen, whose only task is to lay eggs. Drones are male bees, and their only job is to mate with new queens. Worker bees gather food, maintain the hive and feed the queen and her young. Glands in their head produce royal jelly for the larvae. Workers also make honey by regurgitating nectar and spreading it in cells to dehydrate, then capping it with wax.

Being queen A queen bee is the largest bee in the hive. She can live for up to 5 years.

Hard workers Workers are females that cannot breed. They live for only a few weeks.

Bee young Worker bees bring food to the larvae as they mature inside water-resistant waxen cells. These larvae (above) are transforming into pupae, and will emerge as adults.

Honeybee swarm A swarm of bees gathers when an old queen, along with up to 70,000 workers, leaves an established hive to establish a new colony. The swarm waits while scouts find a good location for the nest.

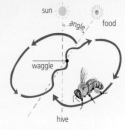

sun
angle
food
waggle
hive

Dance of the bees A worker bee uses a figure-eight dance to convey information about a new food source. The rate of tail-waggling indicates the distance to the food source, while the direction is signaled by the angle of the dance to the sun.

Larva cells Most larvae become workers. They are first fed royal jelly, and later pollen and honey. Queen larvae are fed only royal jelly. Drones develop from unfertilised eggs.

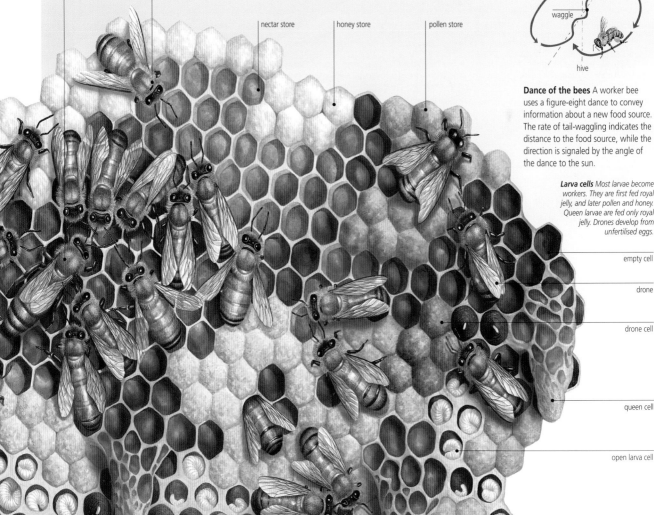

queen bee

worker

nectar store   honey store   pollen store

empty cell

drone

drone cell

queen cell

open larva cell

Anthophorid digger bee
Anthophora parietina,
family Anthophoridae

Halictidae is a large family
of solitary bees that nest
in subterranean tunnels

Mining bees often share
ground nests, but do not
work together or share a queen

Halictid bee
Halictus quadricinctus, family Halictidae

Carpenter bee
Xylocopa violacea,
family Anthophoridae

Mining bee
Colletes cunicularius,
family Colletidae

Sand digger wasp
Ammophila sabulosa,
family Sphecidae

Drags paralysed prey
back to sand burrow

Mason bees build their
nests in empty snail shells

Mason bee
Osmia bicolour,
family Megachilidae

Red-tailed bumblebee
Bombus lapidarius, family Apidae

Bumblebee colonies die out
each autumn, with only young
mated females overwintering
to start new colonies in spring

Paper wasp
builds nest by
rolling balls of
wood particles
and saliva into
paper-thin walls

Common wasp
Vespula vulgaris, family Vespidae

Potter wasp
Eumenes pomiformis,
family Eumenidae

Paper wasp
Polistes gallicus, family Vespidae

FACT FILE

Family Sphecidae This family includes species known as digger wasps, sand wasps, mud-dauber wasps and thread waisted wasps. A female sphecid wasp paralyses arthropod prey with her sting and deposits it in her nest, where her larvae later feed on its body. Most species have their nests underground in burrows, but some use plant stems or rotten wood, and mud daubers build rows of cells from pellets of mud.

Species 8,000

Worldwide; often in sandy soil

Solitary hunter The female bee wolf (Philanthus triangulum) will carry paralysed honeybees back to its sandy burrow

Family Apidae The honeybees, bumblebees and stingless bees in this family live in communal nests centred on a queen. Worker bees forage for nectar and pollen, which they bring back to the nest to feed the queen and her larvae. While honeybees often attach their hives to trees, bumblebees usually create their nests in the soil.

Species 1,000

Worldwide; near flowers

Fierce bee When provoked, a colony of Southeast Asia's giant honeybees (Apis dorsata) is capable of stinging a person to death.

Family Vespidae This family contains all the social wasps, as well as some solitary ones. Hornets, yellow jackets and paper wasps all use chewed wood and saliva to build their papery nests. In most species, the colony dies out in late autumn, leaving only a few mated queens to overwinter and establish new colonies in spring.

Species 4,000

Worldwide

Self-sacrifice To defend its colony, a worker of the social wasp species Brachygastra lecheguana will sting an attacker and may well die when the sting detaches from its abdomen.

Myrmica laevinodis, family Formicidae

Myrmica laevinodis feeds on honeydew produced by aphids in return for protecting them from parasites

Honey ant
Myrmecocystus hortideorum, family Formicidae

Honey ants called repletes store food in their swollen abdomen and hang from the ceiling of the colony's nest

Red wood ant
Formica rufa, family Formicidae

Formica rufa worker

Formica rufa queen

Formica rufa male

Leafcutter workers carry leaf fragments up to three times their own weight

Pharaoh ant
Monomorium pharaonis, family Formicidae

Leafcutter ant
Atta sexdens, family Formicidae

Carpenter ant
Camponotus herculeanus, family Formicidae

Slave-making ant
Polyergus rufescens, family Formicidae

Giant hunting ant
Dinoponera grandis, family Formicidae

Slave-making ant raids nests of closely related species to steal pupae, which then emerge in its own nest and become its workers

Bull ant
Myrmecia forficata, family Formicidae

Weaver ant
Oecophylla smaragdina, family Formicidae

OTHER INSECTS

LUM Arthropoda	
BPHYLUM Hexapoda	
SSES Insecta	
DERS 19*	
MILIES 218*	
CIES >3,000*	

als refer only to the 19 orders
t make up 'Other insects'.

Of the remaining 19 orders of Insecta, 16 are illustrated here. They are a diverse assortment, which include primitive, wingless forms such as silverfish and bristletails; parasites of mammals and birds such as fleas and lice; parasites of insects such as strepsipterans; and crop pests such as thrips. Also included are insects that spend most of their lives in water, such as mayflies, caddisflies, dobsonflies and stoneflies. Stick and leaf insects are plant-feeders; angel insects, snakeflies, ant lions, lacewings, and hanging flies prey on other invertebrates; while rock crawlers, web-spinners, earwigs, booklice and scorpion flies recycle detritus.

Web-spinners The only insects other than danceflies with silk-producing glands in the legs, web-spinners (order Embioptera) use their silk to create a shared network of nests and tunnels. They develop by incomplete metamorphosis, with nymphs resembling their parents.

Earwigs The order Dermaptera contains the earwigs, small flattened insects that feed on detritus. The large 'forceps' extending from the abdomen are used in defence and courtship. Females guard their eggs and newly hatched larvae.

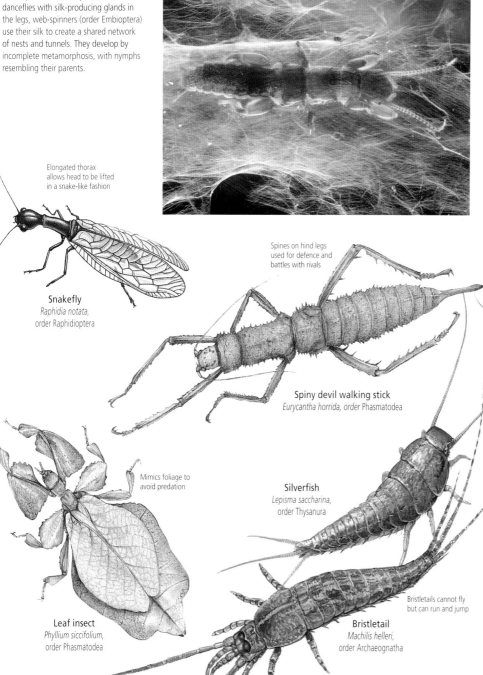

Elongated thorax allows head to be lifted in a snake-like fashion

Snakefly
Raphidia notata,
order Raphidioptera

Spines on hind legs used for defence and battles with rivals

Spiny devil walking stick
Eurycantha horrida, order Phasmatodea

Mimics foliage to avoid predation

Leaf insect
Phyllium siccifolium,
order Phasmatodea

Silverfish
Lepisma saccharina,
order Thysanura

Bristletails cannot fly but can run and jump

Bristletail
Machilis helleri,
order Archaeognatha

Order Thysanura This order contains the silverfish, flightless insects that may closely resemble the earliest insects. They have long antennae on their head, and three 'tails' extending from the abdomen. Silverfish hatch from eggs laid in crevices near food sources.

Species 370

Worldwide; in trees, caves & buildings

House guest *This silverfish (Lepismodes iniquilinus) is often found in houses, where it feeds on paper, glue in book bindings, starched clothing and dry foods.*

Order Phasmatodea The supreme mimics in this order are known as stick insects and leaf insects. They feed on foliage. Most species are wingless, and, when wings are present, they usually are fully developed and functional only in the males. Many females can produce offspring from unfertilised eggs.

Species 3,000

Worldwide, esp. in the tropics; near plants

Stick mimic
When disturbed, stick insects such as Bacillus rossii may freeze for hours or they may sway as if blowing in the wind.

FACT FILE

Order Ephemeroptera The mayflies in this order live very short lives as adults, often lasting only a day. The males form great swarms from which females select mates. Eggs are deposited in or near water, and the nymphs are aquatic. Nymphs leave the water to moult into winged forms, which soon moult again into the adults. Mayflies are the only insects to moult once they have wings.

Species 2,500

Worldwide; in fresh or brackish water

Flying romance
Mayflies mate in flight, with the male using his long forelegs to grasp the female.

Order Megaloptera The dobsonflies and alderflies in this order spend most of their lives as predatory aquatic larvae. They leave the water to pupate, emerging as winged adults that usually do not feed and only live long enough to breed. Eggs are usually laid on rocks or plants beside ponds or streams, and the larvae crawl or fall into the water.

Species 300

Worldwide; in fresh water

Toe-biter *The larva of the dobsonfly Archichauliodes is known as the 'toe-biter'. It breathes through the leg-like gills along its abdomen.*

Order Phthiraptera The parasitic lice in this order are tiny wingless insects that evolved from winged ancestors. They feed on birds and mammals and cannot survive long away from their host. Lice can travel to a new host only when two members of the host species come into contact, which restricts most lice to particular host species. Some lice have sucking mouthparts, while others have chewing mouthparts.

Species 5,500

Worldwide; on bird or mammal hosts

Louse bites dog *The dog-biting louse (Trichodectes canis) uses its chewing mouthparts to feed on the hair, skin and blood of domestic dogs and other canids. Gripping claws on its legs make it difficult to dislodge.*

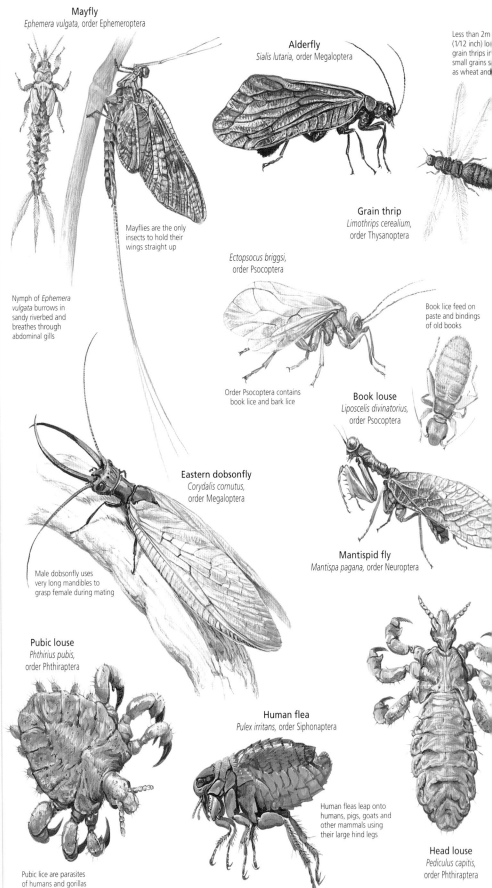

Mayfly
Ephemera vulgata, order Ephemeroptera

Mayflies are the only insects to hold their wings straight up

Nymph of *Ephemera vulgata* burrows in sandy riverbed and breathes through abdominal gills

Alderfly
Sialis lutaria, order Megaloptera

Less than 2m (1/12 inch) lo grain thrips in small grains s as wheat and

Grain thrip
Limothrips cerealium, order Thysanoptera

Ectopsocus briggsi, order Psocoptera

Order Psocoptera contains book lice and bark lice

Book lice feed on paste and bindings of old books

Book louse
Liposcelis divinatorius, order Psocoptera

Eastern dobsonfly
Corydalis cornutus, order Megaloptera

Male dobsonfly uses very long mandibles to grasp female during mating

Mantispid fly
Mantispa pagana, order Neuroptera

Pubic louse
Phthirius pubis, order Phthiraptera

Pubic lice are parasites of humans and gorillas

Human flea
Pulex irritans, order Siphonaptera

Human fleas leap onto humans, pigs, goats and other mammals using their large hind legs

Head louse
Pediculus capitis, order Phthiraptera

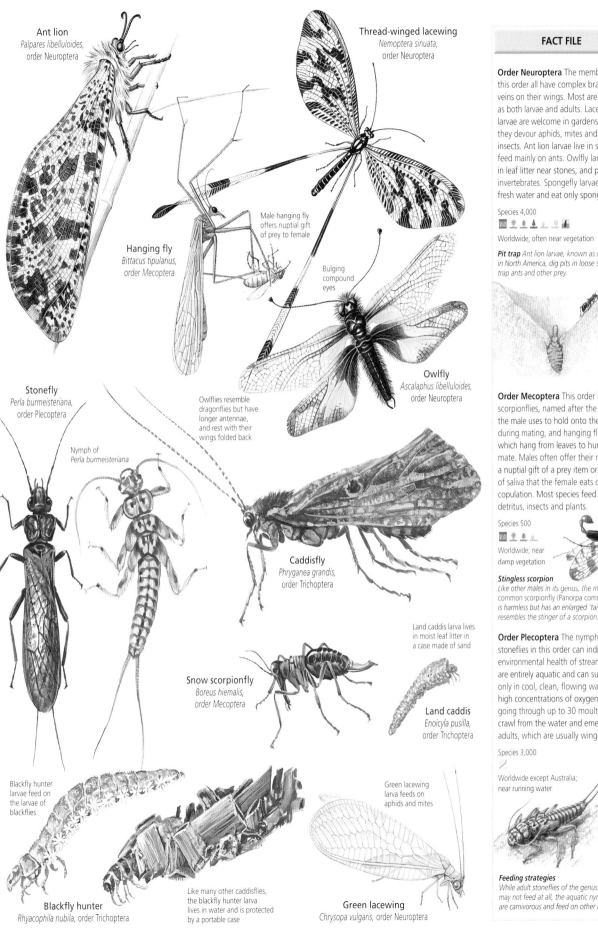

Ant lion
Palpares libelluloides,
order Neuroptera

Thread-winged lacewing
Nemoptera sinuata,
order Neuroptera

Hanging fly
Bittacus tipularius,
order Mecoptera

Male hanging fly
offers nuptial gift
of prey to female

Bulging
compound
eyes

Owlfly
Ascalaphus libelluloides,
order Neuroptera

Stonefly
Perla burmeisteriana,
order Plecoptera

Nymph of
Perla burmeisteriana

Owlflies resemble
dragonflies but have
longer antennae,
and rest with their
wings folded back

Caddisfly
Phryganea grandis,
order Trichoptera

Land caddis larva lives
in moist leaf litter in
a case made of sand

Snow scorpionfly
Boreus hiemalis,
order Mecoptera

Land caddis
Enoicyla pusilla,
order Trichoptera

Blackfly hunter
larvae feed on
the larvae of
blackflies

Green lacewing
larva feeds on
aphids and mites

Like many other caddisflies,
the blackfly hunter larva
lives in water and is protected
by a portable case

Blackfly hunter
Rhyacophila nubila, order Trichoptera

Green lacewing
Chrysopa vulgaris, order Neuroptera

FACT FILE

Order Neuroptera The members of
this order all have complex branching
veins on their wings. Most are predators
as both larvae and adults. Lacewing
larvae are welcome in gardens because
they devour aphids, mites and scale
insects. Ant lion larvae live in sand and
feed mainly on ants. Owlfly larvae live
in leaf litter near stones, and prey on
invertebrates. Spongefly larvae live in
fresh water and eat only sponges.

Species 4,000

Worldwide; often near vegetation

Pit trap Ant lion larvae, known as doodlebugs
in North America, dig pits in loose sand to
trap ants and other prey.

Order Mecoptera This order includes
scorpionflies, named after the large tail
the male uses to hold onto the female
during mating, and hanging flies,
which hang from leaves to hunt and
mate. Males often offer their mates
a nuptial gift of a prey item or a pellet
of saliva that the female eats during
copulation. Most species feed on
detritus, insects and plants.

Species 500

Worldwide; near
damp vegetation

Stingless scorpion
Like other males in its genus, the male
common scorpionfly (Panorpa communis)
is harmless but has an enlarged 'tail' that
resembles the stinger of a scorpion.

Order Plecoptera The nymphs of the
stoneflies in this order can indicate the
environmental health of streams. They
are entirely aquatic and can survive
only in cool, clean, flowing water with
high concentrations of oxygen. After
going through up to 30 moults, nymphs
crawl from the water and emerge as
adults, which are usually winged.

Species 3,000

Worldwide except Australia;
near running water

Feeding strategies
While adult stoneflies of the genus Perla
may not feed at all, the aquatic nymphs
are carnivorous and feed on other larvae.

INSECT ALLIES

Hexapods are arthropods with six legs and a body divided into three parts: head, thorax and abdomen. The vast majority of hexapods are insects, but there are also three classes of non-insect hexapods – the springtails (class Collembola), proturans (Protura) and diplurans (Diplura). Found in soil and leaf litter, these tiny creatures range from 0.5mm to 3cm (¹⁄₅₀ inch to 1¼ inches) in length. They are distinguished from insects by their mouthparts, which are fully tucked into the head. As in the most primitive of insects, the silverfish and the bristletails, these tiny soil-dwellers evolved from a wingless ancestor and they continue to moult throughout their life.

PHYLUM	Arthropoda
SUBPHYLUM	Hexapoda
CLASSES	3
ORDERS	5
FAMILIES	31
SPECIES	8,300

Ready to leap Springtails are ubiquitous, occurring in freshwater, coastal marine and most terrestrial habitats, including deserts and polar zones. They feed mainly on microorganisms. Surface-dwellers tend to be covered in hairs (above) or scales.

PRIMITIVE HEXAPODS

The springtails that make up the class Collembola are named after a forked organ on the abdomen that can propel them up to 100 times their own body length – a quick way to escape danger. They are among the most abundant animals, with populations of 750 million individuals per hectare (300 million per acre) in some grassland habitats.

With a length of less than 2mm (¹⁄₁₂ inch), proturans are rarely seen and were not even discovered until 1907. They live in soil and leaf litter, where they feed on fungi and decaying matter. They are the most primitive of all hexapods and lack eyes and antennae. Instead, the forelegs perform a sensory function and are held out in front of the animal rather than being used for walking. With each moult, proturans gain another segment of abdomen.

Diplurans lack eyes but feel their way around in soil or leaf litter with their long antennae and two tail-like structures known as cerci. In some carnivorous species, the cerci have become powerful pincers that can capture other soil-dwellers. Other species are herbivorous and feed on soil fungi and detritus. Diplurans are able to regenerate some of their body parts.

Entomobrya superba,
class Collembola

Long legs often found on surface-dwelling springtails

Eosentomon ribagai,
class Protura

Adapted to cold and often found in wet places, soil, and snow

Jumping organ (furcula) usually held cocked against the abdomen but can be released to propel the springtail

Isotoma viridis,
class Collembola

Hypogastrura sp.
class Diplura

Measures only 2mm (1/12 inch) long and lives on pond surface

Sminthurus aquaticus,
class Collembola

Campodea fragilis,
class Diplura

Giant springtail
Tetrodontophora bielanensis,
class Collembola

Giant springtail can reach 9mm (⅓ inch) in length and has lost the ability to jump great distances, but deters the attacks of tiger beetles by releasing chemicals

Proturans hold their forelegs out in front of the body

Cerci have developed into pincers

A dipluran can regrow a lost leg, antenna or cerci over several moults

Baculentulus breviunguis,
class Protura

Catajapyx aquilonaris,
class Diplura

ECHINODERMS

HYLUM	Echinodermata
LASSES	5
RDERS	36
AMILIES	145
PECIES	6,000

The sea stars, sea urchins, brittle stars, feather stars and sea cucumbers that belong to the phylum Echinodermata display diverse body forms, but share some defining characteristics. Adults usually have pentamerous symmetry, with the body arranged into a five-part radial pattern around a central axis. Most internal organs are also arranged in this pattern. An internal skeleton of calcareous plates provides protection and support. The plates often bear spines or small lumps – the name echinoderm means 'spiny skin'. The body cavity includes a water-vascular system, a network of water vessels that controls the tube feet used for locomotion, feeding, respiration and sensory functions.

Sticky defence In sea cucumbers, the five-part symmetry is internal and the skeleton is reduced. This leopard sea cucumber (*Bohadschia argus*) has ejected a mass of sticky white threads, known as Cuvierian tubules, to confuse or entangle a predator.

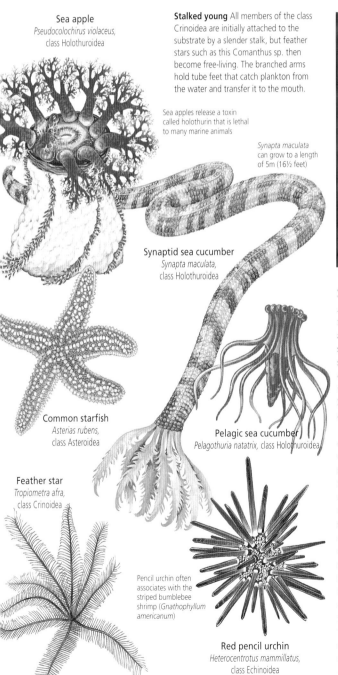

Sea apple
Pseudocolochirus violaceus,
class Holothuroidea

Stalked young All members of the class Crinoidea are initially attached to the substrate by a slender stalk, but feather stars such as this Comanthus sp. then become free-living. The branched arms hold tube feet that catch plankton from the water and transfer it to the mouth.

Sea apples release a toxin called holothurin that is lethal to many marine animals

Synapta maculata can grow to a length of 5m (16½ feet)

Synaptid sea cucumber
Synapta maculata,
class Holothuroidea

Common starfish
Asterias rubens,
class Asteroidea

Pelagic sea cucumber
Pelagothuria natatrix, class Holothuroidea

Feather star
Tropiometra afra,
class Crinoidea

Pencil urchin often associates with the striped bumblebee shrimp (*Gnathophyllum americanum*)

Red pencil urchin
Heterocentrotus mammillatus,
class Echinoidea

SPINY BOTTOM-DWELLERS

All echinoderms are marine and most are mobile bottom-dwellers, although sea lilies are fixed to the sea floor by a long stalk, and a few sea cucumbers float in the open ocean. Echinoderms are found throughout the world at all depths. Sea urchins and sea stars are very commonly seen along the seashore.

The phylum Echinodermata is divided into five classes. Members of the class Crinoidea include the sessile sea lilies as well as the mobile feather stars. They are filter-feeders and, unlike other echinoderms, have their mouth facing away from the substrate. The other echinoderm classes include predators, grazers of algae and deposit-feeders. The sea stars of class Asteroidea and brittle stars of class Ophiuroidea have arms radiating from their body. Their skeletal plates are held together by muscles, which allows flexibility. In the class Echinoidea, sea urchins and sand dollars have a rigid skeleton of fused plates that supports a globular or flattened form, usually featuring

Spiky gathering Many echinoderms, such as these sea urchins, gather in large groups, influenced by the availability of food. The strategy may also provide some protection from predators and enhance reproduction.

prominent spines. Sea cucumbers (class Holothuroidea) are generally soft-bodied, with their skeletons reduced to minute spicules.

Although a few echinoderms can reproduce asexually, most have separate sexes that release eggs and sperm into the water for fertilisation. The larvae are often free-swimming and metamorphose intobottom-dwelling adults. In some species, the larval stage is omitted and the newly hatched young resemble small adults.

FACT FILE

Class Asteroidea Also known as starfish, the sea stars in this class move and feed using the suckered tube feet along their arms. Most are predators that evert their stomach over sessile or slow-moving prey to begin digesting it. Some use their tube feet to prise open the shells of bivalves such as clams. Sea stars are usually vibrant colours such as red, orange or purple and may have a smooth, spiny or ridged surface.

Species 1,500

Worldwide; on the sea floor

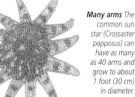

Many arms The common sun star (Crossaster papposus) can have as many as 40 arms and grow to about 1 foot (30 cm) in diameter.

Class Ophiuroidea In contrast to sea stars, in which the arms grade into the central disk, the brittle stars and basket stars of Ophiuroidea have sharply demarcated arms. Rather than using their tube feet to crawl, they move by using any two of their flexible, jointed arms in a breast-stroke action. The class includes predators, scavengers and filter-feeders.

Surface star The brittle star (Ophiura ophiura) usually lives on the surface of sandy or muddy sediment but may also burrow shallowly.

Species 2,000

Worldwide; on the sea floor

Class Echinoidea The sea urchins in this class have a spherical body protected by a skeletal case called a test, and long, movable spines. Sand dollars are flattened and covered in smaller spines. Many echinoids have a system of plates, muscles and teeth known as the Aristotle's lantern, with which they scrape algae from rocks.

Species 950

Worldwide; on or in the sea floor

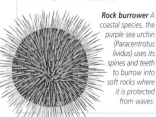

Rock burrower A coastal species, the purple sea urchin (Paracentrotus lividus) uses its spines and teeth to burrow into soft rocks where it is protected from waves.

Spiny starfish
Marthasterias glacialis, class Asteroidea

The spiny starfish can reach a diameter of 70cm (28 inches)

Sand dollar (sea biscuit)
Clypeaster humilis, class Echinoidea

Reef sea urchin
Diadema setosum, class Echinoidea

Black brittle star
Ophiocomina nigra, class Ophiuroidea

The arms of brittle stars are easily broken off, hence the common name

Sea urchins move slowly using their tube feet and spines

Gorgon's head
Astrospartus mediterraneus, class Ophiuroidea

Goose-foot starfish
Anseropoda placenta, class Asteroidea

Heart urchin (sea potato)
Echinocardium cordatum, class Echinoidea

Sea pancake
Echinodiscus auritus, class Echinoidea

Edible sea urchin
Echinus esculentus, class Echinoidea

Cushion star
Culcita novaeguineae, class Asteroidea

An increase in the numbers of this coral predator has devastated large areas of the Great Barrier Reef

Crown-of-thorns starfish
Acanthaster planci, class Asteroidea

African red knob sea star
Protoreaster linckii, class Asteroidea

OTHER INVERTEBRATES

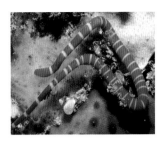

The preceding pages have covered eight major invertebrate phyla, as well as two subphyla of invertebrate chordates. There are, however, another 25 phyla of invertebrates, many of which are profiled in this chapter. Although the phylum Bryozoa contains 5,000 species, most of these minor groups are small – Phoronida (horseshoe worms), for example, contains a mere 20 species. The members of these phyla also tend to be physically small and are often microscopic. Most are marine, although many are found in fresh water and some occur on land. Often overlooked, the minor invertebrate phyla all display fascinating solutions to the challenges presented by their environment.

MINOR INVERTEBRATE PHYLA	
PHYLA	25
CLASSES	> 40
ORDERS	> 60
SPECIES	> 12,000

Ribbon worms Roughly 1,000 species of long ribbon worms make up the phylum Nemertea. The majority are marine, but some live in fresh water or moist soil. They trap or stab their invertebrate prey using a unique projectile proboscis.

Invading comb jelly Native to America's Atlantic coast, the sea walnut (Mnemiopsis leidyi) was accidentally introduced into the Black Sea in the early 1980s. Explosive population growth followed, and soon this predator of zooplankton and fish eggs and larvae had devastated the ecosystem and triggered fishery crashes.

Extreme survivors Water bears such as Echiniscus testudo (shown here magnified) are able to survive environmental stress by entering cryptobiosis, a death-like state. They can survive for years before reviving when conditions become favourable.

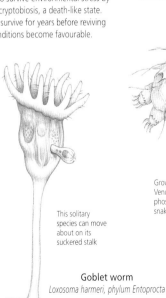

This solitary species can move about on its suckered stalk

Goblet worm
Loxosoma harmeri, phylum Entoprocta

Water bear
Macrobiotus hufelandi, phylum Tardigrada

Growing up to 1.5m (5 feet) long, Venus' girdle glows with a greenish phosphorescence and swims with a snake-like movement

Venus' girdle
Cestus veneris, phylum Ctenophora

FACT FILE

Phylum Entoprocta Attached by a stalk to the substrate, goblet worms use a ring of mucus-secreting tentacles to filter particles from the water. Many species form colonies by budding.

Species 150

Worldwide; mostly on the sea floor

Phylum Tardigrada Unknown until 1773, following the invention of the microscope, water bears crawl over ocean sediment, soil or plants with a slow, bear-like gait. These minute creatures occur in almost all aquatic and moist terrestrial environments.

Species 600

Worldwide; aquatic & moist land habitats

Phylum Ctenophora The marine comb jellies that make up this phylum swim by beating the fused cilia (tiny hairs) arranged in eight comb rows along their body. They engulf their prey directly or capture it with a pair of sticky, retractable tentacles.

Species 100

Worldwide; mostly planktonic

Melon jellyfish
Beroe cucumis, phylum Ctenophora

Can engulf prey (such as other comb jellies) that are as large as itself

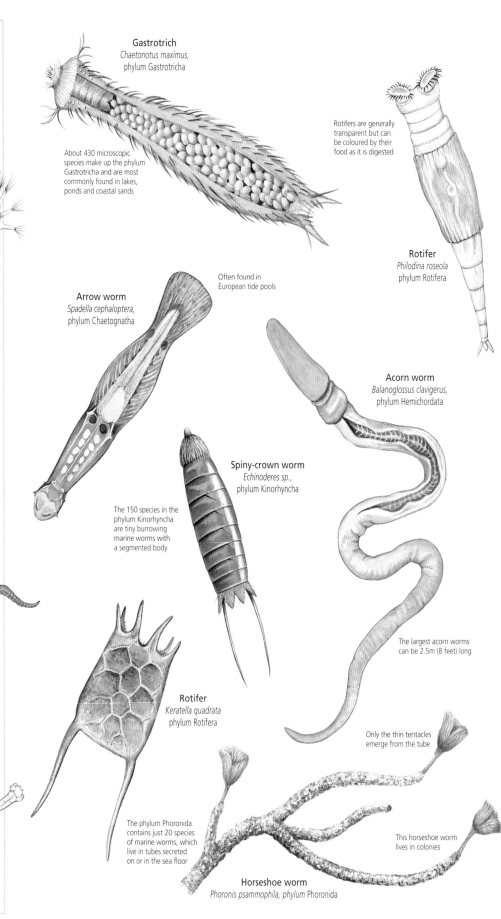

FACT FILE

Phylum Rotifera Sometimes known as wheel animals, rotifers are microscopic aquatic creatures. A crown of cilia (hair-like structures) around the mouth beat rapidly to collect food and propel the rotifer, creating the impression of a whirling wheel. The trunk is often protected by a stiffened epidermis and sometimes bears defensive spines. Most rotifer species are found in fresh water, where they make up much of the zooplankton.

Species 1,800

Worldwide; in aquatic vegetation & moist terrestrial habitats

Swimming rotifer
Many rotifer species, including Brachionus plicatilis, are free-swimming. Others use their cement-producing toes to attach to a surface.

Phylum Hemichordata Known as acorn worms or hemichordates, the members of this phylum have a three-part body made up of a proboscis at the head; a collar in the middle, which bears tentacles in some species; and a trunk containing the digestive and reproductive organs. They feed on small particles, either filtered from the water or consumed with sediment.

Species 90

Worldwide; on the sea floor

Close relatives *Hemichordates, such as Saccoglossus cambrensis, are closely related to the chordates but lack a notochord.*

Phylum Chaetognatha The arrow worms of this phylum are voracious predators. Their head has up to 14 large grasping spines for seizing prey such as copepods or small fishes. When the spines are not in use, a hood formed from the body wall covers the head to protect them. Most species are plank-tonic and many migrate from deeper waters to feed at the surface at night.

Species 90

Worldwide; in plankton & on the sea floor

Torpedo worm
Like other arrow worms, Sagitta setosa has a torpedo-shaped body with dorsal and ventral fins for balance and a tail fin for thrust.

Gastrotrich
Chaetonotus maximus,
phylum Gastrotricha

About 430 microscopic species make up the phylum Gastrotricha and are most commonly found in lakes, ponds and coastal sands

Rotifers are generally transparent but can be coloured by their food as it is digested

Rotifer
Philodina roseola
phylum Rotifera

Often found in European tide pools

Arrow worm
Spadella cephaloptera,
phylum Chaetognatha

Acorn worm
Balanoglossus clavigerus,
phylum Hemichordata

Spiny-crown worm
Echinoderes sp.,
phylum Kinorhyncha

The 150 species in the phylum Kinorhyncha are tiny burrowing marine worms with a segmented body

The largest acorn worms can be 2.5m (8 feet) long

Rotifer
Keratella quadrata
phylum Rotifera

Only the thin tentacles emerge from the tube

The phylum Phoronida contains just 20 species of marine worms, which live in tubes secreted on or in the sea floor

This horseshoe worm lives in colonies

Horseshoe worm
Phoronis psammophila, phylum Phoronida

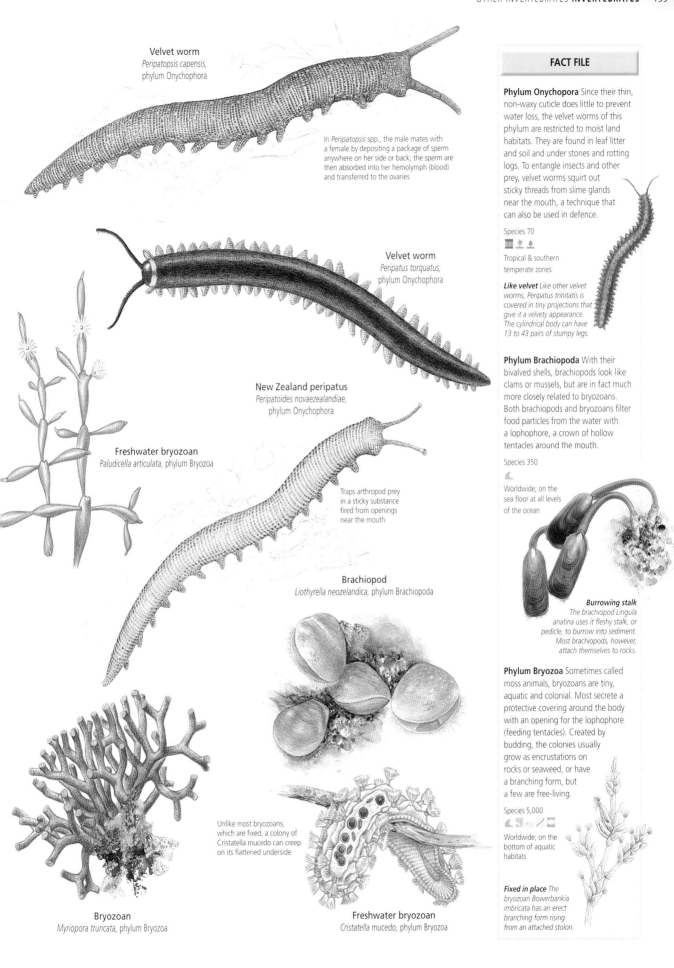

Velvet worm
Peripatopsis capensis,
phylum Onychophora

In *Peripatopsis* spp., the male mates with a female by depositing a package of sperm anywhere on her side or back; the sperm are then absorbed into her hemolymph (blood) and transferred to the ovaries

Velvet worm
Peripatus torquatus,
phylum Onychophora

New Zealand peripatus
Peripatoides novaezealandiae,
phylum Onychophora

Freshwater bryozoan
Paludicella articulata, phylum Bryozoa

Traps arthropod prey in a sticky substance fired from openings near the mouth

Brachiopod
Liothyrella neozelandica, phylum Brachiopoda

Unlike most bryozoans, which are fixed, a colony of Cristatella mucedo can creep on its flattened underside

Bryozoan
Myriopora truncata, phylum Bryozoa

Freshwater bryozoan
Cristatella mucedo, phylum Bryozoa

FACT FILE

Phylum Onychopora Since their thin, non-waxy cuticle does little to prevent water loss, the velvet worms of this phylum are restricted to moist land habitats. They are found in leaf litter and soil and under stones and rotting logs. To entangle insects and other prey, velvet worms squirt out sticky threads from slime glands near the mouth, a technique that can also be used in defence.

Species 70

Tropical & southern temperate zones

Like velvet *Like other velvet worms, Peripatus trinitatis is covered in tiny projections that give it a velvety appearance. The cylindrical body can have 13 to 43 pairs of stumpy legs.*

Phylum Brachiopoda With their bivalved shells, brachiopods look like clams or mussels, but are in fact much more closely related to bryozoans. Both brachiopods and bryozoans filter food particles from the water with a lophophore, a crown of hollow tentacles around the mouth.

Species 350

Worldwide; on the sea floor at all levels of the ocean

Burrowing stalk
The brachiopod Lingula anatina uses it fleshy stalk, or pedicle, to burrow into sediment. Most brachiopods, however, attach themselves to rocks.

Phylum Bryozoa Sometimes called moss animals, bryozoans are tiny, aquatic and colonial. Most secrete a protective covering around the body with an opening for the lophophore (feeding tentacles). Created by budding, the colonies usually grow as encrustations on rocks or seaweed, or have a branching form, but a few are free-living.

Species 5,000

Worldwide; on the bottom of aquatic habitats

Fixed in place *The bryozoan Bowerbankia imbricata has an erect branching form rising from an attached stolon.*

GLOSSARY

abdomen The part of the body containing the digestive system and the reproductive organs. In insects and spiders, the abdomen makes up the rear of the body.

adaptation A change in an animal's behaviour or body that allows it to survive and breed in new conditions.

amphibious Able to live on land and in water.

amplexus A breeding position of frogs and toads, in which the male holds the female with his front legs.

annulus (pl. annuli) A marking resembling a ring, as in turtle scutes, that is used in estimating age.

antenna (pl. antennae) A slender organ on an animal's head, used to sense smells and vibrations around it. Insects have two antennae.

aquatic Living all or most of the time in water.

arachnid An arthropod with four pairs of walking legs; includes spiders, scorpions, ticks and mites.

arboreal Living all or most of the time in trees.

arthropod An animal with jointed legs and a hard exoskeleton.

biodiversity The total number of species of plants and animals in a particular location.

book lungs Lungs found in primitive insects and arachnids, consisting of 'pages' of tissue forming the respiratory surface through which blood and oxygen circulate

camouflage The colours and patterns of an animal that enable it to blend in with the background. Camouflage conceals the animal from predators and helps it to ambush prey.

cephalic Of, relating to, or situated on or near the head.

cephalothorax In arachnids and crustaceans, a region of the body that combines the head and thorax. It is covered by a hard body case.

chelicera (pl. chelicerae) A pincer-like, biting mouthpart, such as a fang, as in spiders, ticks, scorpions and mites.

chitin A hard, plastic-like substance that gives an exoskeleton its strength.

chrysalis The form taken by a butterfly in the pupal stage of its metamorphosis, or the case in which it undergoes this stage.

cloaca An internal chamber in amphibians and reptiles into which the contents of the reproductive ducts and the waste ducts empty before being passed from the body.

clutch The full and completed set of eggs laid by a female reptile or amphibian in a single nesting attempt.

cocoon In insects and spiders, a case made of silk to protect themselves or their eggs. In amphibians, a protective case made of mud, mucus or a similar material, in which the animal rests during estivation.

complete metamorphosis A form of development in which a young insect changes shape from an egg to a larva, to a pupa, to an adult. Insects such as beetles and butterflies develop by complete metamorphosis.

compound eye An eye that is made up from many smaller eyes, each with its own lens; found in most insects, but not in spiders.

crest In lizards, a line of large, scaly spines on the centre of the neck and back. Some lizards can raise or lower the crest as a means of communication with others.

crocodilians Crocodiles, caimans, alligators and gavials. Members of the order Crocodilia.

crustacean A mostly aquatic animal, such as a lobster, crab or prawn, that has a hard external skeleton.

dewlap In a lizard, a flap of skin, sometimes brightly coloured, on the throat. A dewlap usually lies close to the neck and can be extended to communicate with other lizards.

dimorphic Having two distinct forms within a species. Sexual dimorphism is the situation in which the male and female of a species differ in size and/or appearance.

dinosaurs A group of reptiles that dominated Earth from the Triassic to the Cretaceous Period (245–65 million years ago). The largest land animals that ever lived, dinosaurs are more closely related to today's birds and crocodilians than they are to other living reptiles.

dioecious Born either male or female and remaining that way through life.

display Behaviour used by an animal to communicate with its own species, or with other animals. Displays can include postures, actions, or showing brightly coloured parts of the body, and may signal threat, defence or readiness to mate.

diurnal Active during the day. Most reptiles are diurnal because they rely on the Sun's heat to provide energy for hunting and other activities.

dragline A strand of silk that spiders leave behind them as they move about.

drone A male honeybee. Drones mate with young queens but, unlike worker bees, they do not help in collecting food or maintaining the hive.

ecosystem A community of plants and animals and the environment to which they are adapted.

ectothermic Unable to internally regulate the body temperature, instead relying on external means such as the Sun, as in cold-blooded animals such as reptiles.

egg sac A silk bag that some spiders spin around their eggs. Some egg sacs are portable, so the eggs can be carried from place to place. Others are more like a blanket, and are attached to leaves or suspended from twigs.

egg tooth A special scale on the tip of the upper lip of a hatchling lizard or snake. It is used to break a hole in the egg so that the newborn animal can escape. The egg tooth falls off within a few days of hatching.

elytra The thickened front wings of beetles that cover and protect the back wings.

embryo An unborn animal in the earliest stages of development. An embryo may grow inside its mother's body, or in an egg outside her body.

endothermic Able to regulate the body temperature internally, as in warm-blooded animals.

estivate To spend a period of time in a state of inactivity to avoid unfavourable conditions. During times of drought, many frogs greatly reduce their overall metabolic rate and estivate underground until rain falls.

evolution Gradual change in plants and animals, over many generations, in response to their environment.

exoskeleton A hard external skeleton or body case. All arthropods are protected by an exoskeleton.

food chain A system in which one organism forms food for another, which in turn is eaten by another, and so on along the food chain.

fossorial Adapted to digging or burrowing underground.

frill In a lizard, a collar around the neck. Like a crest or dewlap, a frill can be raised to signal to other lizards or to surprise a predator.

gastroliths Stones swallowed by animals such animals as crocodilians, that stay in the stomach to crush food and help digestion.

gestation period The period of time during which a female animal is pregnant with her young.

gills Organs that collect oxygen from water and are used for breathing. Gills are found in many aquatic animals, including some insects and the larvae of amphibians.

global warming The increase in the temperature of Earth and its lower atmosphere due to human activity such as deforestation, land degradation, intensive farming and the burning of fossil fuels.

gravid Full of eggs; pregnant.

grub An insect larva, usually that of a beetle.

habitat The area in which an animal naturally lives. Many different kinds of animals live in the same environment (for example, a rain forest), but each kind lives in a different habitat within that environment.

hatchling A young animal, such as a reptile, that has recently hatched from its egg.

heat-sensitive pit Sense organs in some snakes that detect tiny changes in temperature.

hibernate To remain completely inactive during the cold winter months. Insects may hibernate.

hybrid The offspring of parents of two different species.

incomplete metamorphosis A system of development in which a young insect gradually changes shape from an egg, to a nymph, to an adult.

insectivore An animal that eats only insects or invertebrates.

introduced An animal or plant species imported from another place by humans and deliberately or accidentally released into a habitat.

invertebrate An animal with no backbone. Many invertebrates are soft-bodied animals, such as worms, leeches or octopuses, but most have an exoskeleton, or hard external skeleton, such as insects.

Jacobson's organ Two small sensory pits on the top part of the mouth of snakes and lizards. They use this organ to analyse small molecules picked up from the air or ground with their tongue. keratin A protein found in horns, hair, scales, feathers and fingernails.

larva (pl. larvae) A young animal that looks completely different from its parents. An insect larva, sometimes called a grub, maggot or caterpillar, changes into an adult by either complete or incomplete meta-morphosis. In amphibians, the larval stage is the stage before metamorphosis that breathes with gills rather than lungs (for example, tadpoles).

live-bearing Giving birth to young that are fully formed.

maggot The larva of a fly.

mandibles Biting jaws of an insect.

metamorphosis A way of development in which an animal's body changes shape. Many invertebrates, including insects, and some vertebrates, such as amphibians, metamorphose as they mature.

migration A usually seasonal journey from one habitat to another. Many animals migrate vast distances to another location to find food, or to mate and lay eggs or give birth.

mollusc An animal, such as a snail or squid, with no backbone and a soft body that is often partly or fully enclosed by a shell.

morph A colour or other physical variation within, or a local population of, a species.

moult To shed an outer layer of the body, such as hair, skin, scales, feathers or the exoskeleton.

neoteny The retention of some immature or larval characteristics into adulthood. Some salamander species are usually or often neotenic.

niche The ecological role played by a species within an animal community.

nocturnal Active at night. Nocturnal animals have special adaptations, such as large, sensitive eyes or ears, to help them find their way in the dark.

nymph The young stage of an insect that develops by incomplete metamorphosis. Nymphs are often

similar to adults, but do not have fully developed wings.

ocellus A kind of simple eye with a single lens. Insects usually have three ocelli on the top of their heads.

ovipositor A tubelike organ through which female insects lay their eggs. The stinger of bees and wasps is a modified ovipositor.

ovoviviparous Reproducing by giving birth to live young that have developed from eggs within the mother's body. The embryos may hatch as they are laid or soon after.

paleontology The scientific study of life in past geological periods.

parallel evolution The situation in which related groups living in isolation develop similar structures to cope with similar evolutionary pressures.

parasitism The situation in which an animal or plant lives and/or feeds on another living animal or plant, sometimes with harmful effects.

pedicle The narrow 'waist' that connects an insect's head to its thorax, or a spider's cephalothorax to its abdomen.

pedipalp One of a pair of small, leglike organs on the head of insects and the cephalothorax of spiders and scorpions, used for feeling or for handling food. In spiders, they are also used for mating.

pheromone A chemical released by an animal that sends a signal and affects the behaviour of others of the same species. Many animals use pheromones to attract mates, or to signal danger.

pollen A dustlike substance produced by male flowers, or by the male organs in a flower, and used in reproduction.

pollination The process by which the pollen produced by the male organs of a flower comes into contact with the female parts of the flower, thus fertilising the flower and enabling seeds to form.

pore A minute opening, as in the skin of an animal or the leaf surface of a plant.

predator An animal that lives mainly by killing and eating other animals.

proboscis In insects, a long, tubular mouthpart used for feeding.

pupa (pl. pupae) The stage during which an insect transforms from a larva to an adult.

queen A female insect that begins a social insect colony. The queen is normally the only member of the colony that lays eggs.

rostrum A tubular, beak-like feeding organ on the head of some insects.

rudimentary Describes a simple, undeveloped, or underdeveloped part of an animal, such as an organ or wing.

scutes In a turtle or tortoise, the horny plates that cover the bony shell.

sedentary Having a lifestyle that involves little movement; also used to describe animals that do not migrate.

semi-aquatic Living some of the time in water, and some of the time on land.

silk A strong but elastic substance made by many insects and spiders. Silk is liquid until it leaves the animal's body.

social Living in groups. Social animals can live in breeding pairs, sometimes together with their young, or in a colony or herd of up to thousands of animals.

spawn To release eggs and sperm together directly into the water.

species A group of animals with very similar features that are able to breed together and produce fertile young.

spermatophore A container or package of sperm that is passed from male to female during mating.

spicule A minute, needle-like, siliceous or calcareous body, found in invertebrates.

spinnerets The finger-like appendages of spiders that are connected to silk glands, found near the tip of the abdomen.

spiracle A small opening that leads into the trachea, or breathing tube, of an insect or spider.

stereoscopic vision Vision in which both eyes face forward, giving an animal two overlapping fields of view and thus allowing it to judge depth.

stridulate To make a sound by scraping objects together. Many insects communicate in this way, some by scraping their legs against their body.

stylet A sharp mouthpart used for piercing plants or animals.

symbiosis An alliance between two species that is usually (but not always) beneficial to both. Animals form symbiotic relationships with plants, microorganisms and other animals.

sympatric Of two or more species, occurring in the same area.

taxonomy The system of classifying living things into various groups and

subgroups according to similarities in features and adaptations.

terrestrial Living all or most of the time on land.

tentacles On marine invertebrates, long, thin structures used to feel and grasp, or to inject venom. On caecilians, sensory organs located on the sides of the head, possibly used for tasting and smelling.

territory An area of land inhabited by an animal and defended against intruders. The area often contains all the living resources required by the animal, such as food and a nesting or roosting site.

thorax The middle part of an animal's body. In insects, the thorax is divided from the head with a narrow "waist," or pedicle. In spiders, the thorax and head make up a single unit.

torpid In a sleep-like state in which bodily processes are greatly slowed. Torpor helps animals to survive difficult conditions such as cold or lack of food. Estivation and hibernation are types of torpor.

trachea A breathing tube in an animal's body. Insects and some spiders have many small tracheae that spread throughout the body.

venom Poison injected by animals into a predator or prey through fangs, stingers, spines or similar structures.

venomous Describes an animal that is able to inject venom into another. Venomous animals usually attack by biting or stinging.

vertebrate An animal with a backbone. All vertebrates have an internal skeleton of cartilage or bone. Fishes, reptiles, birds, amphibians and mammals are vertebrates.

vertebral column The series of vertebrae running from head to tail along the back of vertebrates, and which encloses the spinal cord.

vestigial Relating to an organ that is non-functional or atrophied.

vibrissae Specialised hairs, or whiskers, that are extremely sensitive to touch.

worker A social insect that collects food and tends a colony's young, but which usually cannot reproduce.

INDEX

Page numbers in *italics* refer to illustrations, photographs and to information in captions. Species are listed by both their common name/s and scientific name, although page references to scientific names often relate only to mentions in the text of common names.

A

abalone, European edible *140*
Ablepharus kitaibelii 51, 53
Abraliopsis morisii 142
Abronia aurita 57
Acanthaster planci 196
Acanthocardia aculeata 139
Acanthodactylus pardalis 55, 55
Acanthosaura armata 43
Acarus siro 154
Achatina achatina 141
Acrantophis madagascariensis 63
Acrochordus spp. *65*
Acrocinus longimanus 178
Actias selene 183
Actinia equina 134
adders 18, *18*, 20, 67, 75, 76, *76, 78, 79*
Adela reamurella 182
Adenomera andreae 106, *106*
Aeluroscalabotes felinus 46
Aenetus dulcis 183
Afrixalus dorsalis 116
Agalychnis spp. 111, *111*
Agama agama 42
agamas *42*
Agkistrodon spp. 67, *79*
Agriope bruennichi 151
Agrotis infusa 184
Ahaetulla nasuta 72
Aipysurus laevis 77
Alcyonium digitatum 133
alderfly 125, 192, *192*
Algyroides nigropunctatus 55, *55*
Alligator spp. 34, *34*
alligators 14, 33, 34, *34*
Allobates femoralis 115
Alpheus randalli 162
Alytes spp. *102*
Amardillidium vulgare 158, 161, *161*
Amblyrynchus cristatus 39
Ambystoma spp. 94, 96, *96*, 98
Ameiva ameiva 57
ameiva, giant *57*
Ammophila sabulosa 189
Amolops viridimaculatus 118
amphibians 84–119
amphioxus 130
amphipods *161*
amphisbaenians 14, 22, *22*, 36, 60
Amphitretus pelagicus 143
Amphiuma means 93
amphiuma, two-toed *93*
anaconda 23, *23*, *63*
anapsids 14
Anaspides tasmaniae 161
Ancylus fluviatilis 141
Andrias davidianus 93, *93*
Androctonus australis 149
Aneides lugubris 97, *97*
anemones *see* sea anemones
angel insects 125, 191
Anguina tritici 136
Anguis fragilis 56
Anilius scytale 65
Anisoscelis flavolineatus 171
annelids 144, *144*

Anodonta cygnaea 139
anoles 18, *18*, 41, *41*, *44*, *52*
Anolis spp. *41*
Anopheles maculipennis 179
Anseropoda placenta 196
Antalis tarentinum 138
Antaresia childreni 63
Anthaxia hungarica 176
Anthophora parietina 189
Anthrenus scrophulariae 176
Antipathes furcata 134
ant lion 125, 191, 193, *193*
ants 125, 173, 186, 190
   bull ant 190
   carpenter ant 190
   consumption by poison-arrow frogs 115
   giant hunting ant 190
   honey ant 190
   leaf-cutter ant 190
   pharaoh ant 190
   red wood ant 190
   slave-making ant 190
   thief ant 190
   trap-jaw ant 190
   weaver ant 190
anurans *see* frogs; toads
Apalone spp. *27*
Aphantochilus rogersi 151
Aphelinus mali 187
aphids 171, 173, *173*
Aphrodite aculeata 144
Apis spp. *189*
Aplysina aerophoba 131
arachnids 147, 148–55
Araneus diadematus 151
Araniella cucurbitina 151
Araschnia levana 185
Archelon 16, *16*
Architeuthis dux 137, 143
Archosauria 14
Archosauromorpha 16
Arctia caja 183
Argas reflexus 154
Arge ochropus 186
Argiope spp. *152*
Argonauta argo 143, *143*
Argulus foliaceus 160
Argynnis paphia 185
Arion rufus 141
Artemia salina 159, *159*
Arthroleptis wahlbergii 119
arthropods 146–94
Ascaphus truei 102, *102*
Ascaris lumbricoides 136
ascidians 130
Ascothorax ophioctenis 160
Asellus aquaticus 161
Aspidelaps lubricus 76
Aspideretes gangeticus 27, *27*
Aspidites melanocephalus 64, *64*
asps *see* snakes
Astacilla pusilla 161
Asterias rubens 195
Astrospartus mediterraneus 196
Atelopus varius 109, *109*
Atheris squamigera 78
Atractaspis spp. *65*
Atrax robustus 153
Atta spp. *190*
Attacus atlas 183
Attaphila fungicola 168
Atympanophrys shapingensis 103
Atypus muralis 150
Aurelia aurita 133

axolotl 95, *95*
Azemiops faae 78

B

Bachia panoplia 56
bachia, Thomas's *56*
Bacillus rossii 191
backswimmers 174
Baculentulus breviunguis 194
Balanoglossus clavigerus 198
Balanus tintinnabulum 160
banded tulip *140*
bandy-bandy *66*
barnacles 158, 160, *160*
Basiliscus plumifrons 41
Batagur baska 29, *29*
Bathynella natans 161
Bathynomus giganteus 161
Batrachoseps major aridus 94
Batrachuperus mustersi 94
bats 100
bee fly, greater *180*
bee wolf *189*
bees 125, 145, 165, 186, 188–9, *189*
beet fly *181*
beetles 125, 165, 175–8, *181*
   ant-nest beetle *175*
   bee beetle *176*
   bess beetle *178*
   black blister beetle *177*
   blister beetles 177, *177*
   bombardier beetle *175*
   cigarette beetle *177*
   click beetles 177, *177*
   Colourado potato beetle *178*
   common carpet beetle *176*
   convergent lady beetle *176*
   darkling 127, *127*
   Darwin's stag beetle *178*
   diving beetles 174, *175*
   European burying beetle *176*
   European ground beetle *175*
   European splendor beetle *176*
   feather-winged beetle *175*
   fire beetle *177*
   flesh-eating beetle *176*
   frog-legged leaf beetle *178*
   fuscous soldier beetle *176*
   golden rove beetle *176*
   golden spider beetle *177*
   goliath beetle *177*
   greyback cane beetle *107*
   great capricorn beetle *178*
   green scarab *177*
   harlequin beetle *178*
   Hercules beetle *177*
   Java fiddle beetle *175*
   jewel beetles 176, *176*
   lady beetles *165*, 173, *173*, 175, 176, *176*, *177*
   large elm bark beetle *178*
   longhorn (longicorn) beetles *178*
   metallic wood-boring beetle *176*
   rhinoceros dung beetle *177*
   scarab beetles *165*, 175
   seven-spotted lady beetle *176*
   snout beetles *see* weevils
   South American longhorn beetle *175*
   South American sawyer beetle *178*
   spotted cucumber beetle *175*
   stag beetles *175*, *178*, *178*
   tiger beetle *175*
   tobacco beetle *177*
   turnip flea beetle *178*
   water scavenger beetle *176*
   whirligig beetles *174*

axolotl 95, *95*

Beroe cucumis 197
Bhutanitis lidderdalii 184
Bielzia coerulans 137
biology and behaviour
   amphibians 84, 87–8
   invertebrates 126
   reptiles 18–20
Biorrhiza pallida 187
Bipalium kewense 135
bird-cherry ermine *182*
Bitis spp. 67, *79*, *79*
Bittacus tipularius 193
Blaberus giganteus 168
blackfly hunter *193*
Blaniulus guttulatus 157
Blatella germanica 168
bloodworms *179*
blowflies 179, 181, *181*
blue dasher *166*
bluebottles *see* blowflies; jellyfish
Boa constrictor 63, *63*
boas 60, 61, 62, *62*, 63, *63*, 64, *64*
bobtail *see* cuttlefishes
bockadam, New Guinea *71*
Bocydium globulare 172
Boettgerilla pallens 141
Bohadschia argus 195
Boiga dendrophila 72, *72*
Bolitoglossa jacksoni 97
Bolyeria multocarinata 62
Bombina spp. 90, *90*, 102, *102*
Bombus lapidarius 189
Bombylius major 180
boomslang 72, *72*
Boophis madagascariensis 119
Boreus hiemalis 193
Bosmina longirostris 159
botflies 181, *181*
Bothriechis spp. 66, *73*, *81*
Bothriopsis taeniata 81
Bothrops spp. *81*
Botrylloides magnicoecum 130
Botryllus schlosseri 130
brachiopods 125, 199, *199*
Brachygastra lecheguana 189
Brachylophus spp. 39, *39*
Brachynus crepitans 175
Brachypelma albopilosa 150
Brachypoda versicolour 155
Branchionus plicatilis 198
Branchiostoma lanceolatum 130
Branchipus stagnalis 159
Braula caeca 180
Bravicoryne brassicae 173
Breviceps spp. 114, *114*
brine fly *164*
bristletail 125, 191, *191*, 194
bristleworms 144
brittle stars 195, 196, *196*
Brookesia superciliaris 45
brown recluse *153*
bryozoans 125, 197, 199, *199*
Bufo spp. 89, *100*, *101*, 107, *107*, 108, *108*, 109, *109*, 116
bugs 125, 145, *155*, *164*, *171*, 171–4, *172*, *173*
bullfrogs *see* frogs
bumble fly *180*
Bungarus fasciatus 75
bush-crickets *see* crickets
bushmaster 81, *81*
buthid, European *149*
Buthus occitanus 149
butterflies 125, 145, 182–5
   African monarch *185*

Apollo butterfly *184*
Bhutan glory butterfly *184*
brush-footed butterflies 185, *185*
cabbage butterfly *184*
dead leaf butterfly *185*
Helena butterfly *185*
map butterfly *185*
monarch butterflies 185, *185*
moth butterfly *184*
northern jungle queen butterfly *185*
owl butterfly *185*
Rajah Brooke's birdwing butterfly 129, *129*
swallowtail butterfly *146*
Union Jack butterfly *184*
by-the-wind sailor *133*

C

Cacosternum capense 118, *118*
caddisfly 125, 191, *193*
caecilians 84, *84*, 86, 89, *90*, 90, *99*, *99*
Caenorhabditis elegans 136
Caiman crocodilus 35
caimans 33, 34, *34*, 35
Calabaria reinhardtii 62
Calamaria septemtrionalis 70
calango, green *56*
Caligo idomeneus 186
Callagur borneoensis 29, *29*
Calliphora vicina 181
Calloselasma rhodostoma 81
Calopteryx virgo 166
Calosoma sycophanta 175
Calotes spp. 43, *43*
Calumma spp. *45*
Campodea fragilis 194
Camponotus herculeanus 190
Candoia aspera 62
Candona suburbana 160
Canephora hirsuta 182
Canthocamptus staphylinus 159
cantil *79*
Caprella anatifera 161
Captorhinomorpha 16
Carcinus maenas 160, *160*, *163*
Caretta caretta 26
Carettochelys insculpta 27
Carlia triacantha 51, *51*
Caryophyllia smithi 134
Casarea dusumieri 62
Cassiopeia andromeda 133
Catajapyx aquilonaris 194
caterpillars 182, *182*
Catocala nupta 184
Causus lichtensteini 78
caymans *see* caimans
centipedes 127, 146, 157, *157*
Centrolene prosoblepon 112, *112*
Centruroides gracilis 149
Cepaea hortensis 141
Cephalcia albietis 186
cephalopods 123, 137, 142, *143*
Gephenemyia spp. *181*
Cephus pygmaeus 186
Cerambyx cerdo 178
Cerastes cerastes 78
Ceratophrys spp. 105, *105*
Cerberus rynchops 71
Cercopis sanguinolenta 173
Cercosaura ocellata 56
Cereus pedunculatus 134
Cerianthus lloydi 134
Cerocoma meuhlfieldi 177
Cestus veneris 197
Chaetoderma canadense 138

Chaetonotus maximus 198
Chaetopleura apiculata 138
chalcid wasp 187
Chamaeleo spp. 45
chameleons 14, *14*, 18, 21, 37, 38, *38*, 45, *45*
Charina spp. 62
Charinus milloti 149
Charonia tritonis 140
cheese skipper 180, *181*
Chelifer cancroides 149
Chelodina longivollis 25
Chelonia mydas 26, *26*
Chelus fimbriatus 25
Chelydra serpentina 31, *31*
Chiasmocleis ventrimaculata 114, *114*
Chiasognathus grantii 178
chiggers 155
Chioglossa lusitanica 95
Chiromantis xerampelina 119
Chironex fleckeri 133
Chironius monticola 74
Chironomus plumosus 179
Chiroteuthis veranyi 143
Chiton spp. 138
chitons 137, 138, *138*
Chlamydosaurus kingii 37, 42, 52
Chlorohydra viridis 132
Chlorops pumilionis 180
chocolate arion *141*
chopontil *31*
Chromodouris spp. 137
Chrysemys picta 28, *28*
Chrysis ignita 187
Chrysopa vulgaris 193
Chrysopelea paradisi 21, 72
Chrysops caecutiens 180
chuckwala 40
chytridiomycosis fungus 101
cicadas 171, 172, *172*
Cicindela chinensis 175
Cimex lectuarius 172
Cirrothauma murrayi 143
clams 129, *129*, 137, *137*, 139, *139*, 145
classification 17, 86, 124–5
Claudius angustatus 31
Clavelina lepadiformis 130
clearwings 183
Clelia clelia 74
Clemmys spp. 24, 27, *27*, 28, 32
Clypeaster humilis 196
Cnemidophorus spp. 22, 56
cnidarians 124, 127, 132–4
cobras 19, 60, 61, *61*, 66, *73*, 74, 74, 75, *75*
Coccinella septempunctata 176
cockle, spiny *139*
cockroaches 125, 168, *168*
Coelurosauravus 16, *16*
Coenagrion peulla 166
coffin fly *181*
Coleonyx variegatus 46, *46*
Colletes cunicularius 189
Coluber spp. 68
Comanthus spp. 195
comb jellies 125, 197, *197*
Conchoderma auritum 160
conchs 140
Conolophus subcristatus 39
conservation 23
constrictors *see* anaconda; boas
continental drift 16, *16*
Convoluta convoluta 135
cooters, river 28, *28*
copepods 159, *159*
copperhead 79
coqui 102, 106, *106*
Corallium rubrum 134
Corallus spp. 63, 64, *64*

corals 124, 127, 132, 134, 145
  black coral *134*
  bubble coral *134*
  clubbed finger coral *134*
  fire coral *134*
  Formosan soft coral *133*
  mushroom coral *134*
  organ-pipe coral *133*
  red brain coral *134*
  red coral *134*
  West Indian sea fan *134*
Cordylus spp. 49
Coreus marginatus 172
Corophium volutator 161
Corucia zebrata 37, 50
Corydalis cornutus 192
Corynactis viridis 132
Cossus cossus 183
cottonmouth, Florida 67
courtship 18, 88
cowries 140
crabs 127, 128, *128*, 158
  Alaskan king crab *163*
  Chinese mitten crab *163*
  European green crab 160, *160*, 163
  fiddler crab 158, *162*
  giant Japanese spider crab 158, *163*
  hermit crabs 163, *163*
  horn-eyed ghost crab *163*
  red carnation coral crab *146*
  red crab 163, *163*
crane flies 179, *179*, 180
Crangon crangon 162
Craspedacusta sowerbyi 132
crayfish, spinycheek *163*
crickets 125, 145, 170, *170*, 171
crime scene insects 181
crinoids 195, *195*
Cristatella mucedo 199
crocodiles 14, 15, *15*, 27, 33, *33*, 34, 35, *35*
crocodilians 17, 19, *19*, 22, 22, 33–5
Crocodilurus lacertinus 57
Crocodylus spp. 17, *17*, *33*, 34, 35, *35*
Crossaster papposus 196
Crotalus spp. 60, 78, *78*, 79, *79*, 80, *80*
Crotaphytus collaris 40, *40*
crustaceans 125, 146, 158–63
Cryptobranchus alleganiensis 93, *93*
Cryptophia spp. 152
Ctenoglyphus palmifer 155
Ctenosaura similis 39
Ctenotus pulchellus 51
ctenotus, red-sided *51*
Culcita novaeguineae 196
Culex pipens 179
Cuora amboinensis 29
Curculio nucum 178
cushion star *196*
cuttlefishes 142, *142*, 143
Cyanea arctica 133
Cyclommatus imperator 178, *178*
Cyclops strenuus 159
Cyclorana spp. 110, *110*
Cyclura cornuta 39
Cydia pomonella 182
Cylindrophis ruffus 65
Cynops pyrrhogaster 96, *96*
Cypraea tigris 140
Cypris pubera 160
Cyrtodactylus pulchellus 47, *47*
Cyrtophora citricola 153

D

Daboia russelii 78
daddy long legs (crane flies) 179
daddy longlegs (spider) 150
daddy-longlegs (harvestmen) 148, 154, *154*
damselflies 166, *166*
Danaus spp. 185, *185*
danceflies 191
Daphnia pulex 159
darters (Lepidoptera) 183

Dasia smaragdina 50
Dasypeltis scabra 69, 73
Daudebardia rufa 141
dawn dropwing 166
dead man's fingers *133*
Debdroaspis viridis 75
deerflies *see* horseflies
defence
  amphibians 87
  reptiles 20
Deinacrida heteracantha 165
Deinopus spp. 152
Deinosuchus 16, *16*
Delias mysis 184
Delma australus 47
demoiselle, beautiful 166
Dendrelaphis pictus 70, 70
Dendroaspis polylepis 75, *75*
Dendrobates spp. 101, 115, *115*
Dendrocoelum lacteum 135
Dentalium elephantinum 138
Dermacentor marginatus 154
Dermatemys mawii 31, *31*
Dermanyssus gallinae 155
Dermatonotus muelleri 114
Dermochelys coriacea 24, *26*
Dermolepida albohirtum 107
Deroceras reticulatum 141
Derocheilocaris remanei 160
Diabrotica undecimpunctata 175
Diadema setosum 196
diapsids 14
Diastylis rathkei 161
Dicamptodon ensatus 95, *95*
Dicopomorpha echmepterygis 165
Dimetrodon 16, *16*
Diopsis tenuipes 180
Diplodactylus ciliaris 47
Diploglossus fasciatus 57
Diplolepis rosae 187
diplurans 125, 194, *194*
Diporiphora superba 43, *43*
Diprion pini 186
Dipsas catesbyi 74, *74*
Discoglossus spp. 102
Dispholidus typus 72, *72*
dobsonflies 125, 191, 192, *192*
doodlebugs *see* ant lion
Draco quinquefasciatus 43
dragonflies 145, 165, *165*, 166, *166*, 171
dragons (reptiles)
  Boyd's forest dragon 37
  Chinese water dragon 43, *43*
  eastern bearded dragon 42
  five-lined flying dragon 43
  giant forest dragon 43
  Komodo dragon 14, 17, 37, 38, 44, 59, *59*
  semiarboreal tree dragon 43, *43*
  tropical forest dragon 43
Dreissena spp. 139
Drymarchon corais 69, 69
dung beetles *see* beetles
dung fly, yellow *181*
Dutch elm disease 178
dwarf bobtail *142*
Dynastes hercules 177
Dyscophus antongilii 114, *114*
Dysdercus decussatus 171

E

earthworms 144, *144*
earwigs 125, 191, *191*
Echiniscus testudo 197
Echinocardium cordatum 196
Echinoderes 198
echinoderms 123, 125, 127, 195–6
Echinodiscus auritus 196

Echinus esculentus 196
Echis carinatus 78
Ectopsocus briggsi 192
Egernia hosmeri 50, *50*
eggs 15, 19, *19*, 84, 88, *88*, 89
Eirenis modestus 70
Elaphe spp. 68
Elapsoidea loveridgei 76
Elasmosaurus 16, *16*
Eledone moschata 143
Eleutherodactylus spp. 101, 102, 106, *106*
Elgaria multicarinata 56
elm disease 178
Elusor macrurus 32
Elysia crispata 140
Empis tesselata 180
Emus hirtus 176
Emydocephalus annulatus 77
Emydura victoriae 25
Emys orbicularis 28, *28*
endangered species 23, 91, 129
energy transference, via food chain 101
Enhydris enhydris 71, *71*
Enoicyla pusilla 193
Enoplometopus daumi 161
ensatina 97
Ensatina eschscholtzii 97
Entalina 138
Entimus splendidus 178
Entomobrya superba 194
environmental indicators
  corals 134
  frogs 101, 118
Eosentomon ribagai 194
Ephemera vulgata 192, *192*
Epicrates angulifer 64
Epicrionops petersi 99
Epipedobates femoralis 106
Erannis defoliaria 184
Eremias velox 55
Ererpton tentaculatum 71
Ergasilus sieboldi 159
Eriocheir sinensis 163
Eriophyes pini 155
Eriosoma lanigerum 173
Erpeton tentaculatum 71
Erythrolamprus aesculapii 69
Eryx tataricus 62
escargot *141*
Eublepharis macularius 46, *46*
Eucharis adscendens 187
Euchroma gigantea 176
Eudiaptomus vulgaris 159
Eudicella gralli 177
Eumeces spp. 49, *50*
Eumenes pomiformis 189
Eunectes murinus 63
Eunice viridis 144
Euphausia superba 162, *162*
Euplectella aspergillum 131
Euproctus asper 95
Europroctus platycephalus 94
Eurycantha horrida 191
Eurycea lucifuga 97
Euscelis plebejus 173
Euscorpius carpathicus 149
Eusthenopteron 85, *85*
Euthesenopteron 85, *85*
Evania appendigaster 187
evolution 14–15, 84–5, 123, 111, 127, 146
exoskeleton 122, *122*

F

Fannia scalaris 181
fanworms 144
Farancia erytrogramma 74
Fasciolaria hunteria 140
feather stars 195, *195*
ferderlance, Amazon 74, 74
fertilisation 15
fireflies 176, *176*

Flata rubra 173
flatworms 135, *135*
fleas 125, 128, 191, *192*
flesh flies 181, *181*
flies 125, 179–81
fluke, Chinese liver 128, *135*
food
  amphibians 87
  invertebrates 126
  reptiles 20
food chain 101
forensic entomology 181
Formica rufa 190
fritillary, silver-washed (Lepidoptera) *185*
froghopper, red and black 173
frogs 84, 88, 89–91
  Abah River flying frog 119, *119*
  African bullfrog 117
  African goliath frog 100
  African grey tree frog 119
  African ornate tree frog 119
  Amazon river frog 117, *117*
  Australian lace-lid frog 110, *110*
  banded stream frog 118
  barking frog 106, *106*
  barking tree frog 112, *112*
  Bereis' tree frog *112*, 113
  Blue Mountains tree frog 110
  blue poison frog 115, *115*
  Blythe's giant frog 118
  Bongon whipping frog 119
  Borneo splash frog 118
  brilliant-thighed poison frog 115
  brown New Zealand frog 102, *102*
  brown-belly leaf frog 113
  Budgett's frog 105, *105*
  bullfrog 87, 117, *117*
  burrowing tree frog 113
  bush squeaker 119
  Cape clawed frog 103, *103*, 109
  Cape dainty frog 118, *118*
  Carabaya robber frog 106
  casque-headed tree frog 113
  Cayenne slender-legged tree frog *111*
  common clawed frog 103
  common parsley frog 103, *103*
  coqui 106, *106*
  Corsica painted frog 102
  Dahoeping sucker frog 118
  dainty green tree frog 110
  Darwin's mouthbreeder 106
  defining features 100–1, *100*, 108, *108*, 111, *111*
  desert rain frog 114
  dotted humming frog 114, *114*
  Dumeril's striped frog 105
  European common frog 117, *117*
  European tree frog 112, *112*
  eyes 84, *84*
  fringed leaf frog 111
  gastric-brooding frog 104, *104*
  giant banjo frog 104, *104*
  giant burrowing frog 104
  glass frog 113
  golden poison frog 115
  gold-striped frog 106, *106*
  green and black poison frog 115
  green and golden bell frog 91, *91*, 110
  green tree frog *112*
  hairy frog 119, *119*
  harlequin flying tree frog 113
  harlequin frog 109, *109*
  harlequin poison frog 115, *115*
  Hispaniola tree frog 113
  Hochstetter's New Zealand frog 102
  hourglass tree frog 112
  jaguar leaf frog *111*
  Java flying frog 100, 119
  Java whipping frog 119, *119*
  javelin frog 113

Jordan's casque-headed tree
　　frog *111*
Lehmann's poison frog *115*
leopard frog *109*, 117
life cycle *98*
lowland tropical frog 106, *106*
Madagascar bright-eyed frog *119*
Madagascar golden frog *116*
Madagascar reed frog 116, *116*
Malayan horned frog 86, *103*
Malaysian frog *117*
map tree frog *111*
marbled reed frog *116*
marsh frog *117*
marsupial frog *98*, 112, *112*
Mascarene Ridge frog *118*
mass spawning 117, *117*
Mexican tree frog *112*
Mueller's clawed frog *103*
Muller's termite frog *114*
Natal forest tree frog *116*
Natal ghost frog *104*
Nicaragua giant glass frog 112, *112*
northern leopard frog *101*
Nosy Be giant tree frog 114, *114*
ornate chorus frog *112*
ornate rice frog *114*
painted frog *102*
painted Indonesian tree frog *119*
painted-belly leaf frog 111, *111*
paradox frog 89, 110, *110*
Peru robber frog 106, *106*
pickerel frog 117, *117*
pig frog *117*
poison-arrow frogs 115, *115*
rain frogs *114*
red rain frog *114*
redback poison frog 115, *115*
red-banded frog *114*
red-eared frog *117*
red-eyed tree frog 111, *111*
red-legged kassina *116*
rusty tree frog *111*
Schmidt's forest frog *105*
Sehuenca's water frog *105*
Seychelles reed frog *116*
shaping frog *103*
short-footed frog 110, *110*
shovel-headed tree frog 111, *111*
Singapore wart frog 118, *118*
skeleton ghost frog *104*
South American bullfrog 105, *105*
southern bell frog 110, *110*
spotted snout-burrower *118*
spotted-thighed poison frog *106*
strawberry poison frog *115*
striped sand frog *118*
striped spiny reed frog *116*
Sumaco horned tree frog *112*
Surinam horned frog 105, *105*
tailed frog 102, *102*
Thomasset's frog *104*
toads differentiated from 109
tomato frog 114, *114*
Trinidad poison frog *115*
Tulear golden frog 116, *116*
turtle frog 104, *104*
variable robber frog *106*
veined tree frog *111*
Vizcacheras' white-lipped frog *105*
warty tree frog *119*
water-holding frog 110, *110*
Weal's running frog 116, *116*
weeping frog *105*
western marsh frog *104*
White's tree frog *111*
yellow-headed poison frog *115*
yellow-striped reed frog *116*
see also toads
fruit flies 179, *180*
Fungia fungites 134
fungus, frogs endangered by 91, 101
funnel-web spider 153, *153*
Furcifer spp. 45, *45*

G
Galeodes arabs 154
galliwasp, banded *57*
Gallotia spp. 53, *53*
Gambelia sila 40, *40*
Gammarus fossarum 161
Gasteracantha spp. 128, *128*, *153*
Gasterophilus intestinalis 181
Gastropacha quercifolia 183
Gastrophryne olivacea 114
gastropods 123, 137, *137*, 140, 140–1,
　　141 *see also* slugs; snails
Gastrotheca spp. *98*, 112, *112*
gastrotrich 125, *198*
Gavialis gangeticus 35
Gecarcoidea natalis 163, *163*
geckos 21, *21*, 38, *44*, 46
　　African web-footed gecko *46*
　　Anderson's short-fingered gecko *48*
　　banded gecko 46, *46*
　　broad-tailed day gecko *48*
　　Cogger's velvet gecko *46*
　　common leopard gecko 46, *46*
　　common wall gecko 48, *48*
　　common wonder gecko *47*
　　Cradock thick-toed gecko *48*
　　Gray's bow-fingered gecko 47, *47*
　　green tree gecko *46*
　　Henkel's flat-tailed gecko *47*
　　Israeli fan-fingered gecko *48*
　　Kuhl's flying gecko *48*
　　leaf-tailed gecko *38*
　　lined gecko 47, *47*
　　Madagascar day gecko *48*
　　marbled velvet gecko *47*
　　mourning gecko 48, *48*
　　New Caledonia bumpy gecko *46*
　　northern leaf-tailed gecko *46*
　　northern spiny-tailed gecko *47*
　　prehensile tailed gecko *46*
　　Ruppell's leaf-toed gecko *48*
　　Thomas's sticky-toed gecko *46*
　　Tokashiki gecko *46*
　　tokay gecko *47*
　　Wiegmann's striped gecko *48*
Gekko spp. 47, *47*
Geochelone spp. 30, *30*, 32
Geoclemys hamiltoni 29
Geoemyda spengleri 29
Gerrhosaurus major 49
gharials 14, 33, *34*, 35
giant agrippa *184*
Gila monster 37, 38, 58, *58*
Glaphyromorphus crassicaudum 51, *51*
Glaucus atlanticus 140
glistenworm *138*
glow worm *176*
Gnathophyllum americanum 195
gnats 179, *179*
Goliathus meleagris 177
Gonatodes vittatus 48
Gongylophis colubrinu 62
Gongylus gongyloides 167
Goniurosaurus kuroiwae 46
Gonocephalus spp. *43*
Gonyosoma oxycephalum 68
Gopherus polyphemus 30, *30*
Gorgonia flabellum 134
gorgon's head *196*
gout fly *180*
Grantia compressa 131
Graptemys spp. 28, *28*
grasshoppers 125, *147*, 165, *165*,
　　170, *170*
　　long-horned grasshoppers
　　　see katydids
Great Barrier Reef 134, *134*
Gromphadorina portentosa 168
gropers *see* groupers
groundhoppers 170
Gryllotalpa gryllotalpa 170
Gymnophis multiplicate 99
Gymnopholus weiskei 178
Gyrinophilus spp. 97, *97*

H
habitats 21–2, 89–90, 127–8
Hadrurus arizonensis 148
Haldane, J. B. S. 175
Haliclystus auricula 133
Halictus quadricinctus 189
Haliotis tuberculata 140
Halobates spp. 171
hanging flies 180, 191, *193*
Harpesaurus beccarii 43
harvestmen 148, 154, *154*
Heleioporus barycragus 104
Heleophryne spp. *104*
Heliconius melpomene 185
Heliobolus lugubris 55
Helioporus australicacus 104
Helix spp. *141*
hellbender 89, 93, *93*
Heloderma spp. 37, 38, 58, *58*
hemichordates 125, 198, *198*
Hemidactylium scutatum 92, *97*
Hemidactylus flaviviridis 48
Hemikyptha punctata 172
Hemiphractus proboscideus 112
Hemisus guttatus 118
hermaphroditism (snails) 141, *141*
Heterixalus madagascariensis 116, *116*
Heterocentrotus mammillatus 195
Heterodon platyrhinos 67, *74*
Heteronotus reticulatus 173
hexapods 125, 194, *194*
Hildebrandtia ornata 118
Hippodamia convergens 176
Hirudo medicinalis 144
Holaspis guentheri 55, *55*
Homalopsis buccata 71, *71*
Homarus americanus 162
Homopus signatus 30
honeybee 126, 155, *155*, 164, 186,
　　186, 188, *188*, 189
hookworms 136
Hoplodactylus rakiurae 46
Hoplophrys oatesii 146
hoppers 171 *see also* treehoppers
hornets 189
horseflies 179, 180, *180*
horseshoe crabs 146, *147*, 156, *156*
housefly 179, 181, *181*
hoverflies 173, 179, 180, *180*
hula skirt siphonophore *133*
hyalina, Vema 138
hydras *see* hydroids
Hydrodynastes gigas 74, *74*
hydroids 124, 132, *132*, *133*
Hydrolaetare schmidti 105
Hydrometra stagnorum 171
Hydrophis ornatus 77
Hydrosaurus amboinensis 43, *43*
hydroskeleton 122, *122*
hydrozoans 133
Hyla spp. 87, *111*, 112, *112*, 113
Hylidae spp. *101*
Hylonomus 16, *16*
Hymenolepis diminuta 135
Hymenopus coronatus 167
Hynobius chinensis 94, *94*
Hyperolius spp. *116*
Hypnale hypnale 81
Hypogastrura spp. *194*
Hypolimnas misippus 185
Hypsiluris boydii 37

I
Icthyophis spp. *99*
Ichthyosaurus 16, *16*
Idolum diabolicum 167
Iguana spp. 38, *39*
iguanas 38, *44*
　　black iguana *39*
　　Fiji banded iguana 22, *22*, 39
　　Fiji crested iguana 39
　　Galápagos land iguana 39

green iguana 38, 39
green thornytail iguana 41
marine iguana 19, 39
rhinoceros iguana 39
West Indian iguana 39
Ilyocypris gibba 160
Imantodes cenchoa 74
inchworms 184
insects 125, 146, *147*, 164–93
invertebrate chordates 122–30
Ischnopsalis helwigii 154
isopod, giant *161*
Isotoma viridis 194
Ixodes ricinus 154

J
Jacobson's organ 59
Janthina janthina 140
jararacussu *81*
jellyfish 124, 132, *133*
　　box jellies 133
　　freshwater jellyfish 132
　　lion's mane jellyfish 133
　　melon jellyfish *197*
　　moon jellyfish 133
　　purple jellyfish 132
　　stalked jellyfish 133
　　upside-down jellyfish 133

K
Kachuga tecta 29
Kallima inachus 185
Kaloula pulchra 114
Kassina maculata 116
kassina, red-legged *116*
katydids 125, *170*
keelbacks 71
Kentropyx calcarata 56
Keratella quadrata 198
Kinixis belliana 30
knob-tail, stellate *46*
Komodo dragon 14, 17, 37, *38*,
　　44, 59, *59*
kraits 75, *75*, 77, *77*
krill 158, 162, *162*

L
Labyrinthidonts 85
Lacerta spp. 53, *54*
lacewings 125, 173, 191, 193, *193*
Lachesis muta 81, *81*
Lampropeltis spp. 69, *69*
Lampyris noctiluca 176
lancehead, Brazil's *81*
lancelets 130, *130*
land caddis *193*
Lanternaria sp. *172*
lanternflies *172*
Lanthanotus borneensis 58
Laphria flava 180
lappet *183*
large blue (Lepidoptera) *184*
Lasioderma serricorne 177
Laticauda spp. 76, 77, *77*
latrine fly *181*
Latrodectus mactans 153, *153*
Laudakia stellio 42
leaf insect 125, 191, *191*
leaf sucker, apple *173*
lecanium, European fruit *173*
leeches 144
　　medicinal leech *144*
legless lizards 60
　　two-headed legless lizard *36*
Lehmania marginata 141
Leiolepma spp. 102, *102*
Leiopython albertisii 64
leishmania 119
Lepas anatifera 160
Lepidobatrachus laevis 105, *105*
Lepidochelys spp. 26, *26*
Lepidodactylus lugubris 48, *48*
Lepidophyma flavimaculata 54

Lepidoptera *see* butterflies; moths
Lepidosaphes ulmi 173
Lepidosaura 14
Lepisma saccharina 191, *191*
Lepismodes iniquilinus 191
Leptinotarsa decemlineata 178
Leptodactylus spp. 101, 105, *105*
Leptodoura kindtii 159
Leptopelis natalensis 116
lesser wanderer *185*
Lialis burtonis 47
lice 125, 128, 191, *192*
　　bee louse *180*
　　book louse 191, *192*
　　common pill wood louse 158,
　　　161, *161*
　　dog-biting louse *192*
　　freshwater fish louse *160*
　　head louse *192*
　　pubic louse *192*
Lichmophora spp. *135*
Lima hians 139
Limnadia lenticularis 159
Limnodynastes interioris 104, *104*
Limnonectes spp. 118, *118*
Limothrips cerealium 192
limpets *138*, 140, *140*, *141*
Limulus polyphemus 146, *147*, 156, *156*
Lingula anatina 199
Linyphia triangularis 152, *153*
Liothyrella neozelandica 199
Liphistius malayanus 150
Liphyra brassolis 184
Liposcelis divinatorius 191, *192*
Lissemys punctata 27
Lithobius forficatus 157
Lithodytes lineatus 106, *106*
Litoria spp. 110, *110*, 113
Liua shihi 94
lizards 14, 15, 27, 37–60
　　armadillo girdled lizard 37, *49*
　　Asian grass lizard *55*
　　Balkan emerald lizard *53*
　　basilisk lizards 37
　　black crag lizard *49*
　　blue-throated keeled-lizard 55, *55*
　　Burton's snake-lizard *47*
　　Centralian blue-tongued lizard 50, *50*
　　Chinese crocodile lizard 57, *57*
　　Coachella Valley fringe-toed lizard 40
　　collared lizard 21, *21*, 40, *40*
　　Colourado desert fringe-toed lizard 40
　　common green forest lizard 43, *43*
　　common monkey lizard 41
　　common wall lizard 54, *54*
　　common worm lizard 22, *22*, 46
　　Cope's arboreal alligator lizard 57
　　desert night lizard *54*
　　desert spiny lizard *54*
　　Egyptian fringe-fingered lizard 55, *55*
　　European green lizard *53*
　　fence lizards *44*
　　frilled lizard 20, *20*, 37, *42*, *52*
　　Gallot's lizard *53*
　　giant Canary Island lizard 53, *53*
　　glass lizards *44*
　　granite night lizard *54*
　　green basilisk lizard 41
　　Indo-Chinese forest lizard 43
　　Italian wall lizard *54*
　　jeweled lizard *53*
　　Karoo girdled lizard *49*
　　legless lizards *36*, *51*, 60
　　leopard lizard 40, *40*
　　lesser flat lizard *49*
　　long-tail whip lizard *49*
　　Madagascar girdled lizard *49*
　　marble-faced worm lizard *47*
　　Menorca wall lizard *54*
　　Merrem's Madagascar swift *40*
　　Mexican beaded lizard 37, 58, *58*
　　Milo's wall lizard *54*
　　Moroccan dabb lizard *42*

North American island night lizard 54
Radd's rock lizard *54*
rainbow lizard *56*
regal horned lizard 40, *40*
rough-scaled plated lizard *49*
sailfin lizard 43, *43*
sand lizard *53*
sawtail lizard 55, *55*
shingleback lizard *38*, *50*
short-horned lizard 20, *20*, *40*
side-blotched lizard *40*
slender glass lizard *57*
slender sand lizard *55*
slow worm *57*
small-spotted lizard *55*
snake-eyed lizard 55, *55*
southern alligator lizard *56*
stellate knob-tail *46*
Sumatra nose-horned lizard *43*
tiger lizard 53, *53*
Uzzell's rock lizard *54*
viviporus lizard *54*
yellow-spotted night lizard *54*
Zagrosian lizard *53*
Lobophyllia hemprichii 134
lobsters 145, *161*, *162*, *163*, *163*
Locusta migratoria 170
locusts 170, *170*
loggerhead *26*
loggerhead musk turtle *31*
Loligo spp. *142*
Lophelia pertusa 134
louse *see* lice
Loxocemus bicolour 65, *65*
Loxosceles reclusa 153
Loxosoma harmeri 197
Lucilia sericata 181
Lumbricus terrestris 144
Lycaena virgaureae 184
Lycodon laoensis 70
Lycoteuthis diadema 143
Lygnus pratensis 171
Lygosoma bowringii 51
Lymantria spp. *183*
Lymnaea auricularia 141
Lysmata amboinensis 162
Lystrophis semicinctus 74
Lytta vesicatoria 177

M
mabuya, bridled *51*
Mabuya vittata 51
Machilis helleri 191, *191*
Macrelaps microlepidotus 65
Macrobiotus hufelandi 197, *197*
Macrocheira kaempferi 158, *163*
Macrochelys temmincki 31, *31*
Macrodontia cervicornis 178
Macropanesthia rhinoceros 168
Macropisthodon rhodomelas 71
Macrorvipera spp. *79*
Macrotermes natalensis 169
Maculinea arion 184
maggots *179*
Magicicada spp. *172*
Malaclemys terrapin 28, *28*
Malacochersus tornieri 24, *30*
malaria 179, *179*
Malayemys subtrijuga 29
Malpolon monspessulanus 69
Mannophryne trinitatis 115
Mantella spp. 116, *116*
mantids 125, *146*, *165*, *167*, *167*
mantis fly *181*
Mantis religiosa 167
Mantispa pagana 192
mantispid fly *192*
Margaritana margaritifera 139
Marginella cornea 140
marginella, plain *140*
Marthasterias glacialis 196
massasauga 80, *80*
Masticophis flagellum 66, *68*
Mastigoproctus giganteus 149

mastigure, ocellated *42*
matamata 25, *25*
Maticora bivirgata 75
Mauremys caspica 29
mayflies 125, 191, *192*, *192*
mealy bugs 171, *173*
medication *91*
Mediterranean bonnet *137*
Megalodicopia hians 130
Meganyctiphanes norvegica 162
Megaphragma caribea 186
Megascolia maculata 187
Megophrys nasuta 86, *103*
Melanosuchus niger 34, *34*
Meloe violaceus 177
Melongena corona 140
Merodon equestris 180
Meroles anchietae 55
Mertensiella luschani 95
Mesalina guttulata 55
Mesostoma ehrenbergi 135
Messelobatrachus 85, *85*
Meta menardi 151
metamorphosis, invertebrate 122,
   145, *145*
Micaria formicaria 150
Microhyla ornata 114
Microuoides euryxanthus 66, *76*
Micrurus spp. *67*, *76*, *76*
midges 165, 179, *179*
migration
   reptiles 19
Millepora dichotoma 132
millipedes 127, 157, *157*
mimic *185*
Misumena vatia 150
mites 127, 148, 154, 181
   aquatic mites 155
   bulb mite 154
   flour mite 154
   harvest bug 155
   leaf blister mite 155
   pear bud mite 155
   poultry red mite 155
   scabies mite 155
   spider mite 155
   straw itch mite 155
   varroa mite 155, *155*
Mnemiopsis leidyi 197
moccasin, hump-nosed *81*
molluscs 122, 123, 128, 137–43
Moloch horridus 42, *42*
Moma alpium 184
monarchs *185*
monitor lizards 52, 59
monitors 38, *58*, *59*
Monomorium pharaonis 190
Morelia spp. *61*, *64*, *64*, *73*
Morethia ruficauda 51
Mormolyce phyllodes 175
Morpho rhetenor 185
mosquitoes *147*, *165*, *174*, *179*, *179*
moss animals *see* bryozoans
moss neobisid *149*
moths 125, *165*, 182–5
   African moon 126, *126*
   bagworm moth 185
   bent-wing ghost moth 183
   black arches moth 183
   Bogong moth 184
   carpet moth 182
   codling moth 182
   European pine shoot moth 182
   eyed hawk moth 183
   garden tiger moth 183
   geometer moths 184, *184*
   ghost moths 183, *183*
   giant atlas moth 183
   goat moth 183
   inchworm moth 184, *184*
   Indian luna moth 183
   longhorn moth 182
   meal moth 182
   nun moth 183

owl moth 183
owlet moth 184, *184*
   plume moth 165
   Provence burnet moth 183
   red underwing moth 184
   spirit moth 182
   swift moth 183, *183*
   tapestry moth 182
mottled umber *184*
mourning racerunner *55*
mudpuppy 89, 92, 94, *94*
mugger *34*
mulga (snake) *77*
Murex brandarius 140
murex, purple-dye *140*
Musca domestica 179, 181, *181*
mussel shrimp *see* ostracods
mussels 137, 139, *139*
mussurana *74*
Mya arenaria 139
Mycetophila fungorum 179
Myobatrachus gouldii 104, *104*
myriapods 157
Myriopora truncata 199
Myrmecia forficata 190
Myrmecocystus hortideorum 190
Myrmica laevinodis 190
Mysis relicta 161
mystarocarid 160
Mytilus edulis 139

N
Naja spp. 60, 66, *75*, *75*
Nanosella fungi 175
Narceus americanus 157
narcissus fly *180*
Natador depressus 24, *25*, *26*
Natrix natrix 71, *71*, *73*
Naucoris cimicoides 171
Naultinus elegans 46
Nautilus pompilius 142
nautiluses 142, *142*, 143, *143*
Nebalia bipes 161
Necrophorus vespillo 176
Necturus maculosus 92, 94, *94*
nematodes 136
Nematus ribesii 186
Nemoptera sinuata 193
nemtode, wheat seed gall *136*
neobisid, moss 149
Neobisium carcinoides 149
Neomphalus spp. *140*
Neopilina galatheae 138
neoteny 95
Nephila spp. *153*
Nephrurus stellatus 46
Neptune's cup *131*
Nereis diversicolour 144
Nerodia sipedon 71
Nesomantis thomasseti 104
Neurergus kaiseri 95
Neusticurus bicarinatus 56
neusticurus, two-ridged 56
newts 84, *84*, 88, *88*, 92
   banded newt 95
   California newt 96
   common newt 95, *95*
   Japanese firebelly newt 96, *96*
   Luristan newt 95
   red-spotted newt 89, *89*, 92, 95
   Shau Tau Kok newt 96
   Vietnam warty newt 96, *96*
nightcrawler *144*
Niptus hololeucus 177
Norops spp. *41*, *52*
Notaden bennettii 104, *104*
Notechis ater 77
Notophthalmus viridescens 92, 95
Novoeumeces schneideri 49
Nucras tessellata 53, *53*
Nucula nucleus 139
nudibranch *137 see also* sea slugs
nut shell *139*

Nyctimystes dayi 110, *110*
Nyctixalus pictus 119
Nymphon gracile 156

O
Ochthera mantis 181
Octopus vulgaris 143
octopuses 137, 142, 143, *143*
Ocypode ceratophthalma 163
Odontodactylus scyllarus 161, *161*
Odontomachus haematodes 190
Oecophylla smaragdina 190
Oeda inflata 173
Oedipoda coerulescens 170
Oestrus ovis 181
olm 94, *94*
Oligodon octolineatus 70
Oligosoma otagense 50
Ommastrephes sagittatus 142
Oncopeltus fasciatus 172
Onychodactylus fischeri 94
Ophiacomina nigra 196
Ophiodes intermedius 56
Ophion luteus 187
Ophiophagus hannah 61, *73*, *75*
Ophisaurus attenuatus 57
Ophisops elegans 55, *55*
Ophiura ophiura 196
Opilio parietinus 154
Opisthorchis sinensis 135
Oplurus cyclurus 40
orange-barred sulphur *184*
orb weavers 151, *151*, *152*, *153*
Orconectes limosus 163
Orthezia urticae 173
Osmia bicolour 189
Osteocephalus spp. 101, *111*, 113
Osteolaemus tetraspis 34
ostracods 160, *160*
Ostrea edulis 139
Ovula ovum 140
Oxybelis aeneus 72, *72*
Oxyrhopus petola 72
Oxysternon conspicallatum 177
Oxyuranus scutellatus 77, *77*
oysters 137, *137*, 139, *139*

P
Pachliopta hector 184
Pachyachis 16, *16*
Pachydactylus geitje 48
Palinurus vulgaris 162
Pallmatogecko rangeri 46
Palomena prasina 172
Palpares libelluloides 191, *193*, *193*
Paludicella articulata 199
Panchlora nivea 168
Pandinus imperator 149
Panorpa communis 193
Panulirus spp. *162*, *163*, *163*
paper nautilus 143, *143*
Papilio antimachus 184
Papustyla pulcherrima 141
Paracentrotus lividus 196
Paralithodes camtschatica 163
Paramesotriton deloustali 96, *96*
parasites 125, 128, *186*, 187
Parastygocaris andeni 161
Pareus chinensis 69
Parnassius apollo 184
Parthenolecanium corni 173
parthogenesis 22
Patella vulgata 138
pauropods 157, *157*
Pauropus huxleyi 157
Pediculus capitis 192
Pedostibes everetti 109
Pegomya betae 181
Pelagia panopyra 132
Pelagothuria natatrix 195
Pelamis platurus 77
Pelecanus spp. *187*
Pelmatohydra oligactis 133

Pelobates syriacus 103
Pelodytes punctatus 103, *103*
Pelomedusa subrufa 25
Pelusios sinuatus 25
pen shell *137*
Penaeus monodon 162
Penicillus javanus 139
Pennatula spp. *133*, *134*
perentie *59*
Periclimenes imperator 162
Peripatoides novaezealandiae 199
Peripatopsis capensis 199
peripatus, New Zealand *199*
Peripatus spp. *199*
Perla spp. *193*
Phalangium opilio 154
Phalium granulatum undulatum 137
Phelsuma spp. *48*
Philanthus triangulum 189
Philodina roseola 198
Philothamnus semivariegatus 69
Phlebotomus papatasi 179
Phlocus phalangioides 150
Phoebis philea 184
Pholas dactylus 139
Phoronis psammophila 198
Phosphuga atrata 176
Phryganea grandis 191, *193*
Phrynichus spp. *149*
Phrynocephalus persicus 42
Phrynohyas resinifistrix 87, *87*
Phrynohyas venulosa 111
Phrynomantis bifasciata 114
Phrynops hilarii 25
Phrynosoma spp. 40, *40*
Phthiracarus spp. *154*
Phthirius pubix 192
Phyllidia ocellata 140
Phyllium siccifolium 191, *191*
Phyllobates terribilis 115
Phyllomedusa spp. *90*, 111, *111*, *113*
Phylloreta nemorum 178
Physalaemus biligonigerus 105
Physalia physalis 133, *140*
Physignathus cocincinus 43, *43*
Physophora hydrostatica 133
Phytoseiulus persimilis 155
Picromerus bidens 172
Pictodentalium formosum 138
piddock, common *139*
Pieris brassicae 184
pill bugs *see Anaspides tasmaniae*
Pinna nobilis 139
pinworms 136
Piophila casei 180, *181*
Pipa pipa 101, *103*, *103*
pirarucu *see* arapaima
Pisidium amnicum 139
pitvipers *see* rattlesnakes; vipers
Platemys platycephala 25
Platypelis milloti 114, *114*
Platyrhopalopsis mellyi 175
Platysaurus guttatus 49
Platysternon megacephalum 31
Plerogyra sinuosa 134
Plethodon spp. 97, *97*
Pleurodeles poireti 96
Pliocercus spp. *67*, *76*
Podarcis spp. 54, *54*
Podocnemis spp. 25, *25*
Pogona barbata 42
Polistes gallicus 189, *189*
pollution *see* environmental indicators
Polycarpa aurata 130
Polychrus marmouratus 41
Polyergus rufescens 190
Polypedates spp. 119, *119*
Polyphemus pendiculus 159, *159*
Polystoma integerrimum 135
Porites porites 134
Portuguese man-of-war 122, *122*,
   133, *140*
postman, the *185*
Poterion neptuni 131

prawn, black tiger 162 *see also* shrimp
pricklenape, armoured 43
Procolus goryi 178
Proganochelys 16, *16*
Prosthecereaus giesbrechtii 135
Proteus anguinus 94, *94*
proturans 194, *194*
Psammobates tentorius 30, *30*
psammodromus, Algerian 55
Psammodromus algirus 55
Psammophis schokar 69, *69*
Pseudacris ornata 112
Pseudechis australis 77
Pseudemys spp. 28, *28*
Pseudis paradoxa 110, *110*
Pseudobranchus striatus 93
Pseudocerastes persicus 78
Pseudoceros spp. 135
Pseudococcus longispinus 173
Pseudocolochirus violaceus 195
Pseudocordylus melanotus 49
Pseudonaja nuchalis 77
Pseudophryne australis 104
Pseudotrapelus sinaitus 42
Pseudotriton ruber 92
Psylla mali 173
Psyllophryne didactyla 100
Pteranodon 16, *16*
Pterinochilus murinus 150
Pternohyla fodiens 113
pterosaurs 14
Ptychozoon kuhli 48
Ptyodactylus puiseuxi 48
Pulex irritans 192
Pycnogonum spp. 156
Pyemotes ventricosus 155
Pyralis farinalis 182
Pyrophorus noctilucus 177
Pyrosoma atlanticum 130
pyrosome 130
Python spp. 63, *63*, 64, *64*
pythons 15, *15*, 61, *61*, 62, 63
  African rock python 63
  amethyst python 73
  ball python 64
  black-headed python 64, *64*
  blood python 64, *64*
  Calabar ground python *62*
  carpet python 64, *73*
  children's python 15, *15*, *63*
  green tree python *61*, 64, *64*
  Indian python *63*
  Mexican burrowing python 65, *65*
  reticulate python 63, *63*
  white-lipped python *64*
Pyxicephalus adspersus 117

R
racers 66, 69, *69*, 70
racerunners 55
ragworm *144*
Rana spp. 89, *101*, 117, *117*
Ranodon sibiricus 94
Raphidia notata 191, *191*
rattlesnakes 78
  banded rock rattlesnake 79
  black-tailed rattlesnake 80, *80*
  Mojave rattlesnake 80
  prairie rattlesnake 19, 80
  pygmy rattlesnake 79, *79*
  ridge-nosed rattlesnake 80
  speckled rattlesnake 80
  tiger rattlesnake 80, *80*
  timber rattlesnake 60, 80, *80*
  tropical rattlesnake 79
  twin-spotted rattlesnake 80
  western diamondback rattlesnake
    60, 79, *79*
red feather duster *144*
Regina septemvittata 71, *71*
reproduction
  amphibians 88, 89
  invertebrates 122, 123
  reptiles 18

reptiles 14–81
Rhabdophis subminiatus 71
Rhacodactylus auriculatis 46
Rhacophorus spp. 100, 101, *113*,
  119, *119*
Rhagoletis pomonella 180
Rheobatrachus silus 104, *104*
Rheodytes leukops 25
Rhinoclemmys areolata 29
Rhinocoris iracundus 171, *172*, *172*
Rhinoderma darwinii 106
Rhinophis drummondhayi 65
Rhinophrynus dorsalis 103, *103*
Rhizoglyphus echinopus 154
Rhyacionia buoliana 182
Rhyacophila nubila 193
Rhyacotriton olympicus 95
Rhynchocinetes kuiteri 162
rhyncosaurs 16
Rhyssa persuasoria 186
Ricinoides sjoestedti 149
robber fly 179, *180*
rock crawlers 125, 191
rose cynipid 187
rotifers 125, 198, *198*

S
sable fly *181*
Saccoglossus cambrensis 198
Sacculina carcini 160
Sagitta setosa 198
Sagra buqueti 178
salamanders 84, 87, 88, 89, 92, 93
  Apennines salamander 97
  arboreal salamander 97, *97*
  blue-spotted salamander 96
  Californian giant salamander 95, *95*
  cave salamander 97
  Chinese giant salamander 93, *93*
  Chinese salamander 94, *94*
  desert slender salamander 94
  Dybowski's salamander 94
  ensatina 97
  European fire salamander 95, *95*
  Fischer's clawed salamander 94
  four-toed salamander 92, 97
  golden striped salamander 95
  Jackson's climbing
    salamander 97
  Jefferson salamander 98
  Jordan's salamander 97, *97*
  Lake Lerma salamander 94
  life cycle 98
  Luschan's salamander 95
  marbled salamander 96, *96*
  northern dusky salamander 97
  Olympic torrent salamander 95
  Paghman mountain salamander 94
  Pyrenees mountain salamander 95
  red back salamander 97
  red salamander 92
  ringed salamander 96, *96*
  Sardinian brook salamander 94
  Siberian salamander 94
  Sichuan salamander 94
  slimy salamander 97, *97*
  spring salamander 97
  Tennessee cave salamander 97, *97*
  tiger salamander 87, *87*, 96, *96*
Salamandra salamandra 95, *95*
Salamandrella keyserlingii 94
Salticus scenicus 151
Saltuarius cornutus 46
sand dollar 195, *196*
sand fish *49*
sandfly *179*
sand gaper *139*
sandslider, northwestern 51, *51*
Sarcinodes restitutaria 184
Sarcophyton glaucum 133
Sarcoptes scabiei 155
Sauromalus obesus 40
sawflies 125, 186, *186*

scale insects 171, 173, *173*
Scaphiophryne gottlebei 114
scarce copper *184*
Scatophaga stercoraria 181
Sceloporus spp. 40, *44*
Scelotes sexlineatus 51
Schismaderma carens 109
Schistometopum thomense 99, *99*
Schizomus crassicaudatus 149
schnapper *see* snapper, emperor
Scincus scincus 49
Scissurella spp. 140
Scolia procera 187
Scolopendra spp. 157, *157*
Scolytus scolytus 178
scorpionflies 125, 191, 193, *193*
scorpions 127, 146, 148, *148*, 149, *149*
Scutigera spp. 157
Scutigerella immaculata 157
Scyllarus arctus 163
Scytodes thoracica 151, *151*, 153
sea anemones 122, 124, *124*, 128, *128*,
  132, *132*, 134, *134*
sea apple 195
sea biscuit *196*
sea canary *see* beluga
sea cucumbers 125, 195, *195*
sea fans 134, *134*
sea lilies 195
sea monkeys *159*
sea mouse *144*
sea pancake *196*
sea pens *133*, 134, *134*
sea potato 130, *196*
sea skaters 171
sea slugs 126, *126*, 137, *140*
sea spiders 156, *156*
sea squirts 130, *130*
sea stars 125, 195, *196*, *196*
  see also starfishes
sea urchins 125, 195, *195*, *196*, *196*
sea walnut *197*
sea wasp *133*
seed shrimp *see* ostracods
segmented worms 144, *144*
Semiotus distinctus 177
Semnodactylus wealii 116, *116*
Sepia officinalis 142
Sepioteuthis sepioidea 137
Sesia apiformis 183
shield bugs 164, *171*, *172*
Shinisaurus crocodilurus 57, *57*
shrimp *158*
  banded coral shrimp 162
  black tiger prawn 162
  brine shrimp 159, *159*
  brown shrimp 162
  clam shrimp 159, *159*
  cleaner shrimp 162
  emperor shrimp 162
  fairy shrimps 159, *159*
  Kuiter's dancing shrimp 162
  mantis shrimp 161, *161*
  mussel shrimp *see* ostracods
  opossum shrimp 161
  Randall's pistol shrimp 162
  seed shrimp *see* ostracods
  striped bumblebee shrimp 195
  tadpole shrimp 159, *159*
  Tasmanian mountain shrimp 161
Sialis lutaria 192, *192*
sidewinder 78, *78*
Siliquofera grandis 170
  silverfish 125, 191, *191*, 194
Simoselaps calonotus 76
siphonophore, hula skirt *133*
Siphonops annulatus 84, *84*, 99
sipo, mountain *74*
Siren spp. 93, *93*
sirens 89, 92, 93, *93*
Sisturus spp. 79, *79*, 80, *80*
skin
  amphibian 84, *84*
  shedding 15, *15*

skinks 19, 38, *38*, *44*, 50
  Australian blue tongue pygmy
    skink 38, 51
  Boulenger's legless skink 51
  Cape York mulch skink 51, *51*
  Christmas Island grass skink 51
  desert rainbow skink 51, *51*
  emerald skink 50
  five-lined skink 50
  Hosmer's spiny-tailed skink 50, *50*
  juniper skink 51
  lined fire-tailed skink 51
  mole skink 49
  Otago skink 50
  Schneider's skink 49
  six-lined burrowing skink 51
  Solomon Island skink 37, 50
  three-lined burrowing skink 50
skippers 183, *183*
slaters *see* wood lice
sleeping sickness 179, *181*
slider, red-eared 28, 30, *30*
slow worm *56*
slugs
  blue sea slug 140
  grey garden slug 141
  land slug 137
  lettuce sea slug 140
  nudibranch 137
  tree slug 141
  wormslug 141
Smerinthus ocellatus 183
Smilisca baudini 112
Sminthurus aquaticus 194
snail eater, Catesby's 74, *74*
snails
  eared pond snail 141
  escargot 141
  giant tiger snail 141
  land snails 141, *141*
  Manus Island tree snail 141
  purple bubble-raft snail 140
  sea snails 145
  white-lipped garden snail 141
snakefly 125, 191, *191*
snakes 14, 15, 60–81
  Aesculpian false coral snake 69
  Aesculpian snake 68
  Arafura file snake 65
  Arizona coral snake 66, 76
  beaked burrowing asp 65
  beauty snake 68
  black tiger snake 77
  black-banded trinket snake 68
  black-striped burrowing snake 76
  blind snakes 22, 60
  blue Malaysian coral snake 75
  blunthead tree snake 74
  brown vine snake 72, *72*
  bull snake 67
  Cape coral snake 76
  Cape twig snake 72, *72*
  Chinese rat snake 68
  Chinese slug snake 69
  common bronze-back snake 70, *70*
  Cope's false coral snake 76
  coral cylinder snake 65
  coral snakes 61, 66, 67, 69, 75, *75*,
    76, *76*
  corn snake 68
  Crocker's sea snake 76
  crowned leaf-nosed snake 70
  curl snake 76
  Dahl's whip snake 68
  desert whip snake 68
  Drummond-Hay's earth snake 65
  eastern coral snake 76, *76*
  eastern hognose snake 67, 74
  egg-eater snake 73
  European grass snake 71, *71*
  file snakes 22
  forest flame snake 72
  garter snake 70, *70*
  gopher 20, *20*

grass snake 73
grey-banded king snake 69, *69*
green whip snake 68
Hong Kong dwarf snake 70
indigo snake 69, *69*
Laotian wolf snake 70
large whip snake 68
little file snake 65
long-nosed tree snake 72
long-tailed false coral snake 67
Loveridge's garter snake 76
mangrove snake 72, *72*
many-banded coral snake 76
masked water snake 71, *71*
Mayan coral snake 67
Mediterranean cat snake 72
milk snake 69, *69*
Montpelier snake 69
natal black snake 65
northern water snake 71
olive-brown sea snake 77
ornate reef snake 77
paradise flying snake 72
prairie ringneck snake 66
queen snake 71, *71*
rainbow snake 74
rainbow water snake 71, *71*
red cylinder snake 65
red-sided garter snake 70
redtail coral snake 76, *76*
red-tailed green ratsnake 69
rhombic egg-eating snake 69
ringed hognose snake 74
ring-neck snake 70
sea snakes 22, 61, *61*, 75, 77
spotted bush snake 69
striped kukri snake 70
sunbeam snake 65
tentacle snake 71
tropical ratsnake 68
turtle-headed sea snake 77
western brown snake 77
western ground snake 70, *70*
whip snakes 60–1
wood snake 62
yellow-belly sea snake 77
snow fly 180
soldier fly 180
Solen vagina 139
Solenopsis fugax 190
Sonora semiannulata 70, *70*
sow bugs 161
Spadella cephaloptera 198
Spanish fly 177
Spea multiplicata 103, *103*
Speleomantes italicus 97
Speleonectes lucayensis 159
Sphaeridium scarabaeoides 176
spiders 146, 148–54
  black widow 124, 153, *153*
  bolas spider 151, *151*
  Brazilian ant-mimicking spider 151
  brown recluse 153
  camel spider 154
  cave spider 151
  crab spider 150
  daddy-longlegs spider 150
  European buthid 149
  European garden spider 151
  funnel-web 153, *153*
  golden orb weaver 153
  goldenrod spider 150
  ground spider 150
  hooded tick spider 149
  house spider 151
  huntsman spider 150
  jumping spiders 148, 153
  ladybird spider 150
  long-jawed spider 151
  Malaysian trapdoor spider 150
  money spider 151
  net-casting spider 152
  ogre-faced spider 150
  orb weavers 151, *151*, 152, *153*

purseweb spider 150
raft spider 151
red widow 124, *124*
spitting spider 151, *151*, 153
tarantulas 126, *126*, 114, 147, 150, 153, *153*
thorn spider 153
tropical tentweb spider 153
wasp spider 151
water spider 151
whip-spiders 149
wolf spiders 150
woodlouse-eating spider 150
zebra jumping spider 150
see also sea spiders
spiderwebs 152, *152*
Spilotes pullatus 68
spiny devil walking stick *191*
Spirographis spallanzanii 144
Spirula spirula 142
Spondylus americanus 137
sponges 127, 128, *128*, 131, *131*
Spongia officinalis 131, *131*
springtails 125, 194, *194*
squamata 14, 17
squid 137, 142, 143
   Caribbean reef squid 137
   deep-sea vampire squid 143
   European common squid 142
   flying squid 142
   giant squid 137, 143
   long-armed squid 143
   long-finned squid 142
   ram's horn squid 142
stalk-eyed fly 180
starfishes 195, *196 see also* sea stars
Staurois tuberilinguis 118
Staurotypus triporcatus 31
Stegosaurus 16, *16*
stellate knob-tail 46
Stenochiton longicymba 138
Stenodactylus petrii 48
Stenopus hispidus 162
Stephanitis pyri 171
Stichophthalma camadeva 185
stick insects 125, 191, *191*
Stomoxys calcitrans 181
stoneflies 125, 191, 193, *193*
Stratiomys chamaeleon 180
strepsipterans 125, 191
stromatolites 123
Strombus gigas 140
Strongylopus bonaspei 118
Suta suta 76
swallowtails 146, 184, *184*
swift (lizard), Merrem's Madagascar *40*
symphylids 157, *157*
Synanthedon tipuliformis 183
Synapta maculata 195
Syrphus ribesii 180

T

Tabanus bovinus 180
Tachina fera 181
tachinid fly 181
Tachycines asynamorus 170
Tachycnemis seychellensis 116
tadpoles *see* frogs; toads
taipan *61*, 77, *77*
Takydromus sexlineatus 55
tapeworms 128, 135, *135*
Tarentola mauritanica 48, *48*
Taricha torosa 96
Tegenaria domestica 151
tegus 56, *56*, 57
Teius teyou 56
Telescopus fallax 72
Telmatobius yuracare 105
temperature control 14, 87
Teratoscincus scincus 47
termites 125, 169, *169*
Terrapene carolina 28
terrapins 28, *28*, 29, *29*

territoriality 18
testudines 14, 17
Testudo marginata 30
Tetragnatha extensa 151
Tetranychus telarius 155
Tetrodontophora bielanensis 194
Tettigonia viridissima 170
Thamnophis sirtalis 70, *70*
Theloderma asperum 119
Thelotornis capensis 72, *72*
Thelyphonus caudatus 149
Thermosbaena mirabilis 161
thornbugs 171
thorny devil 42, *42*
threadworms 136
thrips 125, *165*, 191, *192*
Thymelicus lineolus 183
Thyridopteryx ephemeraeformis 185
Thysania agrippina 184
Tibicen haematodes 172
ticks 127, 148, *148*, 154, *154*
Tiliqua spp. *38*, 50, *50*, *51*
Timon sp. 53
Titanus giganteus 175
toadlet, red-crowned *104*
toads 84
   Berber toad 108
   Brazilian Izecksohn's toad 100
   brown midwife toad 102
   Cameroon toad 108
   cane toad *107*, 107, 108
   Colombian giant toad 108
   Colourado river toad 108, *108*
   common Asian toad 108, *108*
   crucifix toad *104*, 104
   cururu toad 108
   defining features 100–1, *100*, 108, *108*
   Everett's Asian tree toad 109
   frogs differentiated from 109
   golden toad 91, *91*, 116
   Great Plains narrow-mouthed toad 114
   green toad 109, *109*
   horned toad 109, *109*
   Japanese toad 100
   life cycle 98
   Malaysian narrow-mouthed toad 114
   marine toad *see* cane toad
   Mexican burrowing toad 103, *103*
   Mexican spadefoot toad 103, *103*
   midwife toad 101
   natterjack toad 101
   oak toad 109
   olive midwife toad 102
   oriental firebelly toad 102, *102*
   ornate horned toad 105, *105*
   red toad 109
   red-crowned toadlet 104
   red-spotted toad 109
   Sonoran green toad 109
   South American common toad 109
   square-marked toad 108
   Surinam toad 89, 101, 103, *103*
   Syrian spadefoot toad 103
   Tschudi's Caribbean toad 108
   yellowbelly toad 102
   see also frogs
toe-biter *192*
tortoises 14, 24–32
   Abingdon Island tortoise 32
   African pancake tortoise 24, 30
   African tent tortoise 30, *30*
   Bell's hinge-back tortoise 30
   elongated tortoise 30
   Galápagos tortoises 24, 32
   leopard tortoise 30, *30*
   marginated tortoise 30
   ploughshare tortoise 32
   radiated tortoise 30
   Seychelles giant 15, *15*
   South American red-footed tortoise 30
   speckled cape tortoise 30

Texas tortoise 30, *30*
Torymus bedeguaris 187
Trachemys scripta 28, 30, *30*
Trachycephalus jordani 111
Trapelus persicus 42
Trapezites eliena 183
tree frogs 87, 110–13, *110–13*
   see also frogs; toads
treehoppers 171, *172*, 173
trematodes 135, *135*
Trialeurodes vaporarium 173
Triatroma sanguisuga 172
Trichobatrachus robustus 119, *119*
Trichodectes canis 182
Trichodes apiarius 176
Trichophaga tapetzella 182
Trichuris trichiura 136
trilobites 123, *123*, 146, *146*
Trimeresurus albolabris 81
Trionyx triunguis 27
Triops cancriformis 159
Triprion spatulatus 111, *111*
Trithemis aurora 166
triton, trumpet *140*
Triturus spp. 95, *95*
Trochosa terricola 150
Trogulus tricarinatus 154
Trombidium holosericeum 155
Tropidolaemus wagleri 81, *81*
Tropidophis spp. 62
Tropiometra afra 195
trypanosomiasis 179, 181
tsetse fly 181
Ttidacna gigas 137, 139
tuatara 14, 15, 17, *17*, 27, 36, *36*
Tubipora musica 133
Tubularia indivisa 132
tunicates 130, *130*
Tupinambis teguixin 56, *57*
Turtle Survival Alliance (TSA) 32
turtles 14, 15, 23, *23*, 24–32
   alligator snapping turtle 31, *31*
   Australian pig-nosed turtle 27
   big-headed turtle 31
   black-breasted leaf turtle 29
   bog turtle *see* Muhlenberg's turtle below
   Cagle's map turtle 28
   Caspian turtle 29
   Central American river turtle 31, *31*
   Chelidae Fitzroy turtle 25
   common mud turtle 31
   common snake-necked turtle 25
   common snapping turtle 31, *31*
   eastern box turtle 28
   European pond turtle 28, *28*
   flatback turtle 24, 25, 26
   furrowed wood turtle 29
   Ganges softshell turtle 27, *27*
   giant Amazon river turtle 25, *25*
   green turtle 26, *26*
   hawksbill turtle 26
   helmeted turtle 25
   Hilaire's toadhead turtle 25
   Indian flap-shelled turtle 27
   Indian roofed turtle 29
   Kemp's Ridley turtle 26
   leatherback turtle 14, 17, 24, 26
   loggerhead 26
   loggerhead musk turtle 31
   Malayan box turtle 29
   Malayan river turtle 32
   Malayan snail-eating turtle 29
   Mary river turtle 32
   matamata 25, *25*
   Mexican giant musk turtle 31
   Muhlenberg's turtle 28, 32
   Nile softshell turtle 27
   olive Ridley turtle 26, *26*
   painted turtle 28, *28*
   pond turtles 26, *26*
   razorback musk turtle 31
   red-bellied turtle 28

ringed sawback 28, *28*
scorpion mud turtle 28
sea turtles 14, 19, *19*, 22, 24, 26, 29
serrated turtle 25
smooth softshell turtle 27
spiny softshell turtle 27
spotted pond turtle 29
twist-necked turtle 25
Victoria short-necked turtle 25
wood turtle 24, 27, *27*, 28
tusks (molluscs) 138, *138*
Typhlonectes compressicauda 99
Typhlosaurus vermis 51

U

Uca spp. *158*, 162
Uma spp. 40, *40*
Ungaliophis continentalis 62
Uracentron azureum 41
urchins *see* sea urchins
Uromastyx spp. 42
Uroplatus henkeli 47
Uta stansburiana 40

V

Vampyroteuthis infernalis 143
Varanus spp. *37*, *38*, 44, 58, 59, *59*
Varroa jacobsoni 155, *155*
Velella velella 133
Velia caprai 171
venom 20, 87, 126
Venus' flower basket *131*
Venus' girdle *197*
Vermicula annulata 66
vinegaroons *see* scorpions
Vipera spp. 18, *18*, 78
vipers 60, 61, *61*, 78, 81, *81*
   eyelash viper 66, 73
   Fea viper 78
   green bush viper 78
   hognosed pit viper 81, *81*
   horned viper 78
   Levantine viper 79
   Malayan pit viper 81
   Mauritanic viper 79
   mole viper 65
   Persian horned viper 78
   rhoniceros viper 79, *79*
   Russell's viper 78
   saw-scaled viper 78
   speckled forest pit viper 81
   stiletto vipers 65
   Wagler's palm viper 81, *81*
   Wagner's viper 78
   white-lipped tree viper 81
   yellow-blotched palm pit viper 81
viviparous reptiles 15
Volucella bombylans 180

W

wasps 125, *165*, 186–7, 189
   American pelecinid wasp 187
   bee wolf 189
   clover seed chalcid 187
   common cuckoo wasp 187
   common wasp 189
   cuckoo wasps 187, *187*
   digger wasps 189
   ensign wasp 187
   eucharitid wasp 187
   gall wasps 186, 187
   jewel wasps 187, *187*
   mud-dauber wasps 189
   oak apple gall wasp 187
   paper wasp 189, *189*
   potter wasp 189
   red wasp 187
   rose bedeguar gall 187
   ruby-tailed wasp 187
   ruby-tailed wasps 187, *187*
   saber wasp 186
   sand digger wasp 189

sand wasps 189
scoliid wasps 187, *187*
thread-waisted wasps 189
torymid wasp 187
velvet wasp 187
water bears 125, 197, *197*
water boatmen *174*
water bugs 171
water fleas 158, 159, *159*
water insects 174, *174*
water measurer 171
water scorpions *174*
water striders *174*
waterdogs 92
watering-pot shell *139*
web-spinners 125, 191, *191*
weevils 178
weta, giant *165*
wheel animals (rotifers) 198, *198*
whip-spiders *149*
whiptail lizards 22, 56, *56*
whipworm, human 136
whiteflies 171, *173*
wood lice *see Anaspides tasmaniae*
woolly bear *183*
worms
   acorn worms 198, *198*
   arrow worm 125, 198, *198*
   earthworms 144, *144*
   fanworms 144
   flatworms 135, *135*
   goblet worm 125, 197, *197*
   horseshoe worms 125, 197, 198
   nightcrawler 144
   Palolo worm 144
   ragworm 144
   ribbon worms 125, 197
   roundworms 128, 136, *136*
   segmented worms 144, *144*
   shovel-headed garden worm 135
   spiny-crown worm 125, 198
   torpedo worm 198
   velvet worms 125, 199, *199*
wormslug *141*

X

Xantusia spp. 54, *54*
Xenodon severus 74, *74*
Xenopeltis unicolour 65
Xenophidion schaeferi 62
Xenopus spp. 91, 103, *103*, 109
Xyleutes strix 183
Xylocopa violacea 189

Y

yellow ophion 187
yellowjackets 189
Yponomeuta evonymella 182

Z

Zelotypia stacyi 183
Zonosaurus madagascariensis 49
Zygaena carniolica 183

ACKNOWLEDGEMENTS

t=top; l=left; r=right; tl=top left; tcl=top centre left; tr=top right; cl=centre left; c=centre; cr=centre right; b=bottom; bl=bottom left; bcl=bottom centre left; bc=bottom centre; bcr=bottom centre right; br=bottom right

AAP = Australian Associated Press; APL = Australian Picture Library; APL/CBT = Australian Picture Library/Corbis; APL/MP = Australian Picture Library/ Minden Pictures; AUS = Auscape International; AUST = Austral; BCC = Bruce Coleman Collection; GI = Getty Images; NHPA = Natural History Photographic Agency; NPL=Nature Picture Library; PL = photolibrary.com; SP=Seapics.com; WA = Wildlife Art Ltd.

PHOTOGRAPHS

Front cover GI

1b GI 2l GI 4c GI 8l PL 10cr APL/MP cr SP/Doug Perrine 12c APL/MP 14bl APL/CBT 15bl, br, tl APL/CBT cl GI 17tr APL/CBT 18bl, tr APL/CBT br APL/MP 19br APL/CBT tr GI 20b, cr APL/CBT cl APL/MP 21bcr, r APL/CBT 22br, cr APL/CBT tr GI 23b APL/CBT tr AAP 24bc PL cl APL/ MP cr SP/Doug Perrine 32bc, bl GI br APL/CBT tl PL 33c, cl APL/MP 36bc APL/CBT cr APL/MP 37cr PL 38bc APL/CBT cr GI tl APL/MP 44bl, br, c, tr PL 52c GI tr PL 60bc APL/MP bl APL/CBT 61br, cr PL t APL/MP 66cl APL/MP tl AUS/Jean-Paul Ferrero 67br AUS/Joe McDonald c GI tl PL tr APL/CBT 73bc, cl GI bl APL/MP cr AUS/Paul de Oliveira/OSF tl AUS/Glen Threlfo tr APL/CBT 82c GI 84bc GI c APL/MP tl PL 85tr APL/CBT 86cl GI 87br PL c GI tr APL/MP 88b BCC tr GI 89br APL/CBT tr GI 90bc APL tr GI 91br APL/CBT tr Esther Beaton 92c, t APL/CBT 98cr PL tl APL/CBT 99cr PL 100cl AUS/Satoshi Kuribayashi/OSF cr AUS/Kitchin & Hurst 101c AUS/MichaelFogden/OSF r AUS/Stephen Dalton/OSF tl GI 107b, c APL/CBT cl AUS/Kathie Atkinson tl AUS/Jean-Paul Ferrero 113cl AUS/ Michael Fogden/OSF cr APL/CBT tl APL/MP 120c PL 122br AUS 123bl AUS tr NPL 125br APL/CBT tr PL 126cl GI 127bcl GI bcr APL/MP cr APL/CBT 128bl APL/MP br APL/CBT cl, cr, tr APL/CBT 129tr APL/CBT 130tcl AUS tr APL/MP 131c, tr APL/CBT 132c APL/MP tr GI 135l GI tc PL 136c PL tr GI cl PL 144c APL/CBT tr GI 145cl, cr, tr APL/CBT tl PL 146bc APL/MP c APL/CBT tr PL 147c PL c GI tl APL/CBT 148bc GI cl tr APL/CBT 152bl AUS c PL 156c, cr APL/CBT 157c PL tr APL/CBT 158c, cr APL/CBT 164c PL tl AUS/Andrew Henely tr PL 165bc APL/MP tc GI tl APL/CBT 166c GI cl PL cl PL tr APL/MP 167cl APL/CBT cr, tr PL 168c AUS/Kathie Atkinson 169cl PL tr GI 170c GI tr APL/MP 171c PL cl GI tr AUS/John Cancalosi 174c AUST tl PL tr APL/CBT 175cl PL tr APL/CBT 179cr PL 182c PL tr GI 186c APL/MP tr GI 188tl PL tr PL 191c NHPA tr AUS/Pascal Goetgheluck 194tr APL/CBT 195cr, tr APL/MP cr GI 197c GI cl PL tr AUS 358bc PL

ILLUSTRATIONS

All illustrations © MagicGroup s.r.o. (Czech Republic) - www.magicgroup.cz; except for the following:

Susanna Addario 188bl; **Alistar Barnard/ Frank Knight/John Bull** 98bl, 124br cl, 151br; **Anne Bowman** 33bc, 170tl; **Simone End** 17bc, 124bl cl, 174cl; **Christer Eriksson** 31br, 34bl, 39br, 42cl; **Alan Ewart** 153cr; **Giuliano Fornari** 152cr, 179tr, 185cr, 37c, 169br; **John Francis/ Bernard Thornton Artists UK** 46bl, 61c cl; **Mike Golding** 142cl; **Ray Grinaway** 125tr, 164r; **Robert Hynes** 16br; **Ian Jackson** 168tr; **David Kirshner** 10bc, 85b, 86bcl cr, 165c; **David Kirshner/John Bull** 115bl, 108bl, 109br; **Frank Knight** 25br, 64cl, 138tcr; **James McKinnon** 36c; **Rob Mancini** 124cl, 152cr c cl tl, 153tr; **Tony Pyrzakowski** 17bcr, 163cr; **John Richards** 188cr; **Edwina Riddell** 188c, 25br, 30bl, 38cr tr, 40cl, 48bl, 59tr, 62bl cl; **Barbara Rodanska** 123cr; **Trevor Ruth** 78bl; **Peter Schouten** 51br; **Kevin Stead** 145c, 190bl, 24bl, 26bl, 29br, 35br, 36bl br, 37bl, 39cr, 41cr tr, 43br, 49cr, 50tl, 59br, 60c, 61tl, 65cr, 67cr, 75br, 79cr, 81cr, 98tr, 99cl, 113tr; **Guy Troughton** 52l, 66br; **WA/Robin Bouttell** 123cr; **WA/Sandra Doyle** 124tl, 148c, 150bcl bl, 153br; **WA/Ken Oliver** 46tl, 92bl, 100bl; **WA/Mick Posen** 16tr, 123br; **WA/Chris Shields** 92tl, 151tr cr, 173bl.

CAPTIONS

Page 1 The Amazon poison dart frog displays the kind of brilliant colours and bold patterns normally associated with butterflies. Skin secretions of these small frogs produce the most potent natural toxins known.

Page 2 Horns on the male Jackson's chameleon are not just ornamental. They are used in shoving contests with rivals for territory and mating rights.

Page 4–5 A bee balances on the petals of the cosmos flower, drinking its nectar. As the bee moves on, the dusting of pollen grains caught on its body will pollinate the next flower.

Page 6–7 The colour, delicacy and size of soft coral make it one of the most spectacular animals found on coral reefs.

Page 8–9 Ants are members of a highly social family of insects. The collaborative efforts of leaf-cutter ants ensure they have a constant source of food.

Page 12–13 The green iguana is the largest South American lizard. An agile climber, it is never far from trees.

Page 82–83 A green frog peeps from under a lily pad on Highbank Lake in Manistee National Forest, Michigan, United States.

Page 120–121 Gypsy moth caterpillars are able to consume as much as $0.1 m^2$ (1 sq. ft) of leaves per day. They have become a serious pest to trees such as the oak in the United States.